International law and the use of force

When the United Nations Charter was adopted in 1945, states established a legal 'paradigm' for regulating the recourse to armed force. In the years since then, however, significant developments have challenged the paradigm's validity, causing a 'paradigmatic shift'. *International Law and the Use of Force* traces this shift and explores its implications for contemporary international law and practice.

'This is an important work. It blends traditional conceptions concerning the use of force under international law with new theoretical insights to suggest a new paradigm on the use of force in contemporary international relations. The text is cogently argued, authoritatively documented, concisely written, yet intellectually balanced and comprehensive in scope.

'The authors strive to put into a rigorous theoretical framework a comprehensible construct of the legal implications of using international force in the modern world. In large measure they have admirably succeeded. As both a text and scholarly monograph, this work will be a very welcome and highly useful addition to the international law literature.'

Professor Christopher C. Joyner,
Political Science Department, George Washington University

International Law and the Use of Force will be of great use to all undergraduate and graduate students of international law, international relations and international organizations.

Anthony Clark Arend is Assistant Professor of Government, Georgetown University. **Robert J. Beck** is Assistant Professor of International Law and Organization in the Woodrow Wilson nd Foreign Affairs at the University of Virgi

D0814155

International law and the use of force

Beyond the UN Charter paradigm

Anthony Clark Arend and Robert J. Beck

London and New York

First published 1993
by Routledge
11 New Fetter Lane, London EC4P 4EE

Simultaneously published in the USA and Canada
by Routledge
29 West 35th Street, New York, NY 10001

© 1993 Anthony Clark Arend and Robert J. Beck

Typeset in Garamond by LaserScript, Mitcham, Surrey
Printed and bound in Great Britain by
Mackays of Chatham PLC, Chatham, Kent

British Library Cataloguing in Publication Data
A catalogue reference for this book is available from the British Library

ISBN 0–415–09303–1 (Hbk)
0–415–09304–X (Pbk)

Library of Congress Cataloging in Publication Data
Arend, Anthony C.
  International law and the use of force: beyond the UN Charter paradigm/
  Anthony Clark Arend and Robert J. Beck.
  p. cm.
  Includes bibliographical references and index.
  ISBN 0–414–09303–1: $65.00. – ISBN 0–415–09304–X (pbk.): $19.95
  1. United Nations – Armed Forces. 2. War (International law)
  3. Persian Gulf War, 1991. I. Beck, Robert J., 1961– .
  II. Title
JX1981.P7A7 1993
341.6'2 dc20

92-38903
CIP

ISBN 0–415–09303–1 (Hbk)
0–415–09304–X (Pbk)

DEDICATION

We would like to dedicate this book to

Dr. William V. O'Brien
Professor of Government
Georgetown University

Our teacher, mentor, and friend

Contents

Figures   ix
Acknowledgments   x

Part I Introduction

1 International law and the use of force   1
2 Historical overview: the development of the legal norms relating
   to the recourse to force   11

Part II The United Nations Charter paradigm

3 The United Nations Charter framework for the resort to force   29
4 Collective use of force under the United Nations Charter   47

Part III Challenges to the Charter paradigm

5 Anticipatory self-defense   71
6 Intervention in civil and mixed conflicts   80
7 Intervention to protect nationals   93
8 Humanitarian intervention   112
9 Responding to terrorism   138

Part IV Conclusion: beyond the Charter paradigm

10 International law and the recourse to force: a shift in paradigms   177

Notes and references   203
Index   266

Figures

2.1 League of Nations restrictions on recourse to war   21
6.1 Various forms of civil conflict   83
6.2 Mixed conflict   87

Acknowledgments

This book reflects the contributions of many. As originally conceived, its authors were to have included William T. Parsons, Esq. and Dr. Alberto R. Coll. Governmental commitments, however, prevented our colleagues from participating in the writing. Nevertheless, they provided valuable insights during the conceptualization process. Indeed, the idea of a new work on international law and the use of force originated with Bill.

During the course of the project, a number of individuals and institutions provided vital support. Professors Ken Booth, Christopher C. Joyner, Ruth Lapidoth, and Eugene V. Rostow offered constructive comments on earlier drafts of the manuscript. We have also appreciated the encouragement of our colleagues, including Professors Inis. L. Claude, Jr., Robert J. Lieber, R. K. Ramazani, Abiodun Williams, and Francis X. Winters. Many of our students at Georgetown University, the University of Virginia, and the University of Minnesota contributed to our efforts. These include Elizabeth Anderson, Marc Bernstein, Karen Brown-Thompson, Tania Hanna, April Morgan, Renee Robinson Phillips, Mona Reinhardt, Robert Vander Lugt, Esq., Haleh Vaziri, and Philip Yang. We would like to extend our special thanks to Charles D. McGraw of the University of Connecticut. Our gratitude is also due to Bernadette Beck and Kathleen Grant who exactingly proofread our manuscript.

At our book's inception, crucial institutional support was supplied by the Center for National Security Law at the University of Virginia School of Law, directed by Professor John Norton Moore. Similarly, through a Walsh Research Grant, Georgetown University's Walsh School of Foreign Service and Associate Dean Charles E. Pirtle furnished generous financial assistance.

The enthusiasm of Gordon Smith and the staff of Routledge sustained our efforts over the years. We are indebted particularly to Gordon for his faith in our project and patience with its authors.

Finally, we have dedicated this book to Professor William V. O'Brien. Dr. O'Brien taught international law at Georgetown University for nearly half a century until his retirement in 1993. Both of us are fortunate to be counted among his students, which number in the thousands. Dr. O'Brien instilled in us a concern for the ethical and legal dimensions of armed conflict, the focus of his life's writings. We hope our work will further scholarship in this area and live up to Bill's example.

We would like to thank the following journals for permission to reprint portions of several articles: the *Georgetown Law Journal* for Anthony Clark Arend, 'The United Nations and the New World Order,' vol. 81, 1993; the *Harvard Journal of World Affairs* for Anthony Clark Arend, 'The United Nations and the Termination of the Gulf War,' vol. 1, 1992; and the *Stanford Journal of International Law* for Anthony Clark Arend, 'International Law and the Recourse to Force: A Shift in Paradigms,' vol. 27, 1990.

Part I

Introduction

Chapter 1

International law and the use of force

On August 2, 1990, in one of the most provocative moves of the post-Second World War era, Iraqi troops invaded Kuwait. The invasion force proceeded quickly to subdue Kuwaiti troops and to establish control over the beleaguered state. In a broadcast statement, Baghdad Radio warned other states not to aid Kuwait, claiming that Iraq would 'make Iraq and Kuwait a graveyard for those who launch any aggression.'[1]

The condemnation of Iraq by the world community was instant. US President George Bush referred to the Iraqi invasion as 'naked aggression that violates the United Nations charter.'[2] He specifically criticized Iraqi leader Saddam Hussein, terming 'his behavior intolerable.'[3] The Soviet government called for the restoration of the 'sovereignty, national independence and territorial integrity of the State of Kuwait.'[4]

In the early morning hours after the invasion, the United Nations Security Council convened. This was the body of the world organization charged with the maintenance of international peace and security. While the Iraqi Ambassador attempted to justify the actions of his state, delegate after delegate called Iraq's action a violation of Article 2, paragraph 4 of the United Nations Charter. This provision prohibits the 'threat or use of force against the territorial integrity or political independence of any state or in any other manner inconsistent with the Purposes of the United Nations.'[5] By the end of the meeting, the Council had adopted Resolution 660, which condemned the invasion and called upon Iraq to 'withdraw immediately and unconditionally'[6] from Kuwait. Four days later, on August 6, the Council adopted Resolution 661, imposing sweeping diplomatic and economic sanctions on Iraq.[7] This was the first time in its forty-five year history that the Council had ordered collective sanctions in response to a use of force.[8]

While diplomatic efforts were being made to reach a peaceful settlement to the conflict, the Security Council continued to take action. It adopted further resolutions condemning Iraq's purported annexation of Kuwait (662), demanding the release of non-nationals held in Iraq (664), authorizing the use of force by states to maintain a naval blockade (665), allowing for

UN supervision of food shipments to Iraq (666), and condemning Iraqi incursions into several diplomatic installations (667). Finally, the Security Council adopted Resolution 678, which authorized states to 'use all necessary means to uphold the Security Council Resolution 660 and all subsequent resolutions and to restore international peace and security in the area'[9] if Iraq had not withdrawn from Kuwait by January 15, 1991. On January 16, 1991, when an allied assault was launched, the forcible action was pursuant to Resolution 678.

During the course of the Persian Gulf conflict, world leaders and diplomats constantly referred to norms of international law. In particular, they cited the rules of international law relating to the recourse to force, the so-called *jus ad bellum*. These are the norms that determine when a state may permissibly resort to force against another state. In the Gulf conflict, decision makers were faced with myriad *jus ad bellum* questions. Was the Iraqi invasion of Kuwait, for example, permissible under international law? Were there any plausible legal justifications for the action? If indeed the invasion was illegal, how could the international community lawfully respond to the action? Could other states unilaterally use force to respond to the Iraqi attack? Or was United Nations authorization required before force could be used against Iraq? What was the relationship between the right of self-defense and the authority of the United Nations Security Council?

Although the Gulf War was clearly one of the most dramatic uses of force since 1945, the legal questions it raised are by no means novel. Throughout the period of the modern state system, diplomats and scholars have constantly struggled to understand the legal norms relating to the recourse to force. This book seeks to explore the contemporary *jus ad bellum*: What is it? Where did it come from? And where is it going?

Before we address these essential questions of international law, it is necessary first to set the stage for our inquiry. Accordingly, this chapter will be divided into three sections. In the first, we will characterize the nature of the contemporary international system. International law cannot be understood without an appreciation of the international context within which it operates. In the second section, we will discuss in greater depth the purposes of our book. Here, we will introduce our fundamental argument that the *jus ad bellum* has undergone a 'paradigmatic shift.' In the final section, we will describe our book's methodological approach, setting out our test for the existence of a rule of law.

THE CONTEMPORARY INTERNATIONAL SYSTEM

Force has been a consistent feature of the global system since the beginning of time. Early human beings often resorted to violent means to persuade their fellows to take a certain course of action or in order to obtain something another possessed. As the world began to be organized into political communities, force became a frequent means of interaction among these communities. With the emergence of the modern state system in the seventeenth century,[10] armed conflict of all varieties proliferated. And as technology rapidly advanced, the destructive potential of warfare increased exponentially over the centuries. The machine gun, the airplane, the submarine, and ultimately, the nuclear bomb raised the horrors of war to apocalyptic proportions. In this century alone, there have been two devastating world wars that have resulted in the deaths of over sixty million people[11] and have broken the spirits of entire cultures.

Although the world has been thus far able to avoid another global war, the use of force has not been abandoned. Since the Second World War, there have been myriad uses of force. Professor K. J. Holsti catalogues fifty-eight wars or major armed interventions that have taken place since 1945.[12] And his list excludes both the 1989 US invasion of Panama and the 1991 Gulf War. While some of these conflicts lasted only a few weeks, others were protracted wars, such as the Vietnam War, the Soviet-Afghan War, and the Iran-Iraq War. Taken together, these sixty post-Second World War battles and other 'minor' conflicts that Professor Holsti did not list, have brought death and social upheaval to much of the world. In the relatively brief Gulf War alone, as many as 200,000 persons may have lost their lives.[13] Clearly, the last half of the twentieth century has been no less violent than the first.

The nature of contemporary international relations

The reasons why force has been a perennial factor in international life are many. Indeed, scholars from a variety of disciplines have often undertaken to explore the causes of 'war' and other uses of force.[14] Some of the factors cited by these experts as ultimate causes of international conflict include the inherent aggressiveness of human beings or the sinful nature of humans. But these factors also exist within domestic systems, and yet, generally, domestic authorities have been able to regulate and greatly to limit violence within those systems. Why then does the international system seem to be inherently more violent? The relatively greater incidence of force in the international arena seems to have been due, at least in part, to the very nature of the international system itself.

Unlike a domestic system, where there is a centralized authority with a monopoly of force to deter and punish wrongdoers, the international community is characterized by extreme decentralization.[15] At present, there are over one hundred and eighty states in the world but no international authority with an *effective* monopoly of force to prevent and, if necessary, to punish law breakers. As Professor Robert J. Lieber has explained, there is 'no common power,' 'no overall arbiter or institution to which [states] can turn for settlement of dispute, for enforcement of their rights, or even for effective protection of their basic security and survival.'[16]

There is, of course, the United Nations. But, as will be seen in subsequent chapters, this organization was not actually vested with a monopoly of force at the outset.[17] Moreover, for most of its existence, the UN has been largely unable to use effectively what theoretical power it does possess.

Reinforcing this factual decentralization is the concept of 'sovereignty.'[18] When the state system was emerging in the 1600s, thinkers began developing a theory to justify the de facto arrangement of power. This theory contended that states were to be regarded as juridically equal. No one state was to enjoy greater legal privileges than any other state. Owing to this juridical equality, no state could be subject to the control of another state or of any other temporal authority without that state's consent. States were thus said to be *sovereign*, to have absolute control over activities within their territories. While there may have been certain acknowledged *moral* norms, there were no pre-ordained *legal* norms.[19] Any law that was to be binding on states came not from divine or natural sources,[20] but solely from the states themselves. International law, therefore, if it were to exist, would have to be created by the consent of states. = positivism

THE PURPOSE OF THIS WORK

Over the past several centuries, states have in fact created legal rules to regulate their conduct in a wide variety of areas: international personality; jurisdiction; acquisition of territory; the seas; airspace; outer space; human rights; environmental concerns; economic transactions; and, of course, the use of force. The law relating to the recourse to force, the *jus ad bellum*, developed rather slowly until the beginning of this century. With the devastation wrought by the First World War, however, states redoubled their efforts to impose legal restrictions on the resort to armed force. To this end, both the League of Nations and its successor, the United Nations, sought to establish comprehensive legal regimes.[21]

The League proved to be a short-lived experiment. The United Nations, by contrast, has functioned for nearly half a century as an important actor in the international system. At the same time, the legal framework for the resort to force established by the United Nations Charter has become the most widely accepted framework for describing contemporary law relating to the recourse to force.[22]

In this book, we maintain that the United Nations Charter framework for the *jus ad bellum* represents a 'legal paradigm'.[23] This conclusion is not likely to be disputed. Other scholars have made similar claims.[24] In the years since the Second World War, however, a number of significant developments have challenged the validity of this UN Charter paradigm. These include: problems of Charter interpretation; the changed nature of international conflict; a perceived illegitimacy of institutions for peaceful change and peaceful settlement of disputes; failure of institutions to enforce the law; and a growing preference by states for 'justice' over 'peace.' Most international legal scholars recognize that these post-war developments represent serious threats to the Charter paradigm. Few, if any, contend that these developments are indicative of a 'paradigmatic shift.'[25]

We believe that such a shift has taken place. In this book, we will argue that since 1945 a new legal paradigm has emerged – the 'post-Charter self-help' paradigm. This paradigm, we submit, reflects contemporary international law relating to the recourse to armed force.

The purpose of our book is to explore this shift in paradigms, and to examine the future of the law relating to the recourse to force. To accomplish this task, our work will examine several areas. First, after a brief historical overview, we will describe the United Nations Charter paradigm for the resort to force. Second, we will explore in detail several significant challenges to the Charter paradigm. Third, we will describe the contours of the 'post-Charter self-help' paradigm and assess its capacity to promote international order. Finally, we will explore the future of the *jus ad bellum* and propose a normative framework that will address the problems that have plagued the UN Charter paradigm.

THE APPROACH OF THIS BOOK

Given the purposes outlined above, it is clear that our project will involve two major tasks. First, we will determine what international legal norms relating to the use of force actually exist. Second, we will indicate how these existing norms are at variance with the United Nations Charter paradigm. To accomplish these two tasks, it will be necessary first to set out our methodological approach.

In the decentralized international system, states create legal norms through their consent. The first critical task for any scholar or practitioner, therefore, is to determine what legal norms have in fact been created by states. This undertaking presupposes a fundamental question: How does one determine if a putative rule is genuine 'law?' Where does one look to find 'law?' What, in other words, are the *sources* of international law?

The traditional sources of international law

Traditionally, international legal scholars and world leaders have accepted Article 38 of the Statute of the International Court of Justice as the authoritative enumeration of the sources of international law.[26] While technically this Article is only a list of sources that the Court is to apply in deciding cases before it, most leaders and scholars would agree that Article 38 merely restates those sources that states have already come to acknowledge as authoritative.[27] Under this provision there are three principal sources of international law: 1) *treaties*, 2) *custom*, and 3) *general principles of law.*

There are also two subsidiary means for determining a rule of law: judicial decisions and scholarly writings.

Treaties

The first source listed in Article 38 is treaties, or, as they are referred to in the Article, 'international conventions.' Treaties or conventions are simply written agreements between two or more states and represent one of the most basic and clear ways in which states create rules to regulate their behavior. In a rough sense, treaties may be thought of as somewhat analogous to contracts under domestic law. Just as a contract between individuals creates law for those individuals, so a treaty between states creates law between them. Treaties may be between two states (bilateral) or among more than two states (multilateral). They may deal with many different issues, such as the United Nations Charter, or they may deal with only one subject, such as the 1988 Intermediate Nuclear Forces Treaty between the United States and the Soviet Union.

Treaties normally become law in a process involving several steps.[28] First, the parties enter into negotiations to determine what provisions they would like to include in the treaty. After they reach agreement, they sign the treaty. It is then normally submitted to the domestic ratification processes of each of the parties. In the United States, for example, before the President can ratify a treaty, he or she must submit it to the Senate for advice and consent.[29] Once the domestic procedures are complete, the states submit their instruments of ratification as required by the provisions of the treaty. Instruments of ratification are simply documents certifying that the states intend to be bound by the agreement. In the case of bilateral treaties, the agreement normally becomes binding international law once both sides have deposited their instruments of ratification. Most multilateral treaties specify a particular number of ratifications that must be deposited before a treaty actually becomes binding, or, in more technical language, *enters into force*.

Custom

Another principal source of international law is custom. Article 38 refers to it as 'international custom, as evidence of a general practice accepted as law.' Customary international law is thus created not by a written instrument but rather by state behavior. If, over a period of time, states begin to act in a certain way and come to regard that behavior as being required by law, a norm of customary international law has developed. In other words, for a norm of customary international law to exist, there must be two elements. First there must be state practice. States must comply with the putative rule in their actions. For instance, if there were to be a norm that diplomats were not to be arrested by the host country, states would have to demonstrate a practice of not arresting diplomats. Second, the proposed rule must be perceived to be law. Not only must states actually engage in a practice, they must do so because they believe that the practice is required by law. Thus, in the example given above, states must not only refrain from arresting diplomats, they must do so because they believe that it is *unlawful* to do so.

General principles of law

A final major source of international law listed in Article 38 is 'general principles of law recognized by the civilized nations.' This source is more controversial and difficult to grasp than the other two sources. In fact, international legal scholars seem to disagree on the precise nature of general principles[30]. For those who accept general principles as an independent source of international law, there seem to be at least three plausible definitions, which are not necessarily mutually exclusive.

First, general principles may refer to those basic legal principles that are present in most *domestic* legal systems.[31] Under this interpretation, legal concepts such as prescription,[32] estoppel,[33] and *res judicata*,[34] which are accepted in virtually all domestic systems, would also be applicable principles of international law. The logic is that because states have acknowledged these as important principles in their internal legal systems, they would also accept them as principles in the international legal system.

Second, general principles of law may refer to general principles about the nature of international law that states have come to accept.[35] This interpretation contends that there are certain *a priori* principles that underlie customary international law and treaty law. In other words, in order for customary and treaty law to make sense, there are certain first principles, certain assumptions, about the law-making process that states must accept. Two of these principles that immediately come to mind are sovereignty and *pact sunt servanda*. For law created by custom and treaty to be efficacious, states must first accept the notion that states are sovereign, that they can be bound by no law without their consent, and thus, that they *can* be bound by law *with* their consent. Similarly, the principle of *pacta sunt servanda*, the principle that promises should be kept, is an assumed principle of treaty law. Without first accepting this notion, any particular treaty would have no binding force. These underlying assumptions can be considered as a separate source of international law because they are philosophically prior to norms of custom. One cannot, for example, establish through treaty the principle that treaties should be obeyed.

Finally, a third interpretation of the meaning of general principles of law is that they refer to 'principles of higher law,'[36] such as principles of equity[37] or humanity.[38] Here, general principles would be similar to natural law principles that would fill the gaps left by treaty law and customary law.

Text writers and court cases

In addition to the three principle sources of international law, Article 38 also lists two 'subsidiary means for the determination of rules of law': 'judicial decisions and the teachings of the most highly qualified publicists of the various nations.' These two items are not independent sources of international law, but are rather means by which one can determine the existence of a principal source. In other words, to determine the content of a particular rule of custom, general principle, or the existence and meaning of a treaty, recourse can be had to court decisions and the writings of international legal scholars. Courts and scholars do not 'create' the law, but only give testimony to its existence. It is often quite laborious to undertake an independent assessment of state practice to determine the nature of a particular rule, however. Consequently, it is often convenient to cite credible scholars and generally accepted court decisions that have already reaped the fruits of such an assessment.

Other possible sources of international law

While treaties, custom, and general principles remain the accepted sources of international law, in recent years much attention has been given to the role that resolutions of international organizations play in the formulations of international law.[39] Technically, it is indeed possible for states to create an international organization by treaty and endow a body of that organization with law-making authority over the members. Various organs of the European Community, for example, have such law-creating ability.[40] From the standpoint of universal international organization, this type of law-making authority is quite limited. Resolutions of the United Nations Security Council can be binding on all members of the United Nations if the Council so decides.[41] For a resolution to be adopted, however, it must receive nine affirmative votes from among the fifteen members of the Council. In addition, each of the five permanent members of the Council – the United States, Great Britain, France, Russia (formerly the Soviet Union), and the People's Republic of China – must either vote in the affirmative or abstain for a resolution to be adopted. If any of the permanent members votes in the negative, the resolution is vetoed[42].

General Assembly resolutions, on the other hand, are for the most part only recommendations.[43] Only resolutions dealing with such issues as financial contributions, budgetary matters,[44] and internal housekeeping are binding on member states. General Assembly resolutions are, however, often cited as evidence of state practice. This is normally done in one of two ways. Some scholars contend that if a General Assembly resolution is adopted unanimously, or nearly unanimously, it indicates a belief on the part of states that the principles enunciated in the resolution are 'regarded as

law.'[45] These individuals would, in consequence, be willing to rely on the
resolution as the main indicator of state practice. Other scholars and statesmen would disagree with this interpretation.[46] They would argue that states
vote for United Nations General Assembly resolutions for a variety of reasons
– to appease a domestic audience, to gain international acceptance, to gain
specific favors from other states, and so forth. These reasons may have very
little to do with the perception that the resolution should be regarded as
indicative of state practice. Individuals supporting this interpretation would
contend that generally a General Assembly resolution should be regarded as
but *one* possible indicator of a customary practice that should be taken into
consideration along with the more traditional indicators – daily actions of
states, statements of government officials, behavior of commanders in the
field and the like. These scholars would contend that it would be possible
for a resolution to constitute a codification of existing customary international law. The resolutions could thus be cited as a 'short hand' to denote
the custom, much as treaties that codify customary international law are
cited. To do this, however, it would be necessary to demonstrate that there
was a norm of customary law that existed prior to the adoption of the
resolution and that the states adopting the resolution intend to codify this
norm.

The test of international law

We believe that two criteria should be used to determine if a putative norm
is genuinely 'law': 'authority' and 'control.'[47] First, any rule of international
law must be seen as *authoritative.*[48] States must regard the norm as legitimate;[49] they must perceive it to be 'law.' In the traditional language of
international law, the norm must have *opinio juris.*[50] Second, the prospective
legal norm must be *controlling* of state behavior.[51] Through their practice,
states must actually comply with the requirements of the rule. Neither 100
percent compliance nor a 100 percent perception of authority is necessary.
There must, however, be a *general* perception of authority and a general,
widespread compliance in order for a putative rule to be authentic international law.[52]

It is clear how our two-prong test applies to customary law since authority
and control are simply an alternative method of expressing that a rule of
custom requires a practice (control) regarded as law (authority). This argument is not particularly controversial. We assert, however, that the 'authority-
control' test for 'law' can also be applied to both treaties and general
principles.

It seems reasonable to argue, for example, that states have in practice
effectively withdrawn their consent from a particular provision of a treaty,
and hence, that it is not 'law,' if: 1) the provision is not believed by them to
be authoritative, and 2) there is very little compliance with the provision,

even though the treaty may remain technically 'in force.' Similarly, if a putative general principle is not perceived to be authoritative and is not controlling, it would be impossible to declare that it is truly a 'general principle of law recognized by the civilized nations.' In short, whatever the traditional source of a particular rule of law in question may be, the validity of the rule will be determined by reference to its authority and control.

This approach, while diverging somewhat from the traditional conception of the sources of international law, is grounded firmly in the *positivist* understanding of international law. As the late English jurist J. L. Brierly has explained: 'The doctrine of positivism . . . teaches that international law is the sum of the rules by which states have *consented* to be bound, and that nothing can be law to which they have not consented.'[53] State consent, we maintain, exists only if the rule in question is authoritative and controlling. If there is not a high level of authority and if the putative norm is not reflected to a significant degree in state practice, we posit that the suggested rule is not a norm of international law.

In the absence of a norm restricting state behavior, sovereignty allows states to act as they choose. As a consequence, unless a restrictive norm of international law can be established prohibiting a particular use of force, states are permitted to engage in that use of force. In other words, for the use of force to be prohibited there would need to be a *proscription* that was both authoritative and controlling.

Chapter 2

Historical overview: the development of the legal norms relating to the recourse to force

INTRODUCTION

For as long as human beings have suffered at the hands of one another, there have been efforts to impose restrictions on the recourse to force. The earliest evidence of such efforts can be found in the writings of ancient religions and can be traced through the scholarly writings, customary international law, and international agreements of the succeeding centuries. The purpose of this chapter is to explore this evolution of the norms relating to the recourse to force by examining their development through history. This discussion will set the context for an examination of the UN Charter framework.

In reviewing the history of the law relating to the use of force, legal scholars such as Professor John Norton Moore have found that during particular times a certain normative orientation regarding the recourse to force predominated.[1] In consequence, these scholars have divided history into periods based on the predominant normative orientation. While such division of history is clearly only an approximation and should not be interpreted too strictly, it can prove useful in understanding the historical changes that have occurred in the *jus ad bellum*. Drawing on the work of Professor Moore, six rough historical periods can be identified: 1) the just war period, 2) the positivist period, 3) the League of Nations period, 4) the Kellogg-Briand Pact period, 5) the United Nations Charter period, and 6) the post-United Nations Charter period. Each section of this chapter will discuss the normative developments that occurred during the four periods prior to the Charter Period.

THE JUST WAR PERIOD (c330 BC–AD 1650)

The earliest efforts to provide some form of normative framework for the recourse to force can be seen in the sacred writings of ancient religions. Frequently, these reflected a 'holy war' approach. According to this approach, recourse to force was to be deemed morally permissible when it was divinely ordained. Under the Hebrew conception, a holy war was one that was actually fought by God Himself. In Deuteronomy 20, the Israelites were told not to be fearful in battle because 'the LORD your God is he that goeth with you, to fight for you against your enemies, to save you.' Not all biblical wars, however, were holy wars. Those which were not instituted by God were not holy and were therefore not permissible. From a normative perspective, divine ordination was the sole element that determined the permissibility of the war. Even wars of conquest were acceptable if they were sanctioned by God.[2]

As time passed, the holy war came to be replaced by the just war doctrine proper.[3] Under this idea, recourse to force was deemed to be permissible when there was a just cause. Divine sanction, while still a plausible just cause, was no longer regarded as the *conditio sine qua non* for the use of force.

In reviewing the development of this just war approach, three phases can be identified: the classical phase, the Christian phase, and the secular phase. During each of these phases, different approaches to defining just recourse to war were formulated.

The classical phase (c330 BC–AD 300)

The first major effort to develop a just war doctrine came during the time of the great writers of classical Greece and Rome. One of the first writers to argue that the recourse to force should be circumscribed was Aristotle. In the *Politics*, he strongly criticized those city-states, like Sparta, whose entire orientation was for the prosecution of war. For Aristotle, war was not to be deemed an end in itself, but only a means to the greater end of establishing the 'good life' for the citizens of a political community. He explained that '[w]ar must therefore be regarded as only a means to peace.'[4] Based on this general assumption, Aristotle submitted that training in warfare should be directed toward three ends. These ends were thus the three 'just causes' for waging war.

The first of these ends was 'to prevent men from becoming enslaved.'[5] In contemporary parlance, this would be self-defense. The second reason for preparing individuals for war was 'to put men in a position to exercise leadership – but leadership directed to the interests of the led, and not to the establishment of a general system of slavery.'[6] Here what Aristotle seems to have meant was that it would be permissible to use force to establish a political rule over individuals who would benefit from it.[7] Finally, the third reason that Aristotle gave for preparing for war was 'to enable men to make themselves masters of those who naturally deserve to be slaves.'[8] At first glance, this might seem to contradict his admonition against the establishment of a 'general system of slavery.' But a more thorough understanding of Aristotle's conception of human nature reveals that there really was no contradiction. For Aristotle, some individuals were slaves by nature.[9] These people could only realize their full potential as human beings when they were being subjected to slavery. It would thus be just to use force to establish such a system over these people. Other individuals, however, were not slaves by nature. Hence, it would be unjust for a state to attempt to enslave those individuals.

In the contemporary world, the second and third justifications for using force seem to condone what might be termed imperialism. Nevertheless, in the context of the third century before Christ, Aristotle's effort to limit the recourse to force at all represented a major advance in the thinking about war.[10] But, as Frederick Russell notes, 'Aristotle's theory was not juridical but moral in application.'[11] He was not seeking to define a *lawful* war but rather a *morally* just war.

Another classical thinker to adopt the just war approach was the Roman statesman and philosopher Cicero. For Cicero, as for Aristotle, the ultimate aim of war was to establish peace.[12] In *De Res Publica*, he argued that there were two just causes for engaging in war: 'redressing an injury' and 'driving out an invader.'[13] He also contends that '[n]o war is held to be lawful unless it is officially announced, unless it is declared, and unless a formal claim for satisfaction has been made.'[14] Thus, Cicero, unlike Aristotle, advanced a *legal* argument, contending that war could be lawful if there were a just cause and if the necessary procedural conditions were met.

The Christian phase (cAD 300–AD 1550)

Although the just war doctrine had been advocated by several leading figures in classical thought, it was not immediately embraced by the early Christians. During the first years of the Church, most Christians were pacifists, especially noted thinkers such as Tertullian (160–240) and Origen (185–254). They believed that the return of Christ was imminent and that believers should not preoccupy themselves with the power struggles of this world. As time passed, however, much of this Christian pacifism began to wane. The philosophical shift seems to be attributable to two main factors. The first was the growing realization that the Second Coming would not be soon. Since Christ's return would take a longer time, Christians would have to deal with concrete problems of the here and now. In consequence, they would have to address the problem of obtaining some form of justice through human efforts, sometimes perhaps through force. The second factor that seems to have moved many Christians away from pacifism was the growing influence of Christianity in the Roman Empire. Increasing numbers of Christians began to hold positions of temporal power. With Constantine, the emperor himself was a Christian. In consequence, many began asking how this 'Christian Empire' could exist without the right to use force.[15]

With this change in attitude, the first major Christian figure to take a just war approach was Augustine. While Augustine did not develop a systematic *doctrine* of the just war,[16] he did argue that under certain circumstances recourse to war could be 'just.' In this context, however, 'justice' was not justice in the ultimate, divine sense, but rather justice in the relative, earthly, sense. True justice was only possible with the full realization of the kingdom of God.[17]

Drawing on the work of Augustine, Thomas Aquinas provided a systematic framework for the Christian just war doctrine. Writing in the *Summa Theologiae,* Aquinas argued that recourse to war was morally permissible if it met three conditions. First, there had to be 'proper authority.' By this Aquinas meant that a war was just only if some duly constituted ruler initiated it. Private individuals could not declare war.[18] Second, for a war to be just there had to be a just cause. Aquinas was, however, somewhat vague about what constituted a just cause.[19] He explained that 'there is required a just cause: that is that those who are attacked for some offence merit such treatment.'[20] He then quoted Augustine, who had contended that '[t]hose wars are generally defined as just which avenge some wrong, when a nation or a state is to be punished for having failed to make amends for the wrong done, or to restore what has been taken unjustly.'[21] For Aquinas, therefore, it was sufficient to define a just cause as something that righted a wrong or recaptured stolen property. Third, for a just war it was necessary for the state waging the war to have 'right intention.'[22] Those fighting a just war must be doing so to achieve 'some good' or avoid 'some evil.' War was not to be fought out of malice, hatred, or revenge.[23]

These three conditions for a just war came to be widely accepted by Christian thinkers in the medieval period. As time passed, the late scholastics, such as Francisco Vitoria (1480–1546) and Francisco Suarez (1548–1617), continued to develop the just war doctrine. One clarification that Suarez and Vitoria made to the requirement of a just cause was the addition of the idea of proportionality. Suarez explained that 'it is not every cause that is sufficient to justify war, but only those causes which are serious and commensurate with the losses that the war would occasion.'[24] In other words, the injury suffered by the state must be roughly equivalent to the injuries to be suffered in war in order for it to justify recourse to war. As will be seen later, this concept of proportionality was to continue to play an important role in the development of the *jus ad bellum*.

In examining the Christian phase of the just war doctrine, it would appear that the scholars were more concerned with the *morality* of war rather than with its *legality*. But for the Christian thinkers of the time, if recourse to war were 'unjust,' it would also be illegal. This was because the medieval Christian writers generally accepted a natural law approach.[25] Natural law, according to Aquinas, was 'the rational creature's participation of the eternal law.'[26] In other words, natural law was what a human being through reason could understand of God's eternal law. Human law, which today might be called positive law, was only really 'law' if it conformed to the natural law. In consequence, if a war did not meet the requirements of the *jus ad bellum*, it was not simply immoral, but also legally impermissible. The requirements for just recourse to war can thus be regarded as legal requirements.

The secular phase (c1150–1700)

As the medieval period was coming to an end, the Christian content of the just war doctrine came to receive less emphasis. For the medieval thinkers, war could be just because it conformed to certain theological precepts. Increasingly, however, sixteenth- and seventeenth-century writers began to develop the *jus ad bellum* apart from supernatural concerns. Perhaps the most celebrated writer of this period was Hugo Grotius (1583–1645). Grotius, himself a devout Protestant, took a natural law approach to the recourse to war that dissociated itself from the transcendent. Indeed, he argued that such an approach would be valid even if God were not to exist.

In his work *De Jure Belli ac Pacis*, Grotius set forth his requirements for a just war. He first maintained that for a war to be permissible it needed to be undertaken by a lawful authority. He next discussed just causes for such a war. First, he maintained that it was permissible to use force to defend persons and property.[27] Interestingly enough, however, Grotius allowed for anticipatory self-defense. He explained that it was lawful to use force to respond to 'an injury not yet inflicted, which menaces either person or property.'[28] But, he added, the 'danger . . . must be immediate and imminent in point of time.'[29] A second just cause for initiating war was to inflict punishment on a state that had caused an injury. In *De Jure ac Pacis*, Grotius also discussed several 'unjust' causes of war. These included a 'desire for richer land,'[30] 'a desire for freedom among a subject people,'[31] and 'a desire to rule others against their will on the pretext that it is for their good.'[32]

This secularized version of the just war doctrine continued to be developed by other writers. Noted scholars such as John Locke and Emerich de Vattel formulated their just war approaches to the *jus ad bellum*. One significant aspect about these subsequent formulations was that religion played an increasingly smaller role in the basis of the theory.

THE POSITIVIST PERIOD (c1700–1919)

Even as Grotius and others were writing about the limitations imposed on the recourse to war, the international system was undergoing fundamental changes that were to diminish the acceptance of the just war approach. The most important of these changes were the emergence of the state system and the development of the concept of sovereignty.

Sovereignty and the state system

As the medieval period was coming to an end, the feudal system was being replaced by a new structure. Increasingly, the territorial state was becoming the predominant political unit in the European world. Unlike the hierarchical system that prevailed during feudalism, the new international system was centered around individual, relatively autonomous states, ruled by different monarchs. Many factors contributed to this development, not the least of which were the rise of international trade and the concomitant rise of the merchant class, and the decline of the role of the Catholic Church and the universalism that it helped instill.

With the emergence of the state system, there also developed a new theoretical doctrine to explain the status of the state – the doctrine of sovereignty.[33] Associated with writers such as Jean Bodin (c1529–1596) and Thomas Hobbes (1588–1679), the doctrine came to be regarded as the fundamental ordering principle of the state system. In a nutshell, sovereignty meant three things. First, it meant that the rulers of a particular state – kings, princes, dukes, etc. – had sole authority over their territory. No pope or emperor had temporal control over them. They were 'sovereign' over their state. Second, states were regarded to be juridically equal to one another. As Chief Justice Marshall would later state in the famous *Antelope* case, '[n]o principle of general law is more universally acknowledged than the perfect equality of nations. Russia and Geneva [then an independent state] have equal rights.'[34] Third, and following from these two previous points, sovereignty meant that states were subject to no higher law without their consent. There was no overarching *a priori* law to which states were bound.

In 1648, the doctrine of sovereignty achieved 'codification' with the adoption of the Peace of Westphalia, which brought an end to the devastating Thirty Years War.[35] In the agreements that ended the war, the signatories pledged not to interfere with the determination by local rulers of which religion would prevail in their realm. This was the principle of *cujus regio ejus religio* – he who reigns, chooses the religion. This clearly affirmed the independence of the local ruler; if he could choose the religion of his state – one of the most important issues at the time – he certainly had a significant amount of autonomy.

With the emergence of sovereignty as an ordering principle of the international system, legal scholars formulated the doctrine of positivism.[36] Positivism asserted that since states could be bound by no higher law, the only law that could exist was that which they created by their consent. This they did through treaties, customs, and general principles. With natural law principles increasingly relegated to theological discussion, positivism had a profound influence on the development of norms relating to the use of force.

'War' and the sovereign state system

The major consequence that these developments had for the law relating to the recourse to war was to supplant the just war concept as the predominant *legal* approach to the *jus ad bellum*. Now that states were sovereign, they had a 'sovereign' right to go to war. As the British jurist, William Edward Hall explained in 1880, '[i]nternational law has consequently no alternative but to accept war, independently of the justice of its origin, as a relation which the parties to it may set up if they choose.'[37] In short, even though there might have been certain moral limitations on the recourse to war, legal doctrine came to accept the right of a state to go to war whenever it so desired. States were said to have a *competence de guerre*, a right to war. In the absence of any higher law or authority, there was a legal regime of 'self-help.' States could institute a war at any time to vindicate their rights. The only real qualification of this right to institute war that was accepted by states during this period was the requirement that war be declared.[38] Hence, a state simply declared war, and it was lawful.

Uses of force short of war

Even though recourse to war was essentially unrestricted, a distinction was made between a full-blown war and the use of force 'short of war.' A use of force short of war was a quick action that did not involve major commitment of forces. It took place in the absence of a declaration of war and was thus regulated by the international law of peace. Typical uses of force short of war include reprisals, and self-defense actions.

Reprisals

A reprisal is an action that a state undertakes to redress an injury suffered during time of peace.[39] It is an act that would normally be a violation of international law but is not regarded as such when it is done in response to a prior unlawful act. Reprisals may or may not involve the use of force. For example, if State A violated provisions of an important treaty with State B, State B's termination of another treaty with State A could be regarded as a *non-forcible* reprisal. On the other hand, if State B responded by shelling a naval base owned by State A, such action obviously would be a forcible reprisal.

Over the course of time, customary law came to recognize certain require-ments for a lawful reprisal. The classic enumeration of these criteria for a permissible reprisal can be found in the arbitral decision in the *Naulilaa* case. That case dealt with a German reprisal that occurred in 1914 against Portugal, which was not in a state of war with Germany. The Arbitral Tribunal concluded that for a reprisal to be lawful, three conditions needed to be met. First, there had to be 'a previous violation of international law.'[40] A reprisal was only to be undertaken in response to delictual behavior.[41] Second, the reprisal had to be 'preceded by an unsuccessful demand for redress.'[42] In other words, the injured party had an obligation first to seek redress through pacific means before employing forceful measures. Third, the reprisals 'must be proportionate to the injury suffered.'[43] This does not mean that a precise mathematical correspondence of injury and the response need be calculated, but rather that the response should, on its face, be roughly commensurate to the initial injury. For example, if State A were illegally to sink one small naval vessel of State B, a response by State B that involved the sinking of twenty-five major vessels of State A would likely be disproportionate.

Self-defense

Another use of force short of war that came to be regulated during this period was self-defense. In this context, self-defense does not refer to the response to a major armed attack. Such attack would constitute the initiation of a 'war' and place the injured party in a position where it could simply declare war for its responsive action to be permissible. Instead, self-defense here refers to a protective action aimed at another use of force short of war. It differs from a reprisal in that its purpose is not retaliatory but defensive.

The most celebrated case that dealt with the conditions for permissible self-defense was the *Caroline* case.[44] In 1837, a state of peace existed between the United States and Great Britain. There was, however, an armed insurrection taking place in Canada, and a ship owned by US nationals, the *Caroline*, was allegedly providing assistance to the Canadian rebels. On December 29, 1837, while the *Caroline* was docked on the American side of the Niagara River, Canadian troops boarded the ship, killed several American nationals on board, set the ship on fire, and sent it over the Niagara Falls. Following an American protest, Great Britain claimed that its forces were acting in lawful exercise of the right of self-defense.

Although Britain ultimately apologized for its actions, in the course of the diplomatic correspondence, two criteria for permissible self-defense were articulated: necessity and proportionality. First, for a state to be permitted to use force in self-defense there must be a proven necessity. Secretary of State Daniel Webster explained to the British Foreign Minister that it would have to be demonstrated that the 'necessity of that self-defense is instant, overwhelming, and leaving no choice of means, and no moment of deliberation.'[45] Second, the response would have to be proportionate. The state must not only show the necessity to respond, it must also demonstrate that its actions were not 'unreasonable or excessive.'[46] At the time, these two criteria were accepted by the parties and generally accepted under customary international law.[47]

The use of force to collect contract debts

In addition to the regulations dealing with the use of force short of war that developed under customary international law, there was one interesting treaty limitation imposed on a very specific use of force. This was the prohibition on the use of force to collect contract debts that was established by the second Hague Convention of 1907.[48] In this Convention, the parties pledged 'not to have recourse to armed force for the recovery of contract debts claimed from the Government of one country by the Government of another country as being due to its nationals.'[49] This restriction was, however, qualified. The Convention went on to provide that this prohibition on the use of force did not apply 'when the debtor State refuses or neglects to reply to an offer of arbitration, or, after accepting the offer, prevents any "Compromis" from being agreed on, or, after the arbitration, fails to submit to the award.'[50] Hence, the prohibition established by the Hague Convention was far from absolute.[51]

In sum, during the positivist period there were but few rules limiting the right of states to take recourse to force. Even though norms had developed with respect to uses of force short of war, these restrictions could be circumvented. If a state desired to engage in a prohibited use of force short of war, that state could simply declare 'war,' and its use of force would be permissible.

THE LEAGUE OF NATIONS PERIOD (1919–1928)

In 1914, the liabilities of a system of self-help became obvious when the First World War began. Over the course of its four-year run, the war took a devastating toll. Twice as many people were killed during this relatively brief period than had been killed in all wars combined from 1790–1913. The 'Great War' was truly a war unlike any the world had known. Not surprisingly, when the delegates to the Paris Peace Conference assembled in the Palace of Versailles in the spring of 1919, one of their foremost concerns was to ensure that such a war should never again occur.[52]

In the post-mortem following the First World War, the common belief was that the war had resulted from 'accidental' causes.[53] Most statesmen felt that the war was not caused by the aggressive intent of any one state, but rather that it resulted from a series of miscalculations and misinterpretations, exacerbated by the lack of procedural limitations on the recourse to war. As a consequence of this belief, the delegates to the Paris Conference sought to establish a new, global international organization, that, among other things, would provide the necessary procedural checks to prevent such a war from taking place.[54] And thus the League of Nations was established.

The League system and the recourse to force

Under the League of Nations Covenant, an elaborate set of procedures was established to restrict the recourse to force. First, under Article 12 signatories pledged to submit any dispute 'likely to lead to a rupture' 'to arbitration or judicial settlement or to enquiry by the [League] Council.'[55] A dispute likely to lead to a 'rupture' was presumably one that would have disrupted international peace and led to war. Second, Article 15 provided that if such a dispute were submitted to the League Council, and a report were adopted unanimously by the members of the Council that were not parties to the dispute, the disputants were under an obligation 'not to go to war with any party to the dispute which complies with the recommendations of the report.'[56] Article 13 imposed the same obligation in cases in which there was an arbitral or court decision.[57] Hence, a state could never undertake a war against another state if the second state were abiding by the decision of the dispute resolution body. Third, Article 12 provided that the parties 'agree in no case to resort to war until three months after the award by the arbitrators or the judicial decision or the report of the Council.'[58] This meant that even if the one side did not comply with the report of the Council, or the decision of the arbitral tribunal or court, the other side was required to wait at least three months before it could go to war. The Covenant, in other words, imposed a 'cooling-off' period.

This procedure, while clearly imposing significant restriction compared to the pre-League regime, nevertheless left open substantial rights to take recourse to force.[59] First, if there were no decision by the arbitral body, court, or the League Council, there would be no obligation to refrain from the use of force. In fact, Article 15 of the Covenant explicitly recognized this possibility. It provided that

> [i]f the Council fails to reach a report which is unanimously agreed to by the members thereof, other than the Representatives of one or more of the parties to the dispute, the Members of the League reserve to themselves the right to take such action as they shall consider necessary for the maintenance of right and justice.[60]

Second, if there were a decision by the Council, states would be obliged to refrain from going to war against a state complying with the decision of the settlement body. If, however, one party were not following the decision, the other party could take recourse to war after waiting three months. For example, if there were a dispute between the United States and Canada over fishing rights in the Gulf of Maine that seemed likely to lead to a breach of the peace, both sides would be under an obligation to submit the issue to dispute settlement. Assuming that they submitted the matter to the League Council and the Council handed down a decision, both sides would be under an obligation to carry out the decision. If, however, Canada chose not to follow the decision, after a period of three months, the United States could lawfully resort to war against Canada.

This procedural arrangement established by the League of Nations Covenant can be summarized in Figure 2.1.

These procedural checks[61] were the only *definitive* restraints on the

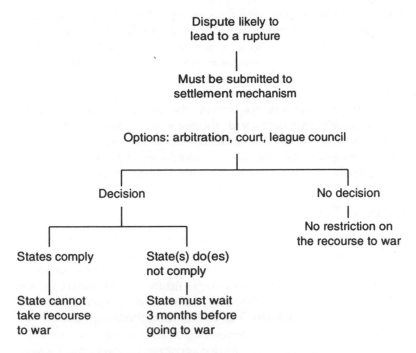

Dispute likely to
lead to a rupture

Must be submitted to
settlement mechanism

Options: arbitration, court, league council

Decision

No decision

No restriction on
the recourse to war

States comply

State(s) do(es)
not comply

State cannot
take recourse
to war

State must wait
3 months before
going to war

Figure 2.1 League of Nations restrictions on recourse to war

recourse to war that existed in the League Covenant. Nonetheless, alongside these requirements were provisions of the Covenant that seemed to be more restrictive of the right of states to use force. Article 10 of the Covenant provided that:

> The Members of the League undertake to respect and preserve as against external aggression the territorial integrity and existing political inde-pendence of all Members of the League. In case of any such aggression or in case of any threat or danger of such aggression, the Council shall advise upon the means by which this obligation shall be fulfilled.[62]

What this meant was that the League was to protect the territorial integrity and political independence of states from aggression. It seemed, thus, to imply that 'aggression' was prohibited. But, as Professor Ian Brownlie points out, if Article 10 did prohibit aggression, it would seem to contradict the provisions of the Covenant discussed above that allowed for recourse to war under certain circumstances.[63] Although the *travaux préparatoires* 'did not provide a conclusive answer,' they 'strongly suggested that Article 10 was intended to be subordinate to Article 15, paragraph 7,' the provision that allowed for recourse to war when the Council was unable to act.[64] Under this interpretation, it would seem that the framers intended that force permitted in accordance with the other provisions of the Covenant (Articles 12 and 15), would not constitute aggression. While subsequent interpretations may have generally affirmed this, the mere presence of Article 10 in the Covenant and the concept of aggression made the League approach to the recourse to war quite confusing.

One final point should also be noted about the League *jus ad bellum*. The League restrictions dealt exclusively with the recourse to 'war.' No provisions were made to limit uses of force that would fall below the threshold of war. In consequence, even under the League Covenant, uses of force short of war would be regulated by the same regime that existed during the positivist period.

Efforts under the League of Nations

The League Covenant was far from the last word on the recourse to war during this period. Soon after the organization began meeting, several other attempts were made to clarify and refine the *jus ad bellum*. These included the 1923 Draft Treaty on Mutual Assistance[65] and the 1924 Protocol for the Pacific Settlement of International Disputes, the so-called Geneva Protocol.[66] Both of these agreements defined 'aggression' as an 'international crime,' and although the Treaty on Mutual Assistance did not go much beyond the League Covenant in its restrictions on the recourse to force, the Geneva Protocol did. Under Article 2 of the Protocol, the parties pledged not to take recourse to war 'except in case of resistance to acts of aggression or when acting in agreement with the Council or Assembly of the League of Nations in accordance with the provisions of the Covenant and of the present Protocol.'[67] In other words, the Protocol sought to limit the circumstances in which there could be a resort to war to two: defense from aggression and when authorized by a competent organ of the League.[68] Unfortunately, even though forty-eight states recommended the ratification of the Protocol in the League Assembly, it failed to receive the number of ratifications necessary to enter into force.[69]

THE KELLOGG-BRIAND PACT PERIOD (1928-1939)

The nature of the Kellogg-Briand Pact
Following these abortive attempts to impose additional restrictions on the *jus ad bellum*, yet another effort was made during the interwar period to regulate the right of states to go to war. This was the Treaty Providing for on the Renunciation of War as an Instrument of National Policy, often referred to as the Pact of Paris or the Kellogg-Briand Pact.[70] The Kellogg-Briand Pact was signed on August 27, 1928 and entered into force on July 24, 1929. Interestingly enough, it is technically still in force, with its parties including the United States and the Soviet Union (presumably now Russia).

Under the Kellogg-Briand Pact, the signatories declared 'in the names of their respective peoples that they condemn recourse to war for the solution of their international controversies, and renounce[d] it as an instrument of national policy in their relations with one another.'[71] They further agreed 'that the settlement or solution of all disputes or conflicts of whatever nature or of whatever origin they may be, which may arise among them, shall never be sought except by peaceful means.'[72] Hence, unlike the League Covenant, which permitted the recourse to war in certain circumstances, the Kellogg-Briand Pact outlawed the resort to war entirely. The text of the Pact nowhere provides for any exception to this general proscription. It was generally recognized by the parties to the Pact, however, that resort to war would be permissible in the case of self-defense.[73] In fact, a number of states, including the United States, presented diplomatic notes prior to the ratification of the Pact indicating their understanding that wars launched in self-defense would be lawful.[74] It also seems safe to assume that war would be permissible when it was authorized by the League Council in accordance with the provisions of the Covenant. Such force would not constitute the use of war 'as an instrument of *national* policy.' Instead, as Professor Yorum Dinstein points out, it would be the use of war as 'an instrument of *international* policy.'[75]

Even though the Kellogg-Briand Pact has frequently been maligned in the literature of international relations,[76] it was actually quite significant in the development of the law relating to the recourse to force.[77] Like the Geneva Protocol,[78] the Pact drew a legal distinction between aggression on the one hand, and self-defense and force authorized by a universal international organization on the other.[79] But unlike the Geneva Protocol, the Kellogg-Briand Pact entered into force and was widely regarded by states as authoritative.[80]

The problems with the Kellogg-Briand Pact

Despite the advances made through the drafting of the Kellogg-Briand Pact, the treaty still presented several major problems. First, the Pact only explicitly outlawed 'war.' It did not, therefore, impose any restrictions on the use of force short of war.[81] Once again, the regime that existed in the pre-League period dealing with these uses of force would continue to apply. Second, since the Kellogg-Briand Pact did not define a self-defense exception, the interpretation of permissible self-defense remained unclear. As noted earlier, many states made explicit statements indicating that they reserved the right to take recourse to war in the exercise of self-defense. But what actions legitimately gave rise to this right? What constituted an offense that would merit the resort to war in self-defense? By not explicitly addressing the issues of self-defense, the Pact left these questions unanswered. Third, as Professor Dinstein observes, the use of the words 'national policy' in the prohibition contained in the Pact left open the possibility that other motivations for the recourse to war might be legal. He argues that 'the "national policy" formula gave rise to the interpretation that other wars – in pursuit of religious, ideological and similar (not strictly national) goals – were also permitted.'[82] Conceivably, states could claim that such wars did not contradict the Pact and were thus permissible.

The Kellogg-Briand Pact in practice

That the Kellogg-Briand Pact ultimately did little to restrain the aggressive powers that brought about the Second World War is well understood. Less well understood, however, is the role that the Pact did play in the interwar development of the *jus ad bellum*. There were, in fact, significant consequences of the Pact. First, it led to further efforts to reaffirm and refine the Pact's obligation.[83] During the interwar period, numerous treaties were concluded that reiterated the obligation to refrain from aggressive war. Such agreements included several 'non-aggression pacts' and the 1933 Convention on the Definition of Aggression.[84] Second, the Pact does seem to have altered the way statesmen thought about, or at the very least *spoke* about, the recourse to war. No longer did their rhetoric reflect a belief in an unrestricted *competence de guerre*. Instead, diplomats and leaders from a variety of states appealed to the Kellogg-Briand Pact as a source of legal obligation.[85] Even after the Second World War had begun, Germany, Italy, and Japan were condemned for violations of the Pact. As late as 1941, American Secretary of War Stimson could still speak of the 'vital change' that 'was made in the system of international law'[86] by the ratification of the Kellogg-Briand Pact. Indeed, it would seem that despite the failure of the Pact to prevent the war, the idea of prohibiting aggressive war had been indelibly planted in the minds of modern world leaders. As will have been seen, this idea would surface again after the war in the form of Article 2(4) of the Charter of the United Nations.

CHAPTER SUMMARY

While it is always difficult to attempt to 'periodize' history, the development of the *jus ad bellum* can be understood in terms of six rough historical periods: the just war period, the positivist period, the League of Nations period, the Kellogg-Briand Pact period, the UN Charter period, and the Post-Charter period. During the *just war period*, there was a sense that recourse to war was permissible if there was a 'just cause.' Even though thinkers differed on the particulars of what constituted a 'just cause,' there was broad agreement that recourse to force was not absolutely unrestricted. As the modern state system began to emerge during the *positivist period*, the just war doctrine began to lose support. With the principle of sovereignty now undergirding the system, states began to articulate a belief that they had a 'sovereign right' to go to war. During this period, customary international law generally recognized that states possessed a *competence de guerre*, even though certain restrictions on the uses of force short of war were acknowledged. Following the First World War, there was a shift away from this approach to the recourse to war. In the *League of Nations period*, a series of procedural checks were established to restrict the resort to war. Due, however, to significant 'gaps' in the League Covenant Framework, subsequent efforts were made to fill these gaps. The most important of these efforts was the Kellogg-Briand Pact. During what might be called the *Kellogg-Briand Pact period*, war as an instrument of national policy was outlawed. The only exceptions to this prohibition that were generally accepted by states were self-defense and wars authorized by the League of Nations.

Part II

The United Nations Charter paradigm

Chapter 3

The United Nations Charter framework for the resort to force

INTRODUCTION

As the Second World War continued to take its toll, the major Allied Powers became convinced that yet another effort should be made to establish a universal international organization charged with the management of international conflict. The League of Nations had failed in this task, but the new organization, it was believed, would be different. And so, in the spring of 1945, the delegates of forty-nine states met in San Francisco to draft the Charter of the United Nations. In this Charter, these delegates pledged their determination 'to save succeeding generations from the scourge of war, which twice in [their] lifetime [had] brought untold sorrow to mankind'.[1]

The purpose of this chapter is to discuss the legal framework created by the United Nations Charter for the regulation of the use of force and to provide an overview of some of the problems of this framework, which will then be discussed in more detail in subsequent chapters. In order to do this, we have divided this chapter into three sections. The first section will examine the normative nature of the Charter; the second section will explain the Charter provisions on the use of force; and the third section will then outline several problems that are challenging the efficacy of these Charter provisions.

THE NATURE OF THE UNITED NATIONS CHARTER

When the UN Charter was written, it established an organization that was given a host of specific tasks, the most important of which was the maintenance of international peace and security. But the Charter was not only an institution-creating document; it was also a norm-creating document. It set forth specific rules intended to regulate the behavior of states, especially with respect to the use of force. These norms are generally regarded as rules of international law from the perspective of both treaty law and customary law.

The Charter as treaty law

The first and most obvious way in which the Charter can be seen as a law-making instrument is through its status as a treaty. Like many multilateral treaties, the Charter was formulated at a conference – the United Nations Conference of International Organization.[2] At the end of this conference, on June 26, 1945, fifty-one states (with the Byelorussian Soviet Republic and the Ukrainian Soviet Republic being considered 'states') signed the Charter, and, on October 24, 1945, when the instruments of ratification of the permanent members of the Security Council and a majority of the other signatories had been deposited, the Charter entered into force.[3] Like any treaty, it is legally binding on all parties that have ratified the document – currently one hundred and eighty states. Those provisions of the Charter, therefore, that impose obligations relating to the use of force constitute treaty law for those states, subject to the general rules of international law concerning treaties.

The Charter as customary international law

Most scholars, while acknowledging that the Charter is treaty law for the states who have ratified it, recognize that certain *portions* of it may also be customary international law, applicable to all states. They argue that over the years, both members and non-members of the United Nations have come to regard particular norms embodied in the Charter to be custom. In order to determine which, if any, Charter rules do, in fact, constitute customary international law, it is necessary to examine state behavior with respect to those provisions to ascertain, first, if states perceive them to be authoritative and, second, if states conform to them in their behavior. As our discussion now turns to the examination of the Charter provisions on the use of force, one of our major objectives will be to determine what authority and control can be accorded to those important Charter rules.

THE CHARTER PROVISIONS ON THE USE OF FORCE

Article 2(4): the general prohibition on the use of force
The most important provision of the United Nations Charter on the recourse to force is Article 2, paragraph 4, which is contained in Chapter I of the Charter, the chapter that defines the purposes and principles of the United Nations. Article 2(4) provides:

> All members [of the United Nations] shall refrain in their international relations from the threat or use of force against the territorial integrity or political independence of any state or in any other manner inconsistent with the Purposes of the United Nations.

Simply put, Article 2(4) establishes a general *proscription* on both the actual use of force and the threat to use such force. It outlaws not only recourse to 'war,' as did the Kellogg-Briand Pact of 1928, but any use of *force* (or threat) that is against the territorial integrity or political independence of another state or that is otherwise inconsistent with the purposes of the United Nations. Hence, even uses of force 'short of war,' such as peacetime reprisals, would be prohibited under Article 2(4).[5]

The Charter exceptions to Article 2(4)

In the United Nations Charter, there are four explicit exceptions to the Article 2(4) prohibition on the use of force: 1) force used in self-defense; 2) force authorized by the United Nations Security Council; 3) force undertaken by the five major powers before the Security Council is functional; 4) force undertaken against the 'enemy' states of the Second World War.

Article 51: individual and collective self-defense

The first explicit exception to Article 2(4) is found in Article 51 of the Charter, which provides:

> Nothing in the present Charter shall impair the inherent right of individual or collective self-defense if an armed attack occurs against a Member of the United Nations, until the Security Council has taken measures necessary to maintain international peace and security. Measures taken by Members in the exercise of this right of self-defense shall be immediately reported to the Security Council and shall not in any way affect the authority and responsibility of the Security Council under the present Charter to take at any time such action as it deems necessary in order to maintain or restore international peace and security.

In other words, if a state experiences an 'armed attack,' that state retains an 'inherent' right to defend itself by using force against the attacking state until the Security Council is able to take action. This right may be exercised either individually or collectively. That is, the victim state may receive the assistance of other states to help ward-off the attacker. Members taking such action in self-defense are also required to report such action immediately to the Security Council.[6]

Chapter VII: enforcement actions authorized by the security council

The second exception to Article 2(4) is contained in Chapter VII of the Charter, which deals with Action with Respect to Threats of the Peace, Breaches of the Peace, and Acts of Aggression (Articles 39–51). Under Article 39, the Security Council is empowered to 'determine the existence of any threat to the peace, breach of the peace or act of aggression.' If the Council so determines, it is authorized under Article 42 to order members of the United Nations to use force against the recalcitrant state. (More will be said about specific procedure for Security Council action in subsequent chapters.)

Article 106: collective use of force before the Security Council is functional

In addition to these two major exceptions to Article 2(4), there are also two other exceptions listed in the Charter. One of these is contained in Article 106, which is found in Chapter XVII on the Transitional Security Arrangements. Article 106 provides:

> Pending the coming into force of special agreements referred to in Article 43 [the Article that provides that states shall conclude agreements with the Security Council in order to make available military contingents to be used in the event of an enforcement action] as in the opinion of the Security Council enable it to begin the exercise of its responsibilities under Article 42, the parties to the Four-Nation Declaration [the United States, Great Britain, the Soviet Union, China] ... and France, shall ... consult with one another and as occasion requires with other Members of the United Nations with a view to such joint action on behalf of the Organization as may be necessary for the purpose of maintaining international peace and security.

In other words, Article 106 allows the five states mentioned, the five permanent members of the Security Council, to take joint military action if the formal procedure for the Security Council to act *has not yet been established.*

Even though no special agreements have been concluded under Article 43, and thus, technically, it could be argued that the organization is still in a period of transition, no joint action has ever been undertaken under Article 106. Moreover, given contemporary conditions, it seems highly unlikely that action under Article 106 will be undertaken in the future. If the five permanent members of the Security Council were to agree on the joint use of force, they would almost certainly do this *through* the Security Council to gain the legitimacy of the organization. In consequence, it seems reasonable to conclude that even though the Article 106 exception could theoretically still be invoked, it is, practically speaking, dead.

Articles 107 and 53: force against 'enemy' states

The final exception to Article 2(4) allows that force may be used against 'enemy' states of the Second World War. This exception is explained in Articles 107 and 53. Article 107 provides:

Nothing in the present Charter shall invalidate or preclude action, in relation to any state which during the Second World War has been an enemy of any signatory to the present Charter, taken or authorized as a result of that war by the Governments having responsibility for such action.

Article 53 further provides that Security Council authorization is not required for

measures against any enemy state ... provided for pursuant to Article 107 or in regional arrangements directed against renewal of aggressive policy on the part of any such state, until such time as the Organization may, on request of the Governments concerned, be charged with the responsibility for preventing further aggression by such a state.

The purpose of these provisions was to permit states to take or continue to take action against the 'enemy' states until the war was ended and to allow for the formation of regional arrangements that could use force against enemy states in the event of a 'renewal of aggression.' Such 'counter-enemy' action would not need to be approved by the Security Council.

In the decades since the Charter was signed, there are still questions about the applicability of these provisions. The western states believe that 'Articles 53 and 107 were only intended to cover the immediate postwar period and are now obsolete.'[7] But, as British international legal scholar Michael Akehurst points out, '[t]his may be true of Article 107, which appears to be a chapter headed "transitional security arrangements", but the temporary character of Article 53 is much less clear.'[8] Theoretically, an act of aggression by a former enemy state, Japan for example, could still give rise to action by an arrangement that would not be subject to Security Council regulation. But since all of the enemy states have been admitted to the United Nations and since various peace treaties have been concluded between most allied states and the enemy states, such action now seems quite unlikely.[9]

In the contemporary world, these last two exceptions are not very significant. They are noted here, however, because they do appear in the Charter and could, conceivably, although not very probably, be raised. For the purposes of the discussion that follows, it will be assumed that self-defense and force authorized by the Security Council are the only *applicable* explicit exceptions to Article 2(4). Given current international conditions, this seems to be a reasonable assumption.

The theory behind the Charter provisions on the use of force

In order to understand the theory behind the Charter framework for the recourse to force, the historical context of the document must be understood. In 1945, the world was just coming out of a devastating war begun by certain states using force to alter violently the existing political and territorial status quo. Based on this experience, the delegates of the San Francisco Conference were convinced that force was simply too destructive to be considered an acceptable means of pursuing changes or advancing other policy. Force was not to be used to gain territory, to change the government of another state – no matter how 'bad' that government may have been – or even to right a past 'wrong.'[10] Such uses of force were considered 'aggression' or, as Professor Myres McDougal terms them, uses of force for 'value extension,'[11] and were prohibited. Instead, force was to be used only for 'value conservation,'[12] for the preservation of the existing political and territorial status quo, either through the exercise of self-defense or as determined by the Security Council.

This legal arrangement meant that the value choice underlying the Charter framework for the use of force was that maintenance of international peace was to be preferred to the pursuit of 'justice'. Justice – the promotion of human rights, the encouragement of self-determination, the rectification of economic problems, the correction of past wrongs, and the equitable resolution of a host of other problems – was to be sought. In fact, the United Nations Charter established mechanisms to facilitate the pursuit of various 'just' goals.[13] Justice, however, was not to be sought at the expense of peace. Undergirding the Charter was a belief that greater harm would be done to the international system by using force to promote justice than by living with a particular injustice. If peaceful means for seeking justice failed, and the choice was between peace and justice, peace was to prevail. Any threat or use of force against the political or territorial order, no matter how just the cause, was to be considered unlawful.[14]

CONTEMPORARY PROBLEMS WITH THE UNITED NATIONS CHARTER FRAMEWORK FOR THE USE OF FORCE: AN OVERVIEW

Over the years, the international community has *seemed* to reaffirm the validity of the Charter provisions on the use of force. The Security Council, for instance, when dealing with cases involving potential or actual armed conflict will often adopt resolutions that cite approvingly the principles contained in Article 2(4). Initial Council action in the Iran–Iraq war is a case in point. In September of 1980, not long after the fighting had begun, the Council adopted Resolution 479, which contained a preambulatory clause proclaiming that the Council was '[m]indful ... that all members are obliged to refrain in their international relations from the threat of or use of force against the territorial integrity or political independence of any State ...'[15] Numerous General Assembly resolutions have also endorsed Article 2(4). One of the most notable is the 1970 Declaration of Principles of International Law Concerning Friendly Relations and Co-operation Among States in Accordance with the Charter of the United Nations (G.A. Res. 2625). The very first 'principle' that this declaration lists is almost a verbatim reiteration of Article 2(4). Following the citation of this principle, the declaration explains that:

> Every State has the duty to refrain in its international relations from the threat or use of force against the territorial integrity or political independence of any State, or in any other manner inconsistent with the purposes of the United Nations. Such a threat or use of force constitutes a violation of international law and the Charter of the United Nations and shall never be employed as a means of settling international issues.[16]

The declaration then goes on to discuss specific activities that may constitute such unlawful threat or use of force.

The other major organ of the United Nations, the International Court of Justice, has also upheld the authority of the Charter prohibition contained in Article 2(4). In its decision in the 1986 *Nicaragua* case,[17] the Court held that the principles of Article 2(4) were not only treaty law, but the substance of customary international law as well.[18]

These bodies of the United Nations, however, are not the only sources of apparent support for the Charter norms of the use of force. States, the actual creators of international law, have also expressed their individual support for Article 2(4). Such expressions of support, moreover, have come from many different sectors of the community of states. Western states, for instance, have often reaffirmed Article 2(4).[19] For example, the United States, in one of its submissions in the *Nicaragua* case, contended that 'the provisions of Article 2(4) with respect to the lawfulness of the use of force *are* "modern customary law" ... and the "embodiment of general principles of international law ..."'[20] Similarly, former socialist states[21] and even less developed states[22] have frequently expressed words of support for Article 2(4).

Yet despite these many reaffirmations of the sanctity of the Charter norms on the use of force, in the years since 1945 a number of problems have seriously challenged the legitimacy and effectiveness of the Charter framework for the use of force. In order to understand the *current* legal status of the Charter norms, it is thus necessary to understand the nature of these problems and how the international community has attempted to respond to them.

Interpretation problems

The meaning of Article 2(4)

Even before the ink was dry on the Charter, questions arose regarding the proper interpretation of provisions relating to the use of force. One set of these questions related to the meaning of Article 2(4). While the Article may have seemed clear on the surface, a closer reading by government officials and scholars has raised a multitude of specific questions.

First, what exactly is a 'threat or use of force'? Is force to be understood as purely *military force* or *armed force* or does it refer to something broader? Would it be possible, for instance, that certain coercive *diplomatic* or *economic* measures could also be considered force? If, to take an example, one state imposed severe economic sanctions on another for the purpose of bringing that country into submission, would that constitute a 'use of force'?

Second, what is a use of force against the 'territorial integrity' or 'political independence' of another state or force that is 'inconsistent with the Purposes of the United Nations'? Is this simply another way of saying *all* use of force, or do these words have a more specific meaning? In the post-Charter world, some individuals have theorized that it might be possible to use force *in* the territory of another state in such a way that it *does not* affect the territorial integrity or political independence of that state or in any other way transgress the purposes of the United Nations. In other words, some scholars and statesmen have suggested that certain uses of force might fall below the 'Article 2(4) threshold.'[23]

The Meaning of Article 51

Similar problems of interpretation have surfaced with respect to Article 51. First, what constitutes an 'armed attack'? Is an armed attack different from an 'act of aggression,' which is mentioned in Chapter VII of the Charter?

Second, does the reference to a state's right to respond in self-defense 'if an armed attack occurs' indicate that a would-be victim must actually wait for the other side to strike *first* before it can respond? What if there were a situation where the troops of one state were amassing on the border and making bellicose statements in obvious preparation for a major attack? Would the soon-to-be aggrieved state be unable to respond until the troops actually crossed the border or the bombs started falling?

Third, is, in fact, an 'armed attack' the only circumstances giving rise to self-defense? Some have argued that since Article 51 refers to self-defense as an 'inherent right,' the purpose of the Article was not to restrict the pre-existing customary right only to cases of armed attack, but rather to make clear that it would *definitely* apply when an armed attack occurs.[24] These individuals suggest that, consequently, an armed attack may be only one of *several* circumstances under which action in self-defense could lawfully be undertaken.[25]

Fourth, how is 'collective self-defense' exercised? Can a state come to the aid of another *without* the request of the victim state? If a request is required, must it take a specific form? Must, for example, the request be made publicly? Must it be pursuant to a pre-existent collective self-defense treaty, like the Rio Pact or the NATO Treaty?

The changed nature of international conflict

Another problem with which the international community has had to contend is the changed nature of international conflict. In formulating the Charter provisions on the use of force, the framers were primarily concerned about overt acts of conventional aggression – instances where a state sends regular troops into another state or launches air strikes or a naval attack against another state. These were the types of conflict with which the delegates at San Francisco were most familiar. The Second World War had begun because Germany, Japan, and Italy had invaded other states.[26] Consequently, it was conflicts of this nature that the framers sought to regulate.

In the world since 1945, however, most conflict has not been of this nature.[27] While there certainly have been conflicts involving overt aggression – the 1956 invasion of Egypt, the 1982 Falklands War, and most recently, the 1990 Iraqi invasion of Kuwait – most breaches of the peace have taken the form of civil conflicts, mixed conflicts, covert actions, or acts of terrorism. Moreover, the ever-present threat of the use of nuclear and other weapons of mass destruction has also challenged traditional assumptions about warfare.

Civil conflict and mixed conflict

Civil conflict refers to situations in which a state is experiencing *domestic* unrest. This internal strife may range in severity from scattered rioting to full-scale civil war. In the latter case, a rebel faction (or factions) is challenging the authority of the established regime to govern the entire country or a portion of it.

A *mixed conflict*[28] exists when there is an outside state (or states) providing some form of assistance (military, economic, etc.) to either the government or the rebels in an existing civil conflict. It is called a mixed conflict because it is at once a *civil* conflict and, since there is outside intervention, an *international* conflict.

Since the Charter provisions on the use of force do not address themselves clearly to these two types of conflict, legal questions abound. Given a civil conflict, for example, what legal rights do outside states have? Is it lawful for an outside state to provide various forms of assistance – diplomatic, economic, military – to one of the parties in the conflict? For example, if there were civil strife in Mexico, could the United States aid the government? Could it aid the rebels? Does the lawfulness of outside aid depend on the *type* of aid being given? For instance, would economic assistance be lawful but military assistance unlawful? Does the lawfulness of aid depend on the severity of the civil strife? Might a state be able to provide certain assistance to the government when there is a low level of civil unrest but not when there is a full-blown civil war? What if the conflict were already a mixed conflict; how would this affect the legal rights of outside states? Does, in other words, the fact that another state has already intervened alter the legality of further outside intervention?

Covert action

Another phenomenon that has grown in frequency since 1945 is covert action. Rather than a state openly committing acts against the territorial integrity or political independence of another state, it may choose covert means to accomplish the same ends. Such activities may include, but are certainly not limited to, efforts to interfere in the domestic political process of another country, such as election rigging or bribery and blackmail of public officials, dissemination of clandestine propaganda, and even assassination.[29] While these activities may violate the sovereignty of a state, how can the aggrieved state respond? Do these covert acts engender the right of the victim state to use force in self-defense? Can such activities be considered to be tantamount to an 'armed attack'?

Terrorism

The rise of terrorist acts in recent years has also presented an unanticipated problem for the Charter framework. The Charter was drafted to deal with the use of force by *states*. Increasingly, however, private individuals, often as part of an organized 'movement,' have used methods of violence against foreign states or nationals of foreign states in an effort to achieve a particular political purpose. Given the Charter's concern with state actions, what is the legal status of terrorist acts? What recourse do states have against terrorists? What if the terrorist group is being supported by a foreign state for the purpose of threatening the territorial integrity or political independence of another state? Can these overt acts of terrorism be considered to be tantamount to an 'armed attack' and thus give rise to the right of self-defense under Article 51? The plain language of the Charter simply does not answer these questions.

Nuclear weapons

Finally, another change in the nature of international conflict that has caused problems in the post-war period is the development and proliferation of nuclear weapons. When the Charter was being drafted in the spring of 1945, the delegates at San Francisco knew nothing of the nature and effects of nuclear weapons. It was not until August of that year, after the Charter had been signed, that the world became aware of the vast destructive potential of the atom. Hence, the provisions of the Charter dealing with the use of force did not assume a nuclear world. As one of the US delegates to the San Francisco Conference, John Foster Dulles, later explained, the United Nations Charter was a 'pre-atomic age charter.'[30] It could not have addressed the threat, proliferation, and potential use of these weapons of mass destruction. Consequently, in the nuclear world of today, many questions arise about the relationship of the Charter norms to the nuclear problem. Under what circumstances do nuclear weapons constitute a 'threat' to the territorial integrity or political independence of another state? Is mere possession such a threat? Is targeting? Because of the radically increased capabilities of these weapons, are the standards for self-defense against them different from those relating to conventional threats? In other words, are there circumstances under which a state *can* use force to respond to the threat of nuclear weapons but would *not* be able to use force to respond to a threat from conventional weapons?

The perceived illegitimacy of institutions for peaceful change and the peaceful settlement of international disputes

While the drafters of the Charter limited the use of force to self-defense and force authorized by the Security Council, they recognized that at times political, economic, and even territorial changes in the international system might be necessary.[31] They also recognized that other disputes would invariably arise among states that would have the potential to threaten international peace and security. In consequence, the framers established a system to serve as an alternative to force whereby states could pursue change and settle their disputes through peaceful means. Under Chapter VI of the Charter, states may bring disputes to the attention of the General Assembly for their recommendations and the Security Council may, on its own initiative, investigate disputes. Moreover, the Charter also establishes the International Court of Justice to consider legal disputes that parties may choose to submit to it.

Since the adoption of the Charter, however, these mechanisms have increasingly been perceived as illegitimate. This perception has manifested itself in several ways. First, many states have come to regard the institutions of the United Nations as politicized organs incapable of rendering an effective judgment in a dispute. This belief is especially strong among the western states, who tend to regard the General Assembly as a radical body dominated by Third World blocs.[32] Recently, even the International Court of Justice is being seen by some as an institution that bows to non-judicial political considerations.[33] Second, even states that are not necessarily troubled by the political orientation of the United Nations often seem to regard the institution slow and ineffective. The General Assembly, which cannot render a binding decision in these matters in any case, frequently deliberates for years on a particular issue without reaching an acceptable solution. The sovereignty question in the Falklands dispute, for example, had been before the Assembly since 1966 before Argentina finally decided to use force in 1982.[34] Similarly, the Security Council is often unable to resolve a dispute to the satisfaction of the parties. The unfortunate consequence of these perceptions of illegitimacy is that states may feel pressure to use force to obtain change or settle another type of dispute, believing that peaceful mechanisms will produce either a politicized solution or no solution at all.

The preference for 'justice' over 'peace'

Despite the severity of all of these post-war problems, the problem that most seriously challenges the Charter norms on the use of force is the growing preference of states for 'justice' over 'peace.' As noted earlier, the Charter provisions were based on an implicit belief that the avoidance of aggressive force was more important than the pursuit of justice when this pursuit involved the use of aggression. In the post-1945 world, however, states have repudiated this hierarchy of values. In many diverse sectors of the international system, claims have been made that force against the existing political and territorial order may, at times, be justified. These claims seem to have manifested themselves in three different ways: 1) claims to use force to promote self-determination; 2) claims to resort to 'just' reprisals; and 3) claims to use force to correct past 'injustices.'

Self-determination

In the post-Charter period, many states have made a claim that force may be used under circumstances other than self-defense if its purpose is to promote self-determination. Many Less Developed Countries, for example, have advocated the use of force to assist peoples fighting against colonial and racist regimes. This can be seen, for example, in the 1974 'Definition of Aggression' Resolution[35] adopted by the United Nations General Assembly. Article 7 of that Resolution, which was included largely at the urging of the Less Developed Countries,[36] states that:

> Nothing in this Definition, and in particular article 3 [which lists acts that generally qualify as aggression], could in any way prejudice the right to self-determination, freedom and independence, as derived from the Charter, of peoples forcibly deprived of the right referred to in the Declaration on Principles of International Law concerning Friendly Relations and Co-operation among States in accordance with the Charter of the United Nations, particularly peoples under colonial and racist regimes or other forms of alien domination; *nor the right of these people to struggle to that end and to seek and receive support*, in accordance with the principles of the Charter and in conformity with the above mentioned Declaration.[37]

Even if this 'right' is limited by the 'principles of the Charter,' its entire thrust, the implication that a state could assist a self-determination movement that is seeking to alter the political order in a state, seems directly to undercut the intention of Article 2(4).[38]

The Third World, however, has not been alone in its cry for the 'just' use of force under circumstances that seem to conflict with Article 2(4). During the immediate post-war period, members of the Socialist Bloc also developed theories for the 'just' use of force against the political independence and territorial integrity of states. They advocated the use of force to support pro-socialist 'wars of national liberation.'[39] They even argued that it was just to use force to prevent a fellow socialist state from 'regressing' into capitalism.[40] This was, in fact, one of the justifications that the Warsaw Pact made for the 1968 invasion of Czechoslovakia. In a letter to the Central Committee of the Communist Party of Czechoslovakia, the Warsaw Pact states explained that they could not 'assent to hostile forces pushing your country off the path of socialism and creating the threat that Czechoslovakia may break away from the socialist commonwealth. This is no longer your affair.'[41] As a Soviet writer subsequently contended, '[t]he sovereignty of individual socialist countries cannot be counterposed to the interests of world socialism and the world revolutionary movement.'[42] In other words, even though the reforms in Czechoslovakia were internal and did not constitute an 'armed attack' against other states, other socialist states had the 'right' to use force to prevent this improper movement away from socialism.

Finally, western states have also demonstrated a preference for justice over peace. The United States, for example, has recently advocated the use of force to correct 'unjust' conditions abroad and to create 'just' societies.[43] When the United States and the Organisation of Eastern Caribbean States invaded Grenada in 1983, three reason for this action were given by the President of the United States. The first was the protection of US nationals, but the others were

> to forestall further chaos [and] to assist in the restoration of conditions of law and order and of governmental institutions to the island of Grenada, where a brutal group of leftist thugs violently seized power, killing the Prime Minister, three Cabinet Members, two labor leaders and other civilians, including children.[44]

While these may well be noble reasons for the invasion, they do not appear to fall within the permissible exceptions to Article 2(4).

Similarly, US actions in Nicaragua were often portrayed as the promotion of 'just' goals. While on the one hand, the Reagan Administration justified support to the contras in terms of collective self-defense,[45] its statements, on the other hand, often reveal a policy that goes beyond pure self-defense. For instance, in a 1986 interview, President Reagan justified aid to the contras in the following terms:

The cancer that has to be excised is Nicaragua. We can try and help those people who want freedom to bring it about themselves. We have a right to help the people of Nicaragua who are demanding what we think are people's rights – a right to determine their own government.[46]

Here the President was suggesting that states do indeed have a right to assist those forcibly fighting for self-determination, even though such actions seek to alter the political status quo.

Perhaps the most recent case in which the United States used self-determination as one justification for the recourse to force was the 1989 invasion of Panama.[47] While self-defense and the protection of American nationals were the main legal justifications for the action,[48] the Bush Administration also claimed that it was acting to 'restore the democratic process.'[49] The Administration contended that because Guillermo Endara was not allowed by Manuel Noriega to assume the presidency, the existing regime was unconstitutional.[50] Hence, American actions were permissible, as President Bush said, 'to defend democracy in Panama.'[51]

Forcible reprisals

Another indication of a growing willingness to use force in certain 'just' circumstances can be seen in the area of reprisals. In the post-Charter period, a forcible reprisal is a quick, limited, forcible response by one state against a prior action by another state that did not rise to the level of an armed attack.[52] Unlike the typical action taken in self-defense, the purpose of a reprisal is not the immediate protection of a state from an on-going attack. Instead, as Professor Derek Bowett has explained,

> reprisals are punitive in character: they seek to impose reparation for the harm done, or to compel a satisfactory settlement of the dispute created by the initial illegal act, or to compel the delinquent state to abide by the law in the future.[53]

Since by definition the injury precipitating a reprisal falls short of an armed attack, scholars have generally agreed that reprisals would thus be prohibited under the UN Charter. As Professor Brownlie has observed, '[t]he provisions of the Charter relating to the peaceful settlement of disputes and non-resort to the use of force are universally regarded as prohibiting reprisals which involve the use of force.'[54]

Notwithstanding this apparent prohibition, states have frequently claimed the right to resort to reprisals when they have believed that such reprisals were 'just.' These claims were most notably chronicled by Professor Bowett in a 1972 article[55] and have been recently up-dated in an article by Professor William V. O'Brien.[56] In these articles, the authors examine such actions as the British air attacks in Yemen in 1964,[57] the Israeli raid on Beirut Airport in

1968,[58] the Israeli raids against Lebanon in 1975,[59] the 1985 Israeli raid on Tunis,[60] and the 1986 US air strike against Libya.[61] While noting that virtually all these uses of force were justified as actions taken in self-defense, the authors explain that the notion of self-defense employed was quite broad.[62] Rather than claiming that the force was necessary for *immediate* protection, the states involved frequently contended that force was being used for purposes of deterrence or punishment.[63] For example, Bowett cites a press report in which a former Israeli Chief of Staff claimed that one purpose of the 1968 Beirut raid was 'to make clear to the other side that the price they must pay for terrorist activities can be very high.'[64] Similarly, in the 1986 air strike against Libya, US officials emphasized that the action was taken in the exercise of the right of self-defense.[65] Much of their argument centered around the notion that the accumulation of actions by Libya taken over a period of time rose to the level of an armed attack.[66] Yet, even as they were making this claim, they contended that 'self-defense' involved more than simply repelling an armed attack. In a statement released from the White House, it was argued that

> [i]n light of this reprehensible [Libyan] act of violence and clear evidence that Libya is planning future attacks, the United States has chosen to exercise its right of self-defense. It is our hope that [US] action will *preempt* and *discourage* Libyan attacks on innocent civilians in the *future*.[67]

President Reagan echoed this theme in his address to the American people, explaining that '[w]e believe that this preemptive action against terrorist installations will not only diminish Colonel Qadhafi's capacity to export terror, it will provide him with incentives and reasons to alter his criminal behavior.'[68]

Irrespective of the merits of any of the cases reviewed by O'Brien or Bowett, their examinations seem to indicate that while states are formally unwilling to depart from the Charter paradigm for justifying their actions, they have expanded the notion of self-defense to include actions undertaken for purposes of deterrence and even punishment. These reasons, while perhaps politically and even morally commendable, seem nevertheless at variance with the Charter value hierarchy of peace over justice.

Correction of past 'injustice'

Finally, despite Article 2(4), states have asserted that it is permissible to use force to rectify unjust conditions in the political or territorial status quo. Even though a fundamental assumption underlying the Charter is that actual change in the international system should only be sought through peaceful means, states have frequently claimed that force is permissible when peaceful means have failed or appear to be ineffective. Several prominent examples should serve to illustrate this point.

In July of 1956, Egyptian President Nassar nationalized the Suez Canal.[69] After several months of multilateral efforts to establish an international regime to regulate the Canal, Israel began military operations against Egypt. This was immediately followed by joint British and French military actions against Nasser. The British and French justifications for their actions proved to be extremely telling. The French representative to the Security Council explained that

> [t]he Governments of France and the United Kingdom ... considered that there existed a serious threat to the Suez Canal and that, unless swift, effective and decisive action was taken immediately, we ran the risk that traffic through the Canal would be seriously impeded for an indefinite period.[70]

The French Ambassador went on to say that France and Great Britain

> took the view that it was their duty to take all necessary steps, even if these steps should, at first, be misunderstood by certain of their friends, in order to safeguard and maintain free passage through the Canal against any interference.[71]

In support of a right of free passage, the British and French cited the 1888 Constantinople Convention,[72] which had been accepted by Egypt.

Here the two states seems to be arguing the classic doctrine of self-help. Because Egypt's nationalization of the Canal threatened freedom of navigation, it constituted an unjust, illegal alteration in the status quo. As such, it was proper to respond to this act through the use of force. In short, despite the Charter's insistence that even just causes take a back seat to the over-riding goal of preventing the recourse to force, Britain and France believed that in this case an exception should be made.

An analogous claim of just recourse to force was made in 1973 by the Arab states who invaded Israel. Their actions, it was contended, were undertaken to win back territory that Israel had unjustly occupied. In the 1967 War, Israel had seized the Sinai Peninsula and the Golan Heights. Accordingly, the Arab states argued that Israel did not have lawful title to these territories and thus force was permissible to regain them. As Professor Shihata has explained, this argument contended that 'Egypt and Syria as the states vested with sovereignty, but illegally deprived of actual control, over territories occupied by Israel were thus legally entitled to seek redress for the protection of their territorial integrity.'[73] When peaceful means proved to be 'in vain,'[74] the Arab states were justified in taking forcible measures.[75] Here again, the Arab states seem to be arguing that if elements of the territorial status quo are so unjust, it is permissible to use force to attempt to correct these elements. But even assuming *arguendo* that the Israeli possession of the territories was illegal, the value system of the Charter would only permit the use of force as authorized by the Security Council or in response to an armed attack. Even if the territories were taken illegally in 1967, once Israeli occupation of them became the status quo, that status quo could only by changed through peaceful mechanisms.

A more recent example of a forcible effort to change the status quo occurred in the 1982 Falklands War. In this case, Argentina's justification for the use of force was quite similar to that taken by the Arab states in 1973. Argentina claimed that the British had illegally seized the Falklands in the 1830s and had thus been in wrongful possession of their territory.[76] In consequence, force was simply being used to recover what was rightly Argentina's territory. Moreover, as Argentine Foreign Minister Costa-Mendez explained to the United Nations Security Council, even though Argentina had 'been accused in this chamber of violating Article [sic] 2 (3) and 4 of the United Nations Charter,' '[n]o provision of the Charter can be taken to mean the legitimization of situations which have their origins in wrongful acts, in acts carried out before the Charter was adopted and which subsisted during its prevailing force.'[77] In other words, Costa-Mendez was contending the Charter prohibition on the use of force did not apply to force used to correct illegitimate acts, or, at the very least, illegitimate acts done before the Charter was adopted.

Taken together, these problems, and others that could be added, have called into question the continuing validity of the Charter framework for the use of force. How has the international community responded to these difficulties? What efforts have been made to provide authoritative inter-pretations of the Charter? How have decision-makers and scholars attempted to adapt the Charter to the changed nature of international conflict? What are the implications of the perceived illegitimacy of mechanisms for peaceful change and peaceful settlement and the growing preference for justice over peace for the current status of the Charter norms? In light of all this, is the Article 2(4) prohibition on the use of force still indicative of existing inter-national law? If not, what norms have taken its place? All these questions, and others that relate to the efficacy of the Charter framework, will be examined in greater detail in subsequent chapters.

CHAPTER SUMMARY

When the United Nations Charter was drafted in 1945, it sought to create legal norms to regulate the behavior of states. These norms are treaty law and many of them may also be customary international law, if states regard them as authoritative and if they are controlling. One set of rules that the Charter contains are rules relating to the recourse to force. The most basic provision of the Charter in this area is Article 2(4), which establishes a general pro-hibition on the use of force by states. The only two exceptions to this rule that still have major significance are self-defense (Article 51) and force authorized by the Security Council (Chapter VII). While states have often proclaimed their support for these Charter provisions, since 1945 several problems have raised many questions about the contemporary status of these norms. These problems include: 1) interpretation problems; 2) the changed nature of international conflict; 3) the perceived illegitimacy of institutions for peaceful change and peaceful settlement; and, 4) the growing preference for justice over peace. It is with these problems that leaders and scholars alike must grapple in order to determine the validity of the Charter framework for the use of force.

Chapter 4

Collective use of force under the United Nations Charter

INTRODUCTION

When any legal system seeks to outlaw particular actions, it is generally desirable for that system to have a mechanism to enforce the law. This mechanism serves not only to punish transgressors of the law, but also, it is hoped, to deter would-be transgressors with the threat of punishment. Not surprisingly, when the UN Charter was being drafted, the framers recognized that if the new international legal order were to prohibit certain uses of force, it would be useful to establish international institutions to enforce the Charter prohibitions. They were troubled, however, by the inability of the League of Nations' institutions to prevent states from using force in violation of the League Covenant. Hence, the delegates at San Francisco sought to create a mechanism for upholding Article 2(4) that would avoid at least some of the pitfalls of the League system.

The purpose of this chapter is to examine the institutions created by the United Nations Charter for the collective use of force and to explore some of the difficulties with these institutions that have developed since 1945. In order to do so, the first section will discuss the Charter framework for the collective use of forces; the second section will discuss some of the problems with this Charter framework, and the third section will then examine efforts to respond to these problems and the implications of these efforts.

THE CHARTER FRAMEWORK FOR THE COLLECTIVE USE OF FORCE

The Charter provisions on the collective use of force

As noted earlier, the major provisions of the United Nations Charter dealing with the collective use of force are contained in Chapter VII of the Charter, which is entitled 'Action with Respect to Threats to the Peace, Breaches of the Peace, and Acts of Aggression.' Broadly speaking, this chapter deals with two aspects of the collective use of force: the authority of the Security Council and the mechanism for imposing collective sanctions.

Chapter VII: the authority of the Security Council

The basic provision of the Charter relating to the authority of the Security Council to deal with conflict is Article 39. This Article provides:

> The Security Council shall determine the existence of any threat to the peace, breach of the peace, or act of aggression and shall make recommendations, or decide what measures shall be taken in accordance with Articles 41 and 42, to maintain or restore international peace and security.[1]

Article 39, therefore, gives the Security Council two functions. First, it gives it the authority to determine if there is a threat to the peace, a breach of the peace, or an act of aggression. Second, it empowers it to make 'recommendations' or decide what 'measures' shall be taken to remedy the situation.

With respect to the first power, no precise definition was provided by the framers as to what constitutes a 'threat to the peace,' a 'breach of the peace,' or an 'act of aggression.'[2] In the practice of the United Nations Security Council, the meaning of these phrases appears to be quite subjective. It seems clear only that in terms of the magnitude of the problems a 'threat to the peace' is the least severe and an 'act of aggression' is the most severe.[3] Moreover, although the Council has never declared the existence of an act of aggression[4], the General Assembly spent years attempting to define aggression[5] and, as noted earlier, in 1974 adopted the 'Definition of Aggression' Resolution,[6] which was, of course, not binding on the Council or states.

The second power enumerated in Article 39, the power to determine what recommendations or other actions should be taken, also requires some explanation. Generally, it seems to have been understood by the framers that the power to make 'recommendations' related to the authority of the Council under *Chapter VII* (Pacific Settlement of Disputes) to recommend action to the *parties* for the peaceful resolution of the underlying dispute.[7] Such recommendations *were not* binding and would not affect any other action ordered by the Council against the recalcitrant state.

This latter action was the heart of Security Council power in the event of a threat to the peace, breach of the peace, or act of aggression and was elaborated in Articles 41 and 42. Article 41 provides:

> The Security Council may decide what measures not involving the use of armed force are to be employed to give effect to its decisions, and it may call upon the Members of the United Nations to apply such measures. These may include complete or partial interruption of economic relations and of rail, sea, air, postal, telegraphic, radio, and other means of communication, and the severance of diplomatic relations.[8]

This provision authorizes the Security Council to impose non-military sanctions on an offending state. Possible sanctions include, but are not limited to those mentioned.

When the Council adopts a resolution mandating these sanctions, the order is binding on all members of the United Nations, or, if the Council so determines, those states necessary to carry out the task. This is in accordance with Article 48, which provides in part that '[t]he action required to carry out the decisions of the Security Council for the maintenance of international peace and security shall be taken by all the Members of the United Nations or by some of them, as the Security Council may determine.'[9]

If the sanctions under Article 41 are deemed insufficient by the Council, military sanctions can be ordered in accordance with Article 42. This Article provides:

> Should the Security Council consider that the measures provided for in Article 41 would be inadequate or have proved to be inadequate, it may take such action by air, sea, or land forces as may be necessary to maintain or restore international peace and security. Such action may include demonstrations, blockade, and other operations by air, sea, or land forces of Members of the United Nations.[10]

Such actions taken under Article 42 are commonly referred to as 'enforcement actions'[11] and are directed against the state that represents a threat to the peace, has breached the peace, or has committed an act of aggression. Like measures under Article 41, actions taken under Article 42 are binding on member states in accordance with Article 48. This provision is in marked contrast to those of the League of Nations Covenant, which stipulated that the League Council could only *recommend* that states take military action against a Covenant-breaking state.

In addition to these powers under Articles 41 and 42, the Security Council is also authorized to take 'provisional measures' under Article 40. Article 40 provides:

> In order to prevent an aggravation of the situation, the Security Council may, before making recommendations or deciding upon the measures provided for in Article 39, call upon the parties concerned to comply with such provisional measures as it deems necessary or desirable. Such provisional measures shall be without prejudice to the rights, claims, or position of the parties concerned. The Security Council shall duly take account of failure to comply with such provisional measures.[12]

In other words, prior to deciding what longer-term action to take, the Council can impose 'provisional measures.' Such measures are not spelled-out, but are rather left to the discretion of the Council. The provision that such measures 'shall be without prejudice to the rights, claims, or position of the parties,' was probably included to indicate that provisional measures were not meant to resolve finally all the underlying issues of a particular dispute, but only to handle the immediate problem of the conflict.[13] A rough analogy can be drawn to an injunction under domestic law, where the court orders a party to refrain from a particular course of action pending resolution of the overall case and without prejudice to the ultimate rights of the parties. Interestingly enough, in practice the Council has taken actions under Article 40 that often have appeared to be dispositive of some of the underlying aspects of a dispute.[14]

The exact legal status of action take by the Council under Article 40 is somewhat uncertain. Charter commentators Goodrich, Hambro, and Simons indicate that '[t]here would appear to be considerable agreement that the parties concerned are obligated to comply with resolutions specifically adopted under Article 40 [and] that other members are obligated to assist in carrying out such resolutions,'[15] but '[t]here is considerable less agreement as to whether these obligations are applicable, if the Council fails to cite Article 40 and/or fails to make a formal determination under Article 39 that a threat to the peace, breach of the peace, or act of aggression exists.'[16]

Chapter VII: the mechanism for imposing military sanctions

In addition to granting the Security Council the authority to order military sanctions, Chapter VII also establishes a mechanism for the Council to use to impose these sanctions. In order to do this, Chapter VII addresses two main issues: the availability of military forces and the means for coordinating the use of these forces.

Since the Council lacked its own 'police force,' it was necessary to create an arrangement so that it could get troops from the member states at times when they were needed. To facilitate this, Article 43 provides that all members of the United Nations were to conclude special agreements with the Security Council through which they would make available to the Council certain contingents of their armed forces.[17] At the time of a conflict, the Council would thus be able to summon these troops without the need for further agreements with the member states. The agreements were to be rather detailed and were to 'govern the numbers and types of forces, their degree of readiness and general location.'[18] They were also to contain provisions relating to other assistance and facilities that the member states might provide to the Council.[19]

In order to coordinate the use of these forces, Article 47 calls for the establishment of a Military Staff Committee.[20] This Committee was

> to advise and assist the Security Council on all questions relating to the Security Council's military requirements for the maintenance of international peace and security, the employment and command of forces placed at its disposal, the regulations of armaments, and possible disarmament.[21]

The Committee was to be composed 'of the Chiefs of Staff of the permanent members of the Security Council or their representatives'[22] and any other members that the Committee may choose to invite. According to Article 47, this Committee was to be 'responsible under the Security Council for the strategic direction of any armed forces placed at the disposal of the Security Council.'[23] Tactical issues 'relating to the command of such forces' were to be 'worked out subsequently.'[24]

The theory behind the Charter provisions on the collective use of force

The United Nations system developed in Chapter VII of the Charter draws upon a well-known approach to conflict management: collective security. In a collective security system, the prevention of aggression, the illegal resort to force, is the primary goal.[25] All states belonging to the system form an international organization and pledge, long in advance of any particular conflict, to act collectively to defeat any aggressor state, irrespective of that state's character or geographic location. The anti-aggressor actions undertaken by the organization would include whatever methods were deemed necessary to defeat the recalcitrant state – diplomatic sanctions, economic sanctions, and, if need be, military sanctions. A body of the organization would be empowered to determine whether an act of aggression had occurred and how the organization should respond. In a pure collective security system, such determinations would be binding on all states. There would also be specific mechanisms established to implement the sanctions. Consequently, the organization would be able to react forcefully and swiftly if an illegal use of force were to take place. Under the theory of collective security, it is hoped that this arrangement would deter any would-be aggressor, since such a state would realize that if it were to commit an act of aggression, the overwhelming power of the rest of the world would be pitted against it.[26]

At first glance, the United Nations would appear to be a perfect representative of a collective security system. States, by their adherence to the Charter, renounce the unilateral use of force. The Security Council is empowered to determine if a threat to the peace, a breach of the peace, or an act of aggression has occurred and is then authorized to decide how the organization shall respond. These decisions of the Security Council are binding on all member states, and there is a mechanism to implement these decisions. Despite these appearances, however, the United Nations was never a true collective security system – not even at its creation.

In a pure collective security arrangement, no state can ever exempt itself from the collective action of the organization. All states, no matter how powerful, would be subject to the imposition of sanctions in the event they committed an act of aggression. In the UN system, this is not the case. Each of the five permanent members of the Security Council – United States, Russia (as successor to the Soviet Union), China, Great Britain, and France –

has a veto in the decision making process of the Council with respect to enforcement actions.[27] If all of the other members of the Council voted in favor of a resolution to institute an enforcement action against a permanent member, that permanent member could simply veto the resolution and it would not pass. Hence, even before the ink was dry on the Charter, it was clear that that document did not establish a true system of collective security. At best, the Charter established only a 'modified' or 'limited' form of collective security.

Collective uses of force by the United Nations

In the history of the United Nations, the Security Council has authorized the use of force against an aggressor in only two conflicts: the Korean War and the Gulf War. Additionally, the Council has authorized the use of force in the Somalian Civil War.

The Korean War

In June of 1950, North Korean forces moved below the 38th parallel into the south. Almost immediately, the United States brought a complaint to the United Nations Security Council. At the time of the invasion, the Soviet Union was boycotting the meetings of the Council in protest at the seating of a representative of the Republic of China (Nationalist China) on the Council. The Soviets had argued that only a representative of the People's Republic of China should be allowed to serve in the China seat. On June 25, the Council adopted Resolution 82 by a vote 9–0, with Yugoslavia abstaining and the Soviet Union absent. In this resolution, the Council noted 'with grave concern the armed attack upon the Republic of Korea by forces from North Korea.'[28] It further called upon 'all Members [of the United Nations] to render every assistance to the United Nations in the execution of this resolution and to refrain from giving assistance to the North Korean authorities.'[29] Pursuant to this resolution, the United States had 'ordered air and sea forces to give cover and support to South Korean troops.'[30]

On June 27, 1950, the Security Council adopted Resolution 83 in which the Council determined 'that the armed attack upon the Republic of Korea by forces from North Korea constitutes a breach of the peace.'[31] Most importantly, however, the resolution indicated further that the Council '[r]ecommend[ed] that the Members of the United Nations furnish such assistance to the Republic of Korea as may be necessary to repel the armed attack and to restore international peace and security in the area.'[32] In other words, the Council authorized states to use force to end the armed attack. A few days later, on July 7, the Council approved Resolution 84 establishing a Unified Military Command under the leadership of the United States. In this resolution, the Council:

3. *Recommend[ed]* that all Members providing military forces and other assistance pursuant to the aforesaid Security Council Resolutions make such forces and other assistance available to a unified command under the United States;

4. *Request[ed]* the United States to designate the commander of such forces;

With this authorization, the United States began to establish this Command under the direction of General Douglas MacArthur.

On July 27, as the United Nations forces were continuing their efforts in Korea, the Soviet delegate returned to the meeting of the Security Council. After making another unsuccessful effort to remove the representative of Nationalist China from the Council, the Soviet representative remained present at all subsequent sessions of the Council and blocked any further resolutions on the Korean War.

This action was the first time the Security Council had authorized states to use force in response to an act of aggression. It should be noted, however, that this action was not a true enforcement action since it was not *binding* on member states but only a *recommendation*. Moreover, the Council was able to reach a decision only because of the fortuitous absence of the Soviet Union.

The Gulf War

The second occasion on which the Security Council was able to authorize the collective use of force came in the wake of the Iraqi invasion of Kuwait in 1990. When the Iraqi army moved into Kuwait on August 2, 1990, the international community responded in an unprecedented fashion. On the day of the invasion, the Security Council adopted Resolution 660 by a vote of 14–0, with Yemen not voting. In this Resolution, the Council condemned the invasion and demanded 'that Iraq withdraw immediately and unconditionally all its forces to the position in which they were located on 1 August 1990.'[33] Four days later the Council adopted Resolution 661 by a vote of 13—0, with Yemen and Cuba abstaining. In this Resolution, the Council, declared itself to be '[a]cting under Chapter VII of the Charter' and imposed sweeping economic sanctions on Iraq.[34]

Shortly thereafter, the Iraqi Revolutionary Command Council proclaimed that it had 'decided to return the part and branch, Kuwait, to the whole and origin, Iraq, in a comprehensive, eternal and inseparable merger unity.'[35] Following Iraq's claim of annexation, the Council unanimously adopted Resolution 662. This Resolution not only reiterated the Council's demand 'that Iraq withdraw immediately and unconditionally all its forces from Kuwait,' but also decided 'that annexation by Iraq under any form and whatever pretext has no legal validity, and is considered null and void' and demanded 'that Iraq rescind its actions purporting to annex Kuwait.'[36]

While these actions were taking place in the Security Council, a military coalition was being formed to respond to the Iraqi actions. Under the coordination of the United States, land, air, and naval forces of states were being deployed in the Persian Gulf area.[37] In order to implement the economic sanctions, the United States began using its naval force to interdict shipping in the Persian Gulf to prevent the movement of goods to and from Iraq or Iraqi occupied Kuwait.[38] This action was justified by the United States as permissible under Article 51 of the Charter. The Americans contended that since an armed attack had taken place against Kuwait, forcible interdiction of shipping would be a permissible act of collective self-defense. A number of individuals, including the Secretary-General of the United Nations, disputed this claim and the United States undertook to obtain Security Council approval for such interdiction. This approval came on August 25, when the Council adopted Resolution 665. This resolution called upon

> those Member States co-operating with the Government of Kuwait which are deploying maritime force to the area to use such measures commensurate to the specific circumstances as may be necessary under the authority of the Security Council to halt all inward and outward maritime shipping in order to inspect and verify their cargoes and destinations and to ensure strict implementation of the provisions related to such shipping laid down in resolution 661 (1990).[39]

The resolution did not explicitly mention the 'use of force.' Nevertheless, it was clear from the negotiations surrounding the resolution's adoption that its intent was to provide authorization for states to use force if necessary.[40]

As time passed during the autumn of 1990, Iraq continued to remain in Kuwait. Even though there was some indication that the economic sanctions might have been having some effect on Iraq, a number of states believed that military force would be necessary to remove Iraq. In light of the belief, and after much negotiations, the Security Council adopted Resolution 678 on November 29, 1990. This resolution

> *Authorizes* Member States co-operating with the Government of Kuwait, unless Iraq on or before 15 January 1991 fully implements ... the foregoing resolutions, to use all necessary means to uphold and implement resolution 660 (1990) and all subsequent relevant resolutions and to restore international peace and security in the area.[41]

Once again, the word 'force' was not explicitly used, but it was clear that the Council intended 'all necessary means' to include the possible use of force.[42] On January 16, 1991, when allied forces began the war against Iraq, it was pursuant to this resolution.[43]

The actions of the United Nations during the Gulf War were truly unprecedented. They represented the first time in the history of the organization that all the permanent members of the Security Council had united to authorize the collective use of force in response to an act of aggression.

As the Gulf War was coming to an end, the United Nations Security Council continued to maintain an active role. On April 2, 1991, it adopted Resolution 687.[44] This Resolution established the conditions for a formal cease-fire and imposed unprecedented requirements on Iraq. In particular, it ordered Iraq to destroy chemical, biological, and nuclear weapons facilities in Iraq and to destroy existing ballistic missiles.[45] The Resolution further required Iraq to submit to international inspections to insure that these actions were carried out.[46] On April 5, 1991, the Security Council adopted Resolution 688. In this resolution, the Council recalled 'Article 2, paragraph 7, of the Charter of the United Nations,'[47] but went on to condemn 'the repression of the Iraqi civilian population in many parts of Iraq.'[48] The Council noted that this treatment of civilians 'led to a massive flow of refugees toward and across international frontiers and to cross border incursions, which threaten international peace and security.'[49] The Council demanded that Iraq 'immediately end this repression' and ordered Iraq to 'allow immediate access by international humanitarian organizations to all those in need of assistance in all parts of Iraq and to make available all necessary facilities for their operations . . .'[50] On April 18, Iraqi Foreign Minister Ahmed Hussein signed a Memorandum of Understanding accepting the Security Council's demands.[51]

These actions by the United Nations are quite remarkable. Even though human rights violations had been condemned before as threats to international peace and security, this was the first time that the United Nations *ordered* a state to receive humanitarian assistance from international agencies. Moreover, as Paul Lewis of the *New York Times* explained, '[n]ever before has the United Nations Security Council held that governments threaten international security if their actions force thousands of their citizens to flee to other lands.'[52]

Since the Gulf War, the Security Council has continued to take a more active role in response to threats to the peace, breaches of the peace, and acts of aggression. It has on two occasions imposed stringent economic sanctions. In April of 1992, the Council imposed economic sanctions on Libya for supporting terrorist groups and refusing to extradite two individuals wanted in connection with the bombing of Pan Am Flight 103.[53] In May of 1992, the Council ordered the imposition of economic sanctions on Serbia for acts of violence against Bosnia-Herzogovina.[54] In late 1992, the Council took action in Somalia.

The Somalian Civil War

The third United Nations' authorization of the collective use of force came in the wake of the devastating civil war in Somalia. For some time, the situation in the east African state had been deteriorating. With the ouster of President Said Barre in January of 1991, the country was plunged deeper into civil strife as rival factions struggled for control. At the urging of Secretary-General Boutros Boutros-Ghali, the United Nations began providing humanitarian assistance to the Somali people. Unfortunately, it became increasingly difficult for the organization to assure that the assistance was reaching the individuals in need as warring groups prevented the delivery of food and other items.

In November of 1992, the United States offered to provide troops to ensure that humanitarian aid would reach its target. In response to this request, the Secretary-General recommended that the United Nations accept the US offer. As a consequence, on December 3, 1992, the Security Council unanimously adopted Resolution 794. In this resolution, the Council 'welcome[d] the offer by a Member State [i.e., the United States] . . . concerning the establishment of an operation to create such a secure environment [for humanitarian assistance].' The Council went on to declare that it was '[a]cting under Chapter VII of the Charter' and, accordingly, 'authoriz[ed] the Secretary-General and Member States cooperating to implement the offer referred to . . . to use all necessary means to establish as soon as possible a secure environment for humanitarian relief operations in Somalia.'[55] As in Resolution 678, the word 'force' was not explicitly used. Nevertheless, it was clear from the surrounding discussion that the intent of Resolution 794 was to permit states to use force if necessary to assure that the relief efforts were successful.[56] Pursuant to this authorization, the United States sent members of its armed forces into the war-torn country.

This authorization to use force was quite novel. Even though not act of aggression had occurred, the Council considered the situation in Somalia 'a threat to international peace and security' and thus could act under Chapter VII. While this action by the United Nations could be considered by some to be an act of 'humanitarian intervention,' this term does not really seem to apply. As will be seen in Chapter 8, 'humanitarian intervention' in the traditional sense refers to a use of force that has not been authorized by the Security Council. In the case of Somalia, even though the purpose of UN action may have been humanitarian in nature, its legal basis was not in some doctrine of humanitarian intervention but rather in the right of the Security Council under Chapter VII to authorize collective force as it sees fit to respond to a threat to the peace.

PROBLEMS WITH THE CHARTER FRAMEWORK FOR THE COLLECTIVE USE OF FORCE

Notwithstanding the actions of the United Nations on the Gulf War, the Security Council has been unable to respond effectively to aggression throughout most of the UN's history. In the world since 1945, several major problems have confronted the system for the collective use of force established by the Charter. While a host of different problems could be listed, three in particular seem to have presented the most difficulties for the effectiveness of the Charter system: the veto, the inability to establish formal mechanisms for collective action, and the rejection of limited collective security.

The Veto: the inability of the Security Council to act

One of the major obstacles to Security Council actions has been the veto. Even though the right of the permanent members to veto resolutions in the Security Council was established by the Charter,[57] the widespread use of the veto, especially in the early days,[58] to block nearly all possible actions by the Security Council against aggression was not anticipated by the framers of the Charter.[59] In the years since 1945, the veto has prevented the Council from taking action against an aggressor in numerous instances. For example, the vetoes by Britain and France precluded action in the 1956 Suez Crisis. Similarly, vetoes by the Soviet Union frustrated Council efforts after the Indian Invasion of Goa in 1961, during the Indian–Pakistani war in 1971, and following the Soviet invasion of Afghanistan in 1979. As noted above, only three times in the history of the United Nations has the Council been able to authorize the use of force against an aggression. The first time it was able to do so only because of the absence of one of the permanent members. The second and third times occurred during the Iraqi crisis. It remains to be seen whether the veto will stymie Council action in the future.

The inability to establish formal mechanisms for collective action

Another problem that has inhibited the collective use of force has been the failure of the United Nations to establish the formal mechanisms envisioned by the Charter. As noted above, all members were to conclude agreements with the Security Council to make available certain contingents of their military for use in enforcement actions. Although efforts were made by the Military Staff Committee in the early sessions of the United Nations to formulate these agreements, none was ever concluded. The main reason for this failure was, not surprisingly, the disagreements that arose between the Soviet Union and the other permanent members of the Security Council and especially between the Soviet Union and the United States.[60] Most of these disagreements centered around the size and composition of the forces that were to be made available to the Council. Underlying these differences seems to have been a fear by the Soviet Union that these forces, which would more than likely have consisted largely of 'western' troops, could ultimately have been used against the Soviet Union.[61] In any event, fruitful negotiations on these Article 43 agreements broke down in mid-1947.[62] Throughout the rest of the Cold War, while the Military Staff Committee continued to meet, it did so 'only as a matter of form.'[63] It was only in the late 1980s and early 1990s that the prospects for enhancing the role of the Committee were raised.[64] Interestingly enough, however, the Committee played no formal role in coordinating activity in the Gulf War.

Following the election of Boutros Boutros-Ghali as Secretary-General of the United Nations in late 1991, efforts were undertaken to attempt to create new mechanisms for the collective use of force. On June 18, 1992, Boutros-Ghali presented a report to the United Nations Security Council outlining his proposal to establish a permanent United Nations force.[65] This force could be sent to areas of potential conflict *before* the outbreak of violence in the hope of deterring a breach of the peace.[66] If such a force is established, it could greatly enhance the organization's ability to fight aggression collectively.

The rejection of limited collective security

But even given these two problems, another development seems to present an even greater challenge to the Charter system for collective action. In the world since 1945, states in general have come to reject the value of limited collective security. For the Charter system to work, nearly all members of the international community have to be committed to use force to fight aggression wherever and whenever it may occur. Throughout most of the life of the United Nations this has not been the case. States are frequently not willing to use force even against actions that they might regard as aggression.[67] When an ally commits aggression, for example, few states would be inclined to use force against it. States are also not disposed to use force against an aggressor who seems to pose only a minimal threat to their own country. They are simply not committed enough to the principle of collective security to be willing to use force in circumstances that seem to have little direct relevance to their own national security goals. Even as the recent United Nation's reaction to the Iraqi attack on Kuwait[68] may indicate a new-found willingness to fight aggression, this action is most notable as a momentous exception in UN practice. Indeed, it is important to note that even in the wake of the euphoria of the Gulf War, the United Nations Security Council took no action in spring of 1991, when rebel forces of the National Patriotic Front of Liberia invaded Sierra Leone.[69]

In short, the institutions established by the framers to ensure that the prohibition on the recourse to force was upheld have not proven very effective. What remains is a restriction with little record of enforcement.

EFFORTS TO RESPOND TO THESE PROBLEMS

In light of these problems that have developed with the Charter framework for the collective use of force, states have attempted to find alternative methods to deal with international conflict. First, as it became clear that the Security Council was going to be unable to function as originally envisioned, states began looking to other international institutions to fight aggression. Second, as efforts to fight aggression in general seemed to be less than successful, international organizations began to use 'peacekeeping' as an alternative to collective security.

The use of other institutions

The General Assembly

As it became apparent that the Security Council would be unable to fulfill much of its duties in the area of conflict management, many states began looking to the General Assembly as a natural substitute. The first effort to assign more responsibility to the General Assembly in the area of peace and security came in 1947 through the creation of the Interim Committee. Theoretically, this body was to deal with issues that would come up during the period between sessions of the General Assembly. But, as Goodrich, Hambro, and Simons explain, '[t]he principal purpose in creating the Committee, largely unstated, was to have in being an organ that could investigate serious situations and summon a special Assembly session when necessary, particular if the Security Council was paralyzed by the veto.'[70] Not surprisingly, the Soviet Union opposed the Interim Committee and refused to attend its sessions. After March of 1951, the Committee stopped meeting.[71]

The second effort to enhance the authority of the General Assembly in the area of peace and security came during the Korean war with the adoption of the so-called 'Uniting for Peace' Resolution. As noted earlier, the Security Council was initially able to recommend that states take action against North Korea because of the absence of the Soviet Union. Once the Soviet Union returned to the Council, however, it effectively blocked any further action. In consequence, when further action was necessary, the United States and several other states decided to take the matter to the General Assembly, where they were able to obtain favorable results.

To empower the Assembly to take such actions in the future, the United States introduced the 'Uniting for Peace' Resolution. This resolution, which was adopted by the Assembly on November 3, 1950, provided, in part, that:

> if the Security Council, because of lack of unanimity of the permanent members, fails to exercise its primary responsibility for the maintenance of international peace and security in any case where there appears to be a threat to the peace, breach of the peace, or act of aggression, the General Assembly shall consider the matter immediately with a view to making appropriate recommendations to Members for collective measures, including in the case of a breach of peace or act of aggression

the use of armed force when necessary, to maintain or restore international peace and security.[72]

In other words, if the Security Council were blocked by a veto, the Assembly was to take up the matter, and if there actually were a breach of the peace or act of aggression, the Assembly could *recommend* that states take collective action against the offending state.

While many had hoped that this resolution would cause the Assembly to take the lead in fighting aggression, this has not proved to be the case. In the years since 1950, the General Assembly has never recommended the collective use of force against a state breaching the peace or committing an act of aggression. As an institution, it has been unable to fill the gap left by the impotence of the Security Council.

Regional arrangements

In addition to attempting to use the General Assembly as a replacement for the Security Council, states have also tried to use regional organizations to manage international conflict, and scholars and government officials have developed various arguments about the lawfulness of such regional actions. Before examining these cases and arguments, it is first necessary to understand the UN Charter provisions relating to regional arrangements.

The Charter provisions on regional arrangements: Chapter VIII

When the Allies began their efforts to develop a post-Second World War international order, a major debate took place over the relationship between regional organizations and the new central organization.[73] Some, like Winston Churchill, favored a series of strong regional councils under the direction of one of the great powers and a rather weak central organization. Others, like American Secretary of State Cordell Hull, believed that regional arrangements could exist, but felt they should be subordinate to a strong centralized universal organization. As it turned out, Hull's position prevailed, and the delegates at San Francisco drafted provisions to ensure that while regional organizations could play a role in conflict management, this role was to be regulated by the Security Council.

The main provisions of the Charter relating to regional arrangements are contained in Chapter VIII, which consists of Articles 52–54. Article 52 allows regional arrangements to deal with 'matters relating to the maintenance of international peace and security' as long as 'such arrangements or agencies and their activities are consistent with the Purposes and Principles of the United Nations.'[74] It also obliges members of such arrangements to 'make every effort'[75] to settle local disputes through these organizations before referring them to the Security Council. Article 53 authorizes the Security

Council to use regional arrangements 'where appropriate'[76] to carry out enforcement actions. But, it provides that 'no enforcement action shall be taken under regional arrangements or by regional agencies without the authorization of the Security Council, with the exception of measures against any enemy state [of the Second World War].'[77] Article 54 simply provides that the Council is to be kept fully informed of any activities undertaken or being contemplated by regional arrangements 'for the maintenance of international peace and security.'[78]

Arguments for the use of force by regional arrangements

In light of these Charter provisions on regional arrangements and given the problems with Security Council action, scholars and others have made a number of claims for the collective use of force by regional arrangements. These include: 1) self-defense; 2) authorized enforcement action; 3) 'not unauthorized' enforcement action; 4) 'recommended' regional action; and 5) regional intervention in civil strife to promote self-determination.

Self-defense One contention that world leaders and scholars make is that it is permissible for regional arrangements to use force in self-defense.[79] This seems to be beyond question. Under Article 51, states retain their right to 'collective,' as well as 'individual,' self-defense in the event of an armed attack 'until the Security Council has taken measures necessary to maintain international peace and security.' In fact, the origins of Article 51 lie in the desire of the Latin American states to ensure that a Latin American regional organization would be able to respond to an attack if the veto paralyzed the Security Council.[80] In one of the earlier drafts of the Charter, there had been no provision akin to Article 51. This troubled the Latin American states, who had met in March of 1945 at the Chapultepec Conference to review the draft. As the result of their concerns, Article 51 was added to the Charter later that spring in San Francisco. Given this evolution, it seems indisputable that if one state belonging to a regional organization were attacked, the organization could collectively use force against the attacker until such time as the Security Council took action. Assuming the Security Council was unable or unwilling to take action, the regional organization could continue its efforts indefinitely. The North Atlantic Treaty Organization (NATO), the Warsaw Treaty Organization (Warsaw Pact – now defunct), the Central Treaty Organization (CENTO – now defunct), and the South East Asian Treaty Organization (SEATO – now defunct) were essentially designed as collective self-defense organizations.

Authorized enforcement action Another possible use of force by a regional arrangement would be an enforcement action that had been authorized by the Security Council. This would be clearly permissible. Article

53 explicitly allows the Council to use regional arrangements to institute enforcement actions. Thus, for example, if one Latin American state used force against another Latin American state, the Security Council could use the Organization of American States (OAS) to carry out an enforcement action. In the history of the United Nations, however, no such use of regional arrangements has been made.

'Not-unauthorized' enforcement action   While collective self-defense and authorized enforcement actions are clearly legally permissible, a number of other claims for the use of force by regional organizations are more debatable. The first of these claims is for the right of a regional arrangement to undertake what might be termed a 'not-*un*authorized' enforcement action. Here the contention is that the use of force by a regional arrangement would be lawful if the Security Council has not *dis*approved it. This was the implication of the arguments made by the US Legal Adviser to the Department of State Abram Chayes and his Deputy, Leonard Meeker, during the Cuban Missile Crisis of 1962.[81] At that time, the United States, with the consent of the Organization of American States, had decided to institute a naval blockade, or 'quarantine' as it was called, to prevent further shipping of nuclear missiles to Cuba. In response to this decision, the Soviet Union introduced a resolution into the Security Council calling for the condemnation of United States actions. The resolution, however, was never voted upon; instead, the Council simply encouraged the parties to seek a peaceful resolution to their dispute.[82]

From these actions, Chayes and Meeker attempted to argue that the Council had effectively *approved* US/OAS actions. Meeker explained that the Security Council 'let the quarantine continue, rather than supplant it' and contended that 'if it were thought that authorization was necessary ..., such authorization may be said to have been granted by the course which the Council adopted.'[83] Chayes went even further to suggest that it was plausible to argue that 'failure of the Council to disapprove regional action amounts to authorization within the meaning of Article 53.'[84] Although this argument has some support,[85] it is generally rejected in the scholarly literature.[86]

'Recommended' regional action   Another somewhat controversial claim also centers around the precise definition of 'enforcement action.' This argument contends that if a regional arrangement *recommends* that its member states use force against another state, such action cannot be considered an *enforcement* action under Article 53 because it is not mandatory. A true enforcement action is one that *requires* states to use force. During the Cuban Missile Crisis, Leonard Meeker advanced this argument, claiming that because the Organization of American States merely *recommended* that its members take action against Cuba, this did not constitute an enforcement action. He explained that '[s]ince the states signatories of the Rio Treaty were not obligated to carry out the resolution recommending the quarantine, it should not be held to constitute 'enforcement action' under Article 53(1) requiring Security Council authorization.'[87]

This argument is clearly based on an exceptionally narrow interpretation of the meaning of 'enforcement action' under Article 53. It does not, however, seem to be consistent with the intent of the framers. Based on the records of the San Francisco Conference, it seems apparent that the purpose of the language in Article 53 was to ensure that regional organizations would not undertake any coercive actions against another state (except in self-defense) without Security Council approval. The fact that such actions had been *recommended* instead of *ordered* would seem to be irrelevant.[88]

Regional intervention in civil strife to promote self-determination   A final argument worth noting relates to the use of force by regional organizations in civil conflict to promote self-determination. As noted in the previous chapter, states from many sectors of the international community have increasingly been claiming a broad right for *individual states* to use force to promote self-determination in a variety of settings. Some officials and scholars, however, while rejecting such a right for individual states, argue that it may be permissible for *regional arrangements* to intervene in civil wars to promote self-determination. One scholar making this contention is John Norton Moore.

Professor Moore argues that when a state is experiencing a high level of civil strife, it is permissible for a regional organization to intervene at the invitation of a 'widely recognized government, or, if there is none, ... [of] a major faction' in the war. Such intervention, Moore contends, is lawful only if the purpose is to promote self-determination 'based on internationally observed elections in which all factions are allowed to participate, which is freely accepted by the major competing factions, or which is endorsed by a competent body of the United Nations.'[89] This action, he explains, would not require Security Council authorization, since it would not be 'directed against any government' and would thus not qualify as an 'enforcement action.'[90] What Moore seems to mean here is that because the intervention was requested by the recognized government, or in its absence, a major faction, the action is not comparable to an 'anti-aggressor' enforcement action; it is not action *against* a state intended to stop external aggression. Rather, it is action intended to restore order *within* a state. Moreover, regional organizations would not be bound by the same set of restrictions against intervening in a civil war as would individual states due to '[t]he greater degree of collective legitimation supplied by regional arrangements.'[91] Moore calls regional action of this nature 'regional peacekeeping,'[92] but it should be noted that 'peacekeeping' is a term of art and generally refers to something quite different.[93] (This will be demonstrated in the next section.)

This theory was used by Moore to justify the actions by the Organization of Eastern Caribbean States (OECS) in Grenada in 1983. In October of that year, following the overthrow and death of Grenadan leader Maurice Bishop, the OECS, with the assistance of the United States, intervened to remove a 'dangerous threat to peace and security' and 'to establish a situation of normalcy in Grenada.'[94] At the time, a number of legal justifications for the action were given, including anticipatory self-defense, the right to protect nationals, and humanitarian intervention. Moore, however, also contended that the OECS/US action was lawful 'regional peacekeeping.' He explained that

> [i]t was undertaken in a context of civil strife and breakdown of govern-
> ment following the brutal murder of Maurice Bishop and members of his
> cabinet in an attempted coup. It was in response to a request for assis-
> tance in restoring human rights and orderly processes of self-
> determination from the only constitutional authority in the island,
> Governor-General Sir Paul Scoon; and the OECS countries are pledged to
> hold free elections and ensure an outcome consistent with the right of
> self-determination for the people of Grenada.[95]

In other words, because there was a request by the Governor-General and because the action was being done to promote self-determination, it did not qualify as a proscribed enforcement action under Article 53.

Moore's proposed norm and its application to Grenada have several problems. First, there seem to be some difficulties with the theory. If inter-vention in a civil war by an individual state is unlawful, why should it be lawful if it is undertaken by a regional arrangement in the absence of Security Council approval? Moore seems to assume that the Charter provisions on regional arrangements permit uses of force short of actual enforcement actions. Yet, with the exception of collective self-defense, the Charter gives no explicit authorization. Moreover, if a state is experiencing a civil war and it is uncertain which faction will ultimately triumph, it could be argued that the state is in the process of pursuing self-determination through civil strife and, therefore, any outside intervention would be against the political independence of the state. Even if there were an invitation from the 'widely recognized' government or a major faction, if the authority of the govern-ment or the faction were being seriously contested, outside intervention would still seem to be interfering with the process of self-determination. Second, aside from the difficulties with the theory itself, the use of the theory to justify OECS action in Grenada also presents problems. One of Moore's theoretical requirements is that the regional arrangement be invited by a widely-recognized government or, if there is none, a major faction. In Grenada, there was no such request. Admittedly, there was an invitation by the Governor-General. But the Governor-General had no effective control of either the government or a major faction. In fact, reports indicate that he was under 'house-arrest' at the time of the request.[96]

But despite the problems with applying this argument to Grenada, there is some indication that the Security Council itself may have acquiesed in the concept of regional intervention in civil conflict. The case in point is the Liberian civil war.

On December 24, 1989, a Liberian ex-patriot named Charles Taylor invaded Liberia with a rebel group known as the National Patriotic Front of Liberia, plunging the country into a bloody civil war. Refugees began pouring over the borders into the Ivory Coast and Guinea.[97] Although this situation could clearly have been labeled a 'threat to the peace,' the United Nations Security Council did not discuss the Liberian crisis until January of 1991.[98] Instead, the issue was addressed by a most unlikely organization – ECOWAS, the Economic Community of West African States.[99] In May of 1990, ECOWAS 'adopted a resolution that called for an end to hostilities and the holding of elections.'[100] It also established 'a standing mediation committee that would intervene promptly whenever a conflict threatened the stability of the region.'[101] Unfortunately, the situation in Liberia worsened. The fighting became increasingly intense. A mediation effort undertaken by the Liberian Council of Churches failed,[102] and the rebels splintered into two factions.[103] Accordingly, in July of 1990, ECOWAS formulated a detailed plan to address the civil war. As Professor Abiodun Williams explains, 'the essential elements' of the plan 'were the declaration of a cease-fire, the deployment of a regional peacekeeping force, the resignation of President Doe, and the establishment of an interim goverment before general elections were to be held.'[104] Despite efforts to secure the acceptance of this plan by all the warring parties, rebel leader Charles Taylor refused to agree to the proposal. Nevertheless, in late August of 1990, an ECOWAS-sponsored 'peacekeeping' force entered Liberia.[105]

Throughout the conflict efforts were made to take the matter to the Security Council.[106] Apparently because the situation was perceived by members of the Council to be an internal issue,[107] the Council did not discuss the matter until its meeting on January 22, 1991. At this meeting, the Council President issued a statement for the Council *endorsing* the efforts of ECOWAS.[108]

Peacekeeping

The theory and practice of peacekeeping

In addition to helping foster a retreat to other institutions, the inadequacies of the Charter system for fighting aggression have also led to the use of peacekeeping. Peacekeeping, as suggested earlier, has a very special meaning in international organizational parlance. Traditionally, it refers to the imposition of a neutral force in an area of conflict once the fighting has stopped. This 'buffer force' serves the purpose of keeping the parties apart, supervising a cease-fire, and/or facilitating a troop withdrawal. Unlike a collective security action, such a peacekeeping mission is undertaken with the *consent* of the state on whose territory the forces will be stationed, and, preferably, the other parties to the conflict as well.[109] In effect, peacekeeping acknowledges that little can be done by an international organization to *stop* aggression, but recognizes that perhaps something can be done after the aggression has ended to prevent it from breaking-out again.[110]

In practice, peacekeeping operations have taken two major forms:[111] observer groups and military contingents. Observer groups generally consist of a small number of individuals who are sent into the area to monitor the situation and report to an international organization. Observer groups have been used in such areas as the Balkans (1947–1949), Indonesia (1947–1951), Kashmir (1959–present), and the Indo–Pakistani Border (1965–1966). Military contingents consist of a larger number of troops and have a broader mandate. They are generally authorized to use force in self-defense if the conflict resumes. UN peacekeeping missions involving major military forces have been used on the Israeli–Egyptian border (1956–1967, 1973–1979), in the Congo (1960–1964), in Cyprus (1964–present), in Lebanon (1978–present), in the Iran–Iraq War (1988–1991), in Central America, (1988–present), in the Gulf War (1990–present) in the Balkans (1991–present), and in Somalia (1992–present). As Secretary-General Boutros Boutros-Ghali observed in June of 1992: 'Thirteen peace-keeping operations were established between the years 1945 and 1987; 13 others since then. An estimated 528,000 military, police and civilian personnel had served under the flag of the United Nations until January 1992.'[112] Moreover, '[t]he costs of these operations have aggregated some $8.3. billion till [*sic*] 1992.'[113]

The lawfulness of peacekeeping

Since peacekeeping was a post-Charter development, numerous questions have surfaced regarding its legality.[114] In the early 1960s, following peace-keeping missions in the Middle East (1956) and the Congo, the Soviet Union and France refused to pay the dues apportioned them for the cost of these missions, contending that the operations were illegal. The heart of their argument rested on the fact that the General Assembly, rather than the Security Council, had played a major role in authorizing these peacekeeping activities. In the case of the Middle East crisis, substantive action by the Council had been blocked by British and French vetoes, so the Council referred the matter to the General Assembly. The Assembly, acting under the 'Uniting for Peace' Resolution, authorized the Secretary-General to set up a peacekeeping operation. In the Congo crisis, even though the initial action was authorized by the Council, the Soviet Union eventually disagreed with the course the operation was taking and began blocking further efforts of the Council. At that point, the General Assembly took up the issue and began managing subsequent activities. But with the Soviets and the French refusing to pay for these operations, the organization soon found itself in a financial crisis.[115]

To put pressure on France and the Soviet Union, the United States obtained a resolution from the General Assembly requesting an advisory opinion from the International Court of Justice on the lawfulness of withholding funds. In the course of its opinion in the so-called *Certain Expenses Case*,[116] the Court ruled that peacekeeping actions authorized by the Security Council *or* the General Assembly were permissible. The Court explained that under the Charter, the Assembly had the right to make recommendations dealing with issues relating to the maintenance of international peace and security as long as the Security Council was not dealing with them. Since the Council was effectively blocked by the veto, this was not the case. Moreover, the Court argued that while it was true that only the Council could *order* states to undertake an enforcement action against another state, the Assembly could *recommend* that states take action that did not amount to an enforcement action. In the case of these peacekeeping missions, since they were undertaken 'at the request, or with the consent, of the States concerned,'[117] they did not qualify as 'coercive or enforcement action'[118] requiring Security Council authorization.

In summary, a UN peacekeeping operation would seem to be lawful under certain circumstances. If it were authorized by the Security Council, there would be little doubt as to its permissibility. Since the Council can authorize an enforcement action against a state, it would seem clear that it could authorize a peacekeeping mission that did not involve action against a state. In addition, a peacekeeping operation authorized by the General Assembly would be permissible if it met three criteria. First, the Security Council could not be considering the issue at the time. Second, the operation could only be established pursuant to a *recommendation* of the General Assembly. Third, it would require the consent of the state on whose territory the forces were to be placed. It would follow logically that a peacekeeping operation undertaken by a regional arrangement also would be lawful as long as it met the same criteria as peacekeeping authorized by the General Assembly.

CHAPTER SUMMARY

When the United Nations was established, an elaborate system for deterring and fighting aggression was set-up. Under Chapter VII of the Charter, the Security Council was empowered to determine if there was a threat to the peace, breach of the peace, or an act of aggression. If the Council so determined, it was authorized to order states to take whatever measures were necessary to end the aggression, including, if need be, collective military measures. To provide for the implementation of these measures, Chapter VII required all states to conclude agreements with the United Nations for the provision of military contingents to be used in enforcement actions. Chapter VII also created the Military Staff Committee to coordinate the collective use of military sanctions. Based on these provisions, the Charter framework for the collective use of force could be considered a limited collective security arrangement.

In the post-Charter world, a number of problems have severely challenged the effectiveness of the Charter framework. These include: 1) the great power veto on the Security Council; 2) the inability to establish formal mechanisms for the collective use of force; and 3) the rejection of even a limited system of collective security. Given these problems, states have attempted to find alternative methods of dealing with international conflict. First, efforts have been made to use other international institutions, including the United Nations General Assembly and regional arrangements. Second, there has also been a widespread use of peacekeeping as an alternative to anti-aggressor action.

Part III

Challenges to the Charter paradigm

Chapter 5

Anticipatory self-defense

On June 7, 1981, Israeli bombers destroyed the Osarik reactor near Baghdad, Iraq.[1] Although Iraq had not used military force against Israel, Israeli authorities claimed that the attack was a lawful exercise of Israel's inherent right of self-defense. According to Israeli officials, Iraq intended to use the reactor, which was not yet operational, to produce nuclear weapons that could ultimately be used against Israel. An official statement of the Israeli government explained that Israel had been 'forced to defend [itself] against the construction of an atomic bomb in Iraq, which itself would not have hesitated to use it against Israel and its population centers.'[2] Echoing this statement, Israeli Prime Minister Menachem Begin explained that the action against the reactor was a 'morally supreme act of national self-defense.'[3] In short, Israel was claiming a right of 'anticipatory self-defense.' Even though Iraq had not launched an actual armed attack, Israel believed that such an attack would follow once the Osarik reactor had begun producing weapons-grade material. Accordingly, Israeli officials argued that its defense necessitated forceful action to preempt future Iraq aggression.

The Israeli justification for the air strike of 1981 raises an important question about the nature of self-defense. Is the right of individual and collective self-defense limited to the occurrence of an actual 'armed attack'? Or can a state exercise this right in an anticipatory fashion? In other words, can a state use force against another state in self-defense before an actual armed attack has occurred?

The purpose of this chapter is to explore the status of anticipatory self-defense under contemporary international law. The first section will examine the nature of the problem. The second section will examine state practice regarding anticipatory self-defense. Finally, the third section will assess the legal status of anticipatory self-defense in the contemporary system.

THE NATURE OF THE PROBLEM

Customary international law and self-defense

As noted in Chapter 2, the right of self-defense is one of the oldest legitimate reasons for states to resort to force. Aristotle, Aquinas, and even the framers of the restrictive Kellogg-Briand Pact all acknowledged that it was permissible to take recourse to arms to defend oneself. Under pre-Charter customary international law, a state could take recourse to force to defend itself not only in response to an actual armed attack, but also in anticipation of an imminent armed attack.[4]

The classic illustration of this right of anticipatory self-defense was the *Caroline* case. In that case, as observed earlier, British troops took action against a ship docked on the American side of the river, claiming that the ship was going to be used to support rebels in Canada. Even though the case dealt with self-defense as a use of force short of war, the criteria it established came to be applied to the claim of self-defense generally, and to anticipatory self-defense in particular. Drawing upon this case, there thus seems to be general agreement among international legal scholars that pre-Charter customary international law recognized a right of anticipatory self-defense provided the conditions of necessity and proportionality were met. First, a state would need to demonstrate that such forceful action was *necessary* to defend itself against an impending attack. It would, in other words, be required to demonstrate that an attack was truly imminent and there were essentially no other reasonably peaceful means available to prevent such attack. Second, the forceful response of the would-be victim would have to be *proportionate* to the threat. While neither of these criteria can be defined with complete precision, they nevertheless provide some basic parameters on the exercise of anticipatory self-defense.

Article 51 and anticipatory self-defense

As we have seen, the United Nations Charter explicitly recognized the right of individual and collective self-defense under Article 51. The language of Article 51, however, calls into question whether this right can be exercised *before* an actual armed attack occurs. Article 51 states that '[n]othing in the present Charter shall impair the *inherent* right of individual or collective self-defense *if an armed attack occurs* against a Member.' Clearly, this language admits of two divergent interpretations. On the one hand, it could be taken to mean that under the Charter states have recourse to force in self-defense only once an actual armed attack has occurred. Under such an interpretation, Article 51 would have the purpose of restricting the pre-existing right of self-defense under customary international law. A state would have to wait until it was struck first before it could respond. On the other hand, by concentrating on the word 'inherent,' Article 51 could be interpreted to mean something very different. Because the word 'inherent' is used to describe self-defense, it could be argued that the framers of the Charter did not intend to circumscribe the pre-existing customary right. Instead, they merely desired to list one situation in which a state could clearly exercise that right.

An examination of the scholarly literature on the question of anticipatory self-defense reveals that most scholars fall into one of two schools of thought. For simplicity's sake, these schools may be called the restrictionist and counter-restrictionist. Restrictionists include such scholars as Brownlie,[5] Dinstein,[6] Henkin,[7] and Jessup.[8] Counter-restrictionists include Bowett,[9] O'Brien,[10] McDougal,[11] and Stone.[12] The restrictionists take the first view expressed above. They argue that Article 51 is the only contemporary source of law on self-defense and, properly interpreted, Article 51 prohibits antici-patory self-defense. The counter-restrictionists refuse to accept this argu-ment. They either reject it either based solely on the variant reading of Article 51, or based on a hybrid argument that combines this particular reading of the Charter with the impact of certain post-1945 developments, such as the failure of collective security.

Unfortunately, in the post-Charter period, there has been no authoritative decision of an international adjudicatory body on the question of antici-patory self-defense. In the *Nicaragua* case, the International Court of Justice did not explicitly address the issue. It simply noted that since 'the issue of the lawfulness of a response to the imminent threat of armed attack has not been raised ... the Court expresses no view on that issue.'[13] Judge Schwebel in his dissent in the *Nicaragua* case did, however, express support for the view that under Article 51 self-defense was not limited to a situation 'if, and only if, an armed attack occurs.'[14] How the Court would have ruled had antici-patory self-defense explicitly been raised is thus unclear.

At present, therefore, there is a real division in the international legal community regarding the efficacy of anticipatory self-defense. Accordingly, a careful examination of state practice is required to assess the current status of anticipatory self-defense under international law.

CONTEMPORARY STATE PRACTICE REGARDING ANTICIPATORY SELF-DEFENSE

Early practice

Following the adoption of the Charter, the question of anticipatory self-defense was raised several times during the early days of the United Nations. One of the first occasions was in 1946, when the Report of the United Nations Atomic Energy Commission was filed. At that time, the Commission was considering some form of international agreement to deal with the new-found problem of nuclear weapons. In the course of these deliberations, the Commission addressed the possibility of a breach of such an agreement by a state preparing for nuclear war. In light of this concern, the Commission noted that '[i]n consideration of the problem of violation of the terms of treaty or convention, it should also be borne in mind that a violation might be so grave as to give rise to the inherent right of self-defence recognized in Art. 51.'[15] According to counter-restrictionist Bowett, this Commission statement constituted a strong endorsement of anticipatory self-defense. He explains that '[i]t cannot be supposed that a treaty violation falls within the definition of an actual armed attack, so that the Commission clearly understood Art. 51 as permitting "anticipatory" self-defense.'[16] Brownlie, on the other hand, sees this support as insignificant, explaining that the Commission's statement 'can hardly be regarded as an authoritative interpretation of the Charter or as an amendment of the Charter by the incidental expression of views by a subsidiary organ of the Security Council.'[17]

Another early case in which the efficacy of anticipatory self-defense was addressed came in 1950 during the Pakistani invasion of Kashmir. At that time, Pakistan justified its action as self-defense. In the consideration of the matter before the Security Council, only India objected to the legitimacy of a claim to anticipatory self-defense.[18] Professor Bowett views this as an important indication that state practice following the adoption of the Charter illustrates no effort to restrict the customary international law conception of self-defense.[19]

Case studies

Following these early considerations of anticipatory self-defense, several prominent uses of force have occurred in which a claim of anticipatory self-defense was made or reasonably could have been made. The three most notable incidents seem to be the Cuban Missile Crisis, the 1967 Middle East War, and the 1981 bombing of the Osarik reactor. Although anticipatory self-defense may have been an element of the legal justification in cases such as the 1983 invasion of Grenada or the 1986 air-strike on Libya, because these actions were justified primarily on other grounds, they will be addressed in other chapters.

The 1962 Cuban Missile Crisis

Much has been written about the 'Thirteen Days'[20] in October of 1962 that shook the international system. As is widely known, on October 16, 1962, information was brought to the attention of American President John F. Kennedy that the Soviets were assembling delivery systems for intermediate range ballistic missiles in Cuba. Regarding this development as 'a deliberately provocative and unjustified change in the status quo,'[21] Kennedy ordered the establishment of a naval blockade, which he termed a 'quarantine,' to prevent the transport of missiles and related matériel to Cuba. In his speech to the American people, Kennedy claimed that he was acting 'in the defense of our own security and of the entire Western Hemisphere.'[22]

Under generally accepted norms of international law, a blockade, whether termed a quarantine or not, constitutes a violation of Article 2(4). As such, it could only be considered permissible if it could be demonstrated that it fell into an exception to the Article 2(4) prohibition. At the time of the Crisis, the official legal justification presented by Legal Adviser to the Department of State Abram Chayes[23] and his Deputy Leonard Meeker[24] focused on the authorization by the Organization of American States as a legitimizing factor. Neverthelesss, in the debate that ensured, the question of anticipatory self-defense was widely discussed in legal scholarship.[25]

During Security Council consideration of the matter,[26] support for American actions seemed generally to fall along Cold War lines. The representatives from Chile, China (Nationalist China), France, Ireland, the United Kingdom, and Venezuela all supported the lawfulness of the quarantine. The representatives from Ghana, Romania, the Soviet Union, and the United Arab Republic opposed the action. In the course of the debate, there was no specific rejection of the concept of anticipatory self-defense. Instead, there seemed to be an underlying acceptance by most members of the Council that in certain circumstances the preemptive use of force could be justified. This can be deduced from the fact that much of the discussion centered around the question of whether the missiles were offensive or defensive.

For the representative from Ghana, the question of the nature of the weapons was decisive. In exploring possible legal arguments that would excuse US actions, Mr Quaison-Sackey of Ghana posed the following questions:

> Are there grounds for the argument that such action is justified in exercise of the inherent right of self-defense? Can it be contended that there was, in the words of a former American Secretary of State whose reputation as a jurist in this field is widely accepted, 'a necessity of self-defense, instant, overwhelming, leaving no choice of means and no moment for deliberation'?[27]

He then went on to answer his questions, concluding that

> My delegation does not think so, for as I have said earlier incontrovertible proof is not yet available as to the offensive character of military developments in Cuba. Nor can it be argued that the threat was of such a nature as to warrant action on the scale so far taken, prior to a reference to this Council.[28]

In short, the Ghanaian delegate clearly accepted the doctrine of anticipatory self-defense, used Webster's formulation from the *Caroline* case, and then applied it to the specifics of the Cuban Missile Crisis as he understood them. Even Cuba and the Soviet Union (at least initially) contended that the missiles were defensive, seemingly giving credence to the argument that if they had been offensive, there might have been some justification for pre-emptive action.

In sum, while the discussions in the Council do not reflect a clear-cut endorsement of anticipatory self-defense, they certainly do not indicate its rejection. Rather, the lack of a specific condemnation of the doctrine, especially by states that opposed American actions, indicates that there may have been, at some level, an acceptance of the notion.

The 1967 Middle East War

Another use of force frequently associated with the concept of anticipatory self-defense was the Israeli action in June of 1967. On June 5, Israeli forces launched attacks against the United Arab Republic (UAR) and quickly defeated the combined Arab forces. Even though no attack had been launched against Israel, Israel felt that its action was a lawful exercise of its right to self-defense. According to Israeli officials, a series of actions by Arab states indicated that military measures against Israel were imminent. The Israeli representative, Aba Eban, told the Security Council that

> [a]n army, greater than any force ever assembled in history in Sinai, had massed against Israel's southern frontier. Egypt has dismissed the United Nations forces which symbolized the international interest in the maintenance of peace in our region, Nasser had provocatively brought five infantry divisions and two armoured divisions up to our very gates; 80,000 men and 900 tanks were poised to move.[29]

In the Security Council debates, only some of the discussion centered around the identity of the aggressor. While the Israelis emphasized the imminent nature of a major Arab attack, they initially left unclear the issue of who exactly began the fighting. As the debate progressed, however, Eban gave more emphasis to the anticipatory nature of Israel's action. Other delegations saw Israel's first strike as clear proof that Israel was the aggressor. The Syrian representative, for example, made the following comments:

> Never once have they [the Israelis] mentioned the aggression committed by the Arabs against Israel in this crisis. What words did the representative of Israel use today? 'Attempts' at aggression and 'threats'. But who committed the aggression? The party that committed the aggression, the party that is definitely the aggressor in this whole crisis is Israel and Israel alone. Israel started the attack on Egypt, Israel on 7 April attacked Syria with large forces, with its air force, and destroyed property and killed civilians.

Similarly, the Moroccan representative seemed to suggest that the initial use of force was decisive. Although he argued that the Arab states were *not* preparing for war, he explained that '[i]t is true that we shall be told that with respect to military measures, it is unnecessary to determine which actions are aggressive and which actions are defensive.'[30] What he seemed to be arguing here was that the intention of military preparation – defensive or aggressive – was not critical to assessing responsibility for aggression. His underlying assumption seems to have been that the first use of force was the aggressive act.

As would be expected, the Soviet delegate to the Security Council was also convinced that Israel was the aggressor. He, too, seemed to emphasize the fact that Israel was the first to use force.[31] At one point, the Israeli delegate read from a letter from Professor René Cassin in which Cassin discussed the Syrian and Soviet statements before the Sixth Committee of the General Assembly supporting a broad definition of aggression that included economic coercion, blockades, and support for armed bands.[32] Calling Cassin 'a supporter of the Zionist point of view,'[33] the Soviet delegate dismissed Israel's argument as 'academic disquisition'[34] and claimed that no progress had been made in the United Nations toward reaching a 'definition of aggression.' In any case, he explained, 'the Security Council at the present time is not engaged in any academic research in the sphere of concepts and terminology.'[35] Instead, 'a very clear and simple fact is before the Security Council: the direct, clear and unconcealed aggression of Israel against the neighbouring Arab States.'[36]

Those delegations that were more sympathetic toward Israel, the United States and Britain, tended to refrain from any discussion of the permissibility of anticipatory self-defense. Hence, the only delegation to examine the legal concept was that of Israel itself.

From these discussions in the Council, it is difficult to glean any consensus on the efficacy of preemptive self-defense. States that were politically opposed to Israel tended to dismiss off-hand Israel's argument. While these states avoided any lengthy discussion of the concept of anticipatory self-defense per se, to the extent that they did discuss the question, they seemed to assume that the first use of force, irrespective of the justification, was illegal. But because of the political posturing involved, it is difficult to conclude that there was a clear consensus opposed to anticipatory self-defense.

The 1981 Israeli bombing of the Osarik reactor

As noted above, one of the most recent cases involving a claim of anticipatory self-defense came in June of 1981, when the Israeli Air Force destroyed an Iraqi nuclear reactor near Baghdad. Immediately following the attack, the Security Council began lengthy deliberations. The first speaker before the Council was the Iraqi Foreign Minister Saadoun Hammadi.

Hammadi roundly condemned the attack as an 'act of aggression.'[37] After Hammadi, the Israeli representative, Mr Blum, made an empassioned argument defending Israel's actions. The basis of his argument focused on the concept of self-defense. After detailing his version of the attempts by the Iraqis to develop nuclear capabilities, Ambassador Blum explained that 'Israel was exercising its inherent and natural right of self-defense, as understood in general international law and well within the meaning of Article 51 of the United Nations Charter.'[38] Blum then cited Sir Humphrey Waldock, Professor Morton Kaplan and Nicholas Katzenbach, and Professor Bowett in support of the notion that anticipatory self-defense was permissible under international law.[39] According to Blum, Israel had attempted to use many diplomatic channels to address the problem.[40] When these efforts had proved ineffective, he contended, Israel was forced to use the military instrument.

All the delegates that followed Ambassador Blum condemned Israel. Many, nevertheless, discussed the issue of anticipatory self-defense. Of the over forty-five delegates that spoke on the issue, several took a restrictionist view of Article 51. The Syrian delegate, for example, told the Council that 'Article 51 of the Charter clearly defines self-defense as an inherent right only if an armed attack occurs against a Member of the United Nations.'[41] He went on to say that the notion of 'pre-emptive strikes' was

> a concept that has been refuted time and again in the Definition of Aggression ... and dismissed as unacceptable, since it usurps the powers of the Security Council as set forth in Article 39 of the Charter and curtails the Council's authority.[42]

Similarly, the Guyanan delegate took a restrictionist view. He explained that

> [w]hile Article 51 of the United Nations Charter does confer upon Member States the right of individual self-defence if an armed attack occurs against them, nowhere does it provide for the use of the pre-emptive strike, which is contrary to the spirit of the Charter and to the purposes and principles of the Organization.[43]

Among the other representatives that seemed to take a restrictionist view were those from Pakistan, Spain, and Yugoslavia.

Yet despite these restrictionist delegates, many representatives expressed views that supported a counter-restrictionist approach to anticipatory self-defense. Typically, these delegates argued that the use of force in a pre-emptive fashion *could* be permissible under the Charter framework provided that it could be demonstrated that there was an imminent threat and that other means of addressing this threat had been exhausted. But Israel, these delegates contended, had not met these criteria. For example, Mr Koroma, the representative from Sierra Leone, rejected Israel's claim of self-defense, explaining that 'the plea of self-defence is untenable where no armed attack has taken place *or is imminent*.'[44] He continued with a quote from Webster's letter in the *Caroline* case, explaining that '[a]s for the principle of self-defence, it has long been accepted that, for it to be invoked or justified the necessity for action must be instant, overwhelming and leaving no choice of means and no moment for deliberation.'[45] 'The Israeli action,' he explained, 'was carried out in pursuance of policies long considered and prepared and was plainly an act of aggression.'[46] In a similar vein, the British delegate, Sir Anthony Parsons, relied heavily on the *Caroline* case. Explained Parsons:

> It has been argued that the Israeli attack was an act of self-defence. But it was not a response to an armed attack on Israel by Iraq. There was no instant or overwhelming necessity for self-defence. Nor can it be justified as a forcible measure of self-protection. The Israeli intervention amounted to a use of force which cannot find a place in international law or in the Charter and which violated the sovereignty of Iraq.[47]

This basic approach was generally supported by delegations from such states as Uganda, Niger, and Malaysia. Many other representatives condemned the Israeli action without explicitly addressing the broader question of the efficacy of anticipatory self-defense. Even Ambassador Kirkpatrick from the United States did not squarely explore the permissibility of anticipatory self-defense.

Given the large number of states that spoke before the Council on the Israeli attack, the debate would seem to be a reasonable indicator of the attitudes of states toward the concept of anticipatory self-defense. Not unlike the debates on the Cuban Missile Crisis and the 1967 War, the deliberations on the Osarik case demonstrated the existence of both restrictionist and counter-restrictionist views. Yet, unlike previous discussions, in the Security Council debates in 1981, there seemed to be a much broader base of support for the counter-restrictionist arguments.

THE LEGAL STATUS OF ANTICIPATORY SELF-DEFENSE

The case studies considered here clearly demonstrate that there continues to be a division within the international legal community regarding anticipatory self-defense. Nevertheless, it is also clear that there are a great many states that take the counter-restrictionist view and support the proposition that in certain circumstances it may be lawful to use force in advance of an actual armed attack. Even though there may not be an established consensus in support of the permissibility of anticipatory self-defense, there is certainly not a consensus opposed to it. In consequence, it would seem to be impossible to prove the existence of an authoritative and controlling norm prohibiting the use of force for preemptive self-defense.

Chapter 6

Intervention in civil and mixed conflicts

INTRODUCTION

On June 27, 1986, the International Court of Justice issued its first decision dealing with the recourse to force since the *Corfu Channel*[1] case of 1949. In the *Nicaragua* case,[2] the Court was forced to address itself to the question of intervention in a civil conflict, or depending upon the interpretation of the facts, a 'mixed' conflict. Nicaragua had alleged that the United States was aiding and abetting the *contra* rebels. This was, in Nicaragua's opinion, impermissible intervention in a civil conflict constituting a violation of Article 2(4). The United States, however, defended its actions by claiming that it was simply taking action against Nicaragua in response to prior Nicaraguan intervention in support of rebels in El Salvador.

Since, as noted in Chapter 3, the Charter provisions on the use of force do not address themselves clearly to conflicts of this nature, the Court found it necessary to take the logic of the Charter restrictions and to attempt to apply it to civil wars and mixed civil/international conflicts. In so doing, the Court was engaging in an activity in which officials and scholars had long been involved: formulating 'norms' of intervention. The result of these efforts to make sense of the Charter has been the development of different 'norms' about the lawfulness of intervention in civil conflicts and mixed conflicts. Since there has been no final authoritative pronouncement on the status of these putative 'norms' of intervention under international law, each 'norm' represents one particular approach to intervention that is endorsed by a certain group of individuals. The ultimate test of each norm, therefore, rests on whether the norm is authoritative and controlling.

The purpose of this chapter is to explore these norms of intervention and to assess the status of each under contemporary international law. Because a fairly coherent set of norms has emerged, this chapter will be constructed slightly differently from previous ones. Rather than concentrating on case studies, it will describe the norms that have developed and explore state practice regarding them. Accordingly, the first section will examine the norms that have developed with respect to civil conflict. Next, the second section will examine norms relating to mixed conflicts. Finally, the third section will evaluate these developments.

INTERVENTION AND CIVIL CONFLICT

The nature of civil conflict

A *civil conflict* exists when a state is experiencing domestic unrest. This domestic unrest may take many forms. Indeed, since the Second World War, scholars have suggested a number of ways to categorize the various forms of civil conflict.[3] The following formulation is an adaptation of several of these proposals.

Low intensity unrest

The term 'low intensity unrest' can be used to characterize the least severe level of civil strife. This would be a situation in which a state was experiencing scattered riots or limited terrorist activities. Certain *organized* groups might exist within the state, but the purpose of these groups would not be 'related to authority structures.'[4] In other words, the purpose of these groups would not be to change the form of government or to take over the existing government. Instead, the groups would either have no real political goals or those goals would be directed toward changing a *particular* policy. An example of this type of civil unrest would be the conditions that existed in the United States during the riots of the late 1960s and early 1970s.

Civil war

In a civil war, a rebel group (or groups) is challenging the authority of the existing government to rule a particular state. The rebels desire to establish themselves as the government of the state in question. This is a fairly familiar type of civil conflict. Ignoring for the moment the question of external intervention, examples of civil wars would include the Spanish Civil War, the FMLN (Farabundo Marti de Liberacion Nacional) challenge to the El Salvadoran government in the 1980s, the *contras'* challenge to the Nicaraguan government, and the Sri Lankan Civil War.[5]

The literature on intervention frequently differentiates between two stages of civil war based on the severity of the conflict: *insurgency* and *belligerency*. Scholarly opinion is not in agreement on the exact definitions of these two terms. The main distinction seems to be the level of international legitimacy accorded the rebels. According to Novogrod, an insurgency exists when the group challenging the government has significant power and size and may even be occupying a significant portion of the territory of the state in question, but has not yet been recognized by other states in the international system as an entity in itself.[6] A belligerency exists when states recognize that there is a 'state of war between ... two quasi-international bodies within the confines of a single juridical entity.'[7]

Wars of secession

A war of secession takes place when a particular group in a state, usually a racial, ethnic, or religious group, wishes to break away from the central government and to form its own state. Recent wars of secession include the failed Biafran secessionist war (1967–1970), the successful Bangladesh war of independence (1971), and the events in Eritrea and Yugoslavia in the early 1990s.

Wars of unification

A final form that civil conflict may take is a so-called war of unification.[8] Here a particular ethnic, racial, or religious group exists in two or more contiguous states and desires to unify to form its own state. If, for example, the Armenians, the Kurds, or the Basques should forcibly seek to form states coterminous to their geographic location, such activity could be characterized as a war of unification. These conflicts can be depicted graphically as shown in Figure 6.1.

Because they involve no foreign intervention, low intensity unrest, civil wars, wars of secession, and wars of unification are all assumed to be purely 'civil.' Accordingly, the United Nations Charter proscriptions have little to say about the *initiation* of force by the government or anti-government groups. Although there are arguable *jus in bello* restrictions that would apply in civil conflict,[9] there is no real law relating to the recourse to force by the domestic parties.[10] The actual *jus ad bellum* questions in civil conflict, therefore, deal not with the use of force by rebels or the government, but rather with the permissibility of another state providing assistance to one of the parties engaged in the civil conflict.

Norms regarding intervention in civil conflict

Over the years, scholars and decision-makers have explored the legal rights an outside party has in civil conflicts. In the course of this examination, several putative norms have been suggested to provide a legal framework for regulating outside intervention. What follows is a description of three of these possible norms that, in one form or another, are most frequently discussed in the literature. These three are by no means the only norms that have been suggested, but simply the most common ones. Moreover, the names assigned to these norms are not sacred. Some individuals may refer to the same effective norm by some other appellation.

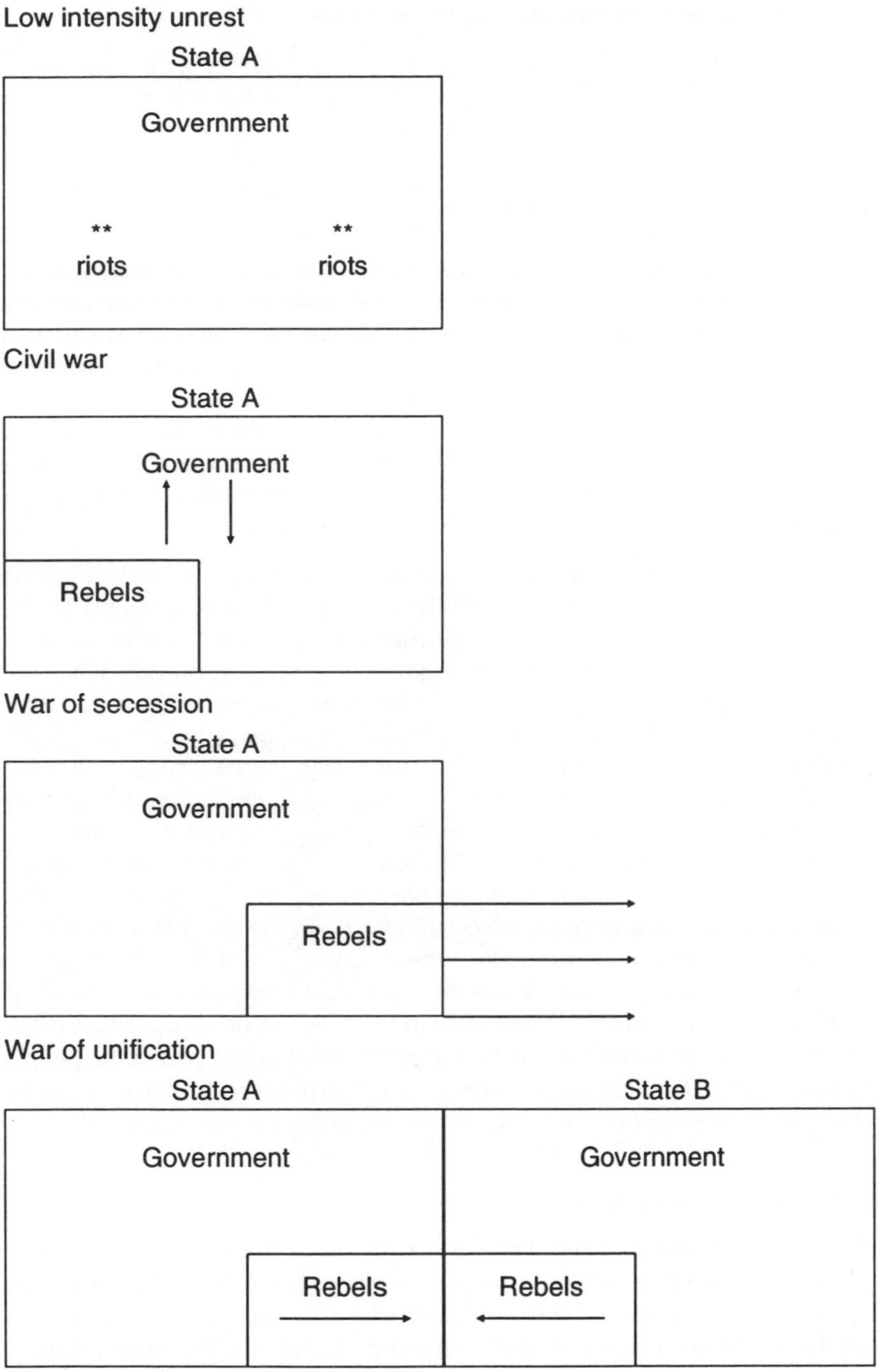

Low intensity unrest

State A

Government

** **
riots   riots

Civil war

State A

Government

Rebels

War of secession

State A

Government

Rebels

War of unification

State A   State B

Government   Government

Rebels   Rebels

Figure 6.1 Various forms of civil conflict

The 'traditional' norm and the 'traditional' rule

One possible approach to the question of permissibility of foreign intervention in civil conflict is what John Norton Moore has referred to as the
'traditional' norm.[11] This traditional rule seems to have emerged under
customary international law prior to the ratification of the United Nations
Charter.[12] Although scholars differ on the precise contours of the norm, its
main points can be summarized as follows.[13]

a   It is permissible to provide assistance to a widely recognized govern-
     ment at its request while there is low-intensity strife or an insurgency.
b   If the civil strife rises to the level of a belligerency, an outside state can
     still lawfully provide assistance to the widely recognized government,
     but the outside state loses neutrality in the conflict.
c   It is impermissible for an outside state to aid the rebels prior to the
     recognition of a belligerency. Once a belligerence is reached, an out-
     side state may aid the rebels, but the outside state will lose neutrality in
     the conflict.

This traditional rule clearly begins with a predisposition toward the existing
regime. Because a regime is widely recognized, it is deemed to be
'legitimate,' and outside states are permitted to provide it assistance at its
request no matter how large the insurgency. Conversely, outside states are
prohibited from providing assistance to the rebels no matter how just their
cause may appear. It is only when a belligerency occurs, when the rebels are
accepted as having certain rights and duties under international law, that the
outside states must behave differently. Under those circumstances, an outside state has the option of either aiding neither side and maintaining its
neutrality or of aiding either the belligerency or the government and losing
its neutrality. If the outside state chooses to aid one of the parties, that
intervening state will become a 'co-belligerent' in the conflict. Under such
circumstances, its actions would be subject to the laws of armed conflict.

    One of the principal difficulties with this norm in the post-Charter world is
that it can be detrimental to self-determination. It allows outside assistance to the
government to combat what may be a genuine effort on the part of the people
to secure self-determination. In consequence, this norm no longer seems to be
the majority position of most contemporary international legal scholars.[14]

The 'neutral non-intervention' rule

Because the traditional rule lacks a sensitivity to the right of peoples to
self-determination, a newer approach to intervention in civil conflict has
emerged since the end of the Second World War. This approach has been
referred to by some as the neutral non-intervention rule. The main tenets of
this rule seem to be as follows.

a It is permissible to aid a widely recognized regime at its request when there is a low level of civil strife.
b It is impermissible to aid even a widely recognized regime at its request if there is an insurgency or belligerency.
c It is always impermissible to provide assistance to the rebels.

This rule attempts to avoid the problems of the traditional approach. It recognizes that when there is a low level of civil strife, there is no serious challenge to the government and outside assistance to the regime would presumably not interfere with self-determination. Thus, for example, if Canada were experiencing minor riots in several locations, it would be permissible for the United States to provide Canada with riot equipment, other material and even troops. If, however, there were a true insurgency, an outside state would have to stay out so as to allow the self-determination process to work itself out. The neutral non-intervention approach assumes that at the point of insurgency, intervention on either side would interfere with the rights of the people to choose, by force if necessary, their own government.

One interesting modification to this rule has been suggested by John Norton Moore. What if, hypothesizes Moore, an outside state is providing assistance to the government of a state experiencing a low level of civil strife and the unrest rises to the level of an insurgency? Must the state aiding the widely recognized regime withdraw its assistance at that point? In Moore's view, the intervenor would be subject to no such requirement. According to him, 'withdrawal of pre-existing military support may amount to intervention on behalf of the insurgents.'[15] When a state would suddenly stop assistance to the government, the effect would be similar to actually aiding the opposition. In consequence, he contends that when a state is providing assistance to the government to combat low level disorders and the unrest rises to the level of an insurgency, the aiding state should simply freeze its assistance at the pre-insurgency level.

The self-determination rule

As noted in Chapter 3, one of the predominant challenges to the United Nations Charter framework has been the growing preference for 'justice' over 'peace.' Since 1945, more and more states have been claiming the right to use force to promote various 'just causes,' even though such uses of force may transgress the territorial integrity or political independence of states. One specific area in which this growing trend has been manifested is in the area of intervention in civil conflict. Alongside the neutral non-intervention rule, some statesmen and scholars seem to be suggesting the emergence of a 'self-determination' rule. The basic elements of this rule can be encapsulated by two propositions.

   a It is permissible for an outside state to provide assistance to the side in a civil conflict that is seeking self-determination of peoples.

   b Either the government or the rebels can be aided.

Support for this norm has come from nearly all sectors of the international community. Third World states have supported the right to intervene in civil conflict to promote decolonization and to fight racist regimes.[16] During the Cold War period, the Soviet Union and its allies contended that they had the right to support 'wars of national liberation.'[17] And western states, particularly the United States, have claimed a right to support groups within states that are struggling for democracy.[18] Indeed, Professor W. Michael Reisman has argued that one of the basic community values undergirding the Charter is the promotion of human rights.[19] If a government becomes destructive of that value, an outside state could permissibly intervene. Article 2(4), in Reisman's interpretation, should not be read as an absolute, but should rather be understood in the context of these larger community goals.

The difficulties with this would-be norm, however, are readily apparent. First, there seem to be many potential definitions as to what constitutes a 'people' seeking 'self-determination.' From the Third World perspective, it is a group fighting racism or colonialism. But even here, what is racism and colonialism? From the Soviet perspective, it was a group waging a 'war of national liberation,' whatever that was. And finally, from the American perspective, it is a group of 'democratic' freedom fighters. Hence, a group worthy of support in the eyes of certain states, such as the *contras*, might not be regarded deserving by other states. From a legal standpoint, this presents a crucial question. How can a norm regarding permissible intervention be developed when there are competing definitions of 'self-determination.' Since there is no common definition of self-determination, the only plausible way to develop such a norm would be to admit that *any* definition of self-determination would be equally valid and thus to acknowledge that states would possess the right to aid a party in a civil conflict seeking self-determination *however defined*. Clearly, such an approach would permit broad rights to intervene, essentially allowing 'self-determination' to be a pretext for nearly any intervention.

A second difficulty with a self-determination rule is that it seems rather squarely to contradict Article 2(4). While the neutral non-intervention rule can be reconciled with the Charter framework, a rule that permits the use of force to promote self-determination runs counter to any reasonable interpretation of 2(4).[20] To acknowledge the validity of this rule would thus be to acknowledge that states can, at least in some circumstances, use force outside the Charter paradigm.

INTERVENTION AND MIXED CONFLICT

The nature of mixed conflicts

When a state is experiencing civil unrest, it is not unusual for one or more of the parties to the conflict to be receiving assistance from another state or states. For example, State A could be fighting a civil war against Rebels R[a], and State B could be providing military support to Rebels R[a]. Such a conflict can be termed a 'mixed' conflict, since it has both a civil and international dimension. It is at once a civil war and an international war. A simple mixed conflict can be depicted graphically as shown in Figure 6.2.

Since, by definition, there has already been outside intervention in a civil conflict, the permissibility of further intervention by a third state – a hypothetical State C, for example – may be subject to a different set of legal tests.

Norms regarding intervention in mixed conflict

In the decades following the adoption of the Charter, much time has been devoted to formulating putative norms regarding the legality of intervention in mixed conflict. The two main events that gave rise to this activity were the Vietnam War and the Central American conflict of the 1980s. As scholars and world leaders debated the legality of American actions, they were forced to develop general norms that sought to apply the basic Charter principles to mixed conflicts. In the course of the debate on Vietnam, many of the most noted international legal scholars offered their particular formulations. Scholars such as John Norton Moore,[21] Richard Falk,[22] Tom Farer,[23] and Quincy Wright[24] all attempted to make sense of the law in this war. Similarly, in the debate over Central America, scholars[25] sought to explore the norms relating to permissible intervention. The main difference in the Central American conflict was the existence of a decision by the International Court

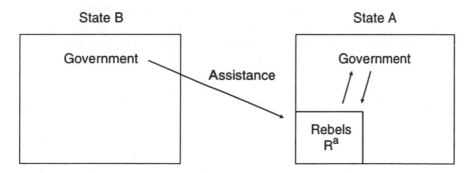

Figure 6.2 Mixed conflict

of Justice – *Nicaragua v. US*.[26] In this case, the Court was asked to assess the legality of US actions in support of the *contras* and with respect to the mining of the Nicaraguan harbors. In order to do so, the Court felt compelled to define the law relating to intervention in mixed conflict.

Taking into consideration the scholarly discussions of these and other conflicts as well as the decision in the *Nicaragua* case, three different normative approaches to intervention in mixed conflict can be identified. Like the norms relating to civil conflict, these are by no means the only possible norms, simply the most common. Moreover, once again, the names used for these norms are not set. They are simply titles that attempt to provide some basic description of the essence of the would-be norm.

The proportionate counter-intervention rule

In the debate that has taken place on the permissibility of intervention in a mixed conflict, the most widely accepted approach might be called the proportionate counter-intervention rule. This rule has, in one form or another, been supported by scholars such as John Norton Moore,[27] Thomas M. Franck,[28] and William V. O'Brien,[29] by the United States Department of State,[30] and by the International Court of Justice in the *Nicaragua* case.[31] Taking the essence of these various positions, this rule seems to have the following tenets.

a It is permissible for a state to provide offsetting assistance to the government of a state if another state has provided assistance to rebels in the state experiencing the civil strife.
b The aid to the government should generally be limited to the territory of the state experiencing the civil strife.
c If, however, the outside aid to the rebels is so great that it rises to the point where it is tantamount to an armed attack, the state supporting the government can respond against the territory of the prior intervening state.

In order to understand prong 'a' of the proportionate counter-intervention rule, the following hypothetical situation may be useful. Nigeria is experiencing a civil conflict due to the challenge posed by the Movement for a Free Nigeria. Botswana decides to support the MFE and begins providing financial and military assistance to this rebel group. Under those circumstances, an outside state, the United States, for example, could provide assistance to the government of Nigeria calculated to offset the Botswanan aid to the rebels. The logic would run as follows. Under international law, there is a right for rebel groups to challenge the existing government. But under the neutral non-intervention norm, an outside state cannot provide assistance to the rebels at any time. Since Botswana has provided assistance to the rebels, the internal struggle for self-determination has been upset. An outside force has improperly weighed-in to support the rebels. Hence, to counter that impermissible intervention, it would be permissible for a third state to provide assistance to the government even if there is a high level of civil strife. This would, it is argued, return the scales to their original position and allow the struggle for self-determination to proceed in accordance with the domestic correlation of forces.

Under prong 'b' of the rule, the state providing the assistance to the government would generally have to restrict its assistance to the territory of the state beset with civil strife. In the hypothetical case, the United States would be required to limit its aid to the territory of Nigeria. The rationale for this restriction is a desire not to expand the locus of the conflict. As much as possible, the boundaries of the conflict should be limited.

Prong 'c,' however, indicates that the limitation imposed by prong 'b' is not absolute. If the Botswanan aid to the rebels is so great that it can be equated to an 'armed attack,' then the United States could take forcible action against the territory of Botswana. The logic of this prong is fairly clear. If the actions of an intervening state are limited to the support of rebels, the intervening state has not committed an 'armed attack' *per se*. Nevertheless, if its actions are as severe as an overt armed attack, an outside state should be able to aid the besieged state in the exercise of its right to collective self-defense. Just as in the case of an overt attack, this assistance could take the form of direct action against the territory of the prior intervening state. The only restriction would be the standard qualification of an action done in self-defense. It would have to be proportionate.

As noted above, this understanding of permissible intervention in mixed conflict was supported by the International Court of Justice in the *Nicaragua* case. In that case, the Court had to deal with allegations by Nicaragua that the United States was violating the territorial integrity and political independence of Nicaragua by providing armed support for the *contras* and by mining Nicaraguan harbors.[32] The United States, while refusing to participate in the discussion of the merits before the Court,[33] argued that it was properly using force in the collective self-defense of El Salvador. According to the American argument,[34] Nicaragua had been providing significant assistance to the El Salvadoran rebels, the FMLN. This assistance took the form of weapons, training, logistical and other support. Taken together, this Nicaraguan aid to the FMLN rose to the level of an 'armed attack' on El Salvador. It thus engendered El Salavador's right under Article 51 of the Charter to individual and *collective* self-defense. Accordingly, the United States could provide military assistance to El Salvador not only in the form of direct assistance to the government of El Salvador, but also in the form of action against the territory of the prior intervening state, Nicaragua. The American mining of the harbors and the assistance to the contras was, according to the US argument, a proportionate action against Nicaraguan territory in light of Nicaragua's 'armed attack' on El Salvador.

While the Court differed considerably with the American interpretation of the facts, it did, in essence, accept the basic premises of the proportionate counter-intervention rule. First, the Court began with the assumption that the use of force against the territory of another state would be not only a violation of Article 2(4) of the Charter but also a violation of customary international law. Such action, however, would be permissible if it could be demonstrated that it constituted the exercise of individual or collective self-defense in response to an armed attack. Then, the Court proceeded to define what constitutes an armed attack. On this point, the Court said that

> it may be considered to be agreed that an armed attack must be under-
> stood as including not merely action by regular armed forces across an
> international border, but also 'the sending by or on behalf of a State of
> armed bands, groups, irregulars or mercenaries, which carry out acts of
> armed force against another State of such gravity as to amount to' (*inter
> alia*) an actual armed attack conducted by regular force, 'or its substantial
> involvement therein.'[35]

In other words, the Court recognized that 'indirect aggression' could be severe enough to be tantamount to an armed attack and give rise to the right of individual or collective self-defense.

But even though the Court and the United States could agree in principle on the contours of the proportionate counter-intervention rule, there was a significant difference on the question of the armed attack threshold. For the United States, and scholars such as John Norton Moore, the provision to rebels of weapons, financial support, logistical support, training, command and control support, and the like can, if sufficiently great, be equated to an armed attack. For the Court, however, such activities in support of rebels, while themselves illegal,[36] can never rise to the level of an armed attack. The Court explained that it 'does not believe that the concept of "armed attack" includes not only acts by armed bands where such occur on a significant scale but also assistance to rebels in the form of the provision of weapons or logistical or other support.'[37] In short, while the Court accepted the proportionate counter-intervention rule, it set the threshold for an armed attack quite high.

The limited counter-intervention rule

Despite the widespread acceptance of the proportionate counter-intervention rule – with either a broad or narrow definition of armed attack – another normative approach to intervention in mixed conflict was also developed in the debates on Vietnam and Central America. This proposed norm might be called the limited counter-intervention rule. During the Vietnam War, this approach was most prominently supported by Professor Richard Falk.[38] In this scholarly discussion on Nicaragua, its use was advocated by Professor Christopher C. Joyner.[39] Drawing upon their writings, this norm has three major elements.

a It is permissible for a state to provide offsetting assistance to the government of a state if another state has provided assistance to rebels in the states experiencing the civil strife.
b The aid to the government must *always* be limited to the territory of the state experiencing the civil strife.
c The state aiding the government can *never* take action against the territory of the prior intervening state no matter how great the assistance to the rebels.

Prong 'a' is exactly the same as the first prong of the proportionate counter-intervention rule. If a state is aiding rebels in a second state, the second state has the right to receive assistance from a third state. It is here, however, that the similarity between the two approaches ends. Under the limited counter-intervention rule, the third state, the state aiding the government of the state beset with civil strife, can never take action against the territory of the prior intervening state. The reason for this restriction is to limit the locus of the conflict to the territory of the state experiencing the civil strife under all circumstances.

Most opposition to this approach stems from the fact that it could be interpreted as severely limiting a state's inherent right of self-defense. If a state is providing extensive support to rebels in another state, the only effective way to respond may be to take action against the territory of the intervening state. But under the limited counter-intervention rule, this would not be legally permissible. Hence, even though indirect aggression could be causing as much harm as an overt attack, no use of force against the territory of the aggressor would be permitted.

The self-determination rule

With the growing trend toward acceptance of a right to intervene in civil conflict to support self-determination, the same normative approach would also seem to be applicable to mixed conflict. In consequence, a self-determination rule for mixed conflict can also be formulated. This norm would have three basic elements.

a It is permissible for an outside state to provide assistance to the side in a mixed conflict that is seeking self-determination of peoples.
b Either the government or the rebels can be aided.
c The existence of prior intervention in support of one or more of the parties would not affect the right of an outside state to aid either side.

In short, for those arguing that there is a right to provide assistance to support self-determination, the existence of a mixed conflict would not change that right.

It is interesting to note that the concept of self-determination figured prominently in the defense of American actions in Nicaragua, even though it was not part of the official legal justification. This was the so-called 'Reagan Doctrine.'[40] As noted in chapter 3, the Reagan Administration claimed that it was permissible to provide assistance to the *contras* because they were 'freedom fighters' seeking to overthrow a repressive, communist regime.

Indeed, as quoted earlier, the President suggested that states had a right to intervene to assist rebels fighting for self-determination, not only as an action in self-defense against the territory of a prior intervening state, but because it was proper to support these groups for their own sake.[43]

CHAPTER SUMMARY

For members of the international legal community, the problem of civil and mixed conflict has been a popular topic for debate. In the course of this debate, many different normative approaches have been formulated. From an examination of these approaches, two conclusions can be drawn.

First, the greatest *official* support is accorded to those norms that are most consistent with the basic Charter principles: the neutral non-intervention rule and the proportionate counter-intervention rule. As the preceding analysis reveals, the neutral non-intervention rule is preferred over the traditional rule because of its recognition of the Charter goal of self-determination. It is preferred over the self-determination rule because it agrees with the Charter in emphasizing 'peace' over 'justice.' In a similar vein, the proportionate counter-intervention rule is more widely accepted than the limited counter-intervention rule because it recognizes that indirect aggression can, at some level, be tantamount to an 'armed attack.' The rule thus preserves the integrity of Article 51 by allowing a forcible response against the territory of the prior intervening state.

Second, despite this official acceptance of the neutral non-intervention rule and the proportionate counter-intervention rule, states increasingly seem to be expressing their *real* support for the self-determination rule for civil and mixed conflict. As noted above, Third World states have claimed the right to intervene to support groups fighting racist or colonialist regimes. The former socialist states, traditionally claimed a right to aid 'wars of national liberation.' And the United States has contended that it has a right to support 'democracy.' These claims clearly contradict the official positions taken by most scholars, world leaders, and, in the case of the proportionate counter-intervention rule, the International Court of Justice.

How long this contradiction will continue is uncertain. One thing, however, is certain. Even though the neutral non-intervention rule and the proportionate counter-intervention rule may still have a good deal of authority, their control, as evidenced by these self-determination claims, has probably slipped away.

Chapter 7

Intervention to protect nationals

INTRODUCTION

On December 20, 1989, the United States launched an invasion of Panama, code-named Operation 'Just Cause.' In a special press briefing given that day, Secretary of State James Baker emphasized that the 'leading objective' of the US military action had been 'to protect American lives.'[1] Earlier on D-Day, President Bush had tersely explained the rationale for his decision to use force: 'Last Friday, [General Manuel] Noriega declared his military dictatorship to be in a state of war with the United States and publicly threatened the lives of Americans in Panama.' On Saturday, 'forces under his command shot and killed an unarmed American serviceman, wounded another, arrested and brutally beat a third American serviceman and then brutally interrogated his wife, threatening her with sexual abuse. That,' said the president, 'was enough.'[2] It was time to act.

The appeal by the Bush Administration to the 'protection of nationals' to justify its use of armed force was far from novel. Indeed, since the UN Charter's entry into force, similar appeals have been advanced by a number of governments, American and otherwise, in support of military incursions across the globe. But is the 'protection of nationals' justification for intervention legally sound, particularly given that it is not explicitly provided for by the United Nations Charter?

The purpose of this chapter is to explore in some detail the concept of intervention for the protection of nationals. The first section will define it, then briefly review those cases since 1945 in which either: 1) states have explicitly invoked the protection of nationals rationale to justify a threat or use of force; or 2) observers have argued that states have had grounds to do so. The second section will consider first the 'restrictionist' theory which holds that intervention to protect nationals is prohibited by the terms of the UN Charter. It will then examine four of the most frequently made arguments in support of the legality of such intervention. This section will conclude by assessing whether the 'protection of nationals' justification for intervention represents an authentic rule of the contemporary *jus ad bellum*.

THE NATURE OF THE PROBLEM

Definition

How properly to define 'intervention,' especially that undertaken to protect nationals, has been the source of great scholarly debate and misunderstanding.[3] Does any interference whatsoever in another state's internal affairs constitute intervention? If a state uses non-military but nevertheless coercive means to protect its nationals abroad, should that action be considered intervention? To what degree must its nationals be at risk before a state can credibly advance a 'protection of nationals' rationale for intervention? For the purposes of this work, intervention for the protection of nationals will be defined as 'the use of armed force by a state to remove its nationals from another state where their lives are in actual or imminent peril.'

Four qualifications of this definition must, however, be added.[4] First, our definition excludes any use of force done with the *consent* of the target state. If, for example, American nationals in Colombia were in danger and the Colombian government granted its permission to the United States to remove them forcibly, such a US action would fall beyond the scope of our definition. Second, even though our definition provides that the threatened nationals be removed from another 'state,' this does not require that those nationals be physically present within the actual *territory* of the target state.[5] They may in some other way lie within the exclusive jurisdiction of that state. For example, they could be imperiled while on its flag ship sailing on the high seas. Third, our definition excludes any state action taken pursuant to a recommendation or decision of a competent organ of the *United Nations*. If, for example, the Security Council authorized a state or states to take military action to protect nationals, such action would lie beyond our definition's ambit. Finally, intervention to protect nationals must be distinguished from *humanitarian intervention*.[6] While intervention to protect nationals suggests humanitarian motives, the concept of 'humanitarian intervention' has a distinct meaning under international law. Humanitarian intervention involves the use of force by a state to protect the citizens of *another state* from threatening situations within their own state. Moreover, unlike many interventions undertaken to protect nationals, humanitarian intervention typically involves a prolonged military action that results in a new government in the target state.[7] This variety of intervention will be explored in depth in Chapter 8.

Post-1945 illustrations

On nearly twenty separate occasions since the close of the Second World War, states have threatened to use force for the 'protection of their nationals,' have actually used force for such purposes, or might arguably have had grounds to do so.[8] The first such occasion took place less than a year after the UN Charter's entry into force.

Early examples in the Middle East

In the summer of 1946, riots erupted in the Persian Gulf state of Iran. When these appeared to threaten installations of the British-owned Anglo-Iranian Oil Company and the British subjects working there, the British government decided that it must act. Accordingly, on August 2, it dispatched a contingent of troops stationed in India to Basra, Iraq – near the Iranian border. The action, done with the consent of the Iraqi government, was undertaken so that armed forces might 'be at hand for the protection, should circumstances warrant it, of Indian, British, and Arab lives, and in order to safeguard British interests in South Persia.' The forces would intervene, the British government pledged, only in the case of 'grave emergency.'[9] Ultimately, intervention proved unnecessary. Nevertheless, Iran protested that Britain's troop movements had constituted an infringement of Iranian sovereignty and of the UN Charter.[10]

Two years later, in 1948, the 'protection of nationals' justification was invoked once again in the Middle East – this time by a number of Arab states and by the new state of Israel. Here, in response to a UN Security Council questionnaire, belligerents from both sides in the war in Palestine justified their recourse to armed force on grounds which included, inter alia, the protection of populations beyond the territory subject to their jurisdiction.[11]

In May of 1951, the United Kingdom again threatened to use force in Iran: first, to prevent the nationalization of the Anglo-Iranian Oil Company;[12] and thereafter, to protect British nationals from volatile circumstances which might jeopardize their safety.[13] At length, the British government sent reinforcements to its airbases in Iraq and warships into Iraqi territorial waters. British Foreign Secretary Morrison argued before the House of Commons that the United Kingdom had 'every right and indeed the duty to protect British lives.' Morrison later told the same body: 'It is the responsibility of the Persian government to see to it that law and order are maintained and that all within the frontiers of Persia are protected from violence.' If that responsibility were not met, the Foreign Secretary asserted, 'it would equally be the right and duty of His Majesty's government to extend protection to their own nationals.'[14] Not surprisingly, the Mossadeq regime rejected British arguments, declaring that the United Kingdom had no right to use Iraqi bases in order to 'intimidate' Iran.[15] The Iranian government was, said Premier Mossadeq, 'completely master of the situation.' As in 1946, Britain did not take recourse to force, though probably only because British nationals had not become seriously endangered.[16]

In January of 1952, rioting seemed again to menace British subjects living abroad – this time, those resident in Cairo, Egypt.[17] The British government pursued a two-track response to this new threat. First, it devised a plan to employ troops stationed along the Suez Canal for an intervention in both Cairo and Alexandria. The scheme was never carried out, however, and not publicized at the time.[18] Second, the government sent a diplomatic note which subtly implied that it might take military action.[19] Anthony Eden, Foreign Secretary at the time, recalled in his memoirs: 'the belief that we had the forces and the conviction that we were prepared to use them were powerful arguments in prodding the Egyptian army to quell the riots.'[20] While the United Kingdom never actually used force in response to the Cairo riots, and although its threat to do so was couched in diplomatic language, its actions then are nevertheless illustrative of state practice.

Four years later, in the autumn of 1956, Britain and France intervened in Egypt, ordering troops to occupy key positions along the Suez Canal.[21] While the French government did not justify its actions then as a protection of its nationals,[22] at times the British government did so, principally in parliamentary debates.[23] Prime Minister Eden declared before the House of Commons, 'there is nothing ... in the Charter which abrogates the right of a Government to take such steps as are essential to protect the lives of their citizens.' In 'an emergency,' states had the right to intervene on the basis of 'self-defense' as provided for by Article 51. In fact, maintained Eden, the right to intervene on behalf of nationals abroad extended even to cases of 'imminent threat.'[24] Such parliamentary rhetoric notwithstanding, the British government made little use of the 'protection of nationals' argument during UN debates before the Security Council and General Assembly.[25] Rather, British representatives suggested that the military action had sought to safeguard international navigation through the canal and to halt fighting between Israel and Egypt.[26]

Africa, 1960–64

On July 10, 1960, little more than a week after the proclamation of Congolese independence, Belgium dispatched paratroopers to its former African colony.[27] In the wake of an army mutiny there, the government of the Congo had been rendered incapable of maintaining law and order, and atrocities had been committed on a number of foreign nationals. Given these frightening circumstances, the Belgian representative to the Security Council explained, his government had 'decided to intervene with the sole purpose of ensuring the safety of European and other members of the population and of protecting human lives in general.'[28] In taking forcible action, Belgium's objective extended beyond simply a protection of its *own* nationals; hence, the incursion might arguably be considered not only an intervention to protect nationals, but also a 'humanitarian intervention.'[29] Italy, the United Kingdom, France and Argentina supported the Belgian claim that its operation had been legally justifiable.[30] However, Tunisia, Ecuador, Poland, and the Soviet Union supported the view of the Congolese government that the Belgian use of force had constituted aggression because it had been undertaken without Congolese consent.[31]

On January 12, 1964, when it received word that the Sultan of Zanzibar had been overthrown in a *coup d'état*,[32] the British government immediately ordered a warship in the vicinity to proceed to the African state and to lie anchored offshore. Unless the lives of British subjects required protection, the captain was directed not to intervene. Five days later, on January 17, British nationals were evacuated from Zanzibar, though apparently with the consent of its new government.[33] Had such consent not been forthcoming, however, and had British citizens been genuinely at risk, it appears likely that the United Kingdom would have taken military action. Hence, though 'not exactly definable as an instance of threat or use of armed force, the British operations in Zanzibar do offer useful elements for the assessment of State practice.'[34]

Also in 1964, four years after the first Belgian intervention in the Congo, both Belgium and the United States sent forces there to save the lives of numerous hostages from Congolese rebels.[35] Among those held were citizens of Belgium, the United States, and several other states. Although statements by the American and Belgian governments underscored that the action had been undertaken with Congolese governmental *approval*, the reactions of other states varied: Ghana and the United Arab Republic suggested that a state was never entitled to use force to protect its nationals; a number of states argued that the action was lawful *only* because the government of the Congo had given its consent; and not surprisingly, Britain maintained that a state had 'a right to land troops in foreign territory to protect its nationals in an emergency if necessary.'[36]

Dominican Republic

On April 28, 1965, a task force of four hundred American Marines landed in Santo Domingo, capital of the Dominican Republic, where a bloody civil conflict was already under way.[37] There, the 'National Reconstruction Government,' composed of forces loyal to former President Reid Cabral, had been fighting forces loyal to the 'Constitutional Party,' which earlier had forced the resignation of Cabral. Because no government had been capable of maintaining law and order, the Dominican Republic was 'to all effects, in the throes of anarchy.'[38] Upon a request by Cabral supporters for direct American intervention, therefore, the United States complied.[39]

Representative Adlai Stevenson explained the rationale for US actions in a statement before the UN Security Council:

In the absence of any governmental authority, Dominican law authority enforcement and military officials informed our Embassy that the situation was completely out of control, that the police and the Government could no longer give any guarantee concerning the safety of Americans or of any foreign nationals, and that only an immediate landing of United States forces could safeguard and protect the lives of thousands of Americans and thousands of citizens of some thirty other countries.[40]

The response by other states to the use of US military force was perhaps predictable. Britain, since 1945 a consistent supporter of intervention for the purpose of protecting nationals, favored the American action, arguing that it had been legally permissible.[41] While expressing reservations about the actual objectives of US intervention, France supported the view that any state might intervene to protect its citizens.[42] Most states which condemned US actions tended to do so for reasons unrelated to law, *per se*.[43] Nevertheless, Jordan questioned whether force might lawfully be used to protect nationals,[44] and a Cuban statement which quoted Jiminez de Arechaga[45] contended that a state was never entitled to use force for such purposes.[46]

The Mayaguez

Ten years later, in the Spring of 1975, the United States once again used force to protect its citizens – now, in South-East Asia. On May 12, Cambodia had seized the US merchant vessel *Mayaguez* while the ship had been passing close to an island claimed both by South Vietnam and Cambodia.[47] The United States responded to the Cambodian action by claiming that the American cargo ship had been seized on the high seas, by dubbing the seizure a piratical act, and by demanding the release of the *Mayaguez* within a twenty-four hour period.[48] After Cambodia failed to comply with the Ford Administration's ultimatum, and following an unsuccessful American aerial strike on May 13, the US launched a second attack the next day by land which recovered the ship and freed its crew.

In reporting to the Security Council, the United States submitted that all its measures had been taken in self-defense and had been consistent with Article 51 of the Charter.[49] Cambodia, meanwhile, characterized the American use of force as 'a brutal act of aggression.' It argued that the *Mayaguez* had been in Cambodian territorial waters while on an espionage mission, and that Cambodian authorities had already begun to prepare for the release of the seized vessel and crew when American military action was taken.[50] Thailand likewise criticized the American use of force, fearing lest it, too, become involved in armed conflict.[51] Meanwhile, China charged that America's actions, *not* those of Cambodia, had constituted 'an act of piracy.'[52]

Lebanon, 1976

On June 28, 1976, during one of the more intense periods of the Lebanese civil war, the United States launched an evacuation by warship of several resident Americans. A month later, on July 27, a US seaborne rescue effort was once again undertaken in Lebanon.[53] Before the first military operation, the United States apparently failed to request the approval of any Lebanese governmental authorities. Before the second, however, the US contacted those in actual control of the operation area: the Palestine Liberation Organization (PLO) and other Palestinian groups – not the Lebanese regime.[54] Although neither American evacuation operation required the engagement of troops in combat *per se*, each may nevertheless be considered a 'particular use of force.'[55]

Entebbe

Also during the summer of 1976, Israel landed airborne commandoes at Entebbe airport in Uganda.[56] The July 3 operation sought forcibly to rescue ninety-six Israelis who had been taken hostage after their June 27 flight to Paris had been hijacked by Palestinian terrorists. Although the Israeli government had not sought prior permission from Ugandan authorities to do so, its commandoes nevertheless freed the hostages, whose lives had explicitly been threatened, and killed their captors. In the process, Israeli troops also destroyed about ten Ugandan military aircraft and killed some Ugandan soldiers.

During subsequent Security Council debate, Israel contended that its actions at Entebbe had been permissible 'self-defense.' When a local state was unwilling or unable to do so, Israel asserted, a state might use force to protect its nationals abroad.[57] While Britain seemed uncharacteristically to equivocate on the 'protection of nationals' question,[58] the US explicitly supported the Israeli view.[59] Meanwhile, Italy, France, and Japan discussed the question of law introduced by Israel but failed to reach a conclusion.[60] A large number of other states, however, were sharply critical of the Israeli action, labelling it an 'aggression'[61] and an 'excessive use of force.'[62] Although the 1976 Israeli action was similar in many regards to other previous uses of force to protect nationals, it differed in one significant respect: nationals had not *voluntarily* entered the jurisdiction of a foreign state. Rather, Israeli citizens had been brought to Uganda against their wills.[63]

Western Sahara

On October 25, 1977, two French technicians were seized following a guerrilla attack upon the Zouerate province of Mauritania, located in the Western Sahara.[64] In a conference convened two days later, the French Defense Minister refused to rule out a use of military force to liberate his countrymen from their 'Polisario Front' captors. In fact, a French parachute corps was dispatched to Senegal, immediately engendering loud protests from both Algeria and Libya. On December 23, the captured French nationals were finally released to the UN Secretary General in Algeria, but only after protracted negotiations and French participation in several air attacks upon Polisario Front forces.

Larnaca

In the winter of 1978, a non-western state for the first time used force in an effort to rescue its nationals held abroad.[65] The stage for this Egyptian action was set on February 18, when Palestinian terrorists attacked a meeting of the Afro-Asian Peoples Solidarity Organization convened in Nicosia, Cyprus. The terrorists killed the Organization's Secretary, an Egyptian national, seized a number of hostages including several Egyptians, and then fled the island by airplane. When the terrorists' jet was denied permission to land elsewhere, it returned on February 19 to the Larnaca airport where negotiations between Cypriot authorities and the terrorists promptly began.

As these talks appeared nearly concluded, an Egyptian military aircraft landed at Larnaca. Shortly thereafter, Egyptian commandoes opened fire on the terrorists' airplane and other targets, prompting Cypriot forces to intervene. In the ensuing melee, a number of Egyptian soldiers were killed or taken prisoner, several Cypriots injured, the terrorists captured, and the hostages freed. Although Egypt had received prior permission to land an aircraft at Larnaca, Cypriot authorities had explicitly forbidden any Egyptian use of force.[66] In light of these circumstances, Cyprus charged that its sovereignty had been violated, and refused Egypt's demands for an apology, the repatriation of captured Egyptian commandoes, and the extradition of two terrorists.[67]

Iranian hostage rescue attempt

Among the most prominent post-1945 attempts to use force solely for the protection of nationals was undertaken by the United States on April 24, 1980.[68] That evening, specially-trained US forces sought unsuccessfully to rescue forty-eight American diplomats and two private citizens who had been held hostage in Iran for six months by a group of student militants. On November 4, 1979, in the wake of the Iranian Revolution, several hundred students had stormed the US Embassy in Teheran and taken numerous hostages, some of whom they released on November 13. With the endorsement of the Ayatollah Khomeini, the remaining US citizens had remained captive despite various non-military initiatives by the US government, *inter alia*: on several occasions in 1979-80, the Carter Administration had sought UN Security Council action; it had instituted proceedings against Iran before the ICJ on November 26, 1979; and it had also ordered frozen all Iranian assets in the US. When these and other efforts to secure the release of the US hostages had apparently failed, a rescue mission was launched on April 24, even as the World Court was rendering its final judgment.

While the United States dubbed its effort 'a rescue operation, not a military action,'[69] Iran called it 'a blatant act of invasion,' though it did not apprise the Security Council of the matter.[70] Perhaps not surprisingly, the reaction of other states varied: several pronounced themselves in favor of the lawfulness of the action, while others declared it legally impermissible.[71] In its judgment of May 24, 1980, the ICJ conceded that the US might 'have had understandable feelings of frustration at Iran's long-continued detention of the hostages.' Nevertheless, the Court could not 'fail to express its concern in regard to the United States' incursion into Iran.' Given its timing, the American operation was 'of a kind calculated to undermine respect for the judicial process in international relations.'[72]

Grenada

On October 25, 1983, the United States launched another significant military operation – this time, aimed in part at protecting US nationals on the tiny Caribbean island of Grenada.[73] On the afternoon of October 19, Prime Minister Maurice Bishop and scores of his countrymen had perished in the bloody aftermath of an unsuccessful effort to return the Grenadian leader to power, only days after a *coup* by 'hardliners' within Bishop's own Marxist-Leninist party had ousted him. Later on October 19, the leader of the Grenadian army, General Hudson Austin, had announced the formation of a 'Revolutionary Military Council' and had proclaimed a four day 'shoot-on-sight' curfew. In light of fears that American citizens might be harmed or taken hostage, and given a request for assistance by the Organization of Eastern Caribbean States (OECS), the Reagan Administration decided to take military action.[74] In addition to evacuating US and other nationals, Operation 'Urgent Fury' sought to restore democracy to Grenada and to expel Cuban influence from the island.[75]

Within a week of the Grenada invasion, seventy-nine governments had condemned, repudiated or in some way expressed disapproval of the American action.[76] On November 2, the UN General Assembly voted 108 to 9 to condemn the American operation as a 'violation of international law.'[77] Reagan responded that the resolution had not 'upset [his] breakfast at all.'[78] The American action had been legally justifiable, the State Department Legal Adviser would later maintain, for three reasons: as a 'protection of nationals'; as a 'collective action under Article 52 of the UN Charter'; and as a response to a request by 'lawful authority,' Grenadian Governor-General Scoon.[79]

Panama

Six years later, on December 20, 1989, the United States launched its largest military operation since the Vietnam War, an invasion of Panama. By the conclusion of Operation 'Just Cause,' ten thousand American troops had taken control of the isthmus state, had seized General Manuel Noriega for trial in the US on drug-trafficking charges, and had installed an alternative Panamanian government headed by Guillermo Endara, whose democratic election had earlier been annulled.[80]

In an address given on D-Day morning, President Bush set out four objectives for the use of force: 'to safeguard the lives of Americans, to defend democracy in Panama, to combat drug trafficking and to protect the integrity of the Panama Canal Treaty.'[81] Of these goals, Secretary of State Baker later told a press conference, protection of American lives had been 'the leading one.' The US military action had been taken in 'self-defense,' Baker asserted. Hence, it had been fully in compliance with international law, and specifically in accord with the Charters of the UN and Organization of American States (OAS).[82]

Notwithstanding such American arguments, the international response to 'Just Cause' was largely negative. Although European reaction was generally muted, the governments of Latin America – Argentina, Brazil, Mexico, Venezuela, Peru, Costa Rica, Guatemala, and Cuba – roundly condemned the US action as an interference in Panamanian sovereignty.[83] A resolution by the OAS likewise criticized the United States.[84] The Soviet Union, meanwhile, called the American invasion 'a violation of the United Nations Charter and of the universally accepted norms of behavior between sovereign states.'[85] Similarly, China dubbed it 'a violation of international law.'[86] Only a veto by the United States, Britain, and France circumvented a condemnatory UN Security Council resolution.[87]

Liberia

In August of 1990, the United States launched Operation 'Sharp Edge,' a heliborne rescue of American and other foreign nationals from war-torn Liberia. In that sub-Saharan African state, two competing rebel forces had been seeking for seven months the ouster of President Samuel K. Doe.[88] On August 4, Prince Johnson, one of the insurgent leaders, ordered the arrest of all foreigners in Monrovia in order to spur international intervention in the civil war. The next day, a contingent of two hundred and fifty-five Marines flew into the Liberian capital to begin an evacuation of US and other foreign dependants, apparently without the formal approval of the Liberian government. A Bush Administration spokesman explained that American forces were in Liberia 'to protect lives' and would remain there 'as long as necessary to insure the safety of US citizens.'[89] The US action did 'not indicate or constitute any intention on the part of the US government to intervene militarily in the Liberian conflict,' however.[90] In the course of the next two weeks, US Marines evacuated about one thousand foreign nationals, including those from Lebanon, Italy, Canada, France, and Iraq.[91] Shortly thereafter, on August 24, a 'peacekeeping' force of three thousand soldiers from Nigeria and four smaller West African states arrived in Liberia to begin an attempt to enforce a cease-fire there.[92]

The character of state practice

Regarding the use of force for the protection of nationals, how can state practice since 1945 most accurately be characterized? What general conclusions, if any, may be drawn? To answer these related questions, at least four factors must be considered: 1) the nature of intervening states; 2) the circumstances of intervention; 3) the scope of intervention; and 4) state justifications for intervention.

The nature of intervening states

From a review of state practice since the UN Charter's entry into force, two features are immediately striking. First, those states which have intervened to protect their nationals, or at least threatened to do so, have been almost exclusively *western*. Of the sixteen prominent cases considered here which did not involve target state consent, thirteen involved uses of force threatened or taken by the United States, Britain, France or Belgium.

Second, only a very *few states* have actually invoked the right to use force for the protection of their nationals abroad – in general, those states with the substantial *capacity* to exercise it. For example, of the sixteen cases since 1945 of threatened or actual military action without target state assent, the United States and the United Kingdom account together for eleven. The US alone accounts for seven: the Dominican Republic in 1965; the *Mayaguez* in 1975; Lebanon in 1976; Iran in 1980; Grenada in 1983; Panama in 1990; and Liberia in 1990. Moreover, only one significant use of force was not employed by either the western powers or by Israel: Egypt's 1978 raid on Larnaca, Cyprus. Such a pattern of state behavior is consistent with what Hedley Bull has observed of intervening states: 'The intervener should be superior in power to the object of the intervention.' Accordingly, 'the great intervening powers of modern history, although by no means the only ones, have been the great powers.'[93]

The circumstances of intervention

Since 1945, the circumstances surrounding uses of force for the protection of nationals have in some respects varied significantly. For example, the *number* of endangered nationals has ranged from hundreds (Grenada) or even several thousands (Congo, Dominican Republic) to only two (the threatened French intervention in the Western Sahara.) The *governmental situation* within the target state has likewise varied. In some cases, such as America's 1965 intervention in the Dominican Republic or its more recent evacuation of Liberia, no government within the state has appeared capable of protecting foreign nationals. In other cases, however, the state government has simply been unwilling to protect threatened aliens, as was apparently the case in the 1976 Entebbe raid and in the 1979–80 Iranian hostage crisis. Finally, the *nationality* of those individuals who have benefited from the use of force of the intervening state has also differed. Specifically, intervening states have at times protected not only the lives of their own citizens, but also those of foreign residents of the target state. In the Congo, Grenada, and Liberia missions, for example, the intervening states rescued not only their own nationals, but those of other states as well.[94]

Despite variations in the circumstances surrounding actual or threatened uses of force, one prominent element of continuity may also be noted: the target states almost exclusively have been areas which before 1945 had been under *'great power'* influence or direct control. Iran, Palestine, Egypt, Cambodia, Dominican Republic, Lebanon, Uganda, Western Sahara, Grenada, and Panama – all experienced threatened or actual 'protection of nationals' interventions and all were once controlled or strongly influenced by Britain, France, or the United States. Such a pattern of intervention would seem to reflect both the political instabilities frequently experienced within the target states and the military inferiorities of target states to intervening states such as Britain and the United States.

The scope of intervention

Of the various uses of force to protect nationals we have considered here, many have been *limited* in their temporal durations, territorial scopes, and political impacts within the target states. In these cases, intervening states have simply entered the territories of target states, have forcibly removed their nationals and perhaps those of other states, and then have rapidly departed.[95] Such abbreviated uses of force as Israel's Entebbe raid in 1976 and America's evacuation of Liberia in 1990 have had narrow territorial foci and have been undertaken without prejudice to the governmental structures of the target states.

Other uses of force for the protection of nationals, however, have been of *more significant* duration, territorial scope, and political impact. In these cases, intervening states have typically remained in their target states for extended periods, have occupied all the territory there, and have helped effect significant political changes within the target states. In the American interventions in the Dominican Republic, Grenada, and Panama, for example, new regimes were in place in the target states prior to the withdrawal of US occupation forces.

State justifications for intervention

The justifications offered by states for their uses of force to protect nationals have varied substantially since 1945. In many instances, states have maintained that they have taken action *solely* to protect the lives of their nationals. Often, however, intervening states have justified their uses of force in terms of *multiple* rationales.[96] This latter tendency would seem to reflect at least four factors: first, the complicated or ambiguous material circumstances which have frequently preceded intervention; second, the desire of states to offer justifications of both legal and political plausibility; third, the multiple objectives which have often been pursued by intervening states; and fourth, the varying audiences toward which justifications for intervention have been directed. Hence, during the Suez crisis of 1956, Britain justified its actions not only by invoking its right to protect nationals, but also by claiming the need to safeguard freedom of navigation through the canal and to halt fighting between Israel and Egypt.[97] Similarly, in October of 1983, the United States asserted that its invasion of Grenada had been legally permissible for three reasons: as a protection of nationals; as a collective action taken with the OECS; and as a response to an invitation by lawful authority.[98] And in 1989, the American invasion of Panama was justified in terms of four principles: protection of American lives; defense of Panamanian democracy; combating drug trafficking; and protection of the integrity of the Panama Canal Treaty.[99]

INTERVENTION TO PROTECT NATIONALS – THE QUESTION OF LEGALITY

The 'restrictionist' theory

A number of prominent scholars have argued that 'intervention to protect nationals' is legally permissible.[100] Nevertheless, the majority of states[101] and the majority of scholars[102] appear now to embrace the 'restrictionist' theory which holds that such intervention is *not* permissible.[103] Accordingly, it is useful first to consider here the 'restrictionist' theory before exploring those arguments which challenge it.

The 'restrictionist' theory is based upon three fundamental tenets.[104] First, the theory holds that the principal goal of the United Nations system is the maintenance of international peace and security. Second, it maintains that the United Nations has a monopoly on the legitimate recourse to force – except in clear cases of state self-defense. Finally, it asserts that if states were allowed to employ force for any purpose other than 'individual or collective self-defense,' they would merely be provided with a ready legal pretext for geopolitical intervention.[105]

Before 1945, customary international law allowed states to use force for the protection of their nationals abroad.[106] This pre-Charter rule, restrictionist scholars contend, was frequently subject to abuse as intervening states invoked it to justify military actions taken strictly for *Realpolitik* purposes.[107] In order to address this problem, restrictionists submit, the framers of the UN system deliberately circumscribed the state's authority to use armed force. In the new international legal order, no use of force for geopolitical objectives would be permitted. 'The whole object of the Charter,' posits restrictionist Ian Brownlie, 'was to render unilateral use of force, even in self-defense, subject to [UN] control.'[108]

For their rendition of the *jus ad bellum*, the restrictionists draw heavily upon Articles 2(4) and 51 of the UN Charter. In their view, the language of Article 2(4) clearly indicates a general prohibition on the use of force by states.[109] No state is permitted to threaten or use force 'against the territorial integrity or political independence of any state, or in any manner inconsistent with the Purposes of the United Nations.' Article 51, which provides for 'individual and collective self-defense,' constitutes merely a narrow exception to the general prohibition of 2(4).[110] States may defend themselves, restrictionists argue, but only after an actual 'armed attack' upon state *territory* has occurred.[111] Typical of the restrictionist view is that described by Waldock, himself a counter-restrictionist: '2(4) prohibits entirely any threat or use of armed force between independent States except in individual or collective self defense under article 51 or in execution of collective measures under the Charter for maintaining and restoring peace.'[112] The UN Charter's prohibition, the French restrictionist Viraly suggests, has 'the broadest range it is possible to imagine.'[113]

An armed attack upon 'nationals abroad' must be legally distinguished, say restrictionists, from one upon 'sovereign territory.' While unfortunate, an attack upon nationals does not justify a self-defense response by their state of nationality. Hence, any state use of force solely to protect its nationals is *per se* illegal, if perhaps 'more or less condonable.'[114]

To bolster their argument that intervention to protect nationals is impermissible,[115] restrictionists invoke the principle of 'non-intervention,' which is supported by two General Assembly Resolutions[116] and by positions set out in debate by various UN member states. Restrictionists recognize, however, that while the actions of the General Assembly may help to indicate or to clarify state views, they nonetheless have no binding legal effect.[117]

'Counter-restrictionist' arguments

Legal scholars who challenge the 'restrictionist' theory can be grouped into different schools or approaches – for example, the proponents of the 'realist theory' and the proponents of the 'self-defense theory.'[118] Although such categorizations are certainly convenient, they tend often to oversimplify and sometimes even to obfuscate. Hence, they will not be employed in this chapter. Rather, we will consider here four basic arguments which support the legality of intervention to protect nationals. For the purposes of analysis, each will be discussed individually. It must be emphasized, however, that scholars typically employ a constellation of these arguments in order to support their challenges to the restrictionist theory.

Survival or revival of the pre-Charter customary rule

Of those scholars who argue that intervention to protect nationals is legally permissible, many contend that the pre-Charter customary rule which permitted such intervention has either survived or been revived in the Charter period.

Derek Bowett is one of the most prominent advocates of the former view.[119] According to Bowett, a reading of the *travaux préparatoires* of the Charter indicates that the UN system's framers intended 'to preserve the pre-existing, customary right of self-defense,'[120] and hence, to preserve the state's right to protect its nationals. The language of Article 2(4), asserts Bowett, 'is in no way incompatible with the right to protect nationals.'[121] Moreover, Article 51's provision for self-defense 'if an armed attack occurs against a Member' was most likely intended *not* to limit uses of force to cases of responses to actual armed attack against state territory. These words of qualification within Article 51, contends Bowett, were used 'illustratively rather than exhaustively.'[122]

Although such textual exegesis is helpful in determining the legal status of intervention for the protection of nationals, the actual practice of states in the post-1945 period is far more persuasive, Professor Bowett asserts. An analysis of Charter practice, he suggests, demonstrates sufficiently 'that some States do still maintain the right to use force abroad in the protection of nationals.'[123] Both the text of the UN Charter and the practice of states during the Charter period indicate, therefore, that the pre-Charter rule has *survived.*

Other legal scholars have claimed that the customary right to protect nationals has *been revived* in the Charter period. In their view, the UN founders mistakenly assumed that 'self-help' would no longer be necessary 'since an authoritative international organization [could now] provide the police facilities for enforcement of international rights.'[124] Unfortunately for the international system, submit Michael Reisman, Richard Lillich, and other scholars, the UN enforcement mechanisms have been confounded at virtually every turn by dissension among the Security Council's permanent membership.[125] Article 2(4)'s prohibition on the threat or use of force, they assert, must hence be conditioned on the United Nation's capacity to respond effectively. When the UN fails to do so, customary law revives and states may intervene to protect nationals.[126]

'A rational and contemporary interpretation of the Charter,' argues Reisman, 'must conclude that Article 2(4) suppresses self-help [only] insofar as the organization can assume the role of enforcer.' Where the United Nations cannot assume such a role, 'self-help prerogatives revive.'[127] To impose a less flexible interpretation on 2(4), Reisman posits, would merely provide 'an invitation to lawbreakers who would anticipate a paralysis in the Security Council's decision dynamics.'[128]

Self-defense under Article 51

Closely related to the 'pre-Charter customary rule' argument is the argument that protection of nationals abroad constitutes permissible 'self-defense' under Article 51. According to this second argument, 'an injury to a national in a foreign State which is unwilling or unable to grant him minimum standards of justice and protection' is legally tantamount to 'an injury to the national's home State.' Such an injury represents 'a breach of a legal duty to the national's State,' and thus, justifies a use of force by the aggrieved state.[129] Article 51's legal effect is not to create this right of self-defense, therefore, 'but explicitly to recognize its [pre-Charter] existence.'[130]

In order for a state lawfully to use force to protect its nationals, however, three criteria must be satisfied.[131] First, the nationals of the state must face an imminent threat of injury. Second, the territorial sovereign must be unwilling or unable to protect the nationals of the state. And finally, and of greatest significance, any state's use of force must be limited solely to the purpose of protecting its nationals.[132] States may not, for example, intervene both to protect their nationals *and* to install a new regime in the target state.

Permissible force below the 2(4) threshold

A third argument in support of the legality of intervention to protect nationals relies upon a rather 'narrow'[133] or 'literal'[134] reading of the provisions of Article 2(4). As we have seen, 2(4) provides that 'All Members shall refrain in their international relations from the threat or use of force against the territorial integrity or political independence of any state, or in any other manner inconsistent with the Purposes of the United Nations.' Several prominent scholars suggest that there may be uses of force which do not infringe upon the long-term territorial integrity and political independence of states, and which are not inconsistent with the UN's purposes.[135]

Such uses of force would *not* involve: a prolonged military presence by the intervening state in the target state; a loss of territory by the target state; a regime change there; or any actions 'inconsistent with the purposes of the United Nations.' Limited uses of force of this kind would fall 'below the 2(4) threshold,' and thus, would not be prohibited by the UN Charter. Specifically, any short-term military intervention undertaken exclusively for the purpose of protecting nationals would be legally permissible. Indeed, it might even be considered 'commendable.'[136]

Human rights

Most international legal scholars agree that the United Nations system has one principal purpose: the maintenance of international peace and security. A few scholars, however, most notably Professors McDougal and Reisman, reject this restrictionist premise.[137] Instead of one major purpose, they submit that the UN has two major purposes, each of *equal* weight: first, the maintenance of international peace and security; and second, the protection of human rights.

To advance this 'humanitarian' argument, proponents typically invoke the Preamble and Articles 1, 55, and 56 of the UN Charter as well as the developing corpus of international human rights law.[138] The Preamble's 'repeated emphasis upon the common interest in human rights,' argue Reisman and McDougal, 'indicates that the use of force for the urgent protection of such rights is no less authorized than other forms of self-help.'[139] Under Article 1(3), they suggest, 'promoting and encouraging respect for human rights' is set out as a fundamental purpose of the United Nations.[140] Similarly, Article 55 of the Charter points to the UN objective of promoting 'human rights' observance, while Article 56 authorizes 'joint and separate action [by Members] in cooperation with the Organization for the achievement of the purposes set out in Article 55.'[141]

Human rights deprivations, Reisman and McDougal contend, might well represent a 'threat to the peace,' thereby prompting the Security Council's Chapter VII jurisdiction.[142] If the Security Council failed to act under such circumstances, 'the cumulative effect of articles 1, 55, and 56 [would be] to establish the legality of unilateral self-help.'[143] Individual states could therefore intervene to protect their nationals abroad, for there exists 'a coordinate responsibility for the active protection of human rights: members may act jointly with the Organization ... or singly or collectively.'[144] Were this interpretation not the case, it 'would be suicidally destructive of the explicit purposes for which the United Nations was established.'[145]

Legal assessment

What is the legal status of intervention for the protection of nationals? Is 'the use of armed force by a state to remove its nationals from another state where their lives are in actual or imminent peril' permissible under the contemporary *jus ad bellum*? In order to answer this question, it is useful to recall both the practice of states since 1945 and the arguments advanced by international legal scholarship.

As we have seen, most scholars[146] – including Professors Akehurst, Brierly, Brownlie, DeLima, Franck, Friedmann, Henkin, Jessup, Kelsen, Rodley, Ronzitti, Tucker, Verdoss, Wehberg, and Wright[147] – accept the 'restrictionist theory' which holds that intervention to protect nationals is impermissible. Notwithstanding this majority view, a number of prominent scholars – including Professors Bowett, Lillich, McDougal, Moore, Reisman, Stone, and Waldcock – argue that a right to intervene for the protection of nationals *does* exist.[148] Meanwhile, most states have maintained that the use of force to protect nationals is unlawful.[149] Nevertheless, those few states which have intervened to protect their nationals or only threatened to intervene, most notably the United States and Britain, have consistently asserted their legal right to do so.[150]

Given these facts, what may be concluded? Of the various interpretations of the UN Charter which have been examined here, the restrictionist theory appears most accurately to reflect both the intentions of the Charter's framers and the 'common sense' meaning of the Charter's text. This judgment may certainly be debated. Indeed, the restrictionist/counter-restrictionist dispute is likely to continue into the foreseeable future. But regardless of how one assesses the cogency of the respective restrictionist and counter-restrictionist textual interpretations, one fact remains clear: a substantial gap separates the *restrictionist views* of most states and legal scholars and the consistent *practice* of those 'states whose interests [have been] specially affected.'[151] The existence of this rather egregious discrepancy would seem to call into question the existence of a rule prohibiting state intervention to protect nationals.

In light of the 'authority-control' test of a putative norm of international law, it is difficult to hold that a rule exists prohibiting intervention to protect nationals. To be sure, since 1945 most states have not intervened to protect their nationals, and most have rejected as illegal such intervention. But only a relatively few states have actually faced circumstances where substantial numbers of their nationals abroad have been threatened. And even fewer states under such circumstances have had sufficient capacity to take military action. Hence, since 1945 there have been relatively few 'states whose interests [have been] specially affected.'[152] Of these states which have had both the *cause* and the *capacity* to use force, however, all appear consistently to have claimed their right to do so. Such behavior, while perhaps not quantitatively significant, is nevertheless qualitatively so. Hence, the actions of Britain, the United States, and a few other 'specially affected' states cannot be ignored in any assessment of state practice *per se*. Their actions suggest that the restrictionist 'norm' is neither authoritative nor controlling.

CHAPTER SUMMARY

This chapter has examined the concept of intervention for the protection of nationals: 'the use of armed force by a state to remove its nationals from another state where their lives are in actual or imminent peril.' The first section reviewed eighteen cases since 1945 in which states either have invoked the 'protection of nationals' rationale to justify a threat or use of force, or might potentially have had grounds to do so. In two of these cases, Zanzibar (1964) and the Congo (1964), the target state actually gave its consent to intervention. A review of state practice during this period indicates that only a relatively few states have intervened or threatened to do so – typically western states with significant military capacities such as the United States and Britain. It also illustrates that the circumstances surrounding intervention, the scopes of intervention, and the justifications offered for intervention have varied substantially.

The second section considered first the 'restrictionist theory' which holds that intervention to protect nationals is prohibited. The 'restrictionist' argument, which appears now to be supported by most states and most scholars, assumes that the UN's principal purpose is the maintenance of international peace and security and that Articles 2(4) and 51 of the Charter substantially limit the state's capacity to take recourse to force.

This section next examined four of the most frequently made arguments in support of the legality of intervention to protect nationals: 1) survival or revival of the pre-Charter customary rule; 2) self-defense under Article 51; 3) permissible force below the 2(4) threshold; and 4) human rights. It then assessed whether the 'protection of nationals' justification for intervention represents an authentic rule of the contemporary *jus ad bellum*. It concluded that there exists a substantial gap between, on the one hand, the 'restrictionist' views of most states and legal scholars, and, on the other, the consistent practice of 'those states whose interests [have been] specially affected.' Such a significant discrepancy would seem to call into question the existence of any authoritative and controlling rule prohibiting state intervention to protect nationals.

Humanitarian intervention

INTRODUCTION

In April of 1975, Khmer Rouge forces assumed governmental control of Cambodia, the western neighbor of Vietnam soon to be dubbed 'Democratic Kampuchea.' Under Pol Pot's unflinching leadership, the new Communist regime sought brutally and systematically to return Cambodian society to its agrarian roots – and at horrific cost. In less than three years, perhaps as many as one-sixth of Cambodia's six million people perished in the hellish torture chambers of Phnom Penh and in the 'killing fields' of the countryside.[1]

When they eventually became publicized, the atrocities committed by the Khmer Rouge appalled many within the international community. In 1979, for example, a number of western states presented a resolution to the UN Commission on Human Rights condemning 'the gross and flagrant violations of human rights which [had] occurred in Democratic Kampuchea.' And the year before, in a Senate subcommittee hearing, George McGovern had wondered aloud whether 'any thought' had been given to 'sending in a force to knock this government out of power, just on humanitarian grounds.'[2]

Senator McGovern's 1978 query was a provocative one, raising a fundamental question of international law. It remains so today. Is it permissible to remove forcibly the government of another state because it is engaged in the deliberate, widespread abuse of the human rights of its own nationals? Can military intervention, to remove a state's regime or merely to protect that state's citizenry, be justified solely on the grounds of humanity?

The purpose of this chapter is to explore in some detail the concept of 'humanitarian intervention'. The first section will define it, then review eleven cases since 1945 in which: 1) states have explicitly justified their uses of force as 'humanitarian interventions' *per se* ; 2) states have justified their uses of force on 'humanitarian' grounds generally; or 3) observers have characterized state uses of force absent UN authorization as potential 'humanitarian interventions'. The section will close with a characterization of state practice. The second section will set out the three most frequently made arguments in support of the legality of humanitarian intervention:

1) protection of human rights; 2) revival of the customary right of humanitarian intervention; and 3) per- missible force below the 2(4) threshold. It will conclude by assessing whether 'humanitarian intervention' represents a legitimate justification for recourse to force under the contemporary *jus ad bellum*.

THE NATURE OF THE PROBLEM

Definition

Because of the tremendous scholarly confusion surrounding intervention generally,[3] and 'humanitarian intervention' specifically,[4] it is essential that our discussion begin with an explicit definition. For the purposes of this work, 'humanitarian intervention' will be defined as 'the use of armed force by a state (or states) to protect citizens of the target state from large-scale human rights violations there.'[5] In theory, a humanitarian intervention can be directed against either governmental or non-governmental actors.[6] In practice, however, a state *government* is typically more capable of violating human rights on the massive scale required to justify an intervention on humanitarian grounds.[7] Hence, while a humanitarian intervention might conceivably achieve its purpose without removing an incumbent regime, this situation would be a rather unusual one.[8] For example, a forcible operation might be launched against a state in which a condition of anarchy prevailed.

To be considered a 'humanitarian intervention' as defined here, an action must satisfy four separate criteria. First, there must be within the target state an 'immediate and extensive threat to fundamental human rights, particularly a threat of widespread loss of human life.'[9] Second, the intervention's specific purpose must be essentially limited to protecting fundamental human rights.[10] Third, the forcible action must *not* be undertaken pursuant to an invitation by the legitimate government of the target state or done with that government's explicit consent.[11] Fourth, properly speaking, a 'humanitarian intervention' *per se* cannot be undertaken upon the authorization of the Security Council, whether by UN forces or by those of Chapter VIII 'regional arrangements.'[12] As we have earlier maintained, humanitarian UN relief operations such as those begun in northern Iraq in 1991 and across Somalia in 1992 are best characterized as simply 'collective uses of force' under the Charter. To describe either United Nations undertaking as a 'humanitarian intervention' is to deprive the term of its traditional core meaning.

Humanitarian intervention must likewise be distinguished from both 'intervention to protect nationals'[13] and 'intervention to facilitate self-determination.'[14] As has been seen in Chapter 7, 'intervention to protect nationals' involves the state's protection of its *own* nationals abroad. In contradistinction, humanitarian intervention involves the state's protection of the nationals *of another state* from inhuman and cruel treatment within their state, typically by their own government. As noted in Chapter 3, 'intervention to facilitate self-determination' involves a state's armed intervention on behalf of a self-determination movement within the target state. There, a group is fighting against the established regime in order to implement the right of self-determination of a people. For example, the movement could be seeking to end colonial, racist, or political domination.[15] By contrast, humanitarian intervention seeks not the creation of a new state *per se*, but only the protection of human rights within an existing state. Moreover, while humanitarian intervention requires that inhuman and cruel treatment take place within the target state prior to any use of force, 'intervention to facilitate self-determination' has no such prerequisite.[16] Finally, state supporters of the legality of intervention to facilitate self-determination 'have been careful not to present this alleged right as an example of a wider right of humanitarian intervention.' Rather, they have been 'often the most vehement in condemning any [other form of] intervention, humanitarian or otherwise, in the affairs of other states.'[17]

Post-1945 illustrations

Since the entry into force of the United Nations Charter, states have taken a number of military actions which they have either justified on general 'humanitarian' grounds or explicitly characterized as 'humanitarian interventions.' States have likewise taken actions which they have not dubbed 'humanitarian interventions' themselves, but which other states or scholarly observers have done so. This section will consider all those uses of force since 1945 which might be considered potential humanitarian interventions.[18] As will be seen, however, genuine instances of humanitarian intervention have been 'few and far between,'[19] if they have occurred at all.[20]

The Palestine conflict, 1948

On May 14, 1948, the state of Israel proclaimed its independence. The following day, a group of Arab states – Egypt, Syria, Lebanon, Transjordan, Saudi Arabia and Iraq – took military action against Israel, to which the new Jewish state promptly responded.[21] Among other grounds offered by the Arab states for their use of force was its ostensibly humanitarian objective.[22] Explained the representative of Egypt before the Security Council,

> [N]ow that the British mandate in Palestine has ended, ... Egyptian armed forces have started to enter Palestine to establish security and order in place of the chaos and disorder which prevailed and which rendered the country at the mercy of Zionist terrorist gangs who persisted in attacking

peaceful Arab inhabitants ... Horrible crimes, revolting to the conscience of humanity, have been perpetrated by these Zionist gangs. Arab women have been assaulted, pregnant women's stomachs ripped open, children killed before the very eyes of their mothers and prisoners tortured and then brutally murdered.[23]

A week later, in response to a May 22 Security Council questionnaire, both Egypt and Israel justified their extra-territorial uses of armed force, at least in part, in humanitarian terms.[24] The Security Council reacted negatively to the actions of all involved, however, especially to those of the Arab states.[25] The Soviet Union argued specifically that 'each government [had] the right to restore order only in its own country.'[26]

For three reasons, the 1948 Palestine conflict should probably not be considered an authentic instance of 'humanitarian intervention.' First, the Arab states appear then to have justified their actions far more on the basis of a request emanating from the 'Palestinian people' than on the basis of the humanitarian intervention doctrine.[27] In particular, Egypt did not recognize the state of Israel, and considered all of Palestine to be the rightful possession of Palestinian Arabs, who had given their assent to the admission of Egyptian armed forces.[28] Second, since the planned establishment of an Arab state in Palestine 'never became a reality, and since none of the neighboring Arab states at that time purported to annex any part of Palestine, Israel could have argued that her military operations in Palestine in May 1948 were not taking place on territory under the sovereignty of another state.'[29] Third, as one scholar has tersely observed, 'the political objectives' of both the Arab and Israeli belligerents in 1948 'are too well-known' and 'need no comment.'[30] The goal of any 'humanitarian intervention,' as we have suggested, must be essentially confined to the protection of fundamental human rights.

Belgian intervention in the Congo

On July 10, 1960, slightly over a week after the proclamation of Congolese independence, Belgium dispatched paratroopers to its former colony.[31] Following an army mutiny there, the government of the Congo had been rendered incapable of maintaining law and order, and atrocities had been committed on a number of individuals. In light of these frightening circumstances, the Belgian representative to the UN Security Council explained, his government had 'decided to intervene with the sole purpose of ensuring the safety of European and other members of the population and of protecting human lives in general.'[32]

In employing armed force, Belgium's purpose extended beyond simply a protection of its *own* nationals. Hence, the incursion might arguably be considered not only an intervention to protect nationals, but also a potential 'humanitarian intervention.' Italy, the United Kingdom, France, and

Argentina supported the Belgian assertion that its operation had been legally justifiable.[33] Indeed, Belgium, France, the United Kingdom, and Italy expressly described the Belgian action as a form of *humanitarian intervention*.[34] Meanwhile, Tunisia, Ecuador, Poland, and the Soviet Union supported the view of the Congolese government that the Belgian use of force had constituted aggression because it had been undertaken without Congolese consent.[35]

While Belgian actions in 1960 might perhaps be judged as a lawful protection of its own nationals, it is rather doubtful that Belgium's use of force constituted a legitimate 'humanitarian intervention.' According to Professor Verwey, Belgian motives appear then to have been not purely humanitarian:

> It has never become quite clear which and how many foreigners were (to be) saved. Clear [it] was, however, that the Belgian troops stayed on until September, and took active part in a civil war on the side of the Katangese rebels who, Belgium hoped, would respect Belgian commercial interests in the minerals-rich province of Katanga, in exchange for its armed support.[36]

Verwey's overall assessment of the 1960 intervention would seem implicitly to be accepted by Professor Tesón, a prominent recent advocate of the legality of humanitarian intervention. In Tesón's 1988 treatise, no mention whatsoever is made of the episode in his extensive chapter on state practice.[37]

The Congo, again

On November 24, 1964, four years after the first Belgian intervention in the Congo, both Belgium and the United States sent armed forces there to save the lives of nearly two thousand hostages from Congolese rebels.[38] Among those held in Stanleyville and Paulis were nationals of the Congo, Belgium, the United States, Britain, Greece, Italy, Canada, and eleven other states.[39] In light of its special circumstances, the three-day operation has been variously labelled by scholars a 'humanitarian intervention,'[40] an 'intervention to protect nationals,'[41] and an 'intervention with the consent of the territorial state.'[42]

Public statements by the US and Belgian governments emphasized that their military action had been undertaken with Congolese governmental consent and that its purpose had been 'humanitarian.'[43] Nevertheless, the reactions of other states varied: Ghana and the United Arab Republic suggested that a state was never entitled to use force to protect its nationals;[44] Bolivia, Brazil, Nationalist China, and Nigeria argued that the action was lawful *only* because the government of the Congo had given its consent;[45] and Britain asserted that a state had 'a right to land troops in foreign territory to protect its nationals in an emergency if necessary.'[46]

But was the combined military action a 'humanitarian intervention' as defined here? Certainly for one reason, but arguably for two, this case must be excluded from the category of bona fide humanitarian interventions. First, the Congolese government gave its *consent* to the intervention.[47] By our definition, a use of force undertaken with the explicit consent of the target state's government is *not* a humanitarian intervention. Second, there is some cause to believe that the intervention's specific purpose was not limited to protecting fundamental human rights. The Sudanese representative to the Security Council, for example, hinted that ulterior motives had informed the intervention. 'In normal circumstances,' he submitted, 'it would be difficult to oppose a rescue mission undertaken for humanitarian purposes.' However, in the present case 'the dropping of paratroopers could only have the effect of a provocation of violence.'[48] Similarly, legal scholars have suggested that American and Belgian motives extended beyond simply the humanitarian desire to protect the lives of Congolese and foreign captives.[49]

Dominican Republic

On April 28, 1965, a US task force landed in the Dominican Republic capital, Santo Domingo, where a violent civil war was in progress.[50] Forces loyal to former President Reid Cabral had been fighting those supporting the 'Constitutional Party,' which earlier had compelled Cabral's resignation. Because no government had been capable of maintaining law and order, Professor Ronzitti maintains, the Dominican Republic was 'to all effects, in the throes of anarchy.'[51]

In its early stages, the American use of force was justified on the grounds that it sought to protect the lives of US and other foreign nationals.[52] Within a few days of the incursion, however, it became apparent to observers that the US action would not be a temporary measure. Once Americans and other foreigners had been evacuated, the United States did not withdraw its troops. Instead, after the US had secured the authorization of the Organization of American States (OAS), a force of over twenty thousand reestablished order in the Republic. Because these military activities were undertaken, 'at least in theory, with the *consent* of both the rival factions in the Dominican Republic,' they probably 'cannot be regarded as a true example of intervention taking place without the consent of the local government.'[53] Nor can American actions in 1965 be considered purely 'humanitarian.' President Johnson, for example, explained his rationale for action in decidedly geopolitical terms: 'The American nation cannot, must not, and will not permit the establishment of another communist government in the Western hemisphere.'[54] In light of this and similar Johnson Administration rhetoric, Professor Dore has called the 'Dominican crisis ... the first instance in which the US carried out an open, public, and outright invasion of another state to preserve hemispheric solidarity.'[55]

East Pakistan, 1971

The Indian intervention in East Pakistan[56] is frequently cited 'as a very significant precedent' by supporters of humanitarian intervention's lawfulness.[57] Accordingly, the 1971 military action, which is perhaps best understood within the broader context of the politics of the Indian subcontinent, merits our close attention here.

Following British withdrawal from the Indian peninsula in 1947, two states came into existence: India and Pakistan, the latter geographically and ethnically divided into East and West. Because of pronounced cultural and linguistic differences between Pakistan's two halves, and more importantly, because of West Pakistan's economic and military domination over more populated East Pakistan,[58] political unrest gradually escalated, as East Pakistanis sought limited autonomy.

In elections held in 1970, the Awami League,[59] the autonomist political party of East Pakistan, obtained the majority of seats in the National Assembly. Apparently because this electoral result was perceived by the central government as a threat to Pakistani territorial integrity, President Yahya Khan decided not to summon the new parliament. This decision engendered significant protests in East Pakistan, to which the government responded with an imposition of martial law. Such a drastic move only further exasperated the autonomist movement.[60] On March 23, Sheikh Muhibur Rahman, leader of the Awami League, issued a 'Declaration of Emancipation.'[61] This proclamation, Professor Teson maintains, constituted 'the final blow to any attempt to settle the conflict peacefully.'[62]

On March 25, 1971, the army of West Pakistan attacked Dacca, the capital of East Pakistan. This military strike inaugurated a several-month period of 'mass murders and other atrocities' that seem to have been directed 'against *all* of the East Pakistani people.'[63] According to the Report of the International Commission of Jurists:

> The principal features of this ruthless oppression were the indiscriminate killing of civilians, including women and children and the poorest and weakest members of the community; the attempt to exterminate or drive out of the country a large part of the Hindu population; the arrest, torture and killing of Awami League activists, students, professional and business men and other potential leaders ... ; the raping of women; the destruction of villages and towns; and the looting of property. All this was done [on] a scale which is difficult to comprehend.[64]

Terrorized by the indiscriminate brutality they had witnessed or more directly experienced, perhaps as many as ten million East Pakistanis sought refuge in India.[65]

On December 5, 1971, India invaded East Pakistan, and the next day, formally recognized Bangladesh as an independent state. By the twelfth day of fighting, December 16, the West Pakistani army in Dacca had surrendered. The Indian use of armed force had quickly prevailed.[66] But how is one properly to characterize that use of force?

According to Professor Akehurst,[67] India first justified her actions to the UN Security Council as a 'humanitarian intervention.'[68] When the final version of the Official Records of the Security Council proceedings was published, however, India appears to have deleted all such justificatory statements, alleging instead that Pakistan had first attacked India.[69] Akehurst maintains that India most probably underwent 'a change of mind and realized that humanitarian intervention was an insufficient justification for the use of force.'[70] To Akehurst's contention, Professor Tesón responds that whether or not 'India amended her initial pro-interventionist statement' is an issue 'of little importance.' What really mattered, according to Tesón, were not Indian objectives, but rather that 'the whole picture of the situation was one that warranted foreign intervention on the grounds of humanity.'[71]

Tesón's argument, though viscerally appealing, must be rejected. International legal scholarship has long recognized that state motives must be taken into account in legal assessments of state practice. For there to be a genuine 'humanitarian intervention,' we have suggested, the intervening state's objective must be essentially *limited* to protecting human rights. Such was simply not the case in India's invasion of Pakistan. Here, 'non-humanitarian motives played a decisive role.'[72] Among these motives were: 1) India's political interest in East Pakistan's secession; 2) India's need to free itself from the heavy economic burden imposed by the influx of Pakistani refugees; and 3) India's need to respond to Pakistan's use of force against India.[73] If the invasion of Pakistan was in some sense 'a humanitarian operation,' it was also clearly 'undertaken by a partisan actor.'[74] Certainly, during Security Council and General Assembly debate, state reactions to India's use of force provided little or no support for the legality of humanitarian intervention.[75]

Indonesian intervention in East Timor, 1975

On December 7, 1975, Indonesian military forces launched a full-scale invasion of East Timor, the Portuguese-controlled half of the South Pacific island of Timor.[76] For nearly half a year, several rival political groups there had been struggling for power in anticipation of Portuguese-promised East Timorese independence. Because it had 'felt called to restore order,'[77] the Indonesian government argued that its use of armed force had been justifiable.

In the light of such apparently 'humanitarian' rhetoric, a few commentators have cited the Indonesian action as a potential case of humanitarian intervention.[78] For several reasons, such an interpretation is highly dubious, however.[79] First, Indonesian forces intervened on behalf of a pro-Indonesian faction after Indonesian government consultations with that group. Second, immediately after its use of force, Indonesia sought to thwart outside inter-ference. Presumably, any state involved in a humanitarian intervention would welcome the assistance of other states. Third, and most damaging to a 'humanitarian intervention' interpretation were Indonesian actions in the months immediately following its invasion. Despite UN Security Council and General Assembly condemnations, Indonesian troops remained in East Timor until July of 1976. Then, Indonesia annexed East Timor. This action would seem to reflect *Realpolitik* motives far more than 'humanitarian' ones. Certainly, East Timor suffered a devastating depopulation as a direct result of the Indonesian invasion. According to one estimate, as many as one hundred thousand people were killed: one-sixth of East Timor's total population.[80]

Angola

The story of South Africa's intervention in Angola is in some respects similar to that of Indonesia's intervention in East Timor. Like East Timor, Angola had long been a colonial possession of Portugal. Even before Angola secured its independence on November 11, 1975, it, too, was racked by civil war. Here, a Soviet-supported group centered in the Angolan capital of Luanda, the MPLA, was pitted against two tribal-based groups, the FNLA and UNITA.[81] During the course of the bloody conflict, in the summer of 1975, several thousand South African troops intervened from neighboring Namibia (South-West Africa). South Africa justified its use of force then on 'humani-tarian' grounds, accusing the MPLA and its Cuban supporters of atrocities committed in parts of Angola held by the FNLA-UNITA front.[82]

Governmental rhetoric notwithstanding, geopolitical motives appear to have played a central role in the South African military action, not humani-tarian ones. Hence, the Angola incursion most probably should not be considered a proper example of 'humanitarian intervention.' Certainly, most international legal scholars exclude the Angola case from their list of potential 'humanitarian interventions.'[83] According to Professor Verwey,

> the alleged concern on the side of the South African Government about the fate of black Angolans – which is not all too credible in the case of a government based upon *apartheid* anyway – was obviously of minor importance when the decision to intervene was taken.

It was 'clearly in South Africa's interest to support the UNITA and to prevent MPLA from taking over control with the help of Cuba.' It was likewise in South Africa's interest to protect hydro-electric facilities located on the Cunene river. Of vital significance to Namibian energy security, these instal-lations had been threatened with imminent destruction by the MPLA.[84]

On March 31, 1976, the UN Security Council rejected the 'humanitarian' justification that had been tendered by South Africa for its intervention. Resolution 387, adopted by a 9–0 vote, branded the South African action an 'aggression' against Angola. Five states abstained in the Security Council vote, including the United States, which insisted that the intervention of Cuba in Angola should be condemned.[85]

Kampuchea, 1978–79

In April of 1975, after years of civil war, Khmer Rouge forces led by Pol Pot finally wrested governmental control of Cambodia (Kampuchea) from Lon Nol.[86] At once, the new communist regime began a program of comprehensive economic and administrative reorganization. During the program's savage course, 'excesses of every kind and the very worst violations of human rights took place: torture, killing and mass deportation.'[87] Within less than three years, perhaps as many as one-sixth of Kampuchea's six million people died at the hands of their own government.[88]

On Christmas Day, 1978, after a lengthy series of border incidents between the two communist states, Democratic Kampuchea was invaded by its eastern rival, the People's Republic of Vietnam.[89] Among the vast contingent of Vietnamese invasion forces were members of the United Front for the National Salvation of Kampuchea, a Cambodian insurgent group 'which had been virtually created by Vietnam itself.'[90] On January 7, 1979, the Vietnamese army captured Kampuchea's capital city of Phnom Penh, and in the months that followed, established effective control over most of Kampuchea's territory. While Pol Pot fled into the mountains where he would later establish rebel bases, Vietnam installed a new government in the rechristened 'People's Republic of Kampuchea,' composed of United Front members and led by Heng Samrin.[91] Kampuchea's nightmare, it seemed to some observers, might at last be over.

Professor Ronzitti argues that Vietnam's use of force against Kampuchea 'is probably the one [precedent] which sheds most light on the relation between the use of force and the protection of human rights.'[92] But how is the Vietnamese invasion properly to be understood? Without a doubt, there was within the target state of Kampuchea an 'immediate and extensive threat to fundamental human rights, particularly a threat of widespread loss of human life.' Literally hundreds of thousands of Kampuchean citizens were wantonly slaughtered by Pol Pot's Khmer Rouge regime, their skulls and bones at times stacked in great heaps. But was Vietnam's 1978–79 action a case of 'humanitarian intervention' as defined here?

In a series of UN Security Council meetings which took place on January 11–15, 1979, Vietnam set out its rationale for taking military action.[93] Perhaps surprisingly, it *never* claimed then to have intervened to reestablish human rights in Kampuchea, nor even to have given military assistance to the United Front rebels there.[94] The Kampuchean conflict, it argued, had actually been composed of two separate ones: first, the conflict between Vietnam and Kampuchea; and second, the Kampuchean civil war *per se.* The People's

Republic of Vietnam had become involved in the former conflict only after prior Kampuchean aggression. Consequently, Vietnam's use of force had been undertaken solely in self-defense. The civil war in Kampuchea, meanwhile, had been fought by the Kampuchean people themselves who eventually overthrew the inhumane Pol Pot regime.

In Security Council meetings, the Soviet Union and its allies repeated the Vietnamese claim that Pol Pot had been ousted from power by Kampuchean United Front rebels.[95] Almost all the other states participating in the January debate, however, held that Vietnam had illegally intervened in Kampuchean internal affairs.[96] While several took note of the appalling violations of human rights committed by the Khmer Rouge government, 'not a single state spoke in favor of the existence of a right of humanitarian intervention.'[97] China submitted a draft resolution condemning Vietnam as an 'aggressor,' but the measure appeared to lack the majority's support and was therefore not brought to a vote.[98] A less specific draft resolution which called upon 'all foreign forces' to withdraw from Kampuchea was introduced by Kuwait and six other states. Although this resolution secured thirteen affirmative votes, it was blocked by a Soviet veto.[99]

During its thirty-fourth session, the General Assembly was likewise compelled to make a political assessment of events in Kampuchea. Here, it had first to determine whose credentials to accept: those of the representatives from Kampuchea's defeated Khmer Rouge regime, or those of the representatives from the new Vietnamese-installed government. The Credentials Committee advised accepting those of the Khmer Rouge representatives, and the General Assembly voted subsequently to accept this recommendation.[100] Also during the General Assembly's thirty-fourth session, the UN body adopted a number of resolutions condemning 'foreign intervention' in Kampuchea and calling for the departure of foreign forces.[101] Professor Akehurst observes that a November 1979 resolution was even supported by

> Greece, the Netherlands, Yugoslavia, and India – states which had previously supported humanitarian intervention. Greece said expressly that Pol Pot's violations of human rights did not justify Vietnam's intervention, and Yugoslavia condemned foreign interference in internal affairs under any pretext whatever.[102]

Although the ouster of the Khmer Rouge regime put an end to Pol Pot's reign of terror, Vietnam's use of force against Kampuchea should not be considered a genuine 'humanitarian intervention.' As we have seen, virtually no state viewed the Vietnamese action in such legal terms. Indeed, according to Akehurst, UN debates then 'provide some evidence that there is now a consensus among states in favor of treating humanitarian intervention as illegal.'[103] Even Vietnam itself did not invoke a humanitarian intervention rationale, preferring instead a self-defense argument. However one assesses this official Vietnamese justification for action, Hanoi's regional hegemonistic motives for invading Kampuchea seem clear.[104] It is perhaps for this reason that Professor Tesón, perhaps the most prominent recent advocate of humanitarian intervention's legality, excludes the Kampuchea case from his lengthy discussion of state practice.[105]

Uganda, 1979

On April 11, 1979, forces from the Ugandan National Liberation Front (UNLF) entered Uganda's capital city of Kampala and formed a provisional government there headed by Professor Yusuk Lule.[106] The rebel action, accomplished only with the direct participation of thousands of Tanzanian troops,[107] ended eight years of brutal dictatorship by Uganda's president, Idi Amin. Under the Amin regime, perhaps as many as three hundred thousand Ugandan citizens had been killed, many after having suffered grisly torture.[108] According to Professor Tesón, the 'arbitrariness, ruthlessness, and cruelty of Amin's rule can hardly be overstated.'[109] But can Tanzania's action to remove the manifestly inhumane Amin be characterized as a proper example of 'humanitarian intervention?'

Tanzania's 1979 use of force against Uganda, notes Tesón, was 'the result of a series of events that took place in the context of strained relations between the two nations over the preceding years.'[110] Perhaps the most formative of these was Uganda's armed attack of Tanzania in October of 1978.[111] In the wake of its invasion from the north, Uganda briefly occupied the Kagera Salient – a Tanzanian region located between the Kagera River and the Tanzania–Uganda border – and advanced territorial claims upon the area.[112] Within a few weeks, however, Tanzania launched a November 15 counter-strike from the south, and by November 29, Uganda had withdrawn all of its troops from Tanzanian territory.[113]

Two months later, on January 20, 1979, Tanzanian military forces struck Uganda itself.[114] As early as December of 1978, Tanzania's President Julius Nyerere appears to have determined that Idi Amin 'would be toppled from power.'[115] By February 23, Tanzanian troops captured Masaka, and on March 11, scored a decisive victory over Amin's forces in Lukaya, a mere 65 miles from the Ugandan capital.[116] Only two weeks later, on March 23–25, the two principal Ugandan groups opposed to Amin's regime, the 'Save Uganda Movement' and the 'Forces of National Revolt,' convened in Tanzania and established the UNLF.[117]

On March 27, 1979, President Nyerere characterized the nature of the armed hostilities that had racked Uganda – in terms rather similar to those employed by Vietnam to describe the Kampuchean conflict.[118] 'Two wars,' he submitted, were being fought. The first, conducted by Tanzania in southern Uganda, was merely a 'continuation' of Tanzania's self-defense action following Uganda's October 1978 aggression. The second was a 'war of liberation' fought in the north by Ugandan revolutionaries. Professor Ronzitti observes:

Humanitarian justifications would seem, then, to have been totally lacking in the Tanzanian intervention. According to Nyerere's statements, the sole aim of Tanzania's military action was the limited one of reacting against the armed attack carried out by Uganda, and not that of overthrowing the Amin regime, which was the task of the Ugandan rebels.[119]

After the April 11 fall of Kampala to Tanzanian and Ugandan rebel forces,[120] Tanzania's justification for its use of force shifted somewhat. No longer, suggests Ronzitti, could it 'deny the obvious and claim that the aim of its intervention [had been] limited.'[121] Now Tanzania indicated that its action had been informed by humanitarian motives. Announced the Tanzanian Foreign Minister on April 12, Amin's fall had been 'a tremendous victory for the people of Uganda and a singular triumph for freedom, justice and human dignity.'[122] Said Nyerere: 'If Africa, as such, is unable to take up its responsibilities, it is incumbent upon each state to do so.' Tanzania's intervention in Uganda had served as 'a lesson to Amin and people of his kind.'[123]

Despite such words, Nyerere's principal justification for Tanzania's use of force was not the overthrow of Amin. Rather, the President of Tanzania maintained that his state had sought to achieve three objectives: to respond to the Ugandan aggression; to punish Idi Amin for his authorization of that attack; and to deter a second Ugandan assault upon Tanzanian territory.[124] Declared Nyerere, 'From the outset, we said our aim was to punish Amin. The aim of uprooting Amin was not our task; it was the task of the people of Uganda.'[125]

International reaction to Tanzania's participation in the ouster of Amin was largely muted. According to Professor Wani, the global community perceived the intervention as 'some kind of blessing.'[126] Hence, although Tanzania's use of force 'was charged as a violation of certain peremptory norms of international law, it was never seriously censured.'[127] At no time, for example, was the action debated in the United Nations, though numerous states were quick to recognize the new Ugandan regime of Yusuf Lule.[128] Nor did the Organization of African Unity (OAU) ever censure Tanzania,[129] even though basic principles of its Charter had been breached by Tanzania's intervention.[130]

At a meeting of the OAU convened in Monrovia on July 17, 1979, the recent events in Uganda were considered. Here, Nyerere circulated a report that articulated Tanzania's grounds for action. According to that document, the 'war between Tanzania and Idi Amin's regime in Uganda [had been] caused by the Ugandan army's aggression against Tanzania and Idi Amin's claim to have annexed part of Tanzanian territory. There [had been] no other cause for it.'[131] With the support of Nigeria, Sudan criticized Tanzania for its invasion of Uganda and for its interference in Ugandan internal affairs. In reply, President Binaisa, the new leader of Uganda, countered that OAU member states ought not to 'hide behind the formula of non-intervention when human rights are blatantly violated.'[132]

How has Tanzania's 1979 recourse to force been interpreted by legal scholarship? In Professor Tesón's view, the Uganda incursion represents 'a precedent supporting the legality of humanitarian intervention in appropriate cases.'[133] More fundamentally, it constitutes 'perhaps the clearest in a series of cases which have carved out an important exception to the prohibition of article 2(4).'[134] Professor Ronzitti, noting the difficulty of giving 'an account of the reasons put forward by Tanzania for its intervention,' argues that the action is not an authoritative precedent for the existence of a right of humanitarian intervention.[135]

Of these two recent assessments, Ronzitti's would seem the better one. Certainly, Amin's actions in Uganda constituted an 'immediate and extensive threat to fundamental human rights, particularly a threat of widespread loss of human life.' Hence, by our definition, they would have fulfilled one of four prerequisites for a 'humanitarian intervention.' Nevertheless, Tanzania frequently emphasized the self-defense grounds (however dubious) of its use of force, not the humanitarian ones.[136] In view of the words of the Tanzanian government itself, therefore, the purpose of Tanzania's use of force was *not* 'limited to protecting fundamental human rights.' Accordingly, the 1979 intervention should not legally be considered a 'humanitarian' one.

Central Africa, 1979

On September 21, 1979, Jean-Bedel Bokassa, the notorious 'Emperor' of the Central African Empire, was overthrown in a bloodless *coup*.[137] Bokassa's deposition, brought about while he was away in Libya, was facilitated by the active support of eighteen hundred French commandoes. Because of the French operation's 'humanitarian motives,' and its 'null cost in human lives,' Professor Tesón has labelled it 'an instance of humanitarian intervention *par excellence*.'[138] Whether France's use of armed force actually merits such a characterization is debatable, however.

In recent studies of humanitarian intervention, legal scholars have variously treated France's Central African incursion, code-named Operation 'Barracuda.' Both Professors Verwey and Ronzitti have ignored it altogether.[139] Professor Akehurst makes merely a brief reference to the case, observing that 'France tried to pretend that her troops arrived in the Central African Empire, at the request of the *new* government, *after* Bokassa had been overthrown.'[140] Only Professor Tesón, a prominent defender of humanitarian intervention's international legality, examines the Central African case in any detail.

According to Tesón, '[a]lthough some early French statements may have given the impression that the French sent their troops after the *coup*, it was soon apparent that the French troops had participated directly in the maneuver.'[141] On September 24, for example, the French Minister of Cooperation publicly acknowledged that France had 'accompanied' the coup.[142]

Moreover, foreign and French commentators at the time uniformly dubbed France's action a military intervention.[143] In Tesón's opinion, 'humanitarian concerns were crucial to the French decision to overthrow Bokassa.'[144] 'French troops provided the necessary and proportionate help the Central African citizens needed to depose a dictator who had undoubtably rendered himself guilty of the gravest crimes against humanity.'[145]

To be sure, during his fourteen years as dictator Bokassa committed a number of atrocities.[146] In April of 1979, for example, the dictator personally ordered the torture and murder of perhaps as many as two hundred children after they had refused to purchase government-mandated school uniforms.[147] And when in May his Central African subjects provided evidence of his actions to a Commission of Inquiry established by the French-African Conference, Bokassa subsequently authorized that reprisals be taken against them.[148]

In view of Bokassa's manifestly loathsome behavior, did France's action in September of 1979 constitute an unambiguous case of humanitarian intervention? For two reasons, the action appears not to have done so. First, the scope of the human rights violations committed by the Bokassa regime seems to have been insufficiently broad to have justified a humanitarian intervention. We have earlier contended that there must be within the target state an 'immediate and extensive threat to fundamental human rights, particularly a threat of widespread loss of human life.' The torture and murder of two hundred people, however appalling, should by itself probably not be considered 'a widespread loss of life' justifying intervention. Second, there is some cause to question the purity of France's 'humanitarian' motives. The French government never invoked, for example, a 'humanitarian intervention' justification for its actions. Indeed, the French at first refused even to acknowledge their direct participation in Bokassa's ouster. Moreover, France had substantial economic interests in Central Africa to protect, including diamonds, uranium, and other strategic minerals.[149] Finally, the French intervention has been interpreted by some African observers as an 'urgent effort to prevent the success of several rival *coups* under preparation' in Central Africa with the support of two communist states, Cuba and the Soviet Union.[150]

Grenada, 1983

As discussed in Chapter 7, on October 25, 1983, the United States launched 'Urgent Fury,'[151] an operation which sought to evacuate American and other nationals from Grenada, to restore democracy to the tiny Eastern Caribbean island, and to expel Cuban influence from there.[152] Because of its special circumstances, several objectives, and multiple state participants, the Reagan Administration use of force has been variously characterized as a 'regional peacekeeping' action,[153] an intervention in response to lawful invitation,'[154] an 'intervention to protect nationals,'[155] and a 'humanitarian intervention.'[156]

The stage for American action was set a week before the actual invasion, on the afternoon of October 19. Then, former Grenadian Prime Minister Maurice Bishop and scores of his countrymen perished in the bloody aftermath of an unsuccessful effort to return Bishop to power – only days after a coup by 'hardliners' within Bishop's own Marxist-Leninist party had ousted him. Later on October 19, General Hudson Austin announced the formation of a 'Revolutionary Military Council.' The leader of the Grenadian army also declared a four day 'shoot-on-sight' curfew. Because of fears that American citizens might be harmed or taken hostage, and pursuant to a request for assistance by the Organization of Eastern Caribbean States (OECS), the Reagan Administration decided on the evening of October 23 to take military action.[157]

The Grenada invasion was overwhelmingly criticized by the international community. Indeed, almost immediately, seventy-nine governments condemned, repudiated or in some way expressed disapproval of the American action.[158] By November 2, moreover, the General Assembly voted 108 to 9 to condemn the US use of force as a 'violation of international law.'[159]

International opinion notwithstanding, did the American invasion of Grenada represent a genuine instance of 'humanitarian intervention?' Early Reagan Administration justifications seemed to emphasize the action's 'humanitarian' dimension.[161] The first spoken and written statements issued by Washington on October 25, for example, emphasized the goals of restoring order and forestalling chaos, surely 'humanitarian' objectives.[162] On October 26, US Ambassador to the OAS J. William Middendorf submitted that the United States had had 'a particularly humanitarian concern.'[163] And a week later, a White House statement claimed that the Grenada action had been 'taken for humanitarian reasons.'[164] In the light of such rhetoric, Professor Teson concludes: the 'whole logic of [the Reagan Administration action], evidenced not only by the conduct of the United States and her Caribbean allies, but also by statements by the highest United States officials, denote[d] the humanitarian underpinnings of the mission.'[165]

Despite such statements by the US government, the Grenada invasion should not be considered a proper example of humanitarian intervention, for several reasons. First, the Reagan Administration never explicitly justified its action on the basis of 'humanitarian intervention.' Indeed, it explicitly rejected the 'humanitarian intervention' rationale for its action in its most carefully crafted legal justification: State Department Legal Adviser Davis Robinson's letter to Professor Edward Gordon.[166] The American action had been legally justifiable, Robinson maintained, for three reasons: as a 'protection of nationals'; as a 'collective action under Article 52 of the UN Charter'; and as a response to a request by 'lawful authority,' Grenadian Governor-General Scoon.[167] Second, geopolitical motives clearly informed the American decision to use military force. As has been suggested, 'Urgent Fury' sought not only to evacuate American and other nationals from Grenada, but also to restore democracy to the island, and to expel the communist influence of Cuba. Finally, if one accepts the view that Sir Paul Scoon's invitation constituted a lawful invitation, then US actions pursuant to Grenadian governmental consent would fall beyond the ambit of our definition of 'humanitarian intervention.'

The character of state practice

With respect to humanitarian intervention, how can state practice since the UN Charter's entry into force most accurately be characterized? What general conclusions, if any, may be drawn from this chapter's historical review? To answer these questions, three factors will be considered in turn: 1) the circumstances of intervention; 2) state justifications for intervention; and 3) state responses to intervention.

The circumstances of intervention

Since 1945, state governments have all too frequently violated human rights – at times, on a massive scale. As we have seen, by 1979 perhaps as many as three hundred thousand Ugandans had perished under Idi Amin's brutal leadership, possibly one million Kampucheans under Pol Pot's. And in 1971, ten million East Pakistanis sought refuge in India after having suffered a seven-month period of atrocities by the West Pakistani army. But despite these and other lamentable cases of widespread human rights abuse by state governments, have there been any genuine instances of 'humanitarian intervention' during the UN Charter period? Professor Ronzitti argues that bona fide examples of such intervention have been 'few and far between.'[168] In view of the various cases considered here, the conclusion drawn in Ronzitti's 1985 treatise seems firmly grounded. Indeed, since the Second World War there may well have been no authentic example of a 'humanitarian intervention.'

We have earlier suggested that a 'humanitarian intervention' must satisfy four criteria:

a there must be within the target state an immediate and extensive threat to fundamental human rights, particularly a threat of *widespread* loss of human life;
b the intervention's specific purpose must be essentially *limited* to protecting fundamental human rights;
c the action must not be pursuant to the *invitation* by the legitimate government of the target state or done with that government's explicit *consent*; and

d the intervention must not be undertaken upon authorization by the
   United Nations Security Council.

Of the eleven post-1945 uses of armed force considered in this chapter, all
satisfied the fourth criterion insofar as none involved an intervention pursuant to UN authorization; we have deliberately not explored here the recent
Security Council-authorized relief operations in northern Iraq and Somalia.
However, not a single use of force we have examined would appear to
satisfy all three of our remaining criteria.

France's 1979 incursion in Central Africa, for example, was not undertaken in response to a sufficiently widespread loss of life to be legitimately
categorized as a 'humanitarian intervention.' Interventions in the Congo
(1964), the Dominican Republic, Angola, and Grenada followed what could
at least arguably be interpreted as target state invitation or consent.[169] And
not one of the interventions reviewed in this chapter appears to have been
informed by exclusively (or perhaps even principally) humanitarian
motives.[170] For example, some interventions seem to have been government
responses to perceived communist threats abroad: in the Dominican
Republic, Angola, Grenada, and possibly Central Africa. Others by India,
Indonesia, South Africa, and Vietnam apparently reflected state desires for
regional hegemony or territorial expansion. Economic considerations may
also have provided an impetus for state recourses to force in the Congo
(1960), East Pakistan, and Central Africa. And two interventions, in Palestine
and Uganda, appear to have been launched at least in part because the
governments of the neighboring target states had been viewed as inimical to
the intervening states' long-term geopolitical interests.

State justifications for intervention

In a 1986 essay, Professor Bowett posited that since the UN Charter's entry
into force, there had been 'no true example of a clear reliance on [the right
of humanitarian] intervention by any state.'[171] Bowett's assessment remains
valid today. To be sure, when taking up arms, intervening states have often
denounced large-scale violations of human rights in their target states: for
example, in East Pakistan, Kampuchea, Uganda, and Grenada. Nevertheless,
they have almost invariably taken care not to submit explicit 'humanitarian
intervention' justifications for their recourses to armed force.[172]

After the American invasion of Grenada in 1983, for example, the United
States at first cited its 'humanitarian reasons' for action[173] but later pointedly
rejected a 'humanitarian intervention' legal rationale.[174] Likewise, although
the Tanzanian Foreign Minister termed Idi Amin's 1979 ouster from power 'a
singular triumph for freedom, justice and human dignity,'[175] a subsequent
Tanzanian report submitted that the 'war between Tanzania and Idi Amin's
regime in Uganda' had been solely 'caused by the Ugandan army's ag-

gression against Tanzania and Idi Amin's claim to have annexed part of Tanzanian territory.'[176] And while in Security Council debate India initially justified its 1971 invasion of East Pakistan as a 'humanitarian intervention,' it later appears effectively to have retracted the argument by editing the Council's provisional records.[177] Hence, one must look all the way back to the 1948 Palestine conflict 'to find an instance of the invocation of the doctrine of humanitarian intervention,' although the Arab states emphasized then that their use of armed force had been solicited by the 'Palestinian people.'[178]

Responses to intervention: target and observer states

Since 1945, how have target states responded to intervention for ostensibly 'humanitarian' purposes? Four of the interventions considered here followed what might be construed as target state invitation or consent: the Congo (1964), the Dominican Republic, Angola, and Grenada. To these uses of force, naturally, target state 'authorities' did not object. However, after the other seven interventions examined in this chapter, those which lacked prior state assent, the governments of the respective target states typically launched prompt and vocal protests.[179] Uganda, for example, sought the assistance of 'all friendly countries' to respond to the 1979 assault of '20,000 soldiers' from Tanzania led 'by mercenaries and a few Ugandan exiles.'[180] Similarly, Pakistan submitted in 1971 that its territorial integrity had been violated by India and called for the pacific settlement of disputes, 'whatever their cause, origin or magnitude.'[181] In 1960, the Congolese government labelled as 'aggression' Belgium's use of armed force then.[182] And in 1979, Democratic Kampuchea announced that it had fallen victim to 'a large-scale act of flagrant aggression' by Vietnam.[183]

It is not surprising that target states have consistently objected to univited uses of force against them. But how have 'observer states,' those neither targets nor intervenors, reacted to instances of intervention for 'humanitarian' purposes? Since the Charter's entry into force, the number of observer states which have censured such interventions, or at least challenged their international legality, has been substantial – far greater than the number of those states which have supported them.[184] Moreover, according to Professor Akehurst, 'the United Nations debates on Cambodia in 1979 provide some evidence that there is now a consensus among states in favor of treating humanitarian intervention as illegal.'[185]

Of those observer states which have actually supported (or at least, failed to condemn) particular acts of intervention, most have refrained from expressly invoking the 'humanitarian intervention' concept. Rather, they have generally preferred to rely upon other, less controversial, legal arguments.[186] After the 1971 Indian intervention, for example, the Soviet Union noted that Pakistan had terrorized and repressed its Bengali population. Nevertheless, it supported India's action as a 'self-defense' response to prior Pakistani attack.[187] In the Ugandan case, numerous states reacted positively to the governmental change in Uganda, as evidenced by their swift recognition of the new regime. However, not one invoked the doctrine of humanitarian intervention.[188] And in 1979, the Soviet Union and other eastern bloc states hailed the ouster of the brutal Khmer Rouge regime as an action accomplished by Kampuchean insurgent forces. Pol Pot's removal was not, they suggested, an operation of the Vietnamese military.[189]

HUMANITARIAN INTERVENTION – THE QUESTION OF LEGALITY

The 'restrictionist' theory

Is 'humanitarian intervention' legal? Certainly, a modest number of prominent scholars have argued that states may lawfully undertake humanitarian interventions.[190] Notwithstanding the opinion of these authorities, however, the majority of scholars[191] and the majority of states[192] now appear to accept the 'restrictionist theory' which posits that such intervention, as well as intervention to protect nationals, is *not* permissible.[193] Hence, we will first review here the restrictionist theory, discussed in greater detail in Chapter 7, before considering counter-restrictionist arguments.

Three basic premises, it will be recalled, underly the 'restrictionist' theory.[194] First, the theory maintains that the fundamental objective of the United Nations system is the maintenance of international peace and security. Second, it holds that except in clear cases of state self-defense, the UN has a monopoly on the legitimate recourse to force. Third, it contends that if states were permitted to take recourse to armed coercion for any purpose other than 'individual or collective self-defense,' they would merely be provided with a ready pretext for geopolitical intervention.[195]

Articles 2(4) and 51 play central roles in the restrictionist rendition of the UN Charter *jus ad bellum*. The language of Article 2(4), restrictionist scholars submit, clearly indicates a general prohibition on the use of force by states.[196] For them, Article 51 represents only a narrow exception to the general prohibition of 2(4).[197] By the terms of these two Charter provisions, therefore, humanitarian intervention has been rendered legally impermissible.[198] Because it does not involve 'individual or collective self-defense' (Article 51), or Security Council enforcement (Chapter VII), humanitarian intervention constitutes a proscribed use of force 'against the territorial integrity and political independence of a state' (Article 2[4]). While all restrictionists view humanitarian intervention as illegal *per se*, some concede that in special situations such a use of force might be 'more or less condonable.'[199]

In order to buttress their argument that humanitarian intervention is not legal,[200] restrictionist scholars invoke the principle of 'non-intervention,' which is supported by two General Assembly Resolutions[201] and by positions set out in debate by various UN member states. Restrictionists acknowledge, however, that although General Assembly resolutions provide evidence of state attitudes, such multilateral statements lack binding legal effect.[202]

'Counter-restrictionist' arguments

Three basic arguments are typically advanced in support of the international legality of humanitarian intervention: 1) protection of human rights; 2) the revival of the customary right of humanitarian intervention; and 3) permissible use of force below the 2(4) threshold. For analytical purposes, each of these counter-restrictionist arguments will be separately discussed here. It must be recognized, however, that legal scholars typically combine these fundamental arguments in order to advance their view that humanitarian intervention constitutes a lawful recourse to force.

Two of the three arguments considered in this chapter, 'protection of human rights' and 'permissible force below 2(4),' are frequently cited by counter-restrictionists to support their view that intervention to protect nationals is legally permissible. A variation of the third argument, 'revival of customary right,' is likewise commonly invoked by advocates of the lawfulness of intervention to protect nationals.[203] Only the 'self-defense under Article 51' argument, advanced in support of the legality of intervention to protect nationals, is *not* employed by those who support humanitarian intervention's lawfulness.[204] Because Article 2(4) does not constitute a general prohibition against the use of force to protect human rights, counter-restrictionists submit, it is unnecessary to invoke Article 51 as an exception to 2(4): 'A right to forcible self-help exists not because it is permitted by Article 51 but because it is not denied by Article 2(4).'[205]

Protection of human rights

As noted in Chapter 7, most international legal scholars agree that the United Nations system has one principal purpose: the maintenance of international peace and security.[206] A few jurists, however – most notably Professors McDougal, Reisman, and Tesón – reject this restrictionist premise.[207] They contend that the UN has two major purposes, both equally significant: first, the maintenance of international peace and security; and second, the protection of human rights. Submits Teson, for example: 'the promotion of human rights is as important a purpose in the Charter as is the control of international conflict.'[208]

To bolster this position, proponents of the 'human rights' argument typically cite the developing corpus of international human rights law as well as the UN Charter's Preamble and Articles 1, 55, and 56.[209] Argue Reisman and McDougal, the Preamble's 'repeated emphasis upon the common interest in human rights indicates that the use of force for the urgent protection of such rights is no less authorized than other forms of self-help.'[210] Under Article 1(3), they suggest, 'promoting and encouraging respect for human rights' is set out as a fundamental purpose of the United Nations.[211] Likewise, Article 55 of the Charter points to the UN objective of promoting 'human rights' observance, while Article 56 authorizes 'joint and separate action [by Members] in cooperation with the Organization for the achievement of the purposes set out in Article 55.'[212]

According to Reisman and McDougal, human rights deprivations might well represent a 'threat to the peace,' thereby prompting the Security Council's Chapter VII jurisdiction.[213] If the Security Council failed to act under such circumstances, 'the cumulative effect of articles 1, 55, and 56 [would be] to establish the legality of unilateral self-help.'[214] Individual states could therefore undertake humanitarian interventions, for there exists 'a coordinate responsibility for the active protection of human rights: members may act jointly with the Organization ... or singly or collectively.'[215] The protection of human rights is of as great an importance as the maintenance of international peace and security. Were this interpretation not the case, advocates of humanitarian intervention's legality submit, it 'would be suicidally destructive of the explicit purposes for which the United Nations was established.'[216]

Revival of the customary right of humanitarian intervention

Closely related to the 'human rights' argument is the argument that the customary right of 'humanitarian intervention' has revived in the period after 1945. Under pre-Charter customary international law, counter-restrictionists often contend, states were permitted to engage in humanitarian interventions.[217] This customary law right was legitimately exercised to protect human rights. It was not invoked as a bogus rationale to support *Realpolitik* actions, as restrictionists typically assert.[218] State uses of force before the Second World War may have exported European economic and political perspectives elsewhere; nevertheless, argues Professor Lillich, this fact *per se* 'does not necessarily impeach the viability of the rules that were established, especially since these rules operated in the interests of the smaller countries as well.'[219]

As noted in Chapter 7, the UN founders, counter-restrictionists argue, assumed that 'self-help' would no longer be necessary 'since an authoritative international organization [could now] provide the police facilities for enforcement of international rights.'[220] Unfortunately for the international system, suggest Professors Reisman, Lillich, and Tesón, the UN enforcement mechanisms have been consistently confounded by discord among the Security Council's permanent membership.[221] Article 2(4)'s prohibition of the threat or use of force, they assert, must consequently be conditioned on the UN's capacity to respond effectively. When the United Nations fails to do so, customary law revives and states may invoke the right of humanitarian intervention.[222]

'A rational and contemporary interpretation of the Charter,' Reisman posits, 'must conclude that Article 2(4) suppresses self-help [only] insofar as the organization can assume the role of enforcer.' Where the United Nations cannot assume such a role, 'self-help prerogatives revive.'[223] To impose a more rigid interpretation on 2(4), Reisman argues, would provide merely 'an invitation to lawbreakers who would anticipate a paralysis in the Security Council's decision dynamics.'[224] Contends Professor Tesón: 'It is indeed unlikely that states would have given up self-help to enforce their rights had they known the UN Security Council would have been unable to adopt the enforcement measures contemplated in the Charter.'[225]

Permissible force below the 2(4) threshold

A third argument in support of the legality of humanitarian intervention – and likewise in support of intervention to protect nationals – relies upon a rather 'narrow'[226] or 'literal'[227] reading of the provisions of Article 2(4). As we have seen, 2(4) prohibits the threat or use of force against the territorial integrity or political independence of any state, or in any other manner inconsistent with the Purposes of the United Nations.' Several scholars suggest that there may be uses of force that do not infringe upon the long-term territorial integrity and political independence of states, and that are not inconsistent with the UN's purposes.[228]

Of necessity, such uses of force would *not* involve: a prolonged military presence by the intervening state in the target state; a loss of territory by the target state; a regime change there; or any actions 'inconsistent with the purposes of the United Nations.' Limited uses of force of this kind would fall 'below the 2(4) threshold,' and thus, would not be prohibited by the UN Charter. Specifically, any short-term military intervention undertaken exclusively for the purpose of protecting human rights would be legally permissible.

According to Tesón, 'A genuine humanitarian intervention does not result in territorial conquest or political subjugation.'[229] So contend Professors Reisman and McDougal:

> Since a humanitarian intervention seeks neither a territorial change nor a challenge to the political independence of the State involved and is not only not inconsistent with the purposes of the United Nations but is rather in conformity with the most fundamental peremptory norms of the Charter, it is a distortion to argue that it is precluded by Article 2(4).[230]

Professor Stone offers a similar opinion. What Article 2(4) prohibits, he maintains, is 'not the use of force as such, but as used against "territorial integrity or political independence of any State," or "in any other manner inconsistent with the Purposes of the United Nations."' The purposes 'expressed in Article 1 itself, moreover, embrace not only collective measures against threats to the peace.' They embrace 'also (and coordinately) the bringing about "by peaceful means, and in conformity with the principles of justice and international law, adjustment or settlement" of peace-endangering disputes.' Concludes Professor Stone, it is

> far from impossible to argue that a threat or use of force employed consistently with *these* purposes, and not directed against the 'territorial integrity of political independence of any state,' may be commendable rather than necessarily forbidden by the Charter.[231]

Legal assessment

What is the legal status of humanitarian intervention? Absent UN Security Council authorization is 'the use of armed force by a state (or states) to protect citizens of the target state from large-scale human rights violations there' permissible under the contemporary *jus ad bellum*? In order to answer this question, it is useful to recall both the practice of states since 1945 and the arguments advanced by international legal scholarship.

A review of state practice during the UN Charter period suggests at least three conclusions. First, although state governments have all too frequently violated human rights, at times on a massive scale, genuine instances of humanitarian intervention have been rare, if they have occurred at all. Our eleven-case study reinforces the conclusion drawn in Professor Verwey's nine-case one: probably no case of putative humanitarian intervention since 1945

> can be considered as a pure humanitarian intervention in the sense that the basic condition of 'relative disinterest' on the side of the intervenor was fulfilled, that humanitarian considerations clearly provided the only major objectives and that no overriding or equally important political or economic considerations were involved.[232]

Second, while sometimes citing humanitarian motives, intervening states have generally eschewed expressly 'humanitarian intervention' rationales for their recourses to armed force. Hence, thus far there has been no unambiguous case of state reliance on the right of humanitarian intervention. India appears at first to have flirted with the legal justification in 1971 Security Council debate, but ultimately to have jettisoned it.[233] Accordingly, one must look all the way back to the 1948 Palestine conflict 'to find an instance of the invocation of the doctrine of humanitarian intervention.' Here, however, the Arab states emphasized that their recourse to force had been solicited by the 'Palestinian people.'[234] Third, most observer states have condemned interventions undertaken for ostensibly 'humanitarian' purposes. Of those states which have supported (or failed to condemn) such uses of armed force, most have refrained from explicitly invoking the 'humanitarian intervention' concept. Instead, they have often preferred to rely upon other more conventional legal arguments such as 'self-defense.'

Most contemporary legal scholars, meanwhile, reject the notion of humanitarian intervention.[235] The relatively few jurists who embrace the concept have expressed their intellectual discomfort with a *jus ad bellum* that prohibits uses of armed force designed to halt large-scale human rights violations. Observes Professor Teson, for example: 'There must be something deeply wrong with an international legal system that protects tyrants like [Idi] Amin.'[236] Teson's assertion may well be true. There may well be something 'wrong' with the contemporary *jus ad bellum*. But if something is in fact wrong, then the answer is to change the law, not to reinterpret it.

We argued in Chapter 7 that the 'restrictionist theory' most accurately reflects both the intentions of the Charter's framers and the 'common sense' meaning of the Charter's text.[237] While conceding that our judgment was debatable, we maintained that a substantial gap exists between the restrictionist theory and the practice of states with respect to intervention to protect their nationals. Such an egregious discrepancy, we concluded, indicates that the restrictionist norm prohibiting intervention to protect nationals is neither authoritative nor controlling.

In this chapter, too, we maintain that the restrictionist theory best expresses the UN Charter *jus ad bellum*. However, in light of our examination of post-1945 state practice, we conclude that the restrictionist norm prohibiting humanitarian intervention *is* both authoritative and controlling. By their words and by their actions, the great majority of target states, observer states, and even intervening states have consistently rejected the 'humanitarian intervention' doctrine. Accordingly, since the Charter's entry into force, it has remained almost exclusively for scholars to articulate counter-restrictionist arguments supporting the lawfulness of humanitarian intervention. Such arguments, grounded far more in theory than in fact, have a certain visceral appeal but must ultimately be rejected. If humanitarian intervention is to be legally permissible, then it is the task of states to render it so.

CHAPTER SUMMARY

This chapter has examined the concept of 'humanitarian intervention': 'the use of armed force by a state (or states) to protect citizens of the target state from large-scale human rights violations there.' The first section reviewed eleven cases since 1945 of potential 'humanitarian intervention': the Palestine conflict of 1948; the Congo in 1960 and 1964; the Dominican Republic, 1965; East Pakistan, 1971; Indonesian intervention in East Timor,

1975; Angola, 1975; Kampuchea, 1978; Uganda, 1979; Central Africa, 1979; and Grenada, 1983. A review of state practice during the UN Charter period suggests several conclusions. First, although state governments have often violated human rights, genuine instances of 'humanitarian intervention' have been rare, if they have occurred at all. Second, while sometimes citing humanitarian motives, intervening states have generally eschewed expressly 'humanitarian intervention' rationales. Hence, there has thus far been no unambiguous case of state reliance on the right of humanitarian intervention. Finally, most states have condemned interventions undertaken for 'humanitarian' purposes. Of those states not condemning such uses of force, most have refrained from explicitly invoking the 'humanitarian intervention' concept, preferring instead to rely upon other legal arguments.

The second section set out the three most frequently made arguments in support of the legality of humanitarian intervention: 1) protection of human rights; 2) revival of the customary right of humanitarian intervention; and 3) permissible force below the 2(4) threshold. It then considered whether 'humanitarian intervention' represents a legitimate justification for recourse to force under the contemporary *jus ad bellum*. In light of state practice since 1945, it concluded that the restrictionist norm prohibiting humanitarian intervention *is* both authoritative and controlling.

Chapter 9

Responding to terrorism

INTRODUCTION

On the day of Ronald Reagan's inauguration, January 20, 1981, American citizens who had languished as hostages in Teheran since November of 1979 were finally released by their Iranian captors.[1] Less than a month later, President Reagan issued an explicit warning to would-be terrorists and their supporters: '[W]hen the rules of international behavior are violated, our policy will be one of swift and effective retribution.'[2] No longer would the United States passively endure acts of international terrorism, suggested Reagan. Now it would act.

Presidential rhetoric notwithstanding, significant American action did not come until over five years later.[3] Then, on April 14, 1986, the Reagan Administration launched Operation 'El Dorado Canyon' – an air assault on the sovereign state of Libya. The half-hour bombing raid struck five terrorist-linked targets in Tripoli and Benghazi,[4] causing the deaths of thirty-seven people and the injury of another ninety-three.[5]

That evening on national television, Ronald Reagan tersely articulated his rationale for using armed force: 'I warned that there should be no place on earth where terrorists can rest and train and practice their skills. I meant it.' The United States had proof of a 'direct' Libyan role in the bombing of a West German discotheque frequented by American servicemen, Reagan maintained. Moreover, it possessed 'solid evidence' that Qadhafi had planned other attacks 'against the United States' installations and diplomats and even American tourists.' Self-defense, concluded the President, 'is not only our right, it is our duty. It is the purpose of the mission undertaken tonight.'[6]

The American attack on Libya, which savored both of self-defense and retaliation,[7] was overwhelmingly supported in the United States. A CBS/*New York Times* poll, for example, found that over three-quarters of the American public favored the action.[8] Perhaps surprisingly, even two of the Reagan Administration's most consistent critics, House Speaker Tip O'Neill and Massachusetts Senator Edward Kennedy, approved of the President's decision to use force.[9]

Such support did not extend far beyond American shores, howe of America's western European allies criticized the attack,[10] the Th.. uniformly condemned it,[11] and Soviet Premier Gorbachev accused the Reagan Administration of 'poisoning' the international atmosphere.[12] UN reaction to the Libya raid was markedly, if predictably, anti-American.[13] The General Assembly adopted a condemnatory resolution by a vote of 79 to 28, with 33 abstentions.[14] A similar Security Council resolution, though vetoed by the United States, Britain, and France, was nevertheless supported by nine states.[15]

Besides those of public opinion, the 1986 US raid on Libya raised a number of profound questions of international law – ones which years later continue to merit close attention.[16] Are terrorist acts, for example, illegal under international law? If so, on what grounds? Under what circumstances may a victim state lawfully respond with armed force to the incidence of terrorism? Are there, in fact, any such circumstances? If armed response is legally permissible, how specifically may a state respond? Are there any particular normative guidelines which should inform state actions taken against terrorism? Toward whom may a state response legitimately be targeted? Individual terrorists? A state which supports or sponsors terrorist groups? A state which merely tolerates terrorist activities within its boundaries? It is upon these essential questions that this chapter will focus.

Any international legal analysis of 'terrorism' should begin with a definition of the rather problematic term. Accordingly, the first section of this chapter will first discuss the difficulties of defining terrorism, then advance a workable definition. Next, the second section will consider the relationship of the contemporary *jus ad bellum* to the problem of international terrorism, addressing specifically three broad questions of law: 1) Are terrorist acts illegal?; 2) Under what circumstances may a state forcibly respond to them?; and 3) How may it do so? To facilitate answering these second and third related questions, the second section will examine both the practice of states since 1945 and the writings of publicists. Finally, it will set forth a number of conclusions about the relevance of the Charter *jus ad bellum* to a world vastly different from that of 1945, one regularly disturbed by international terrorism.

WHAT IS TERRORISM?

'The stamp of terrorism,' Guy Roberts has observed, 'is on our times. It has become a phenomenon of almost everyday occurrence that seems to escalate continually in its violence, horror, and senselessness.'[17] While the threat posed to national security by terrorist activities has sometimes been exaggerated by statesmen and scholars,[18] there can be little doubt of terrorism's brutality or its capacity to capture worldwide attention.

From 1975 until 1985, more than 5,000 'terrorist' incidents were reported worldwide. Those attacks left 8,000 persons wounded and over 4,000 dead.[19] In 1987, a year marked by the absence of 'terrorist spectaculars' in the Middle East,[20] there were alone recorded over 800 separate instances of 'international terrorism.' These episodes resulted in the deaths of 633 persons and the wounding of another 2,272.[21]

The number of US nationals attacked has remained relatively low; nevertheless, by the measure of some observers, American citizens have continued to be the number one target of 'terrorists' worldwide.[22] Between 1976–86, for example, American officials or installations abroad were attacked by 'terrorists,' on the average, once every seventeen days.[23] In a single devastating strike in October of 1983, 241 Marines stationed in Beirut were killed by a 'terrorist' truck bomb. The blast caused by six tons of explosives inflicted the Corps' greatest single-day loss of life since the assault on Iwo Jima.[24] Nor in recent years have servicemen been the only prominent American targets of 'terrorism.' Substantial numbers of American businessmen, educators, and vacation travellers have reportedly been victimized as well. And from 1971–86, 'terrorists' killed as many US diplomats as had been killed in the previous 180 years.[25]

Statistics such as these are useful insofar as they help to suggest terrorism's general contours, but they are also misleading.[26] For what precisely is 'terrorism?' It is tempting here to invoke Justice Stewart's dictum, 'I know it when I see it,'[27] for terrorism, like obscenity, does not admit of an easy or strictly objective definition. This methodological challenge has not deterred scholars, however. Indeed, definitions of 'terrorism' have proliferated over the years.[28] One 1983 study by Dutch political scientist Alex Schmid found that 109 different ones had been advanced between 1936 and 1981.[29] More definitions have since appeared, including a half dozen submitted by the United States government.[30]

In light of such vigorous activity, Professor Levitt has suggested that the search for an authoritative definition of terrorism 'in some ways resembles the Quest for the Holy Grail.'[31] Certainly, the 'quest' for definitional consensus has thus far proved unsuccessful. As Professor Oscar Schachter has noted, 'no single inclusive definition of international terrorism has been accepted by the United Nations or in a generally accepted multilateral treaty.'[32]

Given the multitude and diversity of 'terrorism' definitions which have been advanced, some legal scholars have advocated simply jettisoning the term. The Mallisons, for example, have declared that 'terrorism' does not refer to 'a well-defined and clearly identified set of factual events.' Neither does it 'have any widely accepted meaning in legal doctrine.' Hence, the word does 'not refer to a unitary concept in either law or fact.'[33] Similarly, Judge Richard Baxter lamented: 'We have cause to regret that a legal concept of "terrorism" was ever inflicted upon us. The term is imprecise; it is ambiguous; and above all, it serves no operative legal purpose.'[34] Unfortunately, the problematic term 'terrorism,' like the complicated phenomenon it seeks to describe, will almost certainly persist. As a result, it seems best merely to advance a working definition,[35] one which characterizes both the terrorist *act* and the terrorist *actor.*

A terrorist *act* is distinguished by at least three specific qualities:

a. *violence,* whether actual or threatened;
b. a *'political'* objective, however conceived;[36] and
c. an *intended audience,* typically though not exclusively a wide one.

Virtually all formal definitions of terrorism[37] include these essential elements.[38] Thus, random acts of violence performed without deliberate political objectives should not be considered 'terrorism,' even if they do inspire 'terror.' Neither should non-violent acts, done for political purposes and directed at a specific target group. Nor, properly speaking, should politically-motivated acts of violence, when undertaken without any particular audience in mind – though it is difficult to envision circumstances under which such acts might be done. Hence, an 'act of terrorism' will be defined here as *'the threat or use of violence with the intent of causing fear in a target group, in order to achieve political objectives.'*

Terrorist *actors,* whether individual persons or groups, may be categorized by the strength of their association to states. Inevitably, all have some state association, for terrorist actors must act within a system of sovereign states and virtually always have bases within states. The agents of terrorism differ, however, in the degree to which they are tolerated, supported or sponsored by states.

Along a metaphorical 'scale,' Professor Antonio Cassese identifies six 'degrees' of association between states and terrorist actors:

a. terrorist acts by actual state officials;
b. state employment of unofficial agents for terrorist acts;
c. state supply of financial aid or weapons;
d. state supply of logistical support;
e. state acquiescence to the presence of terrorist bases within its territory; and
f. state provision of neither active nor passive help.[39]

Similarly, Professor John Murphy cites a schema identifying twelve distinct categories of state involvement in international terrorism:

a. State Terrorism;
b. Direct Support;
c. Provision of Intelligence Support;
d. Provision of Training (Specialized Terrorist and Basic Military);
e. Provision of Diplomatic Assets;
f. Provision of High Technology;

g. Provision of Weapons and Explosives;
h. Provision of Transportation;
i. Use of Territory;
j. Financial Support;
k. Tacit Support; and
l. Rhetorical Support.[40]

Comprehensive typologies such as those reported by Professors Cassese and Murphy are worthwhile because they suggest the variety and complexity of state/terrorist actor relationships. However, the fundamental varieties of terrorist involvement with states can probably be reduced to only four:

a. terrorist actors *without state toleration, support or sponsorship*;[41]
b. terrorist actors *with state toleration*, but without state support or sponsorship;
c. terrorist actors *with state support*, but without immediate state sponsorship; and
d. terrorist actors *with state sponsorship*.[42]

Under this simplified scheme, 'only those situations in which [a] state contributes active planning, direction, and control to terrorist operations' constitute 'state sponsorship.'[43] By contrast, 'state support' of terrorist actors includes a state's provision of intelligence, weapons, diplomatic assets, funds, or rhetorical endorsement.[44] A condition of 'state toleration,' meanwhile, can be said to exist when a state does not sponsor or support terrorist groups within its borders, but knows of their existence and fails to suppress them.[45]

Unfortunately, states with some regularity threaten or use violence with the intent of causing fear in target groups, in order to achieve political objectives – employing *conventional governmental organs* such as their militaries or intelligence agencies, but *no* non-state agents. Under these circumstances such state actions should, for definitional purposes, probably not be regarded as 'terrorist' *per se*.[46] If, for example, 'Ruritania' were to send members of its intelligence agency into 'Fredonia' to destroy a hospital, that Ruritanian act would seem better described as a covert act of state 'aggression,' rather than as one of state 'terrorism.' Clearly, if Ruritania were to launch a conventional armed invasion of Fredonian territory, that act should be said to constitute an overt act of state aggression, not one of state 'terrorism.'

THREE QUESTIONS OF LAW

In addition to those of politics, ethics, and military strategy, the terrorism phenomenon raises numerous questions of international law. Three of the most prominent legal ones will be addressed here. First, this section will consider whether or not terrorist acts are *unlawful*. Next, it will consider *under what circumstances*, if any, a state may forcibly respond to an act of terrorism. Finally, it will consider *how*, if at all, a state may forcibly respond to a terrorist act.

Are terrorist acts impermissible under international law?

In their legal analyses, scholars have at times tended to assume that acts of terrorism are *per se* illegal and hence to focus their discussions on questions of permissible response. The illegality of terrorist acts should not be presumed, however. To be sure, terrorist acts are morally repugnant. Nevertheless, for any *international legal* proscription[47] to exist, states must first act together to formulate it.[48]

On at least three basic grounds, terrorist acts have been said to be forbidden under international law. Depending on their circumstances and characteristics, terrorist acts may arguably constitute violations of: 1) 'general principles of law;' 2) custom; or 3) various provisions of prohibitory conventions. Let us examine in succession each of these three proscriptive bases, all of which are fundamentally rooted in state consent.

Illegal as violations of 'general principles of law'

As noted in Chapter 1 Article 38 of the Statute of the International Court of Justice enumerates three principal sources of international law:

a. international conventions ...;
b. international *custom*, as evidence as a general practice accepted as law; and
c. the *general principles of law* recognized by civilized nations.[49]

Of these, the third source, 'general principles of law,'[50] may arguably serve as a basis for proscribing at least some acts of terrorism.

There has been much debate regarding the precise legal meaning of Article 38 (c).[51] Nevertheless, courts and legal scholars have frequently interpreted the phrase 'general principles of law' as referring to 'general principles of law common to the municipal legal systems of states.' According to Professor von Glahn, '[s]uch principles might include the concept that both sides in a dispute should have a fair hearing, that no one should sit in judgment of his own case, and so on.'[52] Under this 'municipal law' interpretation, 'general principles of law' would 'enable a court ... to go outside the generally accepted rules of [conventional and customary] international law and resort to principles common to various domestic legal systems.'[53]

Virtually all of the world's domestic legal systems have banned many of the actions typically undertaken by 'terrorist' actors, *inter alia*: murder; assault; maiming; arson; kidnapping; and malicious destruction of property.[54] Hence, it can be argued that by 'general principles of law,' such

acts are prohibited under international law. Although customary international law and treaty law might not explicitly prohibit a particular terrorist
act, that act might nevertheless be considered impermissible as a violation of
'general principles of law.'

Illegal as violations of customary law

Piracy, the slave trade, and hijacking have come to be regarded as 'universal
crimes' under customary international law. It has sometimes been contended
that terrorism might well have gained such a status.[55] For example, the Third
Restatement of the Foreign Relations Law of the United States stipulates that a

> state may exercise jurisdiction to define and punish certain offenses
> recognized by the community of nations as of universal concern, such as
> piracy, slave trade, attacks on or hijacking of aircraft, genocide, war
> crimes, and perhaps certain acts of terrorism.[56]

In an argument parallel to that suggested by the Restatement, Franz Paasche
maintains that 'acts of terrorism, like acts of piracy, should be declared "crimes
against humanity."'[57] To support this view, he cites three similarities between the
agents of piracy and those of terrorism: 1) they fail to recognize or to act within
the law of nations; 2) they use violence against innocents to intimidate and to
coerce governments; and 3) their actions undermine the legal rules that civilized
peoples have developed to guide the conduct of nations.[58]

At first glance the piracy analogy might seem an apt one. For several
reasons, however, it should be rejected. First, though both the terrorist and
the pirate employ violent methods, the terrorist does so for *political* reasons,
not for material aggrandisement. Because of terrorism's inherently political
character, therefore, states have at times failed to condemn, and occasionally
have even celebrated,[59] violent acts of manifest terrorism. Second, under the
customary law of piracy and its twentieth-century codification, states may
only seize *pirate* vessels and aircraft.[60] State advocates of a forcible response
against terrorism have at times been unwilling to exclude from their legal
reach terrorists aboard foreign vessels and aircraft. Third, as Professor
Schachter has submitted, 'states may apprehend pirates on the high seas,' but
'have no right to enter another state's territory to seize suspected pirates.'
Hence, the piracy analogy 'does not help to answer the problem of extra-
territorial enforcement measures against suspected terrorists.'[61]

Illegal as violations of convention provisions

Global and regional 'comprehensive' treaties

Thus far, no comprehensive treaty covering all varieties of terrorist activity
has yet been able to garner global acceptance.[62] In 1937, such a treaty was

drafted and gained League of Nations approval.[63] However, the Convention for the Prevention and Punishment of Terrorism received only one ratification and was allowed to lapse.[64] Regional treaties addressing in a comprehensive fashion the 'terrorism' phenomenon have likewise proved elusive.[65] Only one, the 1977 European Convention on the Suppression of Terrorism,[66] has thus far entered into force.[67]

Multilateral 'specific' treaties

A number of multilateral agreements contain binding provisions which prohibit specific actions undertaken in *peace-time*, ones typically done by 'terrorists.' According to Professor Yoram Dinstein,

> these instruments cannot be viewed as a systematic effort to come to grips with the challenge posed by terrorism. The conventions were concluded under the auspices of different international organizations, and most of them came about as a reaction to specific events.[68]

Among those acts proscribed by treaty are aircraft hijacking,[69] naval vessel hijacking,[70] aircraft sabotage,[71] attacks on 'internationally protected persons' such as diplomats, heads of state, and heads of government,[72] hostage-taking,[73] the theft of nuclear materials,[74] and the use of the mails for the delivery of explosives or other dangerous substances.[75]

Terrorism, Professor Cassese has observed, 'may be committed in war as easily as it may be committed in the context of peaceful relations.'[76] Accordingly, it is significant that a number of multilateral treaties contain provisions which ban during *wartime* acts of the sort often performed by 'terrorists.' These legal instruments include the 1907 Hague Regulations,[77] the four 1949 Geneva Conventions,[78] and the two 1977 Additional Geneva Protocols.[79]

Common Article 3 of the Geneva Conventions, for example, prohibits certain acts against 'persons taking no active part in hostilities' during an 'armed conflict not of an international character.'[80] Such acts include 'violence to life and person, in particular murder of all kinds, mutilation, cruel treatment and torture ..., taking of hostages ..., outrages upon personal dignity, in particular, humiliating and degrading treatment.'[81] Accordingly, if a terrorist attack upon these protected persons were to occur within the setting of a non-international 'armed conflict,' it would be illegal under the provisions of these conventions. For example, if a terrorist group attacked an unarmed bus occupied by civilians during an armed conflict, such an act would be impermissible.[82]

The UN Charter

The language of Article 2(4) of the Charter prohibits 'Members' of the United Nations from taking forcible action against the territorial integrity and political independence of other states. As a matter of customary international law, this prohibition has been generally held to apply to non-member states of the UN as well.[83] It is unclear, however, whether or not 2(4) can be deemed to be a prohibition on the behavior of *non-state actors* such as 'terrorists.'

If a state directly sponsored a terrorist use of force against the territorial integrity or political independence of another state, that sponsoring state act would seem fairly clearly to have violated the terms of Article 2(4). If, however, the terrorist act in question lacked state involvement, that action would not appear self-evidently to have contravened the UN Charter. Hence, the only prohibition against terrorist acts contained within Article 2(4) would seem to apply to acts performed with manifest *state* involvement.

The only time the UN Security Council has explicitly addressed the question of Article 2(4)'s applicability to state involvement with terrorism came in March of 1992. Here, by a vote of 10–0–5,[84] the Council imposed economic sanctions on Libya for that state's connection with terrorist activities and for its refusal to extradite two Libyan nationals alleged to have participated in the 1988 bombing of Pan Am Flight 103 over Lockerbie, Scotland.[85] The Council affirmed in a preambulatory clause to its Resolution 748 that

> in accordance with the principle in Article 2, paragraph 4 of the Charter of the United Nations, every state has the duty to refrain from organizing, instigating, assisting or participating in terrorist acts in another state or acquiescing in organized activities within its territory directed toward the commission of such acts, when such acts involve a threat or use of force.[86]

The Council clearly construed the Article 2(4) prohibition to encompass what we have characterized here as state 'sponsorship,' state 'support,' and even state 'toleration' of terrorism.

General Assembly Resolutions

Though not legally binding, UN General Assembly Resolutions serve to indicate the prevailing attitudes of states. On December 9, 1985, for example, the General Assembly unanimously approved Resolution 40/61 which '[u]nequivocally condemns, as criminal, all acts, methods and practices of terrorism wherever and by whomever committed, including those which jeopardize friendly relations among states and their security.'[87] The Resolution 'calls upon states to fulfill their obligations under international law to refrain from organizing, instigating, assisting or participating in terrorist acts in other States, or acquiescing in activities within their territory directed towards the commission of such acts.'[88]

In 1987 Professor Yoram Dinstein remarked that General Assembly Resolution 40/61 'would have been unthinkable only a few years ago' and 'could not have been carried out without Soviet support.' Predicted Dinstein then:

In the wake of the Resolution, there is room for mild optimism as to the chances of the conclusion in the not too distant future of a binding convention turning terrorism in all its manifestations into a crime. The chances will increase should there be a greater degree of rapprochement between the Soviet Union ... and the West.[89]

If Professor Dinstein's assumption was a valid one, then the prospects now for a comprehensive treaty on terrorism would seem rather more promising in light of the recent collapse of communism in Eastern Europe and the former Soviet Union.

Under what circumstances may a victim state forcibly respond to an act of terrorism? How may it do so?

More controversial than the question of terrorism's international legality are two other related questions. First, under what circumstances, if any, may a victim state lawfully respond with armed force to the incidence of terrorism? And second: How, if at all, may a state do so? In addressing these, it is necessary to review both the practice of states since 1945 and the writings of publicists during that same period. It is likewise essential to bear in mind that force is only one possible response to terrorism, the most coercive response.[90]

Post-1945 state practice

When have states responded forcibly to terrorism? How have they done so? The answers to these questions depend largely on how one construes the rather contestable concept of 'forcible state response to terrorism.' Among the various activities which have in the past been characterized as 'forcible state responses to terrorism' are the following:

a. *abductions* of suspected terrorists;
b. *assassinations* of particular terrorists;
c. military *strikes against terrorist bases*; and
d. military *strikes against states* allegedly involved in terrorism.

This section will examine in turn each of these four related categories of state action.[91] As will be seen, 'the use of armed force beyond the limits of commando operations has been made rarely,'[92] or at least, relatively so.

Abduction of suspected terrorists

An 'abduction' may be legally defined as 'the forcible, unconsented removal of a person by agents of one State from the territory [or jurisdiction] of another State.'[93] In the post-Charter period, abductions of alleged 'terrorists' have been attempted on at least four separate occasions, thrice by Israel and once by the United States.[94] In three of the four cases, the coercive actions proved futile: the abducting states failed to gain jurisdiction over the individuals they had sought. In all three Israeli cases, the forcible interceptions were greeted with harsh condemnation by the international community.

1973 aircraft interception   On August 10, 1973, Israeli aircraft intercepted a Middle East Airlines flight en route from Beirut to Bagdad, forcing the civilian craft to land at an Israeli military base.[95] After having been compelled to disembark, the crew and passengers were subjected to hours of questioning. Israeli authorities had believed that Palestinian terrorists had been on the flight; however, when the Israelis determined that none in fact were, they permitted the flight of ninety persons to leave.

During subsequent Security Council deliberations, the Israeli delegate argued that the actions of his state had constituted a permissible form of self-defense. Israel, Mr Tekoah submitted, possessed the 'inherent' right to protect its citizens from terrorist attack. The Security Council, meanwhile, unanimously condemned the forcible Israeli action.[96] Even the United States expressed its profound disapproval. Averred Ambassador John Scali: 'The commitment to the rule of law in international affairs ... imposes certain restraints on the methods Governments can use to protect themselves against those who operate outside the law.' The United States government, he concluded, 'believes actions such as Israel's diversion of a civil airliner ... are unjustified and likely to bring about counter-action on an increasing scale.'[97]

The *Achille Lauro* incident   Twelve years later, another abduction of alleged terrorists was undertaken – this time by the United States.[98] The origins of the American action lay in the October 7, 1985 hijacking of the cruise ship *Achille Lauro* by four members of the Palestine Liberation Front (PLF). The group threatened to kill the vessel's passengers, beginning with US nationals, unless Israel promptly released fifty imprisoned Palestinians. After a series of protracted multilateral discussions involving Egypt, Italy, West Germany, and PLO representative Mohammed Abbas ('Abul Abbas'), the Italian liner docked in Port Said, Egypt. There, all but one of the hostages were released. Leon Klinghoffer, a wheel-chair-bound American Jew, had been shot and dumped overboard while the *Achille Lauro* was still at sea.

On the evening of October 10, an Egyptian government-chartered Boeing 737 attempted to transport the Palestinians to Tunis. After the aircraft was denied permission to land by Tunisia and Greece, however, four US Navy F-14 fighters from the carrier *Saratoga* intercepted it over the Mediterranean Sea, forcing the craft to fly to an Italian NATO airbase in Sicily. At Sigonella, US troops surrounded the alleged hijackers, though they never implemented arrest orders. Instead, Italian forces took into custody the hijackers and Abbas, a known terrorist and alleged mastermind of the hostage plot.

While some international legal scholars condemned as illegal the attempted US abduction of the *Achille Lauro* hijackers,[99] international reaction was largely muted. Both Italy and Egypt transmitted notes of protest to Washington: the Italian government argued that its airspace had been violated by a US military jet; the Egyptian government, meanwhile, maintained that its aircraft had been illegally hijacked.[100] Nevertheless, in Security Council discussions on October 11, virtually no mention was made of the American use of force. A Palestinian representative raised the issue briefly, charging that the United States had committed an 'official act of terrorism,' an 'act of air piracy against a civilian aircraft.'[101] The Israeli delegate, in sharp contrast, spoke of the 'courageous American act directed against Palestinian terrorism [which] represents an essential step towards the eradication of global terrorism.'[102] The Secretary-General of the Organization of the Islamic Conference, meanwhile, called the United States action 'a matter which has legal implications which I do not intend to address.'[103]

1986 aircraft interception   On February 4, 1986, Israel launched a 'terrorist' abduction attempt strikingly similar to its unsuccessful 1973 venture.[104] Once again, Israeli fighter jets intercepted a civilian flight – this time, a Libyan craft bound for Damascas – and compelled it to land in Israel. As in 1973, Israeli authorities permitted the intercepted aircraft to depart after having first determined that it held none of the 'terrorists' expected to be on board.

In subsequent debate, the Security Council considered whether to adopt a draft resolution condemning Israel for its forcible action. Here, Israel's delegate submitted that his state had acted in 'self-defense,' as the term 'must be construed in the age of terrorism.'105 In such a time, he maintained, 'a nation attacked by terrorists is permitted to use force to prevent or pre-empt future attacks.' It was 'simply not serious to argue that international law' prohibited states from 'capturing terrorists in international waters or airspace.'[106]

United States Ambassador Vernon Walters responded that the Israeli interception had been legally impermissible because it had been undertaken without adequate prior evidence. Nevertheless, he argued that the United States government was unable to accept a draft Security Council resolution which 'implie[d] that the interception of aircraft is wrongful *per se.*' According to Walters: '[A]s a general principle the United States opposes the interception of civil aircraft.' However, he continued, 'we believe that there may arise exceptional circumstances in which an interception may be justified.' He then articulated the US view of the *jus ad bellum*: 'A State whose territory or citizens are subjected to continuing terrorist attacks may respond with appropriate use of force to defend itself against further attacks.' The state's capacity to undertake forcible action, he concluded, was 'an aspect of the inherent right of self-defense recognized in the United Nations Charter.'[107] This US-Israeli rendition of self-defense against terrorism was not supported by any other Security Council member, however.

The kidnapping of Sheik Obeid Before dawn on July 28, 1989, Israeli helicopters landed secretly in the village of Jibchit, Lebanon.[108] There, a force of twelve commandos abducted Sheik Abdul Karim Obeid and two other men from the Shiite cleric's home, killing one of Obeid's on-looking neighbors.[109] In the wake of the operation, an Israeli government spokesman explained its rationale: as spiritual leader within the pro-Iranian Party of God (Hezbollah), Obeid had passed 'war materiel to Hezbollah fighters in southern Lebanon and [had given] shelter to committers of attacks.'[110] Later, an Israeli Army statement pronounced that the 36-year old Sheik had been 'arrested' as a 'preacher, inciter,' and 'planner of attacks against Israel.'[111]

Israel's abduction of Obeid elicited 'a chorus of international criticism.'[112] In a White House press conference, American President George Bush remarked tersely: 'I don't think kidnapping and violence help the cause of peace.'[113] At the United Nations, Secretary General Javier Perez de Cuellar dubbed the kidnapping 'a violation of Lebanese sovereignty' and demanded that the Sheik be returned to Lebanon. Using even blunter language, Egypt accused Israel of 'state terrorism.'[114]

After prior off-the-record consultations,[115] the Security Council unanimously adopted Resolution 638 on July 31, 1989.[116] In a rather brief resolution, the Council addressed only in general terms the question of hostage-taking and abduction, mentioning explicitly neither 'Israel' nor 'Sheik Obeid.' Instead, the resolution 'condemn[ed] unequivocally all acts of hostage-taking and abduction' as 'offenses of grave concern to all States and serious violations of international law.' Moreover, it 'demand[ed] the immediate safe release of all hostages and abducted persons, wherever and by whomever they are being held.' At the time of Resolution 638's adoption, sixteen Western hostages were believed held in Lebanon, including the American William R. Higgins, whose life had been threatened on July 30 in response to Obeid's seizure.[117]

Assassinations of particular terrorists

Any discussion of state assassinations of alleged 'terrorists' is inherently problematic insofar as such actions have typically remained unacknowleged by their perpetrators.[118] Nevertheless, two prominent cases will be reviewed here: in the first, Israel's involvement was broadly conceded, even by Israel's supporters; in the second, the Israeli government publicly admitted its action.

Khalil El Wazir On April 16, 1988, Khalil El Wazir ('Abu Jihad'), two of his bodyguards, and his driver were killed in El Wazir's home in a Tunis suburb.[119] According to Professor O'Brien, 'although Israel did not officially admit responsibility, the assassination was nonetheless an Israeli operation.'[120] Israel did not participate in subsequent Security Council debate;

nevertheless, its spokesmen observed that El Wazir had been Al Fatah's military chief, had served as chief PLO coordinator with the leaders of the *intifada*, and had borne responsibility for a series of lethal terrorist operations against Israel.[121]

The Security Council charged Israel with El Wazir's assassination, formally condemning it in Resolution 611 of April 25, 1988.[122] The United States abstained in the vote, arguing that the condemnatory resolution

> disproportionately places all the blame for this latest round in the rising spiral of violence in the Middle East on one event only while failing to mention other actions that preceded it. It also includes language which is suggestive of chapter VII sanctions.[123]

Despite its abstention, the United States condemned El Wazir's assassination and all political assassinations, while supporting Tunisia's sovereignty and territorial integrity.[124] State Department Legal Adviser Sofaer would later observe in a 1989 speech: 'a state cannot act secretly and without public justification in its self-defense.'[125]

Sheik Musawi   On the afternoon of February 16, 1992, two Israeli helicopter gunships attacked a seven-vehicle motorcade travelling in southern Lebanon.[126] Killed in the rocket assault were Sheik Abbas Musawi, Shiite imam and leader of Hezbollah, Musawi's wife, their six-year-old son, and five of Musawi's bodyguards. Israel launched its lightning raid in the wake of two other forcible actions: its own pre-dawn airstrike that day on two Palestinian bases in southern Lebanon; and an Arab guerrilla attack the day before on an Israeli Army camp within Israel.

Calling the Party of God a 'murderous, terrorist organization,'[127] Israeli Defense Minister Moshe Arens characterized his state's forcible action against Sheik Musawi as both 'an attack intended to hurt Hezbollah'[128] and 'a message to all the terrorist organizations [that] whoever opens an account with us will have the account closed by us.'[129] Though Arens described Musawi as a 'man with lots of blood on his hands,' Israeli authorities did not explicitly link the attack on him to the earlier Arab raid on an Israeli camp in which three servicemen had died. Nor did they explain the timing of Israel's action against Hezbollah's secretary general.[130] What was clear to observers, however, was that the slain leader of Hezbollah had been 'a symbol of terrorism to [the] West.'[131]

Although Sheik Musawi was killed in the Israeli action, the mission's original objective may well have been 'to kidnap Musawi and bring him to Israel for trial or exchange for an Israeli POW believed held by the Hezbollah.'[132] According to one account, the operation 'went wrong' when Israeli helicopters tracking the Sheik's convey misfired. The missiles had been intended 'to take out the vehicle carrying Musawi's bodyguards, allowing commandos in a backup chopper to land and capture him alive.

Instead, an Israeli missile hit Musawi's car, incincerating everyone in it.'[133] If this report is an accurate one, then Israel's operation is an example of yet another failed abduction attempt.[134] Such a conclusion seems plausible in light of the operation's manifest similarities to Israel's 1989 kidnapping of Sheik Obeid, a former colleague of Musawi.

Despite the lethal character of Israel's 1992 action, international reaction to it was relatively reserved. To be sure, Palestinian spokeswoman Hanan Ashrawi was critical, asking rhetorically, 'To use the air force and state policy to kill women and children, that's not terrorism? But it demonstrates again that this has to stop, and the only way it will stop is to have a peace settlement.'[135] Nevertheless, a US State Department official withheld formal comment, observing simply that 'we regret the loss of lives in Israel and Lebanon in recent days and urge all concerned to exercise maximium restraint.'[136] Similar appeals for restraint were made by a number of states, including Britain, France, and Iran.[137] No discussion of the incident was undertaken by the Security Council.

Military strikes against terrorist bases

Since the mid-1960s, military strikes have been regularly launched against alleged 'terrorist' bases – in virtually all instances by the state of Israel against sites in the nearby states of Jordan, Syria, Tunisia, and Lebanon. In two separate studies on the broader subject of 'reprisals,' Professors Bowett and O'Brien included examinations of these counter-terrorist actions.[138] Bowett reviewed twenty-six cases of 'reprisal' from 1953–70, twenty-two of which involved Israel. Of these Israeli cases, at least eight between 1966–70 might be considered 'forcible strikes against terrorist bases.'[139] O'Brien discussed another fourteen cases of Israeli action from 1971–88 which might be similarly characterized.[140] In lieu of scrutinizing here all twenty-two of these cases and other more recent ones, this section will first recount one of the most prominent contemporary examples, then attempt broadly to characterize state practice.

The 1985 Tunis raid On October 1, 1985, Israel launched an air strike on the PLO headquarters in Borj Cedria, a suburb of Tunis.[141] The attack, which killed or injured more than a hundred persons, came a week after the murder by Palestinian 'terrorists' of three Israelis in Larnaca, Cyprus.[142] Declared Defense Minister Yitzhak Rabin after Israel's assault: 'We decided the time was right to deliver a blow to the headquarters of those who make the decisions, plan and carry out terrorist activities.'[143]

In subsequent Security Council debate, Israeli Ambassador Netanyahu maintained that Tunisia had allowed its territory to be employed as a terrorist base; hence, the North African state had represented a legitimate target for Israel's armed action, one proportionate to past and projected damage inflicted by terrorists on Israel.[144] Though the Soviet Union did not participate actively then in discussions,[145] the Security Council by a 14–0–1 vote passed Resolution 573 condemning Israel's 'active armed aggression.' The instrument urged member States to 'dissuade Israel from resorting to such acts,' supported Tunisia's right to reparations, and demanded that Israel 'refrain from perpetrating such acts of aggression or from threatening to do so.'[146]

The United States abstained from the Council's vote because the draft resolution had made no mention of PLO terrorism. The US government's position then appeared somewhat inconsistent, however. As Professor Reisman would later observe:

> The initial White House response to the action was that it was 'a legitimate response against terrorist attacks.' The next day, Secretary of State Shultz defended the Israeli action, while the White House began to inch away. The subsequent White House statement characterized the raid as 'understandable as an expression of self-defense,' but added that bombing 'cannot be condoned.'[147]

At the Security Council, Ambassador Vernon Walters argued that the United States 'recognize[d] and strongly support[ed] the principle that a state subjected to continuing terrorist attacks may respond with appropriate use of force to defend itself against further attacks.' Such an action, contended Walters, was 'an aspect of the inherent right of self-defense recognized in the United Nations Charter.' The United States promoted the principle, he concluded, 'regardless of attacker, and regardless of victim.'[148] Less than a week after Walter's statement, on October 7, four Palestinians hijacked the cruise ship *Achille Lauro* in retaliation for Israel's Tunis raid.

State attacks on 'terrorist' bases: a summary At least four conclusions may be drawn about state practice with respect to forcible actions directed against 'terrorist' *bases* – as distinct from those against terrorist-linked *states*. First, as has already been observed, such uses of force have been undertaken with some regularity since the mid-1960s. Between 1969 and 1988, for example, counter-base operations were launched on the average about once per year.[149] Second, Israel has been essentially the only state to employ armed coercion against terrorist bases *per se*. Third, most counter-base attacks have been directed against targets in Lebanon. By 1988, Israel had carried out at least sixteen separate major operations there, not including the 1978 Litani raid and the 1982 War.[150] Finally, there would appear to have emerged a 'credibility gap'[151] between the putative Charter rule prohibiting forcible actions against terrorist bases and the actual practice of states. What in 1972 Bowett said of reprisals can today probably be applied to state actions against 'terrorist' bases: 'The law ... is, because of its divorce from actual practice, rapidly degenerating to a stage where its normative character is in question.'[152]

Military strikes against states allegedly involved in terrorism

Thus far, the only prominent military strike to be launched against a *state* purportedly linked to terrorist activity has been the 1986 Libya raid by the United States.[153] The April 15 action, described in this chapter's introduction, constitutes perhaps the quintessential example of a 'forcible state response to terrorism.' Although Operation 'El Dorado Canyon' inflicted significant damage on five terrorist-associated targets in Benghazi and Tripoli, it caused considerable collateral destruction as well.[154] In part because of the aerial bombing's alleged lack of discrimination, in part because of its attendant circumstances, the armed measure's lawfuless was challenged in various international fora by numerous states.[155]

Immediately prior to the air strike,[156] Libya had complained to the Security Council on two grounds: that the United States had formally denounced Colonel Qadhafi's activities; and that it had launched provocative 'Freedom of Navigation' (FON) exercises in the Gulf of Sidra. 'It was in this context,' notes Professor O'Brien, 'that the Council debated the US action.'[157]

In a series of eight meetings, the Security Council considered the raid on Libya.[158] Here, the American recourse to force was criticized on a variety of grounds and by representatives from numerous states including Algeria, Cuba, Czechoslovakia, East Germany, Ghana, India, Oman, Saudi Arabia, the Soviet Union, Syria, the United Arab Emirates, and Qatar. Council delegates maintained that the use of armed force against Libya had been, *inter alia*: 'indiscriminant;' pursuant to no prior 'armed attack', pursuant to no substantiated Libyan involvement in 'terrorist' activities; part of a broader pattern of American aggression against 'progressive' Third World states; designed to thwart Libya's support of 'wars of national liberation;' and exemplary of 'state terrorism.'[159]

Ambassador Walters presented the American position, one later characterized as 'virtually identical with the long-standing Israeli position' on permissible responses to terrorism.[160] The United States had acted in self-defense, he submitted, after its peaceful efforts to respond to Libya's terrorist activities had proved ineffective. Alluding to the April 5, 1986 La Belle discotheque bombing in which two Americans had died and seventy-eight had been injured,[161] Walters maintained:

> In light of this reprehensible act of violence – only the latest in an ongoing pattern of attacks by Libya – and clear evidence that Libya is planning a multitude of future attacks, the United States was compelled to exercise its rights of self-defense.[162]

The American self-defense response, the ambassador explained, had been discriminate, proportionate, and counter-force – deliberately targeting elements of Libya's military infrastructure: 'command and control systems, intelligence, communications, logistics, and training facilities.' Such sites had been employed to execute 'Libya's harsh policy of terrorism, including ongoing attacks against US citizens and installations.'[163]

In a 'very rare instance of acceptance of the basic Israeli position' on permissible state response to terrorism,[164] Britain supported in Security Council debate the American use of force. Ambassador Thomson argued here that terrorism had been a Libyan 'instrument of State policy'[165] and that Qaddafi's allies had fostered his self-perception of being above the law.[166] Sir John submitted that the United States possessed the requisite proof to establish a linkage between Libya and the April 5 discotheque bombing as well as to numerous other prior and future terrorist activities. The British diplomat concluded, in marked contrast to earlier statements by Prime Minister Thatcher,[167] that the United States had acted in self-defense.[168]

Ultimately, a Security Council resolution condemning the United States was vetoed by the United States, Great Britain, and France; Australia and Denmark also rejected the resolution, while Venezuela abstained in the vote.[169] Accordingly, the Council undertook no further action on the case. The UN General Assembly, however, subsequently adopted a resolution condemning the Libya raid by a vote of 79–28–33.[170]

Conclusions about state practice

From a scrutiny of post-1945 practice, a number of general conclusions may be drawn regarding 'forcible state responses to terrorism.' For analytical purposes, four qualities of these coercive actions will be reviewed here: their frequency, locations, agents, and consequences.

Frequency of forcible state actions Excluding actions taken against alleged bases, forcible state responses to terrorism have been rather few in number.[171] Since 1945, for example, there appear to have been just four prominent cases of attempted state abduction of suspected terrorists, two relatively unambiguous cases of state assassination of particular terrorists, and one case of a military strike against a state allegedly linked to terrorism. Only counter-base actions have been conducted with any frequency, on the average about once per year since the mid-1960s, and these often have taken the form of small-scale commando operations or airstrikes.

Locations of forcible state actions Virtually every state response to terrorism has been carried out in or around the Middle East: in the states of Lebanon, Libya, Jordan, Syria, and Tunis; and in the airspace over the eastern Mediterranean Sea. Lebanon has been by far the most common site of counter-terrorist actions. Since 1969, an abduction, an assassination, and at least sixteen strikes against alleged terrorist installations have been carried out there. This tendency has likely reflected Lebanon's popularity as a location for 'terrorist' bases as well as its contiguity to Israel.

Agents of forcible state actions   Thus far only two states have used force in response to terrorism: Israel, on about two dozen instances; and the United States twice, in its 1985 attempt to acquire jurisdiction over the *Achille Lauro* hijackers, and in its 1986 air raid against Libya. Significantly, both Israel and the United States have been conspicuous victims of 'terrorist' activities and both have possessed sufficient military and intelligence capacities to take coercive action. One would expect *only* states with such means and such motives to wield force against terrorist-linked targets.

Consequences of forcible state actions   How best to gauge the operational 'effectiveness' of coercive counter-terrorist acts is subject to dispute. Nevertheless, reasonable observers may conclude that such state measures have often proved tactically unsuccessful or productive of significant collateral casualties. Among those actions which might be so judged are the following: the 1973, 1985, and 1986 aircraft interceptions, after which not a single suspected terrorist was taken into custody by the forcibly acting state; the 1992 assassination of Sheik Musawi, which resulted in the deaths of the Shiite cleric's wife, his six-year-old son, and five bodyguards and which may well have constituted a bungled abduction attempt; and the 1986 American air strike against Libya, in which Colonel Qaddafi's stepdaughter was killed and a number of civilian areas were hit and badly damaged.

Notwithstanding their operational consequences, how have Israeli and American counter-terrorist actions been viewed by the international community? Overall, these coercive operations have been routinely criticized by the vast majority of states.[172] To this general observation, however, several important qualifications must be added.

First, in some notable cases, states have departed from the common practice of explicit and virtually unanimous condemnation of the forcibly acting state. The international responses to the interception of the *Achille Lauro* hijackers and to the assassination of Sheik Musawi, for example, were relatively muted. In the latter instance, the Security Council did not even address the issue. Likewise, after the abduction of Sheik Obeid in 1989, the international response was in some respects limited. Here, the Security Council formally rejected hostage-taking in Resolution 638; nevertheless, it neither condemned Israel nor mentioned Obeid by name. Moreover, after the 1986 Libya raid, both Great Britain and France joined the United States in vetoing a condemnatory Security Council resolution. Australia and Denmark rejected the draft instrument as well.

Second, it is difficult to measure the degree to which condemnations of Israeli and United States actions have been based on the nature of the *acts*, and the degree to which such condemnations have been based on the nature of the *actors* themselves. During much of the Cold War period, both Israel and the United States were fairly regularly attacked in international fora. It would seem likely, therefore, that at least some international criticism of counter-terrorist operations has been informed by geopolitical and ideological considerations, not by strictly legal ones.

Finally, Security Council condemnations of specific forcible acts have frequently been internally inconsistent, emphasizing alternative rationales for condemnation of specific actions.[173] Among other things, this lack of consistency may well indicate a general lack of legal sophistication among observer states. As O'Brien observed in his article on 1971–88 counter-terror operations:

> [T]he Council's record during the period studied is conspicuous for the scarcity of serious legal arguments. No delegate remotely approached the level of [Derek] Bowett's analyses of reprisals and self-defense. No one even cited his 1972 article. Other publicists are seldom cited – except by the Israelis.[174]

In O'Brien's opinion, 'the main rationale for condemning Israeli "reprisals"' has been that the 'Security Council has already condemned them.' At least in the case of Israeli coercive actions, he contended, the matter has effectively been *res judicata*.[175]

The writings of publicists

The literature on the terrorism phenomenon and its *jus ad bellum* ramifications is vast and ever-expanding.[176] Given the immensity of this body of work, it is not surprising that scholarly opinion has varied substantially. Three basic trends within the corpus may nevertheless be identified. First, publicists have lacked a *common analytical framework*. Second, they have failed to agree on the parameters of terrorist behavior engendering a *state's right to use force* in self-defense. Third, they have failed to agree on how a state may legally *respond* with force to terrorist acts. Let us consider each of these trends in succession.

Lack of common analytical framework

Scholars, legal and otherwise, often employ common analytical frameworks to facilitate their discourse and to promote cumulative learning. Such frameworks typically include shared *definitions of key terms* and agreement on what *fundamental questions* merit analysis and investigation. In studies of the *jus ad bellum*, for example, publicists have generally agreed on what is denoted by the term 'anticipatory self-defense.' Accordingly, they have devoted relatively little intellectual effort to definitional disputes. Moreover, in their consideration of anticipatory self-defense's permissibility, scholars have commonly agreed on what fundamental questions are legally significant and therefore worthy of exploration. Virtually all who have written on the subject, for example, have accepted *a priori* the importance of the *Caroline* case and the legal criterion of 'imminent threat.'[177]

In the terrorism literature, however, no common analytical framework has yet emerged. First, as we have seen, publicists have failed to devise a consensus definition of 'terrorism.'[178] As Guy Roberts has tersely observed, 'terrorism is not a legal term of art.'[179] Hence, certain important questions have not yet been answered authoritatively. Among them are these:

a. Is an act undertaken solely by a state organ a 'terrorist' act?[180]
b. Is a terrorist act directed against such state targets as military and diplomatic installations and personnel properly categorized as a 'terrorist' act or as simply an 'act of war?'[181]
c. Must an act be politically-motivated to be considered 'terrorist?'[182]
d. Is 'terrorism' *per se* illegal under international law?[183]

Second, though they have at times employed similar vocabulary, scholars have disagreed on what 'terrorism' questions are legally significant. Among the questions addressed by some, but *not all*, legal scholars are:

a. Is there a legally significant distinction between terrorism *with* state involvement and that *without* it?[184]
b. Does the *motive* for a state's response to terrorism affect the response's permissibility? For example, may a response be taken solely for 'punitive' reasons?[185]
c. Does the *locus* of terrorist act affect the permissibility of armed state reponse? For example, does a terrorist attack on nationals *abroad* engender a different response than a terrorist attack on nationals *within* the state?[186]
d. Must a state response to terrorism be justified solely on the grounds of 'self-defense' or has a *'law of permissible reprisal'* emerged?[187]
f. What *'forcible responses* to terrorism' should be considered in a review of state practice? Rescue missions? Attacks on terrorist bases? Interceptions of aircraft and vessels bearing suspected terrorists? Attacks on state sponsors of terrorism? Covert assassinations of terrorist leaders? Overt assassinations of terrorist leaders?[188]

Because scholars addressing the terrorism question have lacked a common analytical framework, any neat summary of their writings is virtually impossible. In previous chapters of this work, it was feasible to isolate fundamental areas of scholarly agreement and to group writers, if somewhat imperfectly, into different legal 'schools.' For example, in Chapter 8 the 'restrictionist' and 'counter-restrictionist' approaches to humanitarian intervention could be characterized and explored. Here, to employ these or similar labels would be greatly to oversimplify a complicated, inconsistent literature. Instead, this section will attempt principally to illustrate the diversity and range of international legal opinion on the terrorism question. To do so, it will concentrate on the writings of a select, though representative, group of prominent contemporary publicists.[189]

Terrorist acts giving rise to self-defense

All publicists have acknowledged that states have an inherent right to defend themselves in the event of an 'armed attack.' They have disagreed markedly, however, over what specific terrorist actions give rise to the right of self-defense under Article 51. At one end of a broad, multihued spectrum lie publicists supporting a 'high threshold' for permissible armed response. Professor Boyle, for example, has suggested that states may respond only to terrorist attacks *within their own territory*.[190] At the other end of the spectrum are scholars supporting a 'low threshold' for forcible response. Abraham Sofaer, for example, has submitted that at times even *one attack on a state's national abroad* may justify that state's forcible response.[191] Located in between are numerous scholars who favor a more 'moderate threshold.' These include Professor Rowles who has contended that isolated terrorist attacks do not constitute armed attacks justifying the use of force, but that *large-scale, continuing attacks* might do so, depending on the circumstances.[192]

'High' self-defense threshold Following a 1988 seminar on terrorism convened at the Hague Academy of International Law, Professor Frowein summarized the 'present state of research' carried out by the English-speaking section of the Centre for Studies and Research. In his discussion of 'the use of force to protect citizens from terrorist threats,'[193] Frowein outlined what might be characterized as a 'high threshold' argument.

> [I]t is difficult to see how one could accept a threat on citizens on *foreign territory* as being 'an armed attack' ... If words mean anything, there cannot be any question that an armed attack *cannot* consist of a terrorist action against citizens on foreign territory, even if tolerated by the territorial state.[194]

Though Frowein seemed ultimately to reject this narrow interpretation of Article 51,[195] he argued that it had apparently been confirmed by the International Court of Justice in the *Nicaragua* case.[196]

In a panel discussion during the 1987 annual meeting of the American Society of International Law (ASIL),[197] Professor Francis Boyle postulated a similarly high threshold for a state's permissible self-defense. Criticizing a series of recent US counter-terrorist actions,[198] he suggested that under Article 51, 'self-defense could *only* be exercised in the event of an actual or perhaps at least imminent 'armed attack' against the *state itself*.'[199] Given the limits imposed by the UN Charter on a state's right to defend itself, therefore, the bombing of a West Berlin discotheque frequented by American soldiers 'could not possibly serve as any justification for the Reagan Administration's decision to bomb targets in and near the Libyan cities of Tripoli and Benghazi.'[200]

'Low' self-defense threshold In stark contrast to the views of Francis Boyle and other 'high threshold' advocates are those of publicists like Alberto Coll, William O'Brien, and Abraham Sofaer. Professor Coll, for example, participated with Professor Boyle in the 1987 ASIL panel discussion on terrorism. Implicitly challenging here Boyle's 'high threshold' argument, Coll contended that self-defense need not be viewed as 'a straitjacket.'[201] The UN Charter's self-defense provisions, he observed, 'do not address directly the subtler modes of contemporary international violence. Hence, it would be a tragic mistake to interpret Article 51 as an absolute prohibition on military response to terrorism.'[202] Self-defense, argued Coll, consists essentially of 'measures necessary to protect the state and its people from outside armed attack in all its conventional and nonconventional forms' – including terrorism.[203] Among those acts constituting 'terrorism' and therefore justifying self-defense, submitted Coll, are ones directed at such targets as 'tourists on a cruise ship, schoolchildren, scholars or journalists.'[204] Isolated attacks against nationals at home or abroad, he seemed to suggest, would engender a state's right of response. Attacks directed specifically against 'military personnel and other agents of the state,' however, 'are best described as simply acts of war,' providing the victim state 'with ample legal justification under the laws of war' for response.[205]

In his 1990 article, 'Reprisals, Deterrence and Self-Defense in Counter-terror Operations,'[206] Professor O'Brien likewise advanced a 'low threshold' argument. In O'Brien's view, 'there is ample warrant for broad interpretations of Article 51.'[207] The '[m]achinery for peaceful settlement of disputes has been variable and notoriously insufficient,' he submitted, and the UN Charter model of collective security has been problematic.[208] Citing a 1986 article by Professor Coll,[209] O'Brien commented:

> Given that much of contemporary conflict takes the form of subversive intervention, exported revolution, indirect aggression and transnational revolutionary warfare emphasizing terrorism, strict interpretations of the right of self-defense against immediate armed attacks are not compelling.[210]

In his lengthy discussion of state practice, O'Brien suggested[211] that the following 'terrorist' actions might engender a state's right to self-defense: armed attacks against its territory;[212] hostage-taking within its territory;[213] hostage-taking beyond its territory;[214] and armed attacks on its nationals abroad.[215]

In a 1989 lecture before the US Army Judge Advocate General's School,

Judge Sofaer set out perhaps the quintessential 'low threshold' argument.[216] 'The notion that self defense relates only to a use of force that materially threatens a State's "territorial integrity or political independence,"' declared Sofaer, 'ignores the Charter's preservation of the "inherent" scope of that right.'[217] States 'have traditionally defended their military personnel, citizens, commerce, and property from attacks even when no threat existed to their territory or independence.'[218] Moreover, the 'military facilities, vessels and embassies of a nation have long been considered its property, and for some purposes its territory.'[219] Accordingly, the US State Department Legal Adviser submitted:

> [W]here an American is attacked because he is an American, in order to punish the US or to coerce the US into accepting a political position, the attack is one in which the US has a sufficient interest to justify extending its protection through necessary and proportionate actions. *No nation should be limited to using force to protect its citizens, from attacks on their citizenship, to situations in which they are within its boundaries.*[220]

To accept such a high threshold for permissible self-defense, Sofaer averred, would be to 'give terrorists and their state sponsors substantial advantages in their war against the democracies.'[221] He explained:

> A view of the meaning of 'armed attack' that restricts it to conventional, ongoing uses of force on the territory of the victim State would as a practical matter immunize those who attack sporadically or on foreign territory, even though they can be counted on to attack specific States repeatedly.[222]

'Moderate' self-defense threshold Located on our analytical spectrum at various points between the advocates of 'high' and 'low' thresholds are legal scholars such as Professors Rowles and Cassese. Though their opinions have differed, these publicists have all supported a rather 'moderate' threshold for permissible self-defense against terrorist action.

Professor James Rowles, for example, advanced such a 'moderate threshold' argument during his 1987 ASIL panel discussion on terrorism with Professors Boyle and Coll.[223] According to Rowles, military responses to 'terrorist' acts are lawful only when those acts are 'on a scale *equivalent to what would be an armed attack* if conducted by government forces.'[224] Large-scale, continuing campaigns of terrorist attacks, therefore, could give rise to the right of self-defense, depending on the circumstances.[225] 'Isolated terrorist attacks, on the other hand, [would] not constitute armed attacks justifying the use of force.'[226] Among those attacks considered 'isolated' by Rowles and therefore *not* justifying armed state response were ones directed against: the Israeli ambassador in London in 1982; three Israeli citizens in Larnaca, Cyprus in 1985; and the American servicemen in La Belle discotheque in 1986.[227] In general, advocates of a 'low threshold' like Sofaer would accept in principle Professor Rowles' argument that an on-going campaign of terrorism engenders the right of self-defense; they would reject, however, Rowles' argument that isolated terrorist attacks fail to justify a forcible response. Conversely, advocates of a 'high threshold' like Boyle would reject Rowles' argument that an on-going campaign of terrorism, if undertaken against targets beyond the victim state's boundaries, would engender that state's right of self-defense; they would accept, however, Rowles' argument that isolated attacks fail to justify a forcible response.

In his 1989 article, 'The International Community's "Legal" Response to Terrorism,' Professor Cassese set out what might also be characterized as a 'moderate threshold' for permissible response to terrorism.[228] In doing so, he offered a straightforward rendition of the *jus ad bellum*: 'If ... we want to find out whether the use of force is permitted, we must first ascertain whether there has been an "armed attack" on the State using force by the State against which force is used.'[229] According to Cassese: '"Armed attack" in this context means *a very serious attack* either on the territory of the injured State or on its agents or citizens while at home or abroad (in another State or in international waters or airspace).'[230] To his 'very serious attack' criterion, Professor Cassese added a second criterion: 'terrorist acts [must] form part of *a consistent pattern of violent terrorist action* rather than just being isolated or sporadic attacks.' This second criterion is based, Cassese submitted, on the general principle that 'States can only have recourse to military force as a *last resort,* for the goal of international peace must always be the overriding factor in international relations.'[231] Consequently, 'sporadic or minor attacks do not warrant such a serious and conspicuous response as the use of force in self-defense.'[232]

Lawful responses to terrorist acts

To answer adequately the fundamental question of *how* a victim state may respond to a given 'armed attack' by terrorists,[233] at least three subsidiary questions must be addressed:

a. What constitutes a '*timely*' response by a victim state to a terrorist act?
b. What constitutes a '*proportionate*' response by a victim state to a terrorist act?
c. What entities constitute *proper targets* for a victim state response to a terrorist act?

Legal scholars have offered a variety of divergent answers to these important and related questions.

'Timely' response   Once it has begun to suffer an 'armed attack,' at what point may a victim state defend itself? May it only respond 'on-the-spot' to an on-going terrorist act? Must it first exhaust peaceful remedies before forcibly acting? May it respond long after a terrorist attack has ceased? May it take forcible action to deter anticipated future attacks? These are all questions related to the 'timeliness' or 'immediacy' of a self-defense response, and fundamentally, to the 'necessity' of that response. They are questions to which publicists have provided markedly different replies.[234]

During the 1987 ASIL panel discussion on terrorism, for example, Professor Boyle suggested that only 'on-the-spot' responses to terrorist armed attack were permissible.[235] According to Boyle, a state might take action solely 'in the event of an actual or perhaps imminent "armed attack."'[236] Immediate self-defense, '[b]y definition, ... would not include military retaliation and reprisal since they occur *after the fact.*'[237] Boyle rejected *post facto* self-defense measures because an

> expansive reading of the doctrine of self-defense to include retaliation
> and reprisal would provide gratuitously ample grounds for many other
> states to come up with all sorts of justifications and pretexts for engaging
> in the threat and use of force that could significantly undermine inter-
> national peace and security.[238]

Boyle's denial here of the lawfulness of armed reprisal was consistent with prevailing scholarly opinion that reprisals are *per se* illegal.[239]

Professor Mark Baker likewise treated the issue of immediacy in his 1987 article, 'A Call to Amend Article 51.'[240] According to Baker, 'the element of time cannot be ignored when examining the necessity of the response. This temporal element of the requirement of necessity means that a response must be made *close in time* to the actual attack.'[241] Distinguishing individual from state 'self-defense,' he noted that each variety should be judged by a different standard: 'An individual's response is normally spontaneous, whereas a state requires a more calculated response when its "collective life is threatened."'[242]

In his 1989 article,[243] Professor Cassese suggested a view of immediacy slightly different from that of Boyle or Baker. While he did not argue that reprisals were permissible, he submitted that a necessary self-defense response must follow the victim state's exhaustion of 'attempts at achieving a peaceful solution.'[244] Cassese's rendition of necessity, and by extension of 'immediacy,' was derivative of the 'general principle' that 'States can only have recourse to military force *as a last resort,* for the goal of international peace must always be the overriding factor in international relations.'[245] The 'exhaustion of peaceful remedies' requirement for necessary self-defense offered by Cassese implies a concept of 'immediacy' apparently more flexible than that offered by Professor Boyle. It suggests that there may be a gap in time between the incidence of a particular terrorist act and a forcible response by the victim state.[246]

A more controversial rendition of timely response has been submitted by a number of scholars including Coll, O'Brien, and Sofaer – all advocates of a 'low' self-defense threshold.[247] Professor Coll, for example, challenged Boyle during their ASIL panel discussion. Rejecting the customary international law standard for necessity set out after the 1837 *Caroline* incident, Coll argued that 'the key components [of Daniel Webster's definition] have to be interpreted rather broadly, given the radically different world in which we live.'[248] Accordingly, self-defense is not permissible solely 'in response to an imminent terrorist attack or as an on-the-spot reaction to an unexpected threat.'[249] Because 'military responses to terrorism are essentially defensive in character,'[250] Coll argued, 'long-term deterrence and short-term prevention of terrorism' are likewise 'legally justifiable under the general provisions of article 51.'[251] He added that self-defense was not 'the only appropriate justification for military responses in all circumstances,' for there was 'still room for acts of reprisal.'[252] Maintained Coll:

> While many scholars argue that reprisals became illegal under the UN Charter, the point is highly debatable; the lack of consensus suggests that current state practice is the best guide to what is acceptable behavior, and on this issue the evidence seems to suggest the continuing relevance of reprisals in the face of UN impotence to provide its members with protection against illegal uses of force.[253]

In his 1990 article, Professor O'Brien advanced views of necessity and timeliness similar to those of Coll.[254] It was 'unrealistic,' he submitted, to deny 'the element of deterrence to self-defense.'[255] 'Contrary to the prevailing view of publicists and the practice of the United Nations,' the 'reprisal/self-defense distinction and the judgment that reprisals are illegal should be abandoned.'[256] Armed reprisals, O'Brien averred, should be assimilated 'into the right of legitimate self-defense.'[257] Self-defense should therefore be understood 'as taking two forms: on-the-spot reaction; and defensive reprisals at a time and a place different from those of the original attack.'[258]

Judge Sofaer's view of necessity, and hence of immediacy, has paralleled that of O'Brien and Coll. In his 1989 address, 'Terrorism, The Law, and the National Defense,' he observed:

> [The *Caroline* test] exaggerates the test of necessity in a situation where that issue was dicta. More fundamentally, moreover, [it] was applied when war was still a permissible option for states that had actually been attacked. Webster's statement therefore related, in that context, to situations in which no prior attack or other act had occurred.[259]

In Sofaer's judgment, 'The law should not be construed to prevent military planners from implementing measures they reasonably consider necessary to prevent unlawful attacks.'[260] He proposed:

A sound construction of Article 51 would allow any state, once a terrorist 'attack occurs' or is about to occur, to use force against those responsible for the attack in order *to prevent* the attack or to deter further attacks unless reasonable ground exists to believe that no further attack will be undertaken.[261]

'Proportionate' response   Although publicists have generally agreed that a victim state's forcible response must be 'proportionate,' they have failed to agree on how 'proportionality' should properly be calculated. Three basic approaches to the 'proportionality' issue have been advanced. Some scholars have maintained that the victim state must respond proportionately to the specific prior act of terrorism.[262] This first approach might be called 'eye-for-an-eye' or *'tit-for-tat' proportionality.* Other scholars, meanwhile, have contended that the victim state's forcible measures should be proportionate to an aggregation of past illegal acts. This second approach might be called *'cumulative' proportionality.* Still others have submitted that the victim state's use of force must be proportionate to the overall terrorist threat faced by the state. This third approach, which is future-directed, might be called 'eye-for-a-tooth' or *'deterrent' proportionality.*

Greg Intoccia has been one proponent of the 'tit-for-tat' approach.[263] In his 1987 analysis of the US attack on Libya, he posited that the right of self-defense 'is limited by the requirement that the force used must be proportionate to the threat and cannot exceed measures strictly necessary to repel a threat. Even if the requirement of actual necessity is satisfied,' Intoccia observed, 'a claim of self-defense must be rejected if the nature and amount of force used is disproportionate to the character of the *initiating coercion.*'[264] Accordingly, 'any response to an act of aggression which employs a level of violence which is greater than is necessary to counter any *continuing immediate threat* must be viewed as impermissible.'[265] Intoccia rejected the cumulative proportionality approach because, he noted, the UN Security Council had 'formally condemned any attempt to justify totality of violence based upon an "accumulation of events as an illegal reprisal."'[266]

A prominent supporter of 'cumulative proportionality' has been Guy Roberts.[267] In 'Self-Help in Combating State-Sponsored Terrorism,' he argued that '[r]ough equivalence in the number of deaths and extent of property damage remains the *sine qua non* of proportionality.'[268] Beyond this 'rough equivalence' test, Roberts asserted, 'proportionality must be calculated on the basis of *prior* events. Therefore, an *accumulation of small events*, such as minor terrorist attacks, can justify a single larger retaliatory response in certain instances.'[269] However, 'making justifications for reprisal on the basis of a *future* wrong is difficult since the wrong supposedly justifying the retaliatory response has yet to occur.'[270] He explained:

If an unfounded expectation of a massive enemy attack or series of attacks can justify a massive anticipatory thrust *to deter* the imagined onslaught, then the rule of law would be irrelevant. Furthermore, proportionality would have no meaning since preventive application of force ... provides no ready reference point for the calculation of a proportional response.[271]

Hence, the deterrent approach to proportionality should be eschewed.

The arguments advanced by Professors O'Brien, Coll, Schachter, and Baker typify the 'deterrent proportionality' approach rejected by Roberts.[272] Professor O'Brien, for example, has argued that 'counter-terror measures should be proportionate to the purposes of counter-terror deterrence and defense, viewed in the total context of hostilities as well as the broader political-military strategic context.'[273] Hence, 'the referent of proportionality' should be 'the *overall pattern of past and projected acts.*'[274] Professor Coll advanced a similar argument during his 1987 ASIL panel discussion: 'Whereas strict proportionality would seem to parallel the proverbial "eye for an eye, tooth for a tooth,"' Coll declared, 'deterrence requires the threat of "an eye for a tooth."'[275] Though 'deterrence is incompatible with strict proportionality,' he conceded, 'an appropriate standard would be that the violence threatened or actually used in deterring an adversary should be the minimum necessary to persuade him not to undertake aggression in the future.'[276]

In a 1987 panel on the 'Use of Force Against Terrorist Bases,' Oscar Schachter lent support to both the cumulative and deterrent proportionality approaches. Here, he argued that '[t]it for tat' was 'not the only test of proportionality.'[277] Indeed, two other tests were appropriate. One test considers 'the response in relation to a continuing pattern of attack rather than the last one.'[278] The second 'judge[s] proportionality in terms of the end sought, namely, the cessation of attacks, and the means used.'[279] Concluded Schachter:

> If proportionality consists of a reasonable relation of means to ends, it would not be disproportionate if in some cases the retaliatory force exceeded the original attack in order to serve its *deterrent* aim. One might say that the force would have to be sufficient to cause the terrorist to change his expectations about costs and benefits so that he would cease terrorist activity.[280]

Mark Baker offered a like rendition of proportionality in his 1987 article: '[W]hen responding to a continuing series of attacks, ... self-defensive measures should be weighed against *all attacks immediately prior* to the response, and, more importantly, the probability and size of *future* attacks.'[281]

Proper targets for response   Related to the central question of 'proportionality' is a further one: What constitute proper targets for a victim state response? In writings on the subject, virtually all publicists have begun with the fundamental premise that 'innocents' should not be targeted *per se.* Victim states must strive in their forcible efforts, scholars have commonly held, to 'discriminate' between terrorist targets and those uninvolved with terrorist activity.[282] Argued Professor Schachter, for example:

> Self-defense actions against terrorism are not exempt from the humanitarian rules applicable to armed conflict. Thus, the general prohibition[s] against [targeting] non-combatants or excessive destruction of civilian property apply. The fact that terrorist bases are found in the midst of cities, and may therefore be 'shielded' by non-combatants, can give rise to a difficult dilemma. It is nonetheless desirable to recognize legal as well as moral restraints relating to non-combatants.[283]

Judge Sofaer offered a corresponding view. States, he suggested, were obliged 'to utilize the most discriminating measures reasonably possible in exercising self-defense.'[284] A comparable guideline was proposed by Professor O'Brien: 'Discrimination in counterterror measures should be maximized by target selection and Rules of Engagement governing operations.'[285]

Though essentially all legal writers have embraced the 'discrimination' concept, their application of the subjective principle to objective circumstances has varied substantially. The 1986 United States attack on Libya, for example, has been viewed by some scholars as an 'indiscriminate' use of force, by others as a 'discriminate' one. Professor Boyle endorsed the former assessment:

> The Reagan Administration must have known that to launch a large-scale bombing operation on the [Qadhafi] compound in the middle of the night when visibility would have been diminished significantly only could have resulted in the large-scale loss of innocent human lives. In its ruthless attempt to murder Qadhafi and his family, the Reagan Administration was fully prepared to sacrifice a fairly large number of innocent Libyan civilians.[286]

Gregory Intoccia evinced a completely different appreciation of the facts, however:

> The vast majority of areas struck by American bombs in the April strike were military targets.... Due care was ... shown by the one to two percent of bombs dropped which had made an impact in civilian areas. At least some civilian casualties were due to Libyan military structures placed so close to civilian sites. For example, while some of Colonel Qadhafi's family members were among the casualties, the family members were struck during the attack against the legitimate target of Colonel Qadhafi's military headquarters, as the headquarters were also used as the Qadhafi family residence.[287]

Concluded Intoccia:

> While each nation is under an obligation to conduct military operations in a manner which minimizes damage to civilians, no international rule

exists which obligates a nation to forgo a legitimate military target simply because injury to civilian personnel might take place.[288]

As a complement to the fundamental principle of 'discrimination,' legal scholars have also generally accepted the principle that there must be some link between the *target* of forcible response and those *responsible* for the terrorist 'armed attack.'[289] Nevertheless, publicists have addressed the responsibility issue with varying degrees of precision and elaboration. While some have discussed it only in rather general terms, others have employed more sophisticated approaches, some of which take into account differing state/terrorist actor relationships.

In a 1987 article, for example, Jeffrey McCredie offered a straightforward, uncomplicated method for target selection. He declared simply that 'chosen targets must be *verifiably connected* with the illegal activity.'[290] In his view, 'the best standard should require that in all circumstances only the individuals and technology involved in illegal activity should be targeted.'[291] Perhaps because McCredie's analysis concentrated solely on state-sponsored terrorism,[292] he did not distinguish various categories of association between 'states' and 'terrorist' actors.

Other scholars have explored more deeply the issue of state responsibility, and hence, have approached somewhat differently the 'proper target' question. Antonio Cassese, for example, maintained that a state could be targeted if a terrorist 'armed attack' was either 'attributable or imputable' to that state.[293] According to Cassese, state responsibility was clearly engaged if the 'terrorists' were 'officials of the state' or '*de facto* effectively controlled by the state'[294] – circumstances we have defined here as conventional 'state aggression' or 'state sponsorship' of terrorism. However, when 'arms or financial aid, logistical support' or 'mere sanctuary' are given by a state to terrorists – circumstances we have characterized as 'state support' and 'state toleration' – Cassese argued that the law was 'not entirely clear' and that states might 'still have plenty of room for manoeuvre.'[295] Professor Baker's rendition of state responsibility differs from that of Cassese. In his view, 'where the state itself is directly behind the terrorist attacks, its responsibility is clear.'[296] Such 'direct' state involvement, according to Baker, would include the provision to terrorist actors of training, financing, and support.[297] Even if a given state government did not specifically support or approve a particular act of terrorism, however, the act would 'become the responsibility of that government' if the government 'generally tolerated' such activities.[298] Using our typology, therefore, 'state sponsorship,' 'state support,' or even 'state toleration' of terrorism could engender a victim's right of response to an armed attack.

Perhaps one of the most elaborate discussions of state responsibility and its legal implications was undertaken by Judge Sofaer.[299] In his 1989 address, he submitted that victim state self-defense was 'the ultimate remedy for a state's knowingly harboring or assisting terrorists who attack another state or its citizens.'[300] Furthermore, proposed Sofaer, states have the right

> to strike terrorists within the territory of another State where the terrorists are using that territory as a location from which to launch terrorist attacks and where the State involved has failed to respond effectively to a demand that the attacks be stopped.[301]

Like Professor Baker, therefore, Sofaer contended that state 'sponsorship,' 'support,' or 'toleration' (as we have defined the concepts here) could engender a victim state's right to forcible response. The US Legal Adviser addressed also the question of how a victim state might establish proof of another state's involvement in terrorist activities,[302] offering three general rules:

a. When a state learns 'that any *official, agency, or party in a state* is materially involved in an incident [of terrorism], that should be treated as strong evidence of state responsibility.'
b. '[E]ven if no evidence is developed that a state is directly responsible for specific [terrorist] acts, the state's *general and continuing support* for a group known to be engaged in terrorism should suffice to establish responsibility for aiding or conspiring, if not as a principal in the crime itself. Differences in the degree of proof of actual approval by a state should operate to vary the degree of responsibility and the remedies imposed.'
c. 'The *public revelation of sensitive information* should not be considered a routine procedure to which ... states are expected to adhere.'[303]

Concluded Sofaer: 'Our ability to justify actions in self-defense with public proof will inevitably and quite properly affect our willingness to resort to the most serious remedial measures,' but 'no formal requirement of public proof should govern our actions in such cases.'[304]

Summary of scholarly opinion

Legal scholars who have examined the *jus ad bellum* dimensions of the terrorism question would appear to agree on at least four basic principles. Virtually all recognize that: 1) if it has suffered an 'armed attack' by 'terrorist' actors, a state is entitled to defend itself forcibly; 2) a victim state's forcible self-defense measures should be 'timely;' 3) a victim state's forcible self-defense measures should be 'proportionate;' and 4) a victim state's forcible self-defense measures should be 'discriminate' and taken against targets 'responsible' in some way for the armed attack.

Scholars differ widely, however, over how the subjective concepts of 'terrorism,' 'armed attack,' 'timeliness,' 'proportionality,' and 'responsibility' should properly be understood. At one end of a vast spectrum are publicists like Professor Boyle who would permit self-defense responses only to ongoing attacks upon a victim state's territory, provided those responses were on-the-spot, proportionate to the ongoing attack *per se*, and focused narrowly upon the actual attackers. At the other end are publicists like Judge Sofaer who would permit self-defense responses to relatively isolated attacks upon a state's nationals or other targets abroad, allowing that response to take place *post facto*, to serve a deterrent objective, to reflect 'deterrent proportionality,' and to target states with even relatively unproven links to the terrorist actors. This profound divergence of opinion would seem to reflect both the lack of a common analytical framework for the 'terrorism' question, and fundamentally different scholarly appreciations of the 'terrorism' phenomenon and the state's right to self-protection.

Legal assessment

Having reviewed both the practice of states since 1945 and the arguments advanced by publicists, it is possible now to return to this chapter's two principal questions: under what circumstances may a victim state respond forcibly to the incidence of terrorism? And provided it has sufficient legal grounds to do so, how may a state respond?

A scrutiny of state practice during the UN Charter period yields at least three conclusions. First, only two states have thus far used force in response to terrorism, Israel and the United States. Significantly, both states have been conspicuous victims of 'terrorist' activities and both have possessed sufficient military and intelligence capacities to undertake coercive measures. Second, Israeli and American counter-terrorist actions have been rather few in number and have remained restricted to the Middle East region. Only counter-base assaults have been conducted with any frequency, and these exclusively Israeli actions have often taken the form of small-scale commando operations or airstrikes. Third, Israeli and American forcible actions have been fairly routinely condemned by the Security Council. This general trend notwithstanding, international criticism has varied in its scope and intensity from case to case, has at times appeared likely to have reflected geopolitical and ideological considerations, and has frequently been internally inconsistent, emphasizing alternative legal arguments.

Contemporary legal scholarship, meanwhile, has remained bitterly divided over the question of forcible state responses to terrorism. Nothing resembling a *communis opinio doctorum* can be said now to exist, nor is any such consensus likely soon to emerge. Two obstacles to agreement have already been noted: the lack of a common framework for analysis; and a scholarly discourse preoccupied by incompatible appreciations of the 'terrorism' phenomenon and the state's right to defend itself. A third, more fundamental, factor may ultimately thwart consensus: the UN Charter itself. As we and others have argued, the Charter's language simply 'does not address directly the subtler modes of international violence' which have characterized much of the post-Second World War period.[305] Among other miscalculations, the Charter's 'framers did not fully anticipate the existence, tenacity and technology of modern day terrorism.'[306]

In view of the ambiguities of scholarly opinion and state practice, how is one most accurately to characterize the law? At least two contradictory characterizations of 'authoritative state practice' can be advanced.

First, it might be contended that the right to take forcible action is engendered only after the onset of a terrorist attack upon a state's territory. Under such circumstances, a state may only use armed measures which are on-the-spot, proportionate to the ongoing attack per se, and focused narrowly upon the actual attackers. No reprisals may be undertaken, no deterrent actions initiated. This legal interpretation would not be inconsistent with the language of Article 51 and would arguably reflect the Security Council practice of regular condemnation of Israeli and US counter-terror actions.[307]

A second, more controversial, rendition of authoritative state practice would proceed from the North Sea Continental Shelf principle that due regard must be given to the actions of those 'states whose interests [have been] specially affected.'[308] Accordingly, this second approach would ascribe great significance to the practice of Israel and the United States, two states whose interests have clearly been 'specially affected' by the incidence of terrorism.[309] On the basis of a review of Israeli and American practice, as well as that of the UN Security Council, it would conclude that the law prohibiting counter-terrorist 'reprisals' was, 'because of its divorce from actual practice, rapidly degenerating to a stage where its normative character' was 'in question.'[310] So suggested Professor Bowett as early as 1972. So averred Professor O'Brien in 1990:

> The Council's clear, black letter law [has] seemingly ... not affect[ed] Israeli nor, for that matter, US policies to any great extent. If one emphasizes Myres McDougal's 'expectations' element in ascertaining the state of international law, it would seem that the Security Council's ... position on counterterror measures will not guide states confronted with serious threats of terrorist attacks from sanctuary states.[311]

If one defines 'the law' as 'authoritative state practice,' and if one accords substantial weight to the practice of the 'specially affected' states of Israel and the United States, then counter-terror reprisals are not prohibited.[312] Such a conclusion regarding the jus ad bellum may not be very satisfying, but it may be an accurate one.

CONCLUSIONS

This chapter has examined the question of forcible state response to 'terrorism.' Acknowledging the inherently problematic nature of the term, the first section offered working definitions of both 'terrorist' act and 'terrorist' actor. It defined an 'act of terrorism' as 'the threat or use of violence with the intent of causing fear in a target group, in order to achieve political objectives'; next, it categorized terrorist *actors* in terms of the strength of their association to states: terrorist actors with state toleration, terrorist actors with state support, terrorist actors with state sponsorship, and terrorist actors lacking state toleration, support or sponsorship.

The second section examined the relationship of the contemporary *jus ad bellum* to the problem of international terrorism, addressing specifically three broad questions of law: 1) Are terrorist acts illegal? 2) Under what circumstances may a state forcibly respond to them? And 3) How may it do so? In response to the first query, it established that terrorist acts might arguably constitute violations of: 1) 'general principles of law'; 2) custom; or 3) various provisions of prohibitory conventions. It noted that no comprehensive treaty covering all varieties of terrorist activity has yet been adopted.

To facilitate answering the second and third related questions, the second section reviewed both post-1945 state practice and the writings of international legal scholars. Here, it offered three conclusions about state practice: 1) only two states have thus far used force in response to terrorism, Israel and the United States, both conspicuous victims of 'terrorist' activities and both well capable of taking forcible action; 2) aside from a number of counter-base operations (exclusively Israeli and generally small-scale), counter-terrorist actions have been rather few in number; and 3) forcible actions have been fairly regularly condemned by the Security Council, though international criticism has varied in its scope and intensity, has at times likely reflected geopolitical and ideological considerations, and has frequently been internally inconsistent.

The second section next showed that contemporary legal scholarship has remained divided over the question of forcible state responses to terrorism. At one end of a very broad, multihued spectrum are publicists who would permit self-defense responses only to ongoing attacks upon a victim state's territory, provided those responses were on-the-spot, proportionate to the ongoing attack *per se*, and focused narrowly upon the actual attackers; at the other end are those who would permit self-defense responses to relatively isolated attacks upon a state's nationals or other targets abroad, allowing that response to take place *post facto*, to serve a deterrent objective, to reflect 'deterrent proportionality,' and to target states with even relatively unproven links to the terrorist actors.

Given the ambiguities of scholarly opinion and state practice, this section concluded that at least two contradictory characterizations of 'authoritative state practice' could be advanced. The first approach concentrates principally on Security Council practice. It concludes that a state may take forcible action only after the onset of a terrorist attack upon its territory, using measures which are on-the-spot, proportionate to the ongoing attack *per se*, and focused narrowly upon the actual attackers. The second approach attaches great significance to the practice of Israel and the United States, two states whose interests have been 'specially affected' by the incidence of terrorism. It concludes that the putative norm prohibiting counter-terrorist 'reprisals' is of questionable efficacy because it is not reflected in state practice; therefore, the existence of any prohibitive norm cannot be established. Though in some respects an unfelicitous one, this conclusion would seem best to capture the contemporary status of the *jus ad bellum*. Given the Charter's failure to address squarely the 'terrorism' question, such a result was perhaps inevitable.

Conclusion: beyond the Charter paradigm

Chapter 10

International law and the recourse to force: a shift in paradigms

The point is that international law is not higher law or better law; it is *existing* law. It is not a law that eschews force; such a view is alien to the very idea of law. Often as not it is the law of the victor; but it is law withal and does evolve.[1]

Daniel Patrick Moynihan

INTRODUCTION

When the framers of the United Nations Charter met in San Francisco, they hoped to establish a new world order – one in which the recourse to force would be severely restricted. To this end, they formulated the United Nations Charter paradigm for the *jus ad bellum*. Three components set the parameters of this paradigm: 1) a legal obligation; 2) institutions to enforce the obligation; and 3) a value hierarchy that formed the philosophical basis of this obligation.

As noted in Chapter 3, the first of these components, the legal obligation, was embodied in Article 2(4) of the Charter. States were to refrain from any threat or use of force against the political or territorial status quo or in any other way against the principles of the United Nations. The only exceptions to this general prohibition were 1) force used in self-defense as defined in Article 51, and 2) force authorized by the Security Council in accordance with the provisions of Chapter VII.

The second component, the international institutions, were established under Chapter VII of the Charter. Under these provisions, the Security Council is empowered to investigate international conflicts and determine if there is a threat to the peace, a breach of the peace, or an act of aggression. If the Council so determines, it is further authorized to take collective action against the recalcitrant state.

The third element of the Charter paradigm is the underlying value hierarchy. When the Charter was drafted, even though the framers proclaimed many goals for the new international organization, its preeminent goal was the maintenance of international peace and security. This goal of peace was to take priority over other goals of justice. Justice was to be sought, but not at the expense of peace. Given the experience of the first two world wars, the framers believed that more damage was done to the international system by taking up arms to fight for justice than by living with a particular injustice.

The preceding analysis reveals, however, that since the Second World War, a number of significant developments have challenged the validity of this Charter paradigm. These include such problems as the failure of international institutions and the emergence of new values concerning the recourse to force. Although most international legal scholars would contend that these post-war developments represent serious threats to the Charter paradigm, few would claim that they are indicative of a paradigmatic shift. We reject this contention. Our conclusion is that in the world since 1945, a new legal paradigm has indeed emerged: a 'post-Charter self-help' paradigm. This paradigm, we argue, is at present the best framework for understanding the contemporary law relating to the recourse to force. But even as this second paradigm may currently describe existing law, recent events in the Middle East, Eastern Europe, Central America, Africa, and elsewhere suggest that a third paradigm may be emerging, a 'pro-democratic' paradigm.

This chapter will attempt to provide an analytical framework for understanding these conclusions. In order to do so, the first section will outline the contours of the post-Charter self-help paradigm. The second section will explore the possible emergence of a new, pro-democratic paradigm. Finally, the third section will examine the future direction of the *jus ad bellum* and make recommendations for its development.

THE POST-CHARTER SELF-HELP PARADIGM

Not long after the Charter was adopted, changes in the international system began to challenge the efficacy of this framework for the recourse to force, leading ultimately to the emergence of a new paradigm. In order to understand the nature of this paradigm, let us examine three elements: 1) the failure of Charter institutions; 2) the emergence of a new value hierarchy; and, 3) the changed legal obligation.

The failure of Charter institutions

As noted in Chapter 4, since 1945 several major problems have developed with the system for the collective use of force established by the Charter. These include the veto, the inability to establish formal mechanisms for collective action, and the general rejection of limited collective security. Even though world leaders and scholars made efforts to respond to these problems, these efforts showed little promise. Using the General Assembly as a substitute for the Security Council only really worked in the case of

Korea. And in that case, the Security Council has already authorized the initial action. In subsequent uses of force, the Assembly has not been able to respond effectively to challenge an act of aggression. Similarly, the use of regional arrangements has not proved very successful. Such arrangements have responded only selectively to uses of force by states and have frequently been perceived as little more than a fig leaf for great power actions.[2] Finally, peacekeeping, which developed in the wake of the failure of limited collective security, cannot be considered as a substitute. Peacekeeping explicitly recognizes that collective action to fight aggression is unlikely. It comes into play only after the hostilities have ceased and the parties consent to international supervision. Peacekeeping is thus not a legitimate alternative to the Chapter VII approach to collective enforcement.

In short, in the post-Charter period, international institutions have failed to deter or combat aggression. The international community has faltered in its efforts to address this profound problem.

A new value hierarchy

As observed previously, the Charter paradigm for the recourse to force was predicated upon the assumption that 'peace' was more important that justice. In the post-1945 world, however, states have repudiated this hierarchy of values. In many diverse sectors of the international system, claims have been made that force against the existing political and territorial order may, at times, be justified. As noted in Chapter 3, these claims seem to have manifested themselves in three different ways: 1) claims to use force to promote self-determination; 2) claims to resort to 'just' reprisals; and, 3) claims to use force to correct past 'injustices.'

These claims suggest that the members of the international system have rejected the philosophical underpinnings of the Charter paradigm. Rather than believing that more injury to world order occurs when force is used to pursue just goals, states have come to believe that, at certain times, it is better to break the peace in the name of justice, than to live with the injustice. At times, justice must take precedence over peace.

A changed legal obligation

The death of Article 2(4)

The failure of Charter institutions to enforce norms relating to the recourse to force and the changing value hierarchy have obliged many scholars to rethink the status of the contemporary *jus ad bellum*. In short, scholars have been compelled to ask whether Article 2(4) is still good international law. We have argued that a putative norm is a rule of international law only if it is authoritative and controlling.[3] As a consequence, for Article 2(4)'s proscription to be regarded as genuine law, its authority and control must be clearly demonstrated.

A review of scholarship and practice suggests three fundamental approaches to this question. The first has been labelled the 'legalist' approach; the second the 'core interpretist' approach; and the third the 'rejectionist' approach.[4] This section will examine each of these three approaches in turn and conclude that the 'rejectionist' approach reflects most accurately the reality of the international system.

The legalist approach

A significant number of international publicists might be considered 'legalists.'[5] These legal scholars, while recognizing that problems exist, adhere to the basic belief that the principle enunciated in Article 2(4) is still good law.[6] To make this argument, they stress several points. First, they argue that the norm remains authoritative since no state has explicitly suggested that Article 2(4) is not good law. As Professor Louis Henkin has explained '[n]o government, no responsible official of government, has been prepared to pronounce it dead.'[7] Thus, because states have not explicitly repudiated Article 2(4), its authority continues.

Second, legalists argue that despite the problems of Article 2(4), the norm remains controlling of state behavior. Here, they contend that despite violations of the norm, it has *for the most part* exerted a restraining influence on state behavior. In the words of Professor Henkin, 'the norm against the unilateral national use of force has survived. Indeed, despite common misimpressions to the contrary, the norm has been largely observed'.[8] One aspect of this legalist argument seems to be that while it is easy to count the times that a particular norm is violated, it is quite difficult to identify the times when a norm exerted a controlling influence, when states refrained from forcible action because of Article 2(4)'s proscription. Another aspect of this argument is that since most states are not, in fact, using force in violation of the Charter, the norm is generally controlling of behavior.

Finally, the legalists argue that Article 2(4) must be understood as a *treaty* obligation for those states that have ratified the United Nations Charter and not just as an obligation under customary international law. Hence, the procedure for a normative change is much more specific and defined. Professor Edward Gordon has argued that

[t]he rule embodied in Article 2(4) is not just a freestanding rule of customary law; it is also a formal treaty obligation. States may withdraw their consent to be bound by treaty obligations, but may not simply walk away from them.[9]

Explains Gordon, '[t]he existence of an operational code [read 'state practice'] different from the formal commitment may be cause for withdrawing state consent, but it does not supplant the process for withdrawing consent called for by the treaty or by treaty law generally.'[10] Although recognizing that treaties may be 'replaced' if they are 'not followed,' Gordon contends that 'an observer's inference that they are lagging behind actual practice is too subjective and fragile a criterion to replace the formal evidence of withdrawal of state consent as an indicator of the continuing force of treaty obligations.'[11] In other words, states must formally terminate a treaty for it to cease to be binding; mere non-compliance is insufficient.

While there is a certain logic in these arguments advanced by the legalists, there are also problems. First, although it may be true that no state has explicitly declared that Article 2(4) is not good law, this fact alone does not mean that the norm is necessarily authoritative. For obvious political reasons, states have not overtly argued that the Charter norms are invalid. But as noted earlier,[12] states have on numerous occasions claimed the right to use force in circumstances that are, nevertheless, clearly antithetical to the principle enshrined in Article 2(4). Given these claims, it seems incorrect to contend that states still hold 2(4) in very high esteem. Admittedly, the provision may still command some perceptions of legitimacy,[13] but they seem to be far below those required for a healthy rule of law.

Second, the arguments advanced by the legalists for the controlling nature of Article 2(4) also seem to be inconsistent with realities of the international system. Certainly not every state violates Article 2(4), and certainly it is difficult to judge when a particular state's behavior was influenced by the existence of 2(4). Nevertheless, the norm has been violated frequently and with impunity in some of the most important cases of state interaction. Even though legal scholars may disagree as to the precise list of such violations of Article 2(4),[14] there is broad agreement that numerous violations have taken place.[15] For the purposes of this chapter, a representative sampling of such violations would seem to include the following major uses of force:[16] the US action in Guatemala (1954); the Israeli, French, and British invasion of Egypt (1956); the Soviet invasion of Hungary (1956); the US-sponsored Bay of Pigs invasion (1961); the Indian invasion of Goa (1961); the US invasion of the Dominican Republic (1965); the Warsaw Pact invasion of Czechoslovakia (1968); the Arab action in the 1973 Middle East War; North Vietnamese actions against South Vietnam (1960–75); the Vietnamese invasion of Kampuchea (1979); the Soviet invasion of Afghanistan (1979); the Tanzanian invasion of Uganda (1979); the Argentine invasion of the Falklands (1982); the US invasion of Grenada (1983); the American invasion of Panama (1989); and the Iraqi attack on Kuwait (1990).

Even Professor Henkin, in arguing that Article 2(4) is still valid, was forced to deal with a number of these instances. He explains:

> the norm against unilateral force has been largely observed. With the exception of Korea (in some respects an 'internal war'), the brief,

recurrent Arab–Israel hostilities in 1956, 1967, and 1973, the flurry between India and Pakistan over Kashmir in September 1965, the invasion of Czechoslovakia by Soviet troops in 1968, [and in the footnote he says: 'One might add, unhappily, Ethiopia–Somalia and Vietnam–Cambodia–China in 1978–79.'], nations have not engaged in 'war,' in full and sustained hostilities or state-to-state aggression even in circumstances in which in the past the use of force might have been expected.'[17]

These 'exceptions,' and others that have taken place since the time Henkin's book was written, are profound exceptions, not simply minor incidents. These uses of force would seem rather clearly to indicate that when a state judges other foreign policy goals to be at stake, it will generally *not* allow itself to be circumscribed by the prohibition of Article 2(4).

Finally, the legalists' use of the treaty-nature of Article 2(4) is problematic. Even though Article 2(4) is a treaty provision, the same test for determining the validity of customary international law can also be employed. If a treaty provision is greatly lacking in authority and control, it seems quite logical to argue that the provision is no longer authentic 'international law.'[18] In the decentralized system that exists today, international law is constituted through state practice. In 1945, fifty-one states chose to enunciate a particular rule relating to the use of force by ratifying the United Nations Charter. Since then, these states and over one hundred additional ones have, through their actions, chosen to change this rule.[19] Even though there have been no formal acts that have attempted to change the written words of Article 2(4), the behavior of these states has been sufficient to effect a change.

The 'core interpretist' approach

Another approach to understanding the status of Article 2(4) has been called the 'core interpretist' approach. The 'core interpretists' argue that although the narrow, legalistic interpretation of Article 2(4) no longer represents existing law, a 'core' meaning of the Article that is still authoritative and controlling can nevertheless be identified.[20] Naturally, these scholars differ as to what represents this 'core' meaning. Some suggest that the 'core' is very large. They contend that the basic prohibition contained in Article 2(4) is still valid, except as modified by authoritative interpretations confirmed in state practice. Thus, every unilateral use of force is prohibited unless it can be demonstrated that the accepted interpretation of the Charter allows for an exception. These 'core interpretists' argue that permissible exceptions would include such uses of force as anticipatory self-defense, intervention to protect nationals, and humanitarian intervention.[21]

Other 'core interpretist' scholars take a slightly different approach. They contend that the 'core' of Article 2(4) is much smaller. For example, Professor Alberto Coll suggests that insofar as there is a remnant of a legal, as opposed to a moral obligation left in article 2(4), it is a good faith commitment to abstain from *clear aggression* that involves a disproportionate use of force and violates other principles of the Charter.[22]

According to Coll,

[c]lear aggression and the content of article 2(4) and article 51 would, in turn, be defined by reference to established traditions of normative reasoning, such as prudence and just war doctrine, in an open interpretative process similar, in fact, to that already underlying state decisionmaking on the use of force in many situations.[23]

He explains that '[u]nder this interpretative process, *clear aggression* would encompass different typologies of coercive acts which various traditions of ethical reasoning, throughout different periods of history, have condemned in the strongest terms as unlawful and morally reprehensible.'[24] Thus using Coll's approach, 'clear aggression' could include the use of force to gain territory, to achieve political domination, and to perpetrate genocide. The activities of Nazi Germany and Imperial Japan that inaugurated the Second World War would be the most obvious examples of such 'clear aggression.'[25]

But whatever the precise nature of the 'core' that the various scholars identify, the important aspect of this approach is that it continues to affirm Article 2(4) as the existing *jus ad bellum*. All the writers of this school would contend that *some* version of Article 2(4) represents the law, and would reject arguments that 2(4) is now dead. One reason for this desire to hold on to even a shred of Article 2(4) is a belief that rejecting the norm entirely might be premature because states do refrain from certain uses of force. Consequently, such rejection could actually contribute to the dissolution of whatever restraining influence 2(4) still exerts.[26] Another reason seems to be the symbolic nature of 2(4). For many 'core interpretists,' Article 2(4) represents a goal, an aspiration of the post-Second World War era.[27] To claim that it is no longer law, would be to claim that prohibiting the unilateral resort to force was no longer a noble goal worth pursuing.

But despite these laudable aspirations, there is one major problem. Holding on to Article 2(4) may actually be doing more harm than good to the international legal system. Given the severely weakened authority of 2(4) and its manifest lack of control, to use Article 2(4) in any way to describe the law relating to the recourse to force may simply be perpetrating a legal fiction that interferes with an accurate assessment of state practice. It may indeed be true that some 'core' of the Article 2(4) prohibition may remain, such as a prohibition on the use of force for territorial aggrandizement. But the problem is that Article 2(4) was designed to be much more than simply a prohibition on the use of force for that narrow purpose.[28] One of the radical aspects of 2(4) was that it went beyond the Kellogg-Briand Pact,[29] which prohibited recourse to 'war,' by prohibiting *all* uses of *force* that were against the territorial integrity or political independence of a state or otherwise inconsistent with the purposes of the United Nations. Moreover, it even prohibited *threats* of force. In other words, the Article 2(4) prohibition was much broader than simply the 'core.' If only this small sub-set of Article 2(4) still remains, it does not seem appropriate to describe the law by reference to the full set.

The 'rejectionist' approach

The third possible approach to the status of Article 2(4) has been called the 'rejectionist' approach. To take this approach would be to argue that Article 2(4) does not in any meaningful way constitute existing law. The contention would be that because authoritative state practice is so far removed from any reasonable interpretation of the meaning of Article 2(4), it is no longer reasonable to consider the provision 'good law.'

The classical elaboration of the rejectionist approach can be found in Professor Franck's 1970 article on the death of Article 2(4).[30] At that time, Professor Franck argued that '[t]he prohibition against the use of force in relations between states has been eroded beyond recognition'[31] This erosion, according to Franck, was due to three main factors: 'the rise of wars of "national liberation",' 'the rising threat of wars of total destruction,' and 'the increasing authoritarianism of regional systems dominated by a super-Power.'[32] But, he explained, '[t]hese three factors may ... be traced back to a single circumstance: the lack of congruence between the international legal norm of Article 2(4) and the perceived national interests of states, especially the super-Powers.'[33] In short, as states have come to value goals other than those expressed in Article 2(4), the authority and control of the norm have essentially disappeared. As Professor Franck put it in 1970: 'The practice of these states has so severely shattered the mutual confidence which would have been the *sine qua non* of an operative rule of law embodying the precepts of Article 2(4) that, as with Ozymandias, only the words remain.'[34]

Twenty years later, in his *The Power of Legitimacy Among Nations*, Franck reaffirmed his 'rejectionist' understanding of Article 2(4). Acknowledging the egregious lack of control of putative rules dealing with the use of force, he commented:

> the extensive body of international 'law,' oft restated in solemn texts, which forbids direct or indirect intervention by one state in the domestic affairs of another, precludes the aggressive use of force by one state against another, and requires adherence to human rights standards simply, if sadly, is not predictive of the ways of the world.[35]

Later, Franck compared Article 2(4) and the one-time US Government mandated 55-mile per hour national speed limit. Observing that while both rules possess 'textual clarity,' they, nevertheless, 'do not describe or predict with accuracy the actual behavior of the real world.'[36] He explained that

> their determinacy is undermined by a popular perception that they can't mean what they so plainly say. The irrationality of the rules – their incoherence: a failure to be instrumental in relation to the purposes for which they were devised – causes us to believe, and act on the belief, that they have become indeterminate. The rules, therefore, have lost some of their compliance pull.[37]

Apart from Professor Franck, no other major international legal scholar has *explicitly* taken this approach, although several have come close.[38] Yet despite this lack of support, the 'rejectionist' approach seems to offer the most accurate description of the contemporary *jus ad bellum*. The legalist approach seems too removed from the realities of the international system[39] and the core interpretist approach seems to do little more than perpetuate a legal fiction.[40] Based on what states have been saying and what they have been doing, there simply does not seem to be a *legal* prohibition on the use of force against the political independence and territorial integrity of states as provided in even a modified version of Article 2(4). The rule creating process, authoritative state practice, has rejected that norm.

The post-Charter obligation

If Article 2(4) is in fact dead, a larger question remains: what norms have developed in the post-Charter era to replace it? In other words, what rules of behavior have states constituted that *are* regarded as authoritative and are, in practice, controlling? Based on state behavior, several conclusions can be drawn about legal principles that seem to have emerged to fill the gap caused by the death of Article 2(4). The following section will set out these conclusions. We will employ here a 'positivist' approach to international law.[41] That is, we assume that unless a restrictive norm of law can be established prohibiting a particular use of force, states are permitted to engage in that use of force.[42] In short, for any use of force to be prohibited, an authoritative and controlling *proscription* must exist.

Our proposal does not purport to offer the only acceptable formulation of the law; rather, it seeks merely to present one possible description of the post-Charter *jus ad bellum*. In order to do so, we will first discuss those circumstances under which recourse to force seems to be lawful. Then, we will examine those circumstances under which recourse to force appears to be unlawful.

Lawful uses of force

Self-defense (including anticipatory self-defense and reprisals) The first circumstance in which the unilateral use of force would seem to be lawful in a post-Article 2(4) legal system would be self-defense. This is not particularly controversial. Individual and collective self-defense has always been explicitly permitted under Article 51 of the Charter.[43] The major change would be the addition of anticipatory self-defense and reprisals.

Before the Charter was adopted, states had the right under customary international law to use force in self-defense even before an armed attack occurred if it could be demonstrated that such an attack were imminent and that no other recourse was available.[44] With the demise of Article 2(4), it is reasonable to assume that this preexisting right would be rehabilitated. There seems to be no consensus on a rule prohibiting force undertaken for that purpose.[45]

In addition to anticipatory self-defense, it would also seem that reprisals would be permissible. As noted earlier, states have also been using a broadened definition of self-defense to justify reprisals.[46] There seems to be a belief on the part of states conducting such actions that they are proper to punish and deter certain prior illegal acts of the target state, even though such initial acts do not rise to the level of an armed attack.[47] While not all states have endorsed the use of force for these purposes,[48] there appears to be no clear agreement on an authoritative norm prohibiting reprisals.[49]

Promotion of self-determination   In light of the growing preference for 'just' uses of force, described above,[50] the use of force to promote self-determination would also seem to be lawful. But since different states have defined self-determination in different ways,[51] it would be impossible to restrict this right to the promotion of a particular 'type' of self-determination. It would, in other words, be difficult to claim, as Professor Michael Reisman does, that using force to promote 'pro-democratic' self-determination would be permissible, but using force to promote 'pro-socialist' self-determination would be impermissible.[52] Consequently, there would seem to be a right for states to use force to promote self-determination *however* they define it. This would mean that such action as the Soviet 'liberation' of Czechoslovakia and the American 'liberation' of Panama would be lawful. It would also mean that it would be permissible to provide assistance to either side in a civil conflict, with the determination being made by the intervening party as to which side was acting in the true interests of self-determination.

This use of force to promote self-determination is obviously much more controversial than self-defense. It actually constitutes a clear use of force against the political independence and territorial integrity of a state. Nevertheless, as demonstrated earlier,[53] states have come to regard a just pursuit of self-determination as a proper use of force, at least when it is their definition of self-determination. Once again, there seems to be no restrictive rule prohibiting such use of force.

Correction of past injustices   Finally, it would seem to be lawful to employ force to correct injustices that had been inflicted on a particular state at a particular time in the past. This means that if one state had previously seized the territory of another state, had endangered the nationals of that state, or had violated some other major norm of international law, the aggrieved state could use force to rectify the situation. This new rule would legalize such actions as the Argentine invasion of the Falklands[54] and, if they had been done today, the British, French, and Israeli invasion of Egypt in 1956,[55] and the Arab invasion in 1973.[56]

This use of force to correct past injustices also clearly involves action against the political and territorial status quo. States seem to feel, however, that the status quo is often unjust, and that in the absence of other effective means to correct the situation, they have the right to take the matter into their own hands.[57]

Unlawful uses of force: territorial annexation

If states have come to acknowledge that force may properly be used to promote self-determination and to correct past injustices, very little would seem to be prohibited. In fact, in a world without Article 2(4), the only thing that does seem to be proscribed is the use of force for pure territorial aggrandizement. States still appear to believe that it is illegitimate to use force solely for the purpose of gaining territory.

Perhaps the most dramatic example of this belief can be seen in the response of the international community to the August 1990 Iraqi invasion of Kuwait.[58] When Iraq invaded and annexed Kuwait, it justified its actions on the basis of Arab unity.[59] Claiming that colonial borders had been unjustly drawn,[60] the Iraqi Revolutionary Command Council proclaimed that it had 'decided to return the part and branch, Kuwait, to the whole and origin, Iraq, in a comprehensive, eternal and inseparable merger unity.'[61] Yet despite this apparent claim of correcting a past injustice, the international community squarely condemned the invasion and annexation. On August 2, the United Nations Security Council adopted Resolution 660 condemning the invasion by a vote of 14–0, with Yemen not voting.[62] Four days later the Council, acting under Chapter VII of the Charter, imposed economic sanctions on Iraq by a vote of 13–0, with Cuba and Yemen abstaining.[63] Shortly thereafter, following Iraq's claim of annexation, the Council unanimously adopted Resolution 662.[64] This Resolution reiterated the Council's demand 'that Iraq withdraw immediately and unconditionally all its forces' from Kuwait, and decided 'that annexation of Kuwait by Iraq under any form and whatever pretext has no legal validity, and is considered null and void' and demanded 'that Iraq rescind its actions purporting to annex Kuwait.'[65] On November 30, after much negotiation, the Council adopted Resolution 678 authorizing states to use force if Iraq did not comply with the demanded withdrawal.[66]

The Security Council's actions in this case are quite telling. Even though Iraq's actions were veiled in claims of 'justice,' the Council did not hesitate in

condemning the invasion and purported annexation. The justification un-
doubtedly was too much of a transparent 'pretext' for a simple effort at
territorial aggrandizement, reminiscent of justifications used at the beginning
of the Second World War.[67] The reaction would indicate a strong perception
on the part of the overwhelming majority of states that uses of force for pure
territorial aggrandizement are impermissible. Moreover, the fact that such
uses of force have been quite rare in the post-War era,[68] indicate that this
norm does have a high degree of control.[69]

But what all this suggests is that the legal structure that has emerged from
the ashes of Article 2(4) may simply be a modified regime of 'self-help.'
Under such a regime, states can lawfully use force to promote self-
determination as they define it and to correct what they perceive to be
injustices. For these purposes they possess a *competence de guerre*, akin to
that possessed by states before the adoption of the League of Nations
Covenant.[70] Under this paradigm, however, one use of force *is* prohibited –
force for territorial annexation. Of course even here, states could claim that
they were acting for other 'just' reasons when their actual goal was pure
territorial acquisition.

An assessment of the post-Charter obligation

If the international legal system has moved toward a modified regime of
self-help in the post-Charter period, is this evolution good? Does this type of
legal arrangement further the general goals of international law? Assuming
that one of the main purposes of international law is to promote stability and
regularity in the relations among states, the answer would quite clearly be
no. Self-determination and justice are extremely subjective terms. They can
mean virtually anything a particular state chooses them to mean, and they
can be used to justify virtually any use of force. In the world of 'just' causes,
one person's liberator is another person's oppressor, and one person's
freedom fighter is another person's terrorist.

The problem, however, is that while self-determination can mean almost
anything, Article 2(4) has already been stripped of any real meaning. In light
of state practice, to contend that it is still good law is to make *it* mean virtually
anything. Recognizing that Article 2(4) is dead may not be very satisfying, but
it may be accurate. The normative framework suggested above certainly
does not represent the most desirable legal regime, but it may reflect the
existing legal regime.

THE POST-COLD WAR ERA: A NEW PARADIGM?

Critics of the preceding analysis of the post-Charter self-help paradigm might
contend that the discussion has assumed the existence of a particular type of
international system. The paradigm, it could be argued, seems to assume the

continuance of the Cold War and its attendant evils – lack of superpower cooperation, widespread superpower intervention, and the like. Now that the tumultuous year of 1989 has brought an end to the Cold War,[71] the paradigm no longer depicts reality. With the collapse of the Soviet Union, increased cooperation among the permanent members of the Security Council,[72] the rising capital of the United Nations,[73] and the great movements toward democracy,[74] a *laissez-faire* approach to the use of force no longer seems accepted. Instead, it could be argued, a new 'pro-democratic' paradigm is coming to describe the law relating to the recourse to force.

This section will examine the arguments supporting the existence of this would-be paradigm. It will do so by exploring the revitalization of international institutions for conflict management, and the possible emergence of a new value hierarchy, and 'new' legal obligation.

The revitalization of international institutions

As noted earlier, one of the factors contributing to the decline of the Charter framework for the use of force was the failure of international institutions designed to manage international conflict. In recent months, however, these institutions of the United Nations seem to be making a resurgence. This can be seen both in the recent successes of the organization in assisting in the peaceful settlement of several important international conflicts and in serious proposals presented to the United Nations regarding conflict management.

Successes of the United Nations

Since 1988, the United Nations has been experiencing a great deal of success in the area of conflict management. In the Iran–Iraq War, the organization was instrumental in establishing a cease-fire after eight years of bloody conflict.[75] The UN was also able to set-up the United Nations Iran–Iraq Military Observer Group (UNIIMOG),[76] a peacekeeping force designed to monitor this cease-fire. And indeed, while many of the underlying issues still were not resolved[77] until the aftermath of the Iraqi invasion of Kuwait,[78] UN peacekeepers helped ensure that no major fighting has broken-out between the two parties since the cease-fire was instituted.[79] Similarly, the United Nations was crucial in the establishment of an independent Namibia.[80] It has also played a key role in Central America with the creation of the United Nations Observer Group in Central America (ONUCA).[81] This peacekeeping body was originally charged with verifying that aid was not being provided to resistance movements in the region.[82] As time passed, the Security Council expanded its mandate to include assisting in the demobilization of the Nicaraguan resistance in the wake of the February 1990 elections.[83] Even in such trouble spots as Cambodia[84] and the Western Sahara,[85] the United Nations has made significant steps toward resolving these long-standing conflicts.

The most remarkable effort of the United Nations, however, has come in the wake of the Iraqi invasion of Kuwait. As noted earlier,[86] the Security Council has been able to adopt several crucial resolutions condemning Iraqi actions and imposing economic sanctions under Article 41 of the Charter. It was even able to adopt a resolution authorizing the use of force by states to enforce these resolutions. These actions represent the first time that the Security Council has actually ordered sanctions against an aggressor. The sanctions ordered against Rhodesia[87] and South Africa[88] were not in response to acts of aggression and the action taken against Korea was only recommended by the Security Council.[89]

An important reason that the United Nations has been able to have a certain amount of success in these areas has been the willingness of all the permanent members of the Security Council to cooperate and to exert pressure on other states. In the Iran–Iraq War, for example, the five permanent members used their influence to persuade the two belligerents to accept a cease-fire proposal. In the Cambodian conflict, it has been the permanent members who have been leading the United Nations effort. Through a series of meetings, those five states adopted a formula for United Nations administration of Cambodia pending the result of UN-monitored elections.[90] And during the Gulf War, an amazing level of cooperation existed, including an especially close relationship between the United States and the then Soviet Union.[91] This kind of great power cooperation is precisely what was envisioned by the framers of the organization as the necessary condition for effective collective security.[92] If this trend continues, it is possible that the Charter institutions could, as in the Iraqi invasion, continue playing a significant role in enforcing the norms dealing with the recourse to force.

Recent proposals for strengthening the United Nations

As the United Nations has been making these important contributions to world order, a number of states have presented several rather significant proposals for improving the organization's ability to deal with international conflict. First, several proposals have been made to enhance the United Nation's ability to aid in the peaceful settlement of international disputes. One such proposal was an effort in 1990 by the United States and the Soviet Union to enhance the role of the International Court of Justice.[93] Second, a number of suggestions have been advanced to radically improve the organization's capability to deal with uses of force per se. For example, the Soviets proposed a revitalization of the Military Staff Committee and the 'establishment of a UN military reserve.'[94] Even before the Iraqi attack on Kuwait, the Soviets suggested

> the establishment of UN observation posts in explosive areas, the deployment of a UN naval force to patrol the Persian Gulf, and the stationing of

UN forces along the border of any country that seeks to protect itself from outside interference.'[95]

Most recently, the Security Council itself has taken the initiative. On January 31, 1992, the Council, meeting as a Summit, called upon the Secretary-General to provide the Council with 'analysis and recommendations on ways of strengthening and making more efficient within the framework and provisions of the Charter the capacity of the United Nations for *preventive diplomacy*, for peacemaking and for peace-keeping.'[96] In response to this charge, the Secretary-General issued a report to the Council on June 17, 1992.[97] In this report, Boutros-Ghali calls for greater institutionalization of United Nations conflict management. In particular, he strongly urges the establishment of institutions that would help the United Nations prevent hot conflicts. The Secretary-General explains:

> The most desirable and efficient employment of diplomacy is to ease tension before they result in conflict – or, if conflict breaks out, to act swiftly to contain it and resolve its underlying causes. Preventative diplomacy may be performed by the Secretary-General personally or through senior staff or specialized agencies and programmes, by the Security Council or the General Assembly, and by regional organizations in co-operation with the United Nations. Preventive diplomacy requires measures to create confidence; it needs early warning based on information gathering and informal or formal fact-finding; it may also involve preventive deployment and, in some situations, demilitarized zones.[98]

After introducing the subject of preventive diplomacy, Boutros-Ghali goes on to elaborate upon specific suggestions for confidence building measures,[99] fact-finding,[100] early warning,[101] preventive deployment,[102] and demilitarized zones.[103]

While these proposals have yet to be implemented, they do suggest a bright future for the Charter institutions. If, in fact, the institutions can be strengthened, the organization may be better equipped to provide alternatives to force as a means to settling international disputes. Moreover, if positive changes can be made to the collective security function of the United Nations, it may be more able to deter and, if need be, fight aggression.

The emergence of a new value hierarchy?

In the Post-Charter Self-Help paradigm, justice is valued above peace. States are claiming the right to use force to promote certain 'just' goals. The major difficulty with this formulation is that different groups of states have offered differing and often contradictory definitions of what a 'just' goal is. With the ending of the Cold War, however, it could be contended that an international consensus is emerging around certain acceptable 'just' goals. Specifically, it could be argued that in light of recent developments, there is a consensus that it is proper to use force to promote democratic self-determination in the western sense of the term.

This argument could be made in two steps. First, with the decline of the ideological confrontation between the East and the West,[104] there is growing international agreement on what constitutes an 'illegitimate' regime. Such a regime would be one that engages in gross violations of human rights as enumerated in the Covenant on Civil and Political Rights[105] or one which has come to power in total disregard of constitutional processes. Hence, the pre-1989 regimes in Panama, East Germany, Bulgaria, Czechoslovakia, and Romania, to name a few, could be regarded as illegitimate.[106] In support of the notion that agreement on the illegitimacy of certain regimes transcends the East–West divide, proponents of this contention would cite Gorbachev's attitude regarding the Eastern European regimes.[107] They would argue that in his calls for change in Eastern Europe and his tacit acceptance of such change, he reflected a new thinking on the part of the Soviet Union's leadership that those regimes were, in fact, illegitimate.[108] Second, because there could be near universal agreement that a particular government is illegitimate, it could be contended that there is an emerging belief that it is becoming permissible to use force against such regimes to promote the self-determination of the peoples.

Although this argument is only in the initial stages of development, one American scholar, Thomas Franck, has attempted to suggest its contours. In a paper delivered in March of 1990 at the United States Institute of Peace, Professor Franck argued that states 'are gradually coming to agree on a *right* to democratic governance, or freedom from totalitarianism.'[109] He explained that

> [w]hatever decent instincts came to cluster around the magnet of 'self-determination,' creating a widely-accepted exception to article 2(4), must now carry forward, in the post-colonial era, to imbue a new inter-nationally-recognized human right to political freedom.[110]

And, according to Franck, '[k]in to such a right would be another: a right of the democratic members of the international community to aid, directly or indirectly, those fighting for their democratic entitlement.'[111] These 'demo-cratic entitlements,' explained Franck, 'are already spelled out in inter-national instruments, in particular the Covenant in Civil and Political Rights, which may now be regarded as customary international law.'[112] But Franck believes that

> [w]hen the most basic of these rights have been found to have been violated – and *only* then – an enunciated international consensus might now be ready to form around the proposition that the use of some levels of force by states could be justified to secure democratic entitlements for peoples unable to secure them for themselves.'[113]

In short, justice would still be valued over peace, but the definition of justice would not be as subjective as in the self-help paradigm.

The emergence of a 'new' legal obligation?

Based on these institutional and attitudinal changes, it could be argued that a 'new' legal obligation regarding the recourse to force is in the process of emerging. Following Franck, it could be contended that the international community is coming to accept one just cause for the recourse to force aside from self-defense – intervention to remove an 'illegitimate' regime. With the decline of competing ideologies, there is developing a consensus around what constitutes such an illegitimate regime and a growing acceptance of the permissibility to use force, if necessary, to remove such a regime. If this is indeed becoming the case, then the paradigm depicting the *jus ad bellum* may be shifting away from the post-Charter self-help paradigm to a new pro-democratic paradigm. Under such a paradigm, force would be permissible in two circumstances: to engage in individual and collective self-defense and to promote 'pro-democratic' self-determination.

While such a paradigmatic shift may occur at some point in the future, at present, it seems exceptionally premature to assert its imminent arrival. This is true for a number of reasons. First, despite the dramatic developments in Eastern Europe and the former Soviet Union, there still seems to be no real international consensus as to what constitutes an 'illegitimate' regime. While it is true that an apparent agreement developed regarding the illegitimacy of certain Eastern European governments, there seems to be no such consensus with respect to the rest of the world. If fidelity to the International Covenant on Civil and Political Rights is used as a determinant of legitimacy, a substantial number of countries fall short. Even following the remarkable developments of 1989, the human rights organization Freedom House lists fifty-nine states as 'not free.'[114] These states comprise over two billion people and come from nearly every area of the world.[115] Clearly, if over one-third of the states in the international system maintain regimes in which significant political rights and civil liberties, as defined in the West, are denied, it is impossible to argue that there is some consensus on democratic legitimacy.

Second, even assuming there were some emerging agreement on legitimacy, there is clearly no consensus developing on the efficacy of the use of force to remove such a regime. A case in point would be the invasion of Panama by the United States. Even though one argument raised by the United States centered around the illegitimacy of the Noriega regime,[116] there was near universal condemnation for the American action. While certain states believed that the government of Manuel Noriega was indeed illegitimate, there seemed to be a general rejection of US contentions that this illegitimacy gave rise to a unilateral right to invade the country.[117] If this was the case with respect to Panama, it is difficult to envision many other cases in which there could be agreement on the permissibility of force to remove an anti-democratic regime.

In short, despite the dramatic changes that have taken place in international politics over the last several years, there does not yet seem to be the international consensus necessary to support the existence of a pro-democratic paradigm. States have not yet come to accept a *jus ad bellum* that permits intervention for only one particular type of self-determination, self-determination aimed at removing illegitimate, anti-democratic regimes.

THE FUTURE OF THE *JUS AD BELLUM*

Three possible scenarios

In light of the preceding analysis, it is contended that there has been a definite paradigm shift in the post-Charter period. The Charter prohibition on the recourse to force as established in Article 2(4) is simply no longer authoritative and controlling.[118] States have chosen to reject this strict pro-scription in favor of a more permissive norm that prohibits force only in cases of action aimed at territorial aggrandizement and allows forcible efforts to promote self-determination as it is variously defined, to carry-out a just reprisal, and to correct a past injustice. Despite the changes that have taken place in the international system, states have not yet reached a consensus on a more restrictive norm limiting permissible intervention to cases involving 'pro-democratic' self-determination. In other words, the post-Charter self-help paradigm, for good or ill, still describes the existing law relating to the initiation of force.

Given this conclusion, where is the law going? Is the international system evolving toward a pro-democratic paradigm or not? While it is impossible to answer this question with any certainty, three scenarios seem plausible.

First, it is conceivable that there will be no significant change in the post-charter self-help paradigm. States may continue to claim the right to use force to correct injustices and promote self-determination as they determine. While there may be increased great power cooperation, this does not necessarily indicate that all states will refrain from acting to promote self-determination. It should be noted, for example, that even while the Soviet Union was allowing the East European states to go their own way, the United States was acting forcefully in Panama. Moreover, the changed nature of Europe may have little to do with the actions of states in other parts of the world. Islamic states, African states, and others may continue to be motivated by diverse definitions of self-determination and justice and may, when appropriate, use force to realize these claims.[119]

A second possible scenario involves the ultimate acceptance of the pro-democratic paradigm. Even though the international system has not yet come to accept a definition of a legitimate regime, it is possible that the international community is evolving toward such definition. Before 1945, human rights was not even a legitimate topic of conversation in international discourse;[120] now, even though definitions of human rights vary greatly, the notion that individuals have certain rights in the international system is generally accepted.[121] It is possible that over time more refinements will be made in this area of the law and the provisions of instruments such as the Covenant on Civil and Political Rights will begin to be reflected in practice. This may then give rise to an accepted notion of legitimacy and a concomitant right to intervene to promote such legitimacy.

Finally, there is even a possibility that Article 2(4) could be rehabilitated. The recent actions by the United Nations in the Gulf may indicate a willingness to return to a more restrictive approach to force. Even though the Iraqi invasion is an easy case because it involved obvious aggression for territorial aggrandizement, it is possible that the effect of the UN response will be a reinvigoration of the norm. With the world apparently rallying around the Charter in this case, the effect may be to encourage states to be more supportive of Charter norms in the future. Having committed themselves as a matter of principle in this case, states may be more inclined to defend the honor of Article 2(4) in the future. If this were to occur, it could lead to a new consensus on the unilateral use of force. Article 2(4) could actually become reflective of authoritative state practice.

A recommended *jus ad bellum*

Whether these or other plausible scenarios will come about is likely to remain unclear for some time. What is clear, however, is that the current post-Charter self-help regime leaves much to be desired. A system that provides very little in normative restraints on the recourse to force, that allows states to use force to promote self-determination and justice as they may choose to define them, is destructive of world order. For policy makers, a course of action that would promote the return to something more closely resembling Article 2(4) would seem to make sense.

Given the recent developments in the United Nations system, the greater potential for great power cooperation, and the commitment of the international community in the Iraqi conflict, the possibility of reestablishing the Charter framework for the recourse to force seems greater than at any other time since 1945. In consequence, we would recommend the following framework for the law relating to the recourse to force. This proposal, we believe, would move the international system closer to a more stable and predictable normative structure. First, we will set out our suggestions for lawful uses of force. Next, we will examine what we believe should be regarded as unlawful uses of force. Finally, we discuss four advantages of our proposal: its clarity of language; its treatment of the changed nature of international conflict; its recognition of the need for limited self-help; and its capacity to enhance international order.

Lawful uses of force

Self-defense

As under the Charter paradigm, self-defense would be a permissible ground for states to take recourse to force. Our proposal sets out three explicit circumstances under which a state may lawfully use force to defend itself: armed attack; imminent attack; and indirect aggression.

Armed attack   First, states would be allowed to use force in response to an overt armed attack. This would simply reaffirm the language of Article 51. When one state engaged in a clear, obvious armed attack against another, the victim state would have the right to respond with force. The only restriction on this right of the aggrieved state would be the traditional requirements of necessity and proportionality.

Imminent attack   Second, states would be allowed to use force to respond to an 'imminent' armed attack. It seems only logical to assert that states need not be required to wait until the bombs drop or the troops cross their borders before they can take defensive action. Given the technology of modern weaponry, the right of *effective*[122] self-defense could become meaningless if a state were required to weather a first hit before it could respond. In accepting anticipatory self-defense as a permissible ground for the use of force, we posit that the burden of proof should fall upon the state exercising this right. The state must demonstrate that an armed attack is truly 'imminent' and that its preemptive action is necessary.

Indirect aggression   As noted in Chapter 6, the International Court of Justice held in the *Nicaragua* case that indirect aggression could rise to the level of an 'armed attack,' engendering a right of self-defense under Article 51. One of the main difficulties with the Court's decision was that it set the threshold of armed attack unduly high.

We accept the notion that indirect aggression can, in some cases, be tantamount to an armed attack. We would, however, propose a lower threshold than that suggested by the International Court of Justice. In our view, indirect aggression (subject to certain qualifications) can be regarded as an armed attack in three instances: covert actions, interventions in civil/mixed conflicts, and certain terrorist actions.

Covert action. While every covert action not undertaken in self-defense is delictual, not every one constitutes an 'armed attack.' It is impossible to determine with absolute precision when a covert action rises to the level of an armed attack. We nevertheless believe that a reasonable assessment of a covert action's character can be made on the basis of three interrelated factors: the nature of the activities; the severity of the effect of the activities; and the temporal duration of the activities.

Nature of activities. We believe that a host of covert activities could rise to the level of an armed attack. These would include such state actions as assassination, destruction of buildings, attacks against military and civilian targets, sabotage, and other acts of violence. The critical common denominator in all these would be their fundamentally *violent* nature. Covert actions such as bribery of public officials and financial support for political movements would be excluded from this category. Although these non-violent actions would be illegal violations of the sovereignty of the target state, we do not consider them to be equivalent to an armed attack. In short, the necessary precondition for an armed attack is *violence.*

Severity of effect. The effect of the violent covert activities in question should be comparable in severity to the effect of an overt armed attack. This level of severity would obviously vary with the nature of the action. Sabotaging a single small building that contained a limited amount of military equipment would not rise to the level of an armed attack. Assassinating a state's president, destroying a major military compound with explosives, or poisoning a water filtration plant would.

Temporal duration. A third factor to be weighed is the temporal duration of covert activities. A one-time covert act producing an effect of great severity might by itself be sufficient to constitute an armed attack. Activities producing effects of lesser severity, however, might only constitute an armed attack if they were part of an ongoing pattern of behavior. If the head of state were assassinated, that one act *per se* could be equated to an armed attack. The isolated destruction of a single small building might not be sufficient to be considered an armed attack; nevertheless, the destruction of a number of such structures over a period of time could be sufficient.

Support of rebels. At what point does outside state support of a rebel movement rise to the level of an armed attack? This question proved to be one of the most contentious ones debated during the Central American conflict of the 1980s. In order to answer this inherently difficult question, three interrelated factors must be weighed: the nature of outside support; the severity of the effects of outside support; and the attributability of the effects to the intervening state.

Nature of support. As noted above, the International Court of Justice in *Nicaragua* set the 'armed attack' threshold at a very high level. Specifically, it held that only the introduction of 'armed bands' or 'mercenaries' into a target state would rise to the level of armed attack. We disagree. We contend that a whole *range of actions* could cross the armed attack threshold: a state's provision to rebels of significant financial support; a state's provision of weapons and other equipment, intelligence, command and control support, and training; and, of course, a state's introduction of armed bands and mercenaries.

Severity of effect. In determining whether a state's actions constitute an armed attack, the *intention* of the intervening state is not dispositive. Nor, moreover, is the *amount of aid* provided by the intervening state to the rebels. The key element in determining whether a state's support of rebels engenders the right of self-defense is the *effect on the target state* of the outside support. The degree of outside support for rebels must be sufficient to produce 'substantial effects' within the target state. Any 'effects' akin to those caused by a conventional attack by regular armed forces should be regarded as 'substantial' ones. As with covert actions, a temporal factor should affect the determination of what constitutes substantiality. 'Substantial effects' could be the result of a single prominent action or of a series of lesser actions undertaken over a period of time.

Attributability of effects to the intervening state. Unlike effects produced by covert action, effects produced by a state's support of rebels are not directly caused by the intervening state. The intervening state merely provides various forms of assistance to the rebels; the rebels, in turn, undertake actions producing effects within their state. Accordingly, for an 'armed attack' to be attributable to the intervening state, the effects within the target state must be demonstrated to be *directly linked* to the intervenor's assistance. For example, if it were proven that an intervening state provided munitions and logistical support to rebel forces, and that those forces employed that assistance in raids against government targets tantamount to an overt armed attack, then the intervening state should be considered to have effectively committed an 'armed attack.' Under such circumstances, the victim state could use force in self-defense against the intervening state.

Terrorist action   As with covert action, every terrorist act is delictual, though not every terrorist act constitutes an 'armed attack.' It is impossible to determine precisely when a terrorist act rises to the level of an armed attack. We nevertheless believe that a host of terrorist acts can do so. Depending on the attendant circumstances, these might include such actions as assassination, destruction of buildings, attacks against military and civilian targets, and sabotage.

As noted in Chapter 9, a terrorist *act* is distinguished by at least three specific qualities:

a. actual or threatened *violence*;
b. a '*political*' objective; and
c. an *intended audience*.

Random acts of violence performed without deliberate political objectives should not be considered 'terrorism,' even if they do inspire 'terror.' Neither should non-violent acts, done for political purposes and directed at a specific target group. Nor, properly speaking, should politically-motivated acts of violence, when undertaken without any particular audience in mind. Accordingly, an 'act of terrorism' should be considered *'the threat or use of violence with the intent of causing fear in a target group, in order to achieve political objectives.'*

In order to justify a forcible state response, the effect of the terrorist act or acts in question must be comparable to the effect of an overt armed attack. This 'armed attack threshold' varies with three interrelated factors: the *locus* of the terrorist act; the *temporal duration* of the terrorist act; and the *severity of injury* the act inflicts upon the state.

Locus. The locus of a terrorist act may be either within a responding state's territory or outside it. Though scholars have generally not isolated this factor, we believe that it is a critical variable for determining the 'armed attack threshold.' Because it violates a state's 'territorial integrity,' a terrorist act occurring within a state's borders constitutes an inherently greater injury to that state's sovereignty than does an identical act abroad.

Temporal duration. A second factor to be weighed is the temporal duration of terrorist acts. A terrorist act can be a single, isolated occurrence or part of an on-going pattern of behavior. The latter variety of act, irrespective of its locus or severity, is more likely to rise to the level of an 'armed attack' because it causes a continuing injury to the state.

Severity of injury to the state. The 'severity' of injury to the state caused by a terrorist act can range across a broad spectrum of acts, although where precisely an act should be placed on this spectrum is debatable. At one end of the spectrum are acts causing injuries of minor severity to the state. We believe that these acts would include ones such as the temporary detention of a private citizen, the destruction of a private citizen's property, or the destruction of a limited amount of government property. Even the killing of a single national could be considered an act inflicting an injury of minor severity upon *the state.* To contend this is not to diminish the tragic results of such an act; rather, it is to underscore that the severity of the act should ultimately be evaluated in terms of its effect upon the state *per se.*

At the other end of the spectrum are acts causing injury of major severity to the state. We believe that these acts would consist of ones which strike at the core of a state's sovereignty. These would include the assassination of a government official, the destruction of a major government installation, or the killing of a large group of nationals *qua* nationals. While we believe that the killing of one national, or perhaps a small number of them, should not be regarded as inflicting severe injury to the state, we nonetheless contend that the killing of a large group of nationals should be so regarded. When a large number of nationals are attacked solely on the basis of their nationality, such an attack on what can reasonably be considered an embodiment of the state's sovereignty would seem to cause the state an injury of major severity.

In assessing whether the 'armed attack threshold' has been reached, the locus of the act, its temporal duration, and the severity of injury it inflicts upon the state must be considered simultaneously. As each of these three factors varies, so, too, will the assessment of whether an 'armed attack' has occurred. For example, an attack of a given severity occurring abroad might not be tantamount to an 'armed attack,' while one of equal severity occurring within a state's territory might be. Because an act within a state's borders self-evidently violates that state's 'territorial integrity,' it is reasonable to posit a lower standard for 'severity' for terrorist acts occurring there than for acts occurring outside a state's territory. Similarly, a single act producing an injury of great severity to the state might by itself be sufficient to constitute an armed attack, whereas activities producing injuries of lesser severity might only constitute an armed attack only if they were part of an ongoing pattern of behavior. In addition to the question of which terrorist acts engender a right of forcible response is the question of what entities constitute permissible *targets for a self-defense response.* There are two such possible targets: the terrorist actor itself; or a state related in some way to the terrorist actor.

We submit that a self-defense response should be permitted against a terrorist actor under three circumstances. First, force may be employed by a victim state if the terrorist actor is located in that state's jurisdiction or in an area beyond the jurisdiction of any state: for example, the high seas or the airspace over the high seas. Second, a state may take forcible action against a terrorist actor located in another state's jurisdiction if that 'host state' is unable or unwilling to take steps to suppress that actor. Lacking evidence of 'host state' support or sponsorship of the terrorist actor, a victim state may not use force against host state targets *per se.* Rather, its action must be limited to the terrorist actor alone. Third, a victim state may employ force against a terrorist actor located in a state which is supporting or sponsoring the activities of the terrorist actor.

Depending on the circumstances, a self-defense response should also be permitted against a state involved with a terrorist actor. Here, we propose an 'attributability' requirement similar to that which we advanced for state support of rebels. As noted in Chapter 9, a state may support or sponsor terrorist actors. In either of these cases, the effects produced by a state's action are not *directly* caused by the state. Instead, the state merely provides various forms of assistance to the terrorist actors; the terrorists, in turn, undertake actions producing effects on the victim state. Accordingly, for an 'armed attack' to be attributable to the sponsoring or supporting state, the effects on the victim state must be demonstrated to be *directly linked* to the state's assistance. For example, if it were proven that a state provided munitions and logistical support to terrorist actors, and that those terrorists employed that assistance in an action reaching the 'armed attack threshold,' then the sponsoring or supporting state should be considered itself to have effectively committed an 'armed attack.' Under such circumstances, the victim state could use force in self-defense against the terrorist-linked state.

Intervention to protect nationals

Provided that four criteria are satisfied, a state should be permitted to intervene to protect its nationals. First, the nationals of the intervening state must be in imminent danger of loss of life or limb. Second, the target state must be unwilling or unable to protect the nationals of the intervening state. Third, the purpose of the intervention must be limited to the removal of the threatened nationals. The intervention must not be used as a pretext for any other activities in the territory of the target state. Fourth, the force used in the intervention must be proportionate to the mission of removing the nationals. No force may be used beyond that which is required to accomplish that limited task.

Force authorized by the security council

Finally, as in the Charter paradigm, force authorized by the Security Council would be permissible.

Unlawful uses of force

Aside from the uses of force detailed above, all other uses of force by a state would be prohibited. This would include the use of force to gain territory, to correct past injustices, and to promote self-determination. As noted above, there is virtually universal agreement that the use of force for territorial aggrandizement is currently illegal. To permit such a use of force would be to destroy all vestiges of international order. In addition, even though the post-Charter self-help paradigm seems to allow the use of force to correct injustices and to promote self-determination, we believe that the terms 'injustice' and 'self-determination' are excessively subjective. Were states allowed to use force to promote their own brands of justice and self-determination, nearly any use of force could be legitimized.

Advantages of our proposed jus ad bellum

Our proposed *jus ad bellum* may not constitute the 'ideal' regime. Nevertheless, it represents a significant improvement over both the Charter paradigm and the existing post-Charter self-help paradigm. The advantages of our proposal can be evaluated in the light of four criteria: its clarity of language; the degree to which it addresses the nature of international conflict; the degree to which it recognizes the need for limited self-help; and its capacity to enhance international order.

First, our suggested *jus ad bellum* eliminates some of the interpretation problems of the Charter framework. In particular, the proposal attempts to deal with the meaning of Article 51 and the nature of an 'armed attack.' It allows for an explicit recognition of several categories of action that may give rise to the right of self-defense including imminent attack and indirect aggression. Our approach includes a number of subjective elements; nevertheless, we believe that it contains fewer than other approaches.

Second, our proposal addresses the changed nature of international conflict. It responds to both civil and mixed conflicts and to the problem of state-sponsored terrorism. As noted throughout our work, these types of conflict have been prominent features of the post-Second World War system. Any legal framework must specifically address these varieties of conflict if it is to be effective.

Third, our framework recognizes the need for self-help for the protection of nationals. It acknowledges that states are frequently unable to receive the cooperation of the target state when their nationals are in danger and that sometimes they may be required to engage in unilateral action to extricate their citizens. Our proposal would legitimize such action, subject to the criteria set out above.

Fourth, our proposal recognizes the critical importance of a restrictive *jus ad bellum* for international order. As we have consistently emphasized, the post-Charter self-help paradigm is destructive. It is far too subjective and allows states excessive justifications for the resort to force. If international law is to promote international stability, the normative framework for the recourse to force must be as limited and objective as possible. In our proposal, we consider all uses of force to correct past injustices and to promote self-determination to be impermissible. Although any given use of force for these purposes could indeed be just, it seems impossible to devise any realistic criteria that would be both reasonably objective and acceptable to all states. Accordingly, we support a strict prohibition on the unilateral recourse to force for these purposes.

If a particular incident were to arise in which states claimed that force should be used either to correct an injustice or to promote self-determination, we believe that the Security Council would be the most appropriate body to consider the issue. If the Council determined then that the matter were so grave that it constituted a threat to the peace, the Council could authorize forcible measures. Such a multilateral approach would, in our view, be far more preferable to the unilateralism of the post-Charter self-help paradigm. It would not eliminate the subjective aspects of defining justice or self-determination. However, before any forcible action could be undertaken, it would require Security Council endorsement.

Notes and references

1 INTERNATIONAL LAW AND THE USE OF FORCE

1 Murphy, 'Iraqi Invasion Force Seizes Control of Kuwait; US Bans Trade, Joins Allies in Freezing Assets,' *Wash. Post*, Aug. 3, 1990: A1 col. 4.
2 Balz and Devroy, 'Bush Leaves Open Military Options,' *Wash. Post*, Aug. 3, 1991: A1, col. 1, A26, col. 1.
3 Ibid.: col. 2.
4 Cited in Bolen, 'Arms Flow to Iraq Halted by Soviets,' *N.Y. Times*, Aug. 3, 1990: A10, col. 1.
5 *UN Charter*, Art. 2, para. 4.
6 *UNSC Res. 660*, Aug. 2, 1990.
7 *UNSC Res. 661*, Aug. 6, 1990.
8 Even though the Security Council had imposed economic sanctions against South Africa (1963) and Rhodesia (1966), these Security Council actions were not taken in response to an actual use of force by one state against another. For a more complete examination, see Chapter 4 below.
9 *UNSC Res. 678*, Nov. 29, 1990.
10 See J. L. Brierly, *Law of Nations*: 1 (6th Waldock ed. 1963) for a discussion of the origins of the modern state system.
11 See R. Lieber, *No Common Power*: 248 (2nd ed. 1991).
12 K. J. Holsti, *Peace and War: Armed Conflicts and International Order 1648–1989*: 274–278 (1991).
13 'Marullo, War and Militarism,' in G. Ritzer and J. C. Calhoun, *Social Problems* (1992).
14 See, for example, S. Brown, *The Causes and Prevention of War* (1987); E. McNeil, *The Nature of Human Conflict* (1965); M. Small, *Was War Necessary?* (1980); J. Stoessinger, *Why Nations Go To War* (1982); K. Waltz, *Man, The State and War* (1954); Q. Wright, *A Study of War* (2nd ed. 1965).
15 See H. Bull, *The Anarchical Society*: 46–51 (1977).
16 R. Lieber, op. cit.: 5.
17 See Claude, 'The Rejection of Collective Security', in I. Claude, *American Approaches to World Affairs*: 51–67 (1986).
18 The concept of sovereignty will be explored in greater depth in Chapter 2. For an excellent discussion of the origins of this concept, see J. Brierly, *The Law of Nations*: 7–16 (6th Waldock ed. 1962).
19 We use the terms 'legal norm' and 'legal rule' here interchangeably. We recognize, however, that certain international relations scholars have distinguished 'norms' from 'rules.'
     Professor Krasner, for example, defines 'norms' as 'standards of behavior defined

in terms of rights and obligations' and 'rules' as 'specific prescriptions or proscriptions for action.' Krasner, 'Structural Causes and Regime Consequences: Regimes as Intervening Variables,' in S. Krasner (ed.) *International Regimes*: 2 (1983). Professor Young defines 'rules' as 'well-defined guides to action or standards setting forth actions that members are expected to perform (or to refrain from performing) under appropriate circumstances.' O. Young, *International Cooperation*: 16 (1989).

20 For a discussion of 'natural law,' see Chapter 2.

21 We use 'regime' here to connote 'a comprehensive set of legal norms within a particular issue area.' For example, legal scholars commonly refer to the 'Regime of Deep Seabed Mining' or the 'Regime of Outer Space.'

Though in some ways reminiscent, our definition of 'regime' should be distinguished from that advanced by a number of international relations scholars including Stephen Krasner, Robert Keohane, and Oran Young. See, e.g. Krasner op. cit.; R. Keohane, *After Hegemony* (1984); O. Young op. cit.

Professor Krasner, for example, defines regimes as 'sets of implicit or explicit principles, norms, rules, and decision-making procedures around which actors' expectations converge in a given area of international relations.' Krasner op. cit.: 2.

22 Arend, 'International Law and the Recourse to Force: A Shift in Paradigms,' *Stan. J. Int'l L.* 27: 1 (1990).

23 The word 'paradigm' may be one of the most abused terms in the social science literature. Since the publication of Thomas S. Kuhn's *The Structure of Scientific Revolutions*, the word has become a staple of contemporary scholarship in the natural sciences, sociology, political science, economics, and even law. We do not wish to contribute to confusion by employing the concept, but rather employ it as a useful tool to aid in the understanding of law and change.

As we will use the term, a 'paradigm' is a model for understanding reality. It is a '*specific, comprehensive* framework that attempts to explain behavior in a particular area.' In physics, for example, one could speak of the 'Newtonian paradigm.' This paradigm was a particular model for understanding the physical world. Scientists operating within this paradigm shared basic assumptions about the laws of physics. All phenomena were to be understood by reference to the Newtonian paradigm. Similarly, a 'legal paradigm' is a conception of a specific legal regime. It is an understanding of the law in a given area. When scholars or state officials accept a legal paradigm, they accept certain assumptions about what the content of the law is.

Our use of the word 'paradigm' is somewhat different than Kuhn's. In his 1969 'Postscript' to *The Structure of Scientific Revolutions*, Kuhn explains that he uses the term 'paradigm' in 'two different senses.' T. Kuhn, *The Structure of Scientific Revolutions*: 175 (2nd ed. 1970). Explains Kuhn:

> On the one hand, it [paradigm] stands for the entire constellation of beliefs, values, techniques, and so on shared by the members of a given community. On the other, it denotes one sort of element in that constellation, the concrete puzzle-solutions which, employed as models or examples, can replace explicit rules as a basis for the solution of the remaining puzzles or normal science.

Thus, paradigm in the first sense represents a complete framework for a discipline. It constitutes the basic assumptions and methods that the members of a given discipline hold in theory and practice. In the second sense, a paradigm is an 'exemplar,' a model that members of a discipline use to address a given problem or 'puzzle.' Ibid.: 187–191.

For another use of the concept of 'paradigm' in connection with international law, see Falk, 'A New Paradigm for International Legal Studies: Prospects and Proposals,' in R. Falk, F. Kratochwil and S. Mendlovitz (eds) *International Law: A Contemporary Perspective.* 651–702 (1985).

24 In a 1990 article, Professor Tom Farer used the concept of 'paradigm' to refer the United Nations Charter framework for the use of force. Farer, 'Panama: Beyond The Charter Paradigm,' *Am. J. Int'l L.* 84: 503–515 (1990).

25 A 'paradigmatic shift' occurs when one paradigm no longer describes reality and is, accordingly, replaced by a new paradigm.

26 Article 38, paragraph 1 provides:

> The Court, whose function is to decide in accordance with international law such disputes as are submitted to it, shall apply:
>
> a international conventions, whether general or particular, establishing rules expressly recognized by the consenting states;
> b international custom, as evidence of a general practice accepted as law;
> c the general principles of law recognized by the civilized nations;
> d subject to the provisions of Article 59, judicial decision and the teachings of the most qualified publicists of the various nations, as subsidiary means for the determination of the rules of law.
>
> *Statute of the ICJ*, Art. 38, para. 1

27 See M. Akehurst, *A Modern Introduction to International Law.* 23 (6th ed. 1987).

28 On the treaty-making process, see M. Akehurst, op. cit.: 6th ed. 1987 pp. 123–133. L. Henkin, R. Pugh, O. Schachter, and H. Smit, *International Law: Cases and Materials.* 398–414 (2nd ed. 1986).

29 *US Const.*, Art. 2, sec. 2.

30 Michael Akehurst explains that 'there is little agreement about the meaning of the phrase' ['general principles of law recognized by the civilized nations']. M. Akehurst, op. cit. See also, Virally, 'The Sources of International Law,' in Sorensen (ed.) *Manual of Public International Law.* 143 (1968).

31 See Virally, op. cit.: 143.

32 In the *Gentini* case, the Mixed Claims Commission considered prescription as a general principle of international law. *Gentini* Case (Italy v. Venezuela), Mixed Claims Commission, 1903, Ralston, *Venezuelan Arbitrations of 1903:* 720 (1904).

33 See *Chorzow Factory* Case (Germany v. Poland), 1927 *PCIJ*, ser. A., No. 9: 31, in which the Court applied the principle of estoppel.

34 The International Court of Justice used the principle of *res judicata* in *Advisory Opinion, Effects of Awards of Compensation made by the United Nations Administrative Tribunal:* 53, 1954 ICJ.

35 This conception of general principles of law was inspired by Professor William V. O'Brien and is somewhat similar to his approach. See, W. O'Brien, *Law and Morality in Israel's War with the PLO:* 85–86 (1991).

36 See G. Von Glahn, *Law Among Nations.* 23 (5th ed. 1986). See also, W. O'Brien op. cit.: 85–86.

37 See W. Friedmann, *The Changing Structure of International Law*, 197 (1964); L. Henkin, R. Pugh, O. Schachter, and H. Smit, op. cit.: 100–107.

38 See *Corfu Channel* Case (UK v. Albania), *ICJ* 1949d:D 4, 22.

39 M. Akehurst, op. cit.: 37.

40 For a discussion of the binding nature of certain decisions by organs of the European Community, see. F. Kirgis, *International Organizations in their Legal Setting:* 637–653 (1977).

41 *UN Charter*, Art. 25.

42 *UN Charter*, Art. 27. For a discussion of the origins and development of the veto, see L. Goodrich, E. Hambro, and A. Simons, *The Charter of the United Nations*: 215–231 (3rd rev. ed. 1969).
43 *UN Charter*, Art. 10.
44 Ibid., Art. 17.
45 See Falk, 'On the Quasi-Legislative Competence of the General Assembly,' *Am. J. Int'l L.* 60: 782 (1966); Bleicher, 'The Legal Significance of Re-Citation of General Assembly Resolutions,' *Am. J. Int'l L.* 63: 444 (1969).
46 See the comments of a former legal counsel to the United Nations in E. Suy, *Innovations in International Law-Making Process* (1978), cited in G. von Glahn, op. cit.: 18–19.
47 The concepts of 'authority' and 'control' have been prominently developed in the jurisprudence of Myres McDougal, Harold Lasswell and the so-called 'New Haven School.' See McDougal and Lasswell, 'The Identification and Appraisal of Diverse Systems of Public Order,' in M. McDougal (ed.) *Studies in World Public Order*: 13–14 (1960). We believe that these concepts reflect well international law's basis in *state consent*, and hence, are valuable. Our use of the terms 'authority' and 'control,' however, differs in two important respects from that of McDougal and Lasswell.

First, the McDougal-Lasswell approach defines 'international law' as a 'process of authoritative decision-making.' See M. McDougal and M. Reisman, *International Law in Contemporary Perspective*: 1–7 (1981); H. Bull, *The Anarchical Society*: 127–128 (1977) ('McDougal and his school insist that law should be regarded as a social process, more particularly as a process of decision-making that is both authoritative and effective.') As Hedley Bull explains, the McDouglians 'reject the idea of law as a "body of rules" because they hold that this process of authoritative and effective decision-making does not consist simply of the application of a previously existing body of rules, but is shaped by social, moral and political considerations as well.' Ibid. We submit, by contrast, that international law consists of a 'body of rules.' J. Brierly, op. cit.: 10. We contend, nevertheless, that these rules are constituted through a *process* of authoritative state practice.

Second, we posit that *state* officials, national decision-making elites, determine through their policies and formal declarations the 'authority' of putative norms. Accordingly, one can conclude that 'states' hold a particular norm to be 'authoritative' when the words and actions of their leaders over a period of time indicate a perception of 'authority.' Therefore, in our view, the requirement of 'authority' is essentially identical to the traditional positivist requirement of *opinio juris*. In the McDougal jurisprudence, members of the international community determine the authority of putative norms. See, e.g. McDougal, Lasswell, and Reisman, 'Theories About International Law: Prologue to a Configurative Jurisprudence,' reprinted in *International Law Essays*: 43–57 (1981) ('Authority will be sought, not in some mysterious transempirical source of 'obligation' or 'validity,' but rather, empirically, in the perspectives, the genuine expectations, of the people who constitute a given community about the requirements for lawful decision in that community.') Here, the McDouglians seem to mean more than simply the decision-making elites in the various states in the international system. They apparently include other members of the international community: international organizations, transnational groups, individuals, and the like. In adhering to the notion that 'authority' has its roots in *states*, we accept the essential positivist tenet that states remain the primary actors in the international system and that international law is created through state consent.
48 In our view, a rule is 'authoritative' when it is perceived to be legitimate. With an understanding of law as process, McDougal and Lasswell define 'authority' as 'the

structure of expectations concerning who, with what qualifications and mode of selection, is competent to make decisions by what criteria and what procedures.' Ibid.: 13. Professor Anthony D'Amato has explained, '[the members of the New Haven School] seem to view "authoritative" so broadly as to encompass just about any decision made by any international decision-maker.' A. D'Amato, *International Law: Process and Prospect*: 11–12 (1987).

49 Professor Thomas M. Franck has most recently developed the concept of legitimacy in connection with international rules. See T. Franck, *The Power of Legitimacy Among Nations* (1990).

50

> Not only must the acts concerned amount to a settled practice, but they must also be such, or be carried out in such a way, as to be evidence of a belief that this practice is rendered obligatory by the existence of a rule of law requiring it. The need for such a belief, i.e. the existence of a subjective element, is implicit in the very notion of *opinio juris sive necessitatis*. The states concerned must therefore feel that they are conforming to what amounts to a legal obligation.

'North Sea Continental Shelf Cases' (FRG v. Den.) (FRG v. Neth.), 1969 *ICJ* 4, para. 77.

51 McDougal and Lasswell explain that '[b]y control we refer to an effective voice in decision, whether authorized or not.' McDougal and Lasswell, op. cit.: 14. In our view, a rule is 'controlling' when it is followed, irrespective of whether or not it is perceived to be authoritative. When a would-be norm *is* both authoritative and controlling, it can be considered law: 'The conjunction of common expectations concerning authority with a high degree of corroboration in actual operation is what we understand by law.' Ibid.

52 Cf. Moore, 'Prolegomenon to the Jurisprudence of Lasswell-McDougal,' *Va. L. Rev.* (1971).

53 J. Brierly, op. cit.: 51.

2 HISTORICAL OVERVIEW THE DEVELOPMENT OF LEGAL NORMS RELATING TO THE RECOURSE TO FORCE

1 See Moore, 'Development of the International Law of Conflict Management,' in J. Moore, F. Tipson, and R. Turner (eds) *National Security Law* 47, 51–83 (1990).

2 For a discussion of the Holy War concept, see J. Walsh, *The Mighty From Their Thrones: Power in the Biblical Tradition* (1987).

3 Much has been written on the Just War doctrine. See, e.g. J. Johnson, *Just War Tradition and the Restraint of War* (1981); W. O'Brien, *The Conduct of Just and Limited War* (1981); P. Ramsay, *The Just War: Force and Political Responsibility* (1968); R. Tucker, *The Just War* (1960); M. Walzer, *Just and Unjust Wars* (1977).

4 Aristotle, *The Politics*: 317 (E. Barker ed. 1971).

5 Ibid.: 319.

6 Ibid.

7 In his translation of Cicero, George Sabine explains that for Aristotle war is justified 'to establish political rule over those who would be benefited thereby.' M. Cicero, *On the Commonwealth*: 216 at n. 71 (G. Sabine and S. Barney trans. 1976).

8 Aristotle, op. cit.: 319.

9 Ibid.: 3.

10 Moore, op. cit.: 53.

11 F. Russell, *The Just War in the Middle Ages*: 12 (1975).

12 Cicero, 'De Officiis,' in *Cicero in Twenty-Eight Volumes* 16: 37 (Walter Miller trans. 1913).
13 Cicero, *On the Commonwealth*, op. cit.: 217.
14 Ibid.
15 See Russell, op. cit.
16 W. Stevenson, *Christian Love and Just War: Moral Paradox and Political Life in St. Augustine and His Modern Interpreters* (1987).
17 M. Paolucci (ed.) *The Political Writings of St. Augustine*: 38–43.
18 T. Aquinas, 'Summa Theologiae, Seconda Secundae,' Q. 40 (Art. 1), in A. D'Entreves, *Aquinas: Selected Political Writings*: 159 (J. Dawson trans. 1948).
19 See W. O'Brien, op. cit. 19–20 for a discussion of Aquinas's conception of just cause.
20 T. Aquinas op. cit.: 159.
21 Ibid.
22 T. Aquinas, op. cit.: 161.
23 Ibid. See also W. O'Brien, op. cit.: 33–35.
24 F. Suarez, 'A Work on the Three Theological Virtues: Faith, Hope, and Charity,' in J. B. Scott (ed.) *F. Suarez, Selections from Three Works* 2: 816 (1944).
25 On the natural law approach, see H. Rommen, *The Natural Law* (R. Hanley trans. 1947).
26 T. Aquinas, Summa Theologica, Q. 91 (Art. 2), A. Pegis (ed.) *Introduction to St. Thomas Aquinas*: 618 (1948).
27 J. B. Scott (ed.) *H. Grotius, De Jure Belli ac Pacis, Libri Tres*: 169–186 (F. Kelsey trans., 1925).
28 Ibid.: 172.
29 Ibid.: 173 (footnote omitted).
30 Ibid.: 550.
31 Ibid.: 551.
32 Ibid.
33 For an examination of the concept of sovereignty, see J. Brierly, *The Law of Nations*: 7–16 (6th Waldock ed. 1981).
34 'The Antelope,' (Wheat. 10: 66 (1825).
35 For a discussion of the Peace of Westphalia, see K. Holsti, *Peace and War: Armed Conflicts and International Order 1648–1989*: 25–42 (1991).
36 See J. Brierly, op. cit: 51–56.
37 W. Hall, *Int'l Law*.: 52 (1880).
38 Ibid.: 315.
39 G. Hackworth, *Digest of International Law* 6: 152–154 (1943).
40 'The Naulilaa,' *UN Reports of Arbitral Awards* 2: 1011, cited in M. Whiteman, *Digest of Int'l Law* 149 (1971).
41 W. O'Brien, op. cit.: 24–25.
42 The Naulilaa, op. cit.
43 Ibid.
44 'The Caroline,' J. Moore, *Digest of Int'l Law* 2: 412 (1906).
45 Ibid.
46 Letter from Mr Webster to Mr Fox (Apr. 24, 1841), *Brit. & For. St. Papers* 29: 1129, 1138 (1857).
47 See J. Brierly, op. cit.: 406.
48 Convention Respecting the Limitation of the Employment of force for the Recovery of Contract Debts, Hague Convention II of 1907, *Stat.* 36: 2241, *Malloy's T.S.* 2: 2248.
49 Ibid.: art. 1.
50 Ibid.
51 See G. Hackworth op. cit. for a discussion of this convention.

52 On the First World War and the League of Nations, see H. Foley, *Woodrow Wilson's Case for the League of Nations* (1923); F. P. A. Walters, *A History of the League of Nations* (1952).
53 I. Claude, *Swords into Plowshares*: 45–46 (4th ed. 1971).
54 Ibid.
55 *Covenant of the League of Nations*, Art. 12, reprinted in I. Claude, op. cit.: 453–462.
56 Ibid.: Art. 15.
57 Ibid.: Art. 13.
58 Ibid.: Art. 12.
59 See Moore, op. cit.: 65–68 for an elaboration of these problems.
60 *Covenant of the League of Nations*, Art. 15.
61 Professor Moore has described this approach as '[l]argely procedural.' Moore, op. cit.: 52.
62 *Covenant of the League of Nations*, Art. 10.
63 I. Brownlie, *International Law and the Use of Force by States*: 62 (1963).
64 Ibid.: 63.
65 See ibid.: 68–69.
66 See ibid.: 69–70.
67 *Protocol for the Pacific Settlement of International Disputes*, Art. 2, cited in ibid.: 69–70.
68 Y. Dinstein, *War, Aggression and Self-Defence*: 80 (1988).
69 I. Brownlie, op. cit.: 71.
70 Kellogg-Briand Pact, Aug. 26, 1928, *Stat* 46: 2343, *T.S.* No. 796, *L.N.T.S.* 94: 57.
71 Ibid.: Art. 1.
72 Ibid.: Art. 2.
73 See Wright, 'The Meaning of the Pact of Paris,' *Am. J. Int'l L.* 27: 39, 42–43; see also Moore, op. cit.: 68–71.
74 Y. Dinstein, op. cit.: 81–82.
75 Ibid.: 82.
76 See, e.g. G. Kennan, *American Diplomacy, 1900–1950*: 83 (1951).
77 Moore, op. cit.: 71.
78 I. Brownlie, op. cit.: 70.
79 See Moore, op. cit.: 70–71.
80 I. Brownlie, op. cit.: 74–80.
81 Moore, op. cit.: 71.
82 Y. Dinstein, op. cit. 82.
83 I. Brownlie, op. cit.: 76.
84 Ibid.
85 Ibid.: 74–80.
86 Cited in G. Hackworth, op. cit.: 680.

3 THE UNITED NATIONS CHARTER FRAMEWORK FOR THE RESORT TO FORCE

1 *UN Charter*, preamble.
2 On the formulation of the United Nations Charter, see I. Claude, *Swords Into Plowshares*: 57–80 (4th ed. 1970); R. Russell and J. Muther, *A History of the United Nations Charter: The Role of the United States, 1940–45* (1958).
3 *UN Charter*, Art. 110.
4 [This reference has been deleted from the text.]
5 Professor Brownlie has explained that '[t]he provisions of the Charter relating to the

peaceful settlement of disputes and non-resort to the use of force are universally regarded as prohibiting reprisals which involve the use of force.' I. Brownlie, *International Law and the Use of Force*. 281 (1963).

6   Article 51 goes on to provide that '[m]easures taken by Members in the exercise of this right of self-defense shall be immediately reported to the Security Council and shall not in any way affect the authority and responsibility of the Security Council under the present Charter to take at any time such action as it deems necessary in order to maintain or restore international peace and security.' *UN Charter*, Art. 51.

7   M. Akehurst, *A Modern Introduction to International Law*. 225 (5th ed. 1984).

8   Ibid.

9   Ibid.: 225–226.

10 This is the generally accepted understanding of the Charter framework. As Professor Schachter has argued, '[f]orce could meet force [i.e. in self-defense] but, unless authorized by the Security Council, force could not answer a non-forcible deprivation of rights.' Schachter, 'In Defense of International Rules on the Use of Force,' *U. Chi. L. Rev.* 53: 113, 126 (1986) (footnote omitted).

11 M. McDougal and F. Feliciano, *Law and Minimum World Public Order: The Legal Regulation of International Coercion*: 18–19 (1961).

12 Ibid.

13 In the Preamble to the United Nations Charter, the parties affirm their dedication 'to establish conditions under which justice and respect for the obligations arising from treaties and other sources of international law can be maintained.' UN Charter, Preamble. Moreover, Article 1(2) of the Charter provides that one of the purposes of the Charter is '[t]o achieve international co-operation in solving international problems of an economic, social, cultural, or humanitarian character, and in promoting and encouraging respect for human rights and for fundamental freedoms for all without distinction as to race, sex, language, or religion.' *UN Charter*, Art. 1, para. 2.

14 See Schachter, op. cit.: 126 (footnote omitted). Professor William V. O'Brien has been even more forceful than Professor Schachter. He contends that 'modern international law has sacrificed justice in its attempt virtually to eliminate the competence of the state to engage in war unilaterally.' W. O'Brien, *The Conduct of Just and Limited War*. 23 (1981). Professor Inis L. Claude, Jr. approaches the issue somewhat differently. He seems to suggest that the Charter has not completely eliminated 'justice' as a legitimate reason to use force. It has simply limited the number of 'just causes' to one: self-defense. Claude, 'Just Wars: Doctrines and Institutions,' *Pol. Sci. Q.* 95: 92–94 (1980).

15 *S.C. Res. 479* (Sept. 28, 1980).

16 Declaration on Principles of International Law Concerning Friendly Relations and Co-operation Among States in Accordance with the Charter of the United Nations, *G.A. Res. 2625*, UN GAOR Supp. (No. 28) 25: 121, *UN Doc. A/8028* (1970).

17 Military and Paramilitary Activities in and against Nicaragua (Nicar. V. US), *Merits*, 1986 *ICJ* 14 (Judgment of June 27) [hereinafter cited as Nicaragua case].

18 Ibid.: paras 187–192.

19 See Higgins, 'The Attitude of Western States Towards Legal Aspects of the Use of Force,' in A. Cassese, *The Current Legal Regulation of the Use of Force*. 435 (1986) ('the West has regarded the general scope of Art. 2(4) and Art. 51 of the UN Charter as satisfactory, and has been reluctant to see elaboration of these principles through codification, lest the balance change.')

20 Counter-Memorial of the United States (Nicar. v. US), cited in Nicaragua case: para. 187.

21 See, Bokor-Szegö, 'The Attitude of Socialist States Towards the International Regulation of the Use of Force,' in A. Cassese, op. cit.: 453.

22 Sahovic, 'Non-Aligned Countries and the Current Regulation of the Use of Force,' in A. Cassese, op. cit.: 479.
23 This is a phrase used by Professor John Norton Moore. For a discussion of this argument, see N. Ronzitti, *Rescuing Nationals Abroad Through Military Coercion and Intervention on Grounds of Humanity.* 1–3 (1985).
24 See D. Bowett, *Self-Defense in International Law.* 184–193 (1958); M. McDougal & F. Feliciano, op. cit.: 233–241; J. Stone, *Aggression and World Order.* 92–101 (1958); Moore, 'The Secret War in Central America and the Future of World Order,' *Am. J. Int'l L.* 80: 23, 82–83 (1986).
25 Moore, ibid.: 83.
26 See Moore, 'The Use of Force in International Relations: Norms Concerning the Initiation of Coercion,' in J. Moore, F. Tipson, and R. Turner (eds), *National Security Law.* 139–140 (1990).
27 See Moore, 'Toward an Applied Theory for the Regulation of Intervention,' in J. Moore (ed.) *Law and Civil War in the Modern World.* 3 (1974).
28 'Mixed conflict' is an abbreviated form of Professor Moore's term 'mixed civil-international' conflict. Ibid.
29 For a discussion of forms of covert actions, see K. Holsti, *International Relations: A Framework for Analysis.* 248–280 (4th ed. 1983).
30 Dulles, 'Address Before the American Bar Association, Aug. 26, 1953,' *State Dept. Release* No. 458: 6.
31 See Dulles, 'The General Assembly,' *For. Aff.:* 1 (1945).
32 For a discussion of this viewpoint, see T. Franck, *Nation Against Nation.* 184–204 (1985); A. Gerson, *The Kirkpatrick Mission* (1991).
33 See Reisman, 'Termination of the United States Declaration Under Article 36(2) of the Statute of the International Court of Justice,' in A. Arend (ed.) *The United States and the Compulsory Jurisdiction of the International Court of Justice.* 71–103 (1986).
34 See I. Claude, 'UN Efforts at Settlement of the Falkland Islands Crisis,' in A. Coll and A. Arend (eds) *The Falklands War: Lessons for Strategy, Diplomacy, and International Law.* 118–131 (1985).
35 *G.A. Res. 3314, UN GAOR Supp.* (No. 31) 29, *UN Doc. A/9631:* 141 (1974) [hereinafter cited as Definition of Aggression].
36 For a discussion of the origins of Article 7 of the Definition of Aggression resolution, see B. Ferencz, *Defining International Aggression: The Search For World Peace* 2: 47–49 (1975).
37 *Definition of Aggression*, op. cit., Art. 7, [Emphasis added.]
38 Ferencz explains that '[t]hose who are so inclined may find in the formulation of Article 7 and the related texts, sufficient ambiguity to justify an assertion that any force may legitimately be applied to overthrow alien oppressors who deprive 'peoples' of an inherent right to self-determination, freedom and independence.' B. Ferencz, op. cit.: 48 (footnote omitted).
39 As Professor Edwin Brown Firmage has explained '[t]he term [war of national liberation] has been variously used by Soviet jurists and apologists to justify war in three situations: first, in defense of the homeland; second, to liberate a people from capitalism; and third, to accomplish the separation of a colony from governance by a colonial power.' Firmage, 'The "War of National Liberation" and the Third World,' in J. Moore (ed.) *Law and Civil War In The Modern World.* 304, 309 (1974) (footnote omitted). See also, Ginsburg, 'Wars of National Liberation and the Modern Law of Nations – The Soviet Thesis,' *L. & Contemp. Prob.* 29: 910 (1964); Reisman, 'Criteria for the Lawful Use of Force in International Law,' *Yale J. Int'l L.* 10: 280 ('the Soviet Union announced, in effect, that it did not accept Article 2(4); "Wars of national

liberation," an open-textured conception essentially meaning wars the Soviets supported were not, in the Soviet conception violations of Article 2(4).')

40 This contention has often been referred to as the 'Brezhnev Doctrine.' For a general discussion of this doctrine, see B. Meissner, *The Brezhnev Doctrine* (1970).

41 Letter from the Warsaw Pact governments to the Czechoslovak Communist Party Central Committee (July 15, 1968), reprinted in B. Meissner, op. cit.: 40, 41.

42 Kovalev, 'Sovereignty and the Internationalist Obligations of Socialist Countries,' *Pravda*, Sept. 26, 1968, reprinted in English in B. Meissner, op. cit.: 50, 51.

43 See generally, Rosenfeld, 'The Guns of July,' *For. Aff.* 64: 698 (1986).

44 Statement by the President and by the Prime Minister of Dominica Eugenia Charles on US Involvement in Grenada (Oct. 5, 1983), reprinted in J. Moore, *Law and the Grenada Mission*: 91 (1984). As time passed, the United States provided more traditional legal justification for the invasion. In a letter to Professor Edward Gordon, Davis R. Robinson, the Legal Adviser to the Department of State, explained:

> The United States, both before and after the collective action, regarded three well established legal principles as providing a solid legal basis for the action: (1) the lawful governmental authorities of a State may invite the assistance in its territory of military forces of other states or collective organizations in dealing with internal disorder as well as external threats; (2) regional organizations have competence to take measures to maintain international peace and security, consistent with the purposes and principles of the UN and OAS Charters; and (3) the right of States to use force to protect their nationals.

'Letter from Davis R. Robinson, Legal Adviser, US Department of State to Professor Edward Gordon Reiterating US Legal Position Concerning Grenada' (Feb. 10, 1984), reprinted in J. Moore, *Law and the Grenada Mission* op. cit.: 125–126 (1984).

45 Counter-Memorial of the United States of America (Nicar. v. US) 220, para. 517 (submitted by the US government to the Court Aug. 17, 1984); Davis R. Robinson, 'Letter to the Editor in Chief,' *Am. J. Int'l L.* 79: 423 (1985).

46 *Time*, March 31, 1986: 16. See also, Rowles, '"Secret Wars," Self-Defense and the Charter – A Reply to Professor Moore,' *Am. J. Int'l L.* 80: 568, 576–577 (1986) for a discussion of this rationale for US actions.

47 On the legality of the American invasion of Panama, see, e.g. D'Amato, 'The Invasion of Panama Was A Lawful Response to Tyranny,' *Am. J. Int'l L.* 84: 516 (1990); Farer, 'Panama: Beyond the Charter Paradigm,' in ibid.: 503; Nanda, 'The Validity of United States Intervention in Panama under International Law,' in ibid.: 494.

48 When asked for the legal justification for the action on the day of the invasion, Secretary of State James Baker told the press that '[t]he actions that we have taken ... in our view are fully in accordance with international law. The United States, under international law, has an inherent right of self-defense, as recognized in Article 51 of the United Nations Charter and Article 21 of the OAS Charter, which entitles us to take measures necessary to defend our military personnel, our United States nationals and US installations.' Excerpts from 'Statement by Baker on US Policy,' *Wash. Post*, Dec. 21, 1989: A19, col. 5. See also, 'A Transcript of Bush's Address on the Decision to Use Force in Panama,' reprinted in ibid.: col. 1.

49 'Text of Statement by [Marlin] Fitzwater,' *Wash. Post*, Dec. 21, 1989: A19, col. 2.

50 See 'Transcript of Bush's Address on the Decision to Use Force in Panama,' op. cit.: col. 1.

51 Ibid.

52 Professor William V. O'Brien explains that a reprisal refers to 'the use of force as an

act of retaliation by one State against another in the absence of an actual armed attack.' O'Brien 'Reprisals, Deterrence and Self-Defense in Counterterror Operations,' *Va. J. Int'l L.* 30: 421 (1990) fn 1. For other definitions of reprisals, see M. Whiteman, *Digest of International Law* 12: 148–187 (1971).

53 Bowett, 'Reprisals Involving Recourse to Armed Force,' *Am. J. Int'l L.* 66: 1 (1972).

54 I. Brownlie, *International Law and the Use of Force by States* 281 (1963). Professor Bowett echoed this sentiment in his 1972 article, explaining that 'few propositions about international law have enjoyed more support than the proposition that, under the Charter of the United Nations, the use of force by way of reprisals is illegal.' Bowett op. cit.: 1.

55 Ibid.

56 O'Brien op. cit.

57 Bowett op. cit.: 8, 34.

58 Ibid.: 10, 13–14.

59 O'Brien, op. cit.: 432–433.

60 Ibid.: 460–463.

61 Ibid.: 463–467.

62 See Bowett, op. cit.: 2–10.

63 In cataloguing Israeli justifications for various uses of force, Bowett explains that, interestingly enough, 'Israel has relied less and less on a self-defense argument and has taken action which is openly admitted to be a reprisal.' Ibid.: 10. He explains that '[t]he Beirut raid of December 28, 1968, is the obvious example of an action not really defended on the basis of self-defense at all. Indeed, even as a reprisal, the motivation for reprisals seems to have shifted from that of punishment for previous act to deterrence of future possible acts.' Ibid. (footnotes omitted).

64 Ibid.: 10 fn. 38.

65 In a letter to Congress, President Reagan explained that '[t]hese strikes were conducted in the exercise of our right to self-defense under Article 51 of the United Nations Charter.' Letter from Ronald Reagan to the Congress, Apr. 16, 1986, reprinted in *Dep't St. Bull.* 86: 8 (1986).

66 See O'Brien, op. cit.: 463–465.

67 White House Statement, Apr. 14, 1986, reprinted in ibid.: 1 (emphasis added).

68 President's Address to the Nation, Apr. 14, 1986, reprinted in ibid.: 2.

69 On the Suez Crisis, see B. Avram, *The Evolution of the Suez Canal Status* (1958); P. Johnson, *The Suez War* (1957); D. Watt (ed.) *Documents on the Suez War* (1957).

70 *UN SCOR, 751st mtg* 11: 10, *UN Doc. S/P.V.* 1360 (1856) (statement by Mr Guiringaud of France).

71 Ibid.: 10–11.

72 On the Treaty of Constantinople, see G. Hackworth, *Digest of International Law* 2: 816 (1941). This agreement was signed by Great Britain, Germany, Austria-Hungary, France, Russia, the Netherlands, Italy, Spain and Turkey. Ibid. When Egypt regained its independence, it pledged to abide by the 1888 Agreement. Ibid.: 822–826.

73 Shihata, 'Destination Embargo of Arab Oil: Its Legality Under International Law,' *Am. J. Int'l L.* 68: 591, 607 (1974).

74 Ibid.: 607.

75 Shihata explains:

> Governmental action taken by a state within its own territory for the restoration of legal order disrupted by unauthorized acts of others certainly falls within the inherent territorial jurisdiction of each sovereign state. Although such action may be based on the exercise of the state's traditional right to self-help under customary international law or under a broad reading

of the UN Charter provisions on self-defense, one need not argue the relevance of such concepts in regard to the Egyptian and Syrian measures. The denial to Egypt and Syria in the particular circumstances of the situation, of the right to take individual or collective action would have resulted in depriving them indefinitely of their essential right to territorial integrity, guaranteed by the UN Charter.

Ibid.: 608 (footnotes omitted).

76 *UN SCOR, 2315th mtg,* 37 *UN Doc. S/P.V. 2350.* 5 (statement of Mr Costa-Mendez of Argentina).
77 Ibid.: 11. For a further discussion of this argument, see Coll, 'Philosophical and Legal Dimensions of the Use of Force in the Falklands War,' in A. Coll and A. Arend (eds) op. cit.: 34, 39–46.

4 COLLECTIVE USE OF FORCE UNDER THE UNITED NATIONS CHARTER

1 *UN Charter,* Art. 39.
2 L. Goodrich, E. Hambro, and A. Simons, *Charter of the United Nations.* 295 (3rd ed. 1969).
3 Ibid.: 295–300.
4 Ibid.: 299. Even in the Iraqi invasion of Kuwait, the Security Council did not term the action an act of aggression.
5 See B. Ferencz, *Defining Aggression: The Aggression: The Search for World Peace* 1–2 (1975) for a discussion of efforts to define aggression.
6 *G.A. Res. 3314, UN GAOR Supp.* (No. 31) 29, *UN Doc. A/9631:* 141 (1974).
7 L. Goodrich *et al.* op. cit.: 300.
8 *UN Charter,* Art. 41.
9 Ibid.: Art. 48.
10 Ibid.: Art. 42.
11 L. Goodrich *et al.* op. cit.: 300–301.
12 *UN Charter,* Art. 40.
13 See L. Goodrich *et al.* op. cit.: 302–310 for a discussion of Article 40.
14 Ibid.
15 Ibid.: 306.
16 Ibid.
17 *UN Charter,* Art. 43.
18 Ibid.: para. 2.
19 Ibid.
20 Ibid.: Art. 47.
21 Ibid.: para. 1.
22 Ibid.: para. 2.
23 Ibid.: para. 3.
24 Ibid.
25 See I. Claude, *Swords into Plowshares.* 245–285 (4th ed. 1971) for the classic discussion of collective security. We have been heavily influenced by Claude's work on this subject.
26 This is essentially Claude's definition of collective security. Ibid.
27 *UN Charter,* Art. 27.
28 *UNSC Res. 82* (June 25, 1950).
29 Ibid.
30 R. Higgins, *United Nations Peacekeeping* 2: 161–162 (1970).

31 *UNSC Res. 83* (June 2, 1950).
32 Ibid.
33 *UNSC Res. 660*, reprinted in *I.L.M.* 29: 1323, 1325 (1990).
34 *UNSC Res. 661*, reprinted in *I.L.M.* 29: 1323, 1325 (1990).
35 'Excerpts from Iraq's Statement on Kuwait,' *Wash. Post*, Aug. 9, 1990: A18, col. 1.
36 *UNSC Res. 662*, reprinted in *I.L.M.* 29: 1323, 1327; see also 'Resolution Says Iraq Must Reverse Step,' *Wash. Post*, Aug. 10, 1990: A30, col. 1. The resolution provides in full:

>   THE SECURITY COUNCIL,
>   RECALLING its resolutions 660 and 661 (1990);
>   GRAVELY alarmed by the declaration by Iraq of a 'comprehensive and eternal merger' with Kuwait;
>   DEMANDING, once again, that Iraq withdraw immediately and unconditionally all its force to the positions in which they were located on 1 August 1990;
>   DETERMINED to bring the occupation of Kuwait by Iraq to an end and to restore the sovereignty, independence and territorial integrity of Kuwait;
>   1. DECIDES that annexation of Kuwait by Iraq under any form and whatever pretext has no legal validity, and is considered null and void;
>   2. CALLS UPON all states, international organizations, specialized agencies not to recognize that annexation, and to refrain from any action or dealing that might be interpreted as an indirect recognition of the annexation;
>   3. FURTHER DEMANDS that Iraq rescind its actions purporting to annex Kuwait;
>   4. DECIDES to keep this item on its agenda and to continue its efforts to put and early end to the occupation.

37 See Rosenthal, 'Bush Sends US Force to Saudi Arabia as Kingdom Agrees to Confront Iraq,' *Wash. Post*, Aug. 8, 1990: A1, col. 6.
38 Coll, 'US Starts Interdiction of Iraqi Cargo Vessels,' *Wash. Post*, Aug. 18, 1990: A1, col. 6.
39 *UNSC Res. 665*, reprinted in *I.L.M.* 29: 1329–1328 (1990).
40 'UN Votes Use of Force to Halt Iraqi Trade,' *N.Y. Times*, Aug. 26, 1990, A1, col. 6. See also, Sciolino, 'How US Got UN Backing For Use of Force in the Gulf,' *N.Y. Times*, Aug. 30, 1990: A1, col. 4.
41 *UNSC Res. 678*, reprinted in *I.L.M.* 29: 1565 (1990).
42 Lewis, 'UN Gives Iraq Until Jan. 15 to Retreat or Face Force: Hussein Says He Will Fight,' *N.Y. Times*, Nov. 30, 1990: A1, col. 6; Goshko, 'UN Authorizes Use of Force Against Iraq,' *Wash. Post*, Nov. 30, 1990: A1, col. 4.
43 Atkinson and Broder, 'US Allies Launch Massive Air War Against Targets in Iraq and Kuwait,' *Wash. Post*, Jan. 17, 1991: A1. col. 1.
44 *UNSC Res. 687* (Apr. 2, 1991).
45 In Resolution 687, the Council decided that Iraq shall unconditionally accept the destruction, removal, or rendering harmless, under international supervision, of:

>   (a) all chemical and biological weapons and all stocks of agents and all related substances and components and all research, development, support and manufacturing facilities;
>   (b) all ballistic missiles with a range greater than 150 kilometres and related major parts, and repair and production facilities.

    Ibid.
46 Ibid.
47 *UNSC Res. 688* (Apr. 5 1991).

48 Ibid.
49 Ibid.
50 Ibid.
51 Memorandum of Understanding signed on April 18 1991, reprinted in 30 *Int'l Legal Materials* 860–862 (1991).
52 Lewis, *UN Votes to Condemn Handling of Iraq Rebels, New York Times*, Apr. 6, 1991, at 6.
53 See Rowe, 'UN Votes to Put Embargo on Libya,' *Wash. Post*, Apr. 1, 1992, at A1, col 2; 'Resolution on Libya Embargo: Barring Takeoff and Landing "to Any Aircraft,"' *N.Y. Times*, Apr. 1, 1992: A12, col. 1.
54 See Lewis, 'UN Votes Trade Sanctions Against Yugoslavia 13–0; Air Travel and Oil Curbed,' *N.Y. Times*, May 31, 1992: A1, col. 6. See also, 'Excerpts from UN Resolution: "Deny Permission,"' ibid.: A8, col. 3.
55 UNSC Res. 694 (1992)
56 See, for example, Letter from Secretary-General Boutros-Ghali to the President of the Security Council, 29 Nov. 1992, U.N. Doc. S/24868; Goshko, 'UN Orders US-Led Force Into Somalia,' *Wash. Post*, Dec. 4, 1992: A1, col. 4.
57 *UN Charter*, Art. 27, para. 3.
58 See T. Franck, *Nation Against Nation*: 20–24 (1985).
59 Ibid.
60 L. Goodrich *et al.* op. cit.: 320.
61 Ibid.: 319–324.
62 Ibid.: 324.
63 Ibid.
64 See Chapter 10 below.
65 Rowe, 'UN Seeks Permanent Armed Force,' *Wash. Post*, June 19, 1992: A1, col. 6.
66 Ibid.
67 See Claude, 'The Rejection of Collective Security,' in I. Claude, *American Approaches to World Affairs*: 51–67 (1986).
68 See Chapter 10 below.
69 See Williams, 'Regional Peacemaking: ECOWAS and the Liberian Civil War,' *Dip. Rec.* 2 (1991).
70 L. Goodrich *et al.* op. cit.: 122.
71 Ibid.
72 *G.A. Res. 377a, UN GAOR Supp.* (No. 20) 5: 10, *UN Doc. A/1775* (1950).
73 On this debate, see Claude, 'The OAS, the UN and the United States,' reprinted in J. Nye (ed.) *International Regionalism* 3 (1968).
74 *UN Charter*, Art. 52.
75 Ibid.
76 Ibid., Art. 53.
77 Ibid.
78 Ibid., Art. 54.
79 Moore, 'The Role of Regional Arrangements,' in J. Moore, *Law and the Indochina War*: 296, 333–334 (1972).
80 See Claude, 'The OAS, the UN and the United States,' in J. Nye op. cit.: 6–13.
81 Meeker, 'Defensive Quarantine and the Law,' *Am. J. Int'l L.* 57: 515, 522 (1963); see the discussion of this approach in Moore, op. cit.: 343–345.
82 Moore, op. cit.: 343.
83 Meeker, op. cit.: 522.
84 Chayes, 'Law and the Quarantine of Cuba,' *For. Aff.* 41: 550, 556 (1963).
85 See Halderman, 'Regional Enforcement Measures and the United Nations,' *Geo. L. J.* 52: 89, 105–111 (1963).

86 Moore, op. cit.: 344–345.
87 Meeker, op. cit.: 522.
88 See L. Goodrich *et al.* op. cit. 365–367.
89 Moore, 'Toward an Applied Theory for the Regulation of Intervention,' in J. Moore (ed.) *Law and Civil War in the Modern World*: 3, 27 (1974).
90 Ibid.
91 Ibid.
92 Ibid.
93 See I. Claude, *Swords into Plowshares*: 314 (4th ed. 1971).
94 'Statement on the Grenada Situation from the OECS Secretariat,' reprinted in J. Moore, *Law and the Grenada Mission*: 89 (1984).
95 J. Moore, *Law and the Grenada Mission*: 32 (1984).
96 See R. Beck, *International Law and 'Urgent Fury'* (1993).
97 Professor Abiodun Williams reports that '[b]y March [of 1991] an estimated 200,000 refugees had fled to the Ivory Coast and Guinea.' Williams, 'Regional Peacemaking: ECOWAS and the Liberian Civil War,' in *Dip. Rec.*: 200, 205 (1991).
98 Professor Williams explains that 'the organization did not consider the Liberian civil war until January 1991 when the Security Council adopted a resolution on the matter.' Ibid.: 207.
99 On ECOWAS generally, see U. Ezenwe, *ECOWAS and the Economic Integration of West Africa.* The members of the organization are: Benin, Burkina Faso, Cape Verde, Gambia, Ghana, Guinea, Guinea-Bissau, the Ivory Coast, Liberia, Mali, Mauritania, Niger, Nigeria, Senegal, Sierra Leone, and Togo. Williams, op. cit.: 215, fn. 1.
100 Ibid.: 205.
101 Ibid.: 205.
102 Ibid.: 206–207.
103 As Professor Williams explains:

> '[a] development that was to complicate the situation still further also occurred with a rift in the ranks of the NPFL. Prince Yormie Johnson, a Gio [a Liberian ethnic group] from Nimba County and former commander of the NPFL's special forces, formed a rival group known as the Independent National Patriotic Front of Liberia (INPFL).'
>
> Ibid.: 206.

104 Ibid.: 208.
105 Williams explains:

> On August 24, a peacekeeping force known as the ECOWAS Monitoring Group (ECOMOG) and under the command of General Arnold Quainoo of Ghana left Freetown [Sierra Leone] for Liberia. Composed of 3,000 troops from Gambia, Ghana, Guinea, Nigeria, and Sierra Leone, its mandate was that of 'keeping the peace, restoring law and order and ensuring that the cease-fire is respected.'
>
> Ibid.: 210

106 The Liberian delegate told the Security Council on January 22, 1991 that '[i]t will be recalled that seven months ago we made efforts to have the Council seized with the deteriorating situation in Liberia.' *UN SCOR, 2974th mtg*: 47 3, *UN Doc. S/PV. 2974* (1991) (statement of Mr Bull).
107 The Liberia representative to the Council indicated that the Council did not take up the issue for fear of encroaching on a matter of domestic jurisdiction. On January 22, he told the Council:

> That a response is now being made, more that one year since the conflict started, raises, in my opinion, the imperative need to review, and perhaps reinterpret, the Charter, particularly its provision which calls for non-interference in the internal affairs of Member States.
>
> Regrettably, the strict application of this provision has hampered the effectiveness of the Council and its principal objective of maintaining international peace and security. As a result, millions of innocent men, women and children have continued to be victimized by conflicts throughout the world, and this world body, which has the moral obligation and authority, has been prevented from averting these human tragedies.
>
> Ibid.

108 This statement read, in part:

> The members of the Security Council commend the efforts made by the ECOWAS Heads of State and Government to promote peace and normalcy in Liberia.
>
> The members of the Security Council call upon the parties to the conflict in Liberia to continue to respect the cease-fire agreement which they have signed and to co-operate fully with the ECOWAS to restore peace and normalcy in Liberia.
>
> Ibid.: 9 (statement of the President, Mr. Bagbeni Adeito Nzengeya)

109 R. Riggs and J. Plano, *The United Nations*: 134 (1988) ('A peacekeeping force is deployed only with the consent of the sovereign of the territory where it operates, and usually with the consent or acquiescence of all the governments concerned.').

110 On peacekeeping, see I. Claude, *Swords into Plowshares*: 312–333 (4th ed. 1971); A. Bennett, *International Organization*: 145–152 (4th ed. 1988).

111 See Riggs and Plano, op. cit.: 134–145.

112 An Agenda for Peace: Preventive diplomacy, peacemaking and peace-keeping, Report of the Secretary-General pursuant to the statement adopted by the Summit Meeting of the Security Council on 31 January 1992, *UN Doc. A/47/277, S/24111*, June 17, 1992, para. 47.

113 Ibid.

114 For a discussion of the financial crisis, see T. Franck, op. cit.: 83–87.

115 On the financial crisis, see T. Franck, op. cit.: 82–87.

116 'Certain Expenses of the United Nations,' *ICJ*: 163 (advisory opinion of 20 July 1962).

117 Ibid.: 164.

118 Ibid.

5 ANTICIPATORY SELF-DEFENSE

1 See Shipler, 'Israeli Jets Destroy Iraqi Atomic Reactor; Attack Condemned by US and Arab Nations,' *N.Y. Times*, June 9, 1981: A1, col. 6.

2 'Israeli and Iraqi Statements on Raid on Nuclear Plant,' reprinted in ibid.: A8, col. 1 (unofficial translation).

3 Shipler, 'Begin Defends Raid, Pledges to Thwart a New "Holocaust,"' *N.Y. Times*, June 10, 1981: A1, col. 6, A12, col. 6.

4 As Professor Dinstein explains:

> While some commentators believe that customary international law [permits self-defense only after an armed attack occurs], the more common view is that the customary right of self-defense is also accorded to States as a

preventive measures (taken in 'anticipation' of an armed attack, and not merely in response to an attack that has actually occurred).

Y. Dinstein, *War, Aggression and Self-Defence*: 172 (1988) (footnotes omitted).

5 I. Brownlie, *International Law and the Use of Force by States*: 275–278, 278 (1963) ('It can only be concluded that the view that Article 51 does not permit anticipatory action is correct and that the arguments to the contrary are either unconvincing or based on inconclusive pieces of evidence.') Brownlie does argue, however, that there are certain 'difficult though somewhat academic cases in which preventive action of a small scale might be justified.' Ibid.: 278.

6 Y. Dinstein, op. cit.: 173 ('Recourse to self-defense under the Article [51] is not vindicated by any violation of international law short of an armed attack.')

7 L. Henkin, *How Nations Behave*: 140–144 (2nd ed. 1979). Henkin argues forcefully against any reading of Article 51 that permits anticipatory self-defense. He does, however, suggest that anticipatory self-defense might be permissible in one, narrow circumstance:

> If there were clear evidence of an attack so imminent that there was no time for political action to prevent it, the only meaningful defense for the potential victim might indeed be the pre-emptive attack and – it may be argued – the scheme of Article 2(4) together with Article 51 was not intended to bar such attack. But this argument would claim a small and special exception for the special case of surprise nuclear attack; today, and one hopes for a time longer, it is meaningful and relevant principally only as between the Soviet Union and the United States and, fortunately, only for a most unlikely eventuality. But such a reading of the Charter, it should be clear, would not permit (and encourage) anticipatory self-defense in other, more likely situations between nations generally.

Ibid.: 143–144

8 P. Jessup, *A Modern Law of Nations*: 166 (1948) ('Under the Charter, alarming military preparations by a neighboring state would justify a resort to the Security Council, but would not justify resort to anticipatory force by the state which believed itself threatened.')

9 D. Bowett, *Self-Defence in International Law*: 184–193, (1958) ('It is not believed, therefore, that Art. 51 restricts the traditional right of self-defence so as to exclude action taken against an imminent danger but before "an armed attack occurs".')

10 O'Brien, 'International Law and the Outbreak of War in the Middle East, 1967,' *Orbis* 11: 716, 721 (1967).

11 M. McDougal and F. Feliciano, *Law and Minimum World Public Order*: 232–244 (1961).

12 J. Stone, *Aggression and World Order*: 98–100 (1958).

13 'Military and Paramilitary Activities in and against Nicaragua' (Nicar. v. US), *Merits, ICJ*: 14 (Judgment of June 27, 1986) at para. 194.

14 Ibid. (Dissenting Opinion of Judge Schwebel).

15 *UN Doc. AEC/18/Rev. 1*: 24.

16 Bowett, op. cit.: 189.

17 I. Brownlie, op. cit.: 276–277 (footnote omitted).

18 Bowett, op. cit.: 189, fn 1.

19 Ibid.

20 This is the title of Robert F. Kennedy's personal account. R. Kennedy, *Thirteen Days: A Memoir of the Cuban Missile Crisis* (1968).

21 Address by President Kennedy, reprinted in ibid.: 153.

22 Ibid.: 156.
23 Chayes, 'The Legal Case for US Action on Cuba,' *Dept. St.* Bull 46: 763 (1962).
24 Meeker, 'Defensive Quarantine and the Law,' *Am. J. Int'l L.* 57: 515 (1963).
25 For the scholarly discussion of the question, see Christol and Davis, 'Maritime Quarantine: The Naval Interdiction of Offensive Weapons and Associated Matériel to Cuba, 1962,' *Am. J. Int'l L.* 57: 525 (1963); Wright, 'The Cuban Quarantine,' *Am. J. Int'l L.* 57: 546 (1963); Comment [McDougal], 'The Soviet-Cuban Quarantine and Self-Defense,' *Am. J. Int'l L.* 57: 597 (1963).
26 *UN Doc S/PV. 1022–1025* (1962).
27 Statement of Mr Quaison-Sackey (Ghana), *UN Doc. S/PV. 1024:* 51 (1962).
28 Ibid. The delegate continued to contend:

> Even from a strictly juridical point of view my delegation cannot agree that in this particular case self-defense can be invoked to justify the exercise of authority by the United States on the high seas, for the concept of freedom on the open seas, enshrined in numerous international instruments, entails absolute freedom of navigation for vessels of all nations in time of peace.

29 Statement of Mr Eban, *UN Doc. S/OV. 1348:* 71.
30 Statement of Mr Benhima of Morocco, *UN Doc. No. S/PV. 1348:* 122.
31 Statement of Mr Fedorenko of the Soviet Union, *UN Doc. No. S/PV. 1351:* 61.
32 Statement of Mr Rafael of Israel, *UN Doc. No. S/PV. 1353:* 56–57.
33 Statement of Mr Fedorenko of the Soviet Union, *UN Doc. No. S/PV. 1353:* 76.
34 Ibid.
35 Ibid.: 77–80.
36 Ibid.
37 Statement of Mr Hammadi, *UN Doc. No. S/PV. 2280,* June 12, 1981: 16.
38 Statement of Mr Blum, *UN Doc. No. S/PV. 2280,* June 12, 1981: 52.
39 Ibid.: 53–55.
40 Ibid.: 38–40, 56.
41 Statement of Mr El-Fattal, *UN Doc. No. S/off. rec. 2284,* June 16, 1981: 6.
42 Ibid.
43 Statement of Mr Sinclair, *UN Doc. No. S/PV. 2286:* 11.
44 Statement of Mr Koroma, *UN Doc. No. S/PV. 2283:* 56 (emphasis added).
45 Ibid.: 57.
46 Ibid.
47 Statement of Sir Anthony Parsons, *UN Doc. No. S/PV. 2282:* 42.

6 INTERVENTION IN CIVIL AND MIXED CONFLICTS

1 'The Corfu Channel Case' (UK v. Alb.), *ICJ* 4 (Judgement of April 9, 1949).
2 'Military and Paramilitary Activities in and against Nicaragua' (Nicar. v. US), *Merits, ICJ* 14 (Judgment of June 27, 1986) [Hereinafter cited as Nicaragua case].
3 See, for example, Falk, 'Introduction,' in R. Falk (ed.) *The International Law of Civil War:* 1, 18–19 (1971); Moore, 'The Control of Foreign Intervention in Internal Conflict,' *Va. J. Int'l L.* 9: 205, 256–258 (1969); Moore, 'Toward an Applied Theory for the Regulation of Intervention,' in J. Moore *Law and Civil War in the Modern World:* 3, 21–24 (1974).
4 Moore, 'The Control of Foreign Intervention in Internal Conflict,' in J. Moore, *Law and the Indo-China War:* 179–180 (1972).
5 For a discussion of the Sri Lankan Civil War, see P. Brogan, *The Fighting Never Stopped:* 227–234 (1990).
6 Novogrod, 'International Strife, Self-Determination and World Order,' *Jag J.* 23: 65

(Dec. 1968–Jan. 1969), reprinted in M. Whiteman, *Digest of International Law* 12: 234 (1971).

7 Ibid.

8 See Moore, 'Toward an Applied Theory for the Regulation of Intervention,' in J. Moore, *Law and Civil War in the Modern World*: 23.

9 Common Article 3 of the 1949 Geneva Conventions provides that certain minimum standards apply in the conduct of an armed conflict 'not of an international character.' Geneva Convention Relative to the Protection of Civilian Persons in Time of War, opened for signature Aug. 12, 1949, *US T. 3516, TIAS* 6: No. 3365, 75 *UNTS*: 287. For a discussion of Common Article 3, see Elder, 'The Historical Background of Common Article 3 of the Geneva Conventions of 1949,' *Case W. Res. J. Int'l L.* 11: 37 (1979).

10 Lauterpacht's Oppenheim states that 'the Law of Nations does not treat civil war as illegal.' M. Lauterpacht (ed.) *L. Oppenheim, International Law* 2: 249 (7th ed. 1952).

11 Moore, 'The Control of Foreign Intervention in Internal Conflict,' in J. Moore, *Law and the Indo-China War*. 161 (1972).

12 Ibid. See also, Borchard, '"Neutrality" and Civil Wars,' *Am. J. Int'l L.* 31: 304, 306 (1937); O'Rourke, 'Recognition of Belligerency and the Spanish War,' *Am. J. Int'l L.* 31: 398, 410 (1937).

13 See Moore's formulation; Moore, 'The Control of Foreign Intervention in Internal Conflicts,' in J. Moore, *Law and the Indo-China War*. 161–162 (1972).

14 Ibid.

15 Ibid.: 197.

16 This can be seen, for example, in the 1974 'Definition of Aggression' Resolution adopted by the United Nations General Assembly. Article 7 of that Resolution, which was included largely at the urging of the Less Developed Countries,[36] states that:

> Nothing in this Definition, and in particular article 3 [which lists acts that generally qualify as aggression], could in any way prejudice the right to self-determination, freedom and independence, as derived from the Charter, of peoples forcibly deprived of the right referred to in the Declaration on Principles of International Law concerning Friendly Relations and Co-operation among States in accordance with the Charter of the United Nations, particularly peoples under colonial and racist regimes or other forms of alien domination; *nor the right of these people to struggle to that end and to seek and receive support*, in accordance with the principles of the Charter and in conformity with the above mentioned Declaration.

> *G.A. Res. 3314, UN GAOR Suppl* (No. 31) 29, *UN Doc. A/9631*: 141 (1974) [hereinafter cited as Definition of Aggression] [Emphasis added.] Even if this 'right' is limited by the 'principles of the Charter,' its entire thrust, the implication that a state could assist a self-determination movement that is seeking to alter the political order in a state, seems directly to undercut the intention of Article 2(4).

17 See, Firmage, 'The 'War of National Liberation' and the Third World,' in J. Moore *Law and Civil War in the Modern World*: 309, (footnote omitted) (1974). See also, Ginsburg, 'Wars of National Liberation and the Modern Law of Nations – The Soviet Thesis,' *L. & Contemp. Prob.* 29: 910 (1964); Reisman, 'Criteria for the Lawful Use of Force in International Law,' *Yale J. Int'l L.* 10: 279, 280 (1985).

18 For example, when the United States and the Organisation of Eastern Caribbean States invaded Grenada in 1983, three reasons for this action were given by the President of the United States. The first was the protection of US nationals, but the others were 'to forestall further chaos' and 'to assist in the restoration of conditions

of law and order and of governmental institutions to the island of Grenada, where a brutal group of leftist thugs violently seized power, killing the Prime Minister, three Cabinet Members, two labor leaders and other civilians, including children.' Statement by the President and by the Prime Minister of Dominica Eugenia Charles on US Involvement in Grenada (Oct. 25, 1983), reprinted in J. Moore, *Law and the Grenada Mission*: 91 (1984). While these may well be noble reasons for the invasion, they do not appear to fall within the permissible exceptions to Article 2(4).

19 Comment, 'Coercion and Self-Determination: Construing Charter Article 2(4),' *Am. J. Int'l L.* 78: 642 (1984).

20 See, e.g. L. Goodrich, E. Hambro and A. Simons, *Charter of the United Nations* 54–55 (3rd ed. 1977).

21 See Moore, *Law and the Indo-China War* (1972); Moore, 'The Lawfulness of Military Assistance to the Republic of Viet-Nam,' *Am. J. Int'l L.* 61: 1 (1967). Moore, 'International Law and the United States Role in the Viet Nam War: A Reply,' *Yale. L. J.* 75: 1051–94 (1967).

22 See, Falk, 'International Law and the United States Role in the Viet Nam War,' *Yale L. J.* 75: 1122–60 (1967): Falk, 'International Law and the United States Role in the Viet Nam War: A Response to Professor Moore,' *Yale L. J.* 75: 1095–1158 (1967).

23 See, 'Intervention in Civil Wars: A Modest Proposal,' Colum. L. Rev. 67: 266–79 (1967).

24 Wright, 'Legal Aspects of the Viet-Nam Situation,' *Am. J. Int'l L.* 60: 750 (1966).

25 See, e.g. Joyner and Grimaldi, 'The United States and Nicaragua: Reflections on the Lawfulness of Contemporary Intervention,' *Va. J. Int'l L.* 25: 621 (1985); Moore, 'The Secret War in Central America and the Future of World Order,' *Am. J. Int'l L.* 80: 43 (1986).

26 Nicaragua Case: 14.

27 See, Moore, 'Toward an Applied Theory for the Regulation of Intervention,' in J. Moore (ed.) *Civil War and the Modern World*: 3 (1972).

28 Interview with Professor Thomas M. Franck, Oct. 30, 1984, quoted in 'Note, A Framework for Evaluating the Legality of the United States Intervention in Nicaragua,' *NYUJ Int'l L. & Pol.* 17: 155, 178 (1984).

29 See O'Brien, *US Military Intervention: Law and Morality* (1979).

30 The United States argument in *Nicaragua* was based on this understanding.

31 Nicaragua Case: para. 195.

32 Ibid.

33 See 'Dep't of State, Statement on the US Withdrawal from the Proceedings Initiated by Nicaragua in the International Court of Justice, Jan. 18, 1985,' reprinted in *Int'l L. Materials* 24: 246 (1985).

34 For a discussion of the American argument, see Moore, 'The Secret War in Central America and the Future of World Order,' *Am. J. Int'l L.* 80: 43 (1986).

35 Nicaragua Case: para. 195.

36 Ibid.

37 Ibid.

38 See Falk, 'International Law and the United States Role in the Viet Nam War,' *Yale L. J.* 75: 362.

39 Joyner and Grimaldi, op. cit.: 680–681.

40 For a discussion of the Reagan Doctrine, see Kirkpatrick and Gerson, 'The Reagan Doctrine, Human Rights, and International Law,' in L. Henkin, S. Hoffman, J. Kirkpatrick, A. Gerson, W. Rogers and D. Scheffer, *Right v. Might: International Law and the Use of Force*: 19 (1989).

41 'Reagan: "We Have A Right to Help"', *Time*, March 31, 1986 at 16.

7 INTERVENTION TO PROTECT NATIONALS

1 *N.Y. Times*, Dec. 21, 1989: 9. For legal analyses of the Panama invasion, see D'Amato, 'The Invasion of Panama was a Lawful Response to Tyranny,' *Am. J. Int'l L.* 84: 494 (1990); Farer, 'Panama: Beyond the Charter Paradigm,' *Am. J. Int'l L.* 84: 503 (1990); Nanda, 'The Validity of US Intervention in Panama under International Law,' *Am. J. Int'l L.* 84: 494 (1990); and Terry, 'Law in Support of Policy in Panama,' *Nav. War Col. Rev.* 43: 110 (1990).

2 Ibid.

3 N. Ronzitti, *Rescuing Nationals Abroad Through Military Coercion and Intervention on Grounds of Humanity:* xvii–xix (1985). See also Hoffmann, 'The Problem of Intervention,' in H. Bull (ed.) *Intervention in World Politics:* 7 (1984); and Higgins, 'Intervention and International Law,' in H. Bull (ed.) op. cit.: 29.

4 Akehurst, 'The Use of Force to Protect Nationals Abroad,' *Int'l Rel.* 5: 3, 4–5 (1977); N. Ronzitti, op. cit.: xviii–xix.

5 Ibid.: xix.

6 Bowett, 'The Use of Force for the Protection of Nationals Abroad,' in A. Cassese (ed.) *The Current Legal Regulation of the Use of Force:* 49 (1986).

7 N. Ronzitti, op. cit.: xv.

8 For good summaries of state practice, see Akehurst, 'Humanitarian Intervention,' in H. Bull (ed.) op. cit.: 99–104; and N. Ronzitti, op. cit.: 26–49.
   Our review of practice includes examples of state uses of force which should not properly be considered 'interventions to protect nationals.'

9 *Keesing's Contemporary Archives* 6: 8084–8085 (1946–48); *Royal Institute of International Affairs, Survey of International Affairs, The Middle East 1945–50:* 76 (1954).

10 N. Ronzitti. op. cit.: 26.

11 *UN SCOR, 3rd Yr. 301st mtg:* 7, 10 (1948).

12 A. W. Ford, *The Anglo-Iranian Oil Dispute:* 58 (1954).

13 Statement by British Foreign Secretary in the House of Commons, *Hansard, Parl. Debates (H.C.)* 488: 43; 489: 1010. See also D. Bowett, *Self-Defence in International Law:* 103 (1958); I. Brownlie, *International Law and the Use of Force by States:* 296–297 (1963).

14 Statement by British Foreign Secretary op. cit.

15 *Keesing's Contemporary Archives* 8: 11603 (1950–52); *Yearbook of the United Nations:* 813 (1951).

16 Waldock, 'The Regulation of the Use of Force by Individual States in International Law,' *Recueil des Cours* 81: 503 (1952).

17 In fact, nine were killed during the course of the civil disturbances in that Egyptian city. N. Ronzitti, op. cit.: 28.

18 A. Eden, *Full Circle:* 232 (1960).

19 N. Ronzitti, op. cit.: 28.

20 Eden, op. cit.: 231–232.

21 See generally, D. Bowett, *Self-Defence in International Law:* 104 (1958); I. Brownlie, op. cit.: 297; and T. Robertson, *Crisis: The Inside Story of the Suez Conspiracy* (1965).

22 *Annuaire Français de Droit International* 3: 831 (1957); *Review Generale de Droit International Public* 28: 153–154 (1957); *GAOR, First Emergency Special Session, 561st plenary mtg:* paras. 220ff.

23 *Hansard, Parl. Debates (H.C.)* 588: 1275, 1277, 1377, 1566–1567; *(H.L.)* 199: 1353–1356, 1359; D. Bowett, *Self-Defence in International Law:* 15, 104 (1958); I. Brownlie, op. cit.: 297; T. Robertson, op. cit.

24 Lauterpacht, 'The Contemporary Practice of the United Kingdom in the Field of

International Law – Survey and Comment, III August 16–December 31, 1956,' *Int'l & Comp. L. Qtly* 6: 326 (1957).

25 The British representative to the Security Council observed, 'we should certainly not want to keep any forces in the area for one moment longer than is necessary to protect our nationals.' *UN SCOR, 749th mtg* 11: 24.

26 Akehurst, op. cit.: 6.

27 G. Abi-Saab, *The UN Operation in the Congo 1960–1964* (1974).

28 Statement by the Belgian representative, M. Loridan in *UN SCOR, 15th Yr 873rd mtg*: 34.

29 See Chapter 6 above.

30 The supporters of Belgium 'declared that, since Belgium had intervened for humanitarian reasons, it was not possible to consider it as an aggressor.' N. Ronzitti, op. cit.: 31–32.

31 Congolese Foreign Minister Bomboko had consented to the Belgian action, but had subsequently been overruled by Prime Minister Lumumba. Akehurst, op. cit.: 7.

32 *Keesing's Contemporary Archives* 14: 19952 (1963–64); *Hansard, Parl. Debates (H.C.)* 687: 38.

33 *The Times* (London), Jan. 18, 1964, cited by N. Ronzitti, op. cit.: 171.

34 N. Ronzitti, op. cit.: 32.

35 See generally Brownlie, 'Humanitarian Intervention,' in J. Moore (ed.) *Law and Civil War in the Modern World*: 22 (1974); Fairley, 'State Actors, Humanitarian Intervention, and International Law: Reopening Pandora's Box,' *Ga. J. Int'l & Comp. L.* 10: 48–50 (1980); Lillich, 'Forcible Self-Help by States to Protect Human Rights,' *Iowa L. Rev.* 53: 338–340 (1967); Weisberg, 'The Congo Crisis 1964: A Case Study in Humanitarian Intervention,' *Va. J. Int'l L.* 12: 261 (1972).

Congolese government *consent* was given to this US–Belgian use of force. Hence, it is not strictly an example of 'intervention to protect nationals.' See Gerard, 'L'operation Stanleyville-Paulis devant le Parlement belge et les Nations Unies,' *Revue Belge de Droit International* 3: 265 (1967).

36 Akehurst op. cit.: 7–8.

37 US Representative Adlai Stevenson in *UN SCOR 20th Yr, 1196 mtg*: 14.

See generally Brownlie, op. cit.: 221; Ehrlich, 'The Measuring Line of Occasion,' *Stan. J. Int'l Stud.* 3: 27, 35–37 (1968); Franck and Rodley, 'After Bangladesh: The Law of Humanitarian Intervention by Military Force,' *Am. J. Int'l L.* 76: 287 (1973); McLaren, The Dominican Crisis: An Inter-American Dilemma, *Can. Y. B. Int'l L.* 4: 178 (1966); Nanda, 'The United States Action in the 1965 Dominican Crisis: Impact on World Order–Part 1,' *Denver L. J.* 43: 439 (1966).

For the US Legal Adviser's justification see Meeker, 'The Dominican Situation in the Perspective of International Law,' *Dep't St. Bull.* 53: 60 (1965).

38 Ronzitti, op. cit.: 33.

39 Dupuy, *Annuaire Français de Droit International* 11: 71, 76–77 (1965); UN Document S/6310; UN SCOR 20th Yr, 1196th mtg: 14; M. Whiteman, *Digest of International Law* 12: 824 (1971); P. Geyelin, *Lyndon B. Johnson and the World*: 43, 244–245, 250, 252, 255 (1966).

40 US Representative Adlai Stevenson in *UN SCOR, 20th Yr, 1196th mtg*: 14.

41 *British Practice in International Law* 13: (1965); *UN SCOR, 1198th mtg*: 13.

42 *UN SCOR, 1198th mtg*: 24.

43 Akehurst op. cit.: 9.

44 *UN SCOR, 1200th mtg*: 3.

45 J. Arechaga, *Derecho Constitutional de las Naciones Unidas* (1958).

46 *UN SCOR, 1196th mtg*: 26, 29.

47 Fairley, op. cit.: 53; Finch, 'Pueblo and Mayaguez, 'A Legal Analysis,' *Case W. Res. J.*

Int'l L. 9: 79 (1977); Friedlander, 'The Mayaguez in Retrospect: Humanitarian Intervention or Showing the Flag?' *St. Louis L.J.* 22: 601 (1978); Paust, 'The Seizure and Recovery of the Mayaguez,' *Yale L.J.* 85: 774 (1976); *Dep't St. Bull.* 72: 720 (1975).

48 Ibid.: 719.

49 Ibid.: 770.

50 *US House, Subcmt. on Intl. Rels., 94th Cong., 1st sess., Seizure of the Mayaguez:* 232–235.

51 Ibid.: 241–242.

52 *N.Y. Times,* May 17, 1975: 11.

53 *Keesing's Contemporary Archives* 22: 28119 (1976); Dept. St. Bull. 75: 90 (1976).

54 Ibid.

55 Frank, 'After the Fall: The New Procedural Framework for Congressional Control over the War Power,' *Am. J. Int'l L.* 71: 620 (1977); N. Ronzitti, op. cit.: 37.

56 Margo, 'The Legality of the Entebbe Raid in International Law,' *S. Afr. L.J.* 94: 306 (1977); Salter, 'Commando Coup at Entebbe: Humanitarian Intervention or Barbaric Aggression?,' *Int'l Law* 11: 331 (1977); Note, 'Use of Force for the Protection of Nationals Abroad: The Entebbe Incident,' *Case W. Res. J. Int'l L.* 9: 117; Akehurst, op. cit.: 3; **UN Yearbook**: 319–320 (1976).

57 *S/PV. 1939.* 51–55.

58 *S/PV. 1940.* 48; N. Ronzitti, op. cit.: 38.

59 *S/PV. 1941:* 31.

60 *S/PV. 1942.* 28–30; *S/PV. 1943:* 28–31, 36–37; Akehurst, op. cit.: 20.

61 Kenya, Qatar, China, Libya, Guinea, Guyana, Somalia, Yugoslavia, Tanzania, Pakistan, Panama, Romania, India, and Cuba. *S/PV. 1939, S/PV. 1940, S/PV. 1941;* and *S/PV. 1943.*

62 Uganda, Mauritania, Cameroon, Mauritius, Benin, Pakistan, and the Soviet Union. *S/PV. 1939, S/PV. 1940,* and *S/PV. 1941.*

63 Akehurst, op. cit.: 21.

64 N. Ronzitti. op. cit.: 40; *Keesing's Contemporary Archives* 24: 28820–28821 (1978); Hollick, 'French Intervention in Africa in 1978,' *The World Today* 35: 75–76 (1979).

65 *Africa Contemporary Review* 10: B46 (1977–78); *Keesing's Contemporary Archives* 24: 29035 (1978).

66 *N.Y. Times,* Feb. 22, 1978: 7; *N.Y. Times,* Feb. 23, 1978: 3.

67 N . Ronzitti, op. cit.: 41.

68 See Note, 'Resort to Force by States to Protect Nationals,' *Va. J. Int'l L.* 21: 485 (1981); Stein, 'Contempt, Crisis, and the Court,' *Am. J. Int'l L.* 76: 499–531 (1982); Rubin, 'The Hostages Incident: The United States and Iran,' *Y.B. World Aff.* 36: 213 (1982); and G. Sick, *All Fall Down* (1985).

69 *Dep't St. Bull.* 80: 38 (1980).

70 *N.Y. Times,* Apr. 26, 1980: A10.

71 See N. Ronzitti, op. cit.: 45–48.

72 United States Diplomatic and Consular Staff in Teheran, Judgment, *ICJ Reports* (1980).

73 Books on the Grenada invasion include: S. Davidson, *Grenada: A Study in Politics and the Limits of International Law* (1987); W. Gilmore, *The Grenada Intervention* (1984); and J. Moore, *Law and the Grenada Mission* (1984).

Articles include: Boyle, Chayes and Dore 'International Lawlessness in Grenada,' *Am. J. Int'l L.* 78: 172 (1984); Dieguez, 'The Grenada Invasion: "Illegal" in Form, Sound as Policy,' *NYU J. Int'l L. & Pol.* 16: 1167 (1984); Dore, 'The US Invasion of Grenada: Resurrection of the "Johnson Doctrine?"' *Stan. J. Int'l L.* 20: 173 (1984); Doswald-Beck, 'The Legality of the US Intervention in Grenada,' *Neth. Int'l L. Rev.*

31: 362 (1984); Fraser, 'Grenada: The Sovereignty of the People,' *W. Indian L.J.* 7: 205 (1983); Gordon *et al*.., 'International Law and the United States Action in Grenada,' *Int'l L*. 18: 331 (1984); Joyner, 'Reflections on the Lawfulness of Invasion,' *Am. J. Int'l L*. 78: 131 (1984); Karas and Goodman, 'The United States Action in Grenada: An Exercise in Realpolitik,' *U. Miami Inter-Am. L. Rev.* 16: 53 (1984); Levitin, 'The Law of Force an the Force of Law; Grenada, the Falklands, and Humanitarian Intervention,' *Harv. J. Int'l L*. 27: 621 (1984); Moore, 'Grenada and the International Double Standard,' *Am. J. Int'l L*. 78: 145 (1984); Nanda, 'The United States Intervention in Grenada – Impact on World Order,' *Cal. Western Int'l L. J*. 14: 395 (1984); Quigley, 'The United States Invasion of Grenada: Stranger than Fiction,' *U. Miami Inter-Am. L. Rev.* 18: 271 (1986–87); Riggs, 'The Grenada Intervention: A Legal Analysis,' *Mil. L. Rev.* 1: 1 (1985); Smart, 'Revolutions, Constitutions and the Commonwealth: Grenada,' *Int'l & Comp. L. Qtly* 35: 950 (1986); Vagts, 'International Law Under Time Pressure: Grading the Grenada Take-Home Examination,' *Am. J. Int'l L*. 79: 169 (1984); Waters, 'The Invasion of Grenada, 1983, and the Collapse of Legal Norms,' *J. Peace Research* 23: 229–246 (1986); and Wheeler, 'The Grenada Invasion: Expanding the Scope of Humanitarian Intervention,' *Bos. C. Int'l & Comp. L. Rev.* 8: 413 (1985).

74 R. Reagan, *An American Life* 449–458 (1990).
75 *Wash. Post*, Nov. 6, 1983: A1; Beck, 'The McNeil Mission,' *Nav. War Col. Rev.* 42: (1991).
76 A. Payne, *et al*., *Grenada: Revolution and Invasion*: 168 (1984).
77 See Moore, op. cit.: 153.
78 *Dep't St. Bull*. 83: 78–79 (1983).
79 Letter of Davis Robinson to Edward Gordon, in Moore, op. cit.: 125–129 (1984).
80 *N.Y. Times*, Dec. 21: A1. For legal analyses, see D'Amato, op. cit.: 494; Farer, op. cit.: 503; Nanda, op. cit.: 494; and Terry, op. cit.: 110.
81 Ibid.: 9.
82 Ibid.
83 Ibid.: 24.
84 *N.Y. Times*, Dec. 23, 1989: 15.
85 *N.Y. Times*, Dec. 21, 1989: 24.
86 *N.Y. Times*, Dec. 22, 1989: 22.
87 *N.Y. Times*, Dec. 24, 1989: 8.
88 *N.Y. Times*, Aug. 5, 1990: 19; *N.Y. Times*, Aug. 6, 1990: 1; *N.Y. Times*, Aug. 8, 1990: 3.
89 *N.Y. Times*, Aug. 6, 1990: A2.
90 *Wash. Post*, Aug. 6, 1990: A1.
91 *Wash. Post*, Aug. 6, 1990: A17; *N.Y. Times*, Aug. 20, 1990: A9.
92 *N.Y. Times*, Aug. 26, 1990: 13.
93 H. Bull, *Intervention in World Politics*: 1 (1984).
94 Such actions notwithstanding, '*the presence in foreign territory of the subjects of the intervening State* is one of the constants' of intervention to protect nationals. N. Ronzitti, op. cit.: 24.
95 Ibid.: 24.
96 Ibid.: 25.
97 Ibid.: 25.
98 Robinson letter to Gordon, op. cit.: 125–129.
99 *N.Y. Times*, Dec. 20, 1989: 9.
100 N. Ronzitti, op. cit: 1–6. See also notes 119–145 below.
101 See generally, R. Higgins, *The Development of International Law Through the Political Organs of the United Nations*: 167–230 (1963); Fonteyne, 'Forcible

Self-Help by States to Protect Human Rights: Recent Views from the United Nations,' in R. Lillich (ed.) *Humanitarian Intervention and the United Nations* 197 app. B, 209–216 (1973).

102 N. Ronzitti, op. cit.: 1: Akehurst, op. cit.: 3. See generally M. Akehurst, *A Modern Introduction to International Law* 313–314 (2nd ed. 1971); J. Brierly, *The Law of Nations* 413–432 (6th ed. 1963); I. Brownlie, *International Law and the Use of Force by States* 432–434 (1963); P. Delima, *Intervention in International Law* 210–218 (1971); L. Henkin, *How Nations Behave* 135–164 (2nd ed. 1979); P. Jessup, *A Modern Law of Nations* 100–150 (1948); H. Kelsen and R. Tucker, *Principles of International Law* 64–87 (2nd ed. 1966); Oppenheim, *International Law* 2: 154 (7th H. Lauterpacht, ed. 1952); Verdross, *Hague Recueil de Cours* 83: 1 (1953): 14; Wehberg, *Hague Receuil de Cours* 78: 7, 70; Wright, 'The Legality of Intervention Under the UN Charter,' *Proc. Am. Soc'y Int'l L.* 51: 79, 86 (1957).

103 Note, 'Resort to Force by States to Protect Nationals,' *Va. J. Int'l L.* 21: 487 (1981); N. Ronzitti, op. cit.: 1.

104 Note, op. cit.: 487. Ian Brownlie's work is exemplary of the 'restrictionist' school. See I. Brownlie, op. cit.: 272; Brownlie, 'Humanitarian Intervention,' in J. Moore (ed.) *Law and Civil War in the Modern World* 217, 219 (1974); and Brownlie, 'Thoughts on the Kind-Hearted Gunman,' in R. Lillich (ed.) *Humanitarian Intervention and the United Nations* 139, 146 (1973).

105 Note, op. cit.: 487.

106 D. Bowett, op. cit.: 87; I. Brownlie, *International Law and the Use of Force by States* 289–296 (1963); N. Ronzitti, op. cit.: 21–23; UN *Rep'ts of Int'l Arbtrl Awards* 2: 641; Waldcock, op. cit.: 499–503; Fitzmaurice, 'The General Principles of International Law,' *Recueil des Cours* 92: 172–174 (1957).

107 Franck and Rodley, op. cit.: 275; Falk, 'Historical Tendencies, Modernising and Revolutionary Nations, and the International Legal Order,' *How. L.J.* 8: 128, 133 (1962).

108 I. Brownlie, op. cit.: 273.

109 See, e.g. Ibid.: 265–268.

110 Ibid.: 271–272; H. Kelsen and R. Tucker, op. cit.: 66–67.

111 I. Brownlie, op. cit.: 278.

112 Waldock, op. cit.: 493. Because he considers intervention to protect nationals permissible self-defense, Waldcock should probably be considered a 'counter-restrictionist.'

113 Viraly, Article 2, paragraph 4, in J. Cot and A. Pellet (eds) *La Charte des Nations Nuies* 114 (1985) ('les termes employes dans l'article 2, paragraphe 4, lui confierent la partie la plus etendue qui se puisse imaginer').

114 Statement by Prof. W. Friedmann, Conference Proceedings, R. Lillich (ed.) in *Humanitarian Intervention and the United Nations* 115 (1973).

115 Note, op. cit.: 490.

116 See the Declaration on the Inadmissibility of Intervention in the Domestic Affairs of States and the Protection of Their Independence and Sovereignty, *G.A. Res. 2131, UN GAOR 20, Annexes* (Agenda Item 107) 3: 9, *UN Doc. A/6220* (1965); and the Declaration on Principles of International Law Concerning Friendly Relations and Co-operation Among States in Accordance with the Charter of the United Nations, *GA Res. 265, UN GAOR Supp.* (No. 28) 25: 121, *UN Doc. A/8028* (1970).

117 See, e.g. H. Lauterpacht, *International Law and Human Rights* 397–408 (2nd ed. 1973); Fonteyne, op. cit. and H. Kelsen and R. Tucker, op. cit.: 67 n. 59.

118 See, e.g. Note, op. cit.: 491–501.

119 See. e.g. D. Bowett, op. cit.: 185; and Bowett, 'The Use of Force for the Protection of Nationals Abroad,' in A. Cassese (ed.) *The Current Legal Regulation of the Use of Force.*

120 Bowett, op. cit.: 40.
121 Ibid.
122 Ibid.
123 Ibid.: 41.
124 M. Reisman, *Nullity and Revision*: 848 (1971).
125 Lillich, op. cit.: 335; Reisman and McDougal, 'Humanitarian Intervention to Protect the Ibos,' in R. Lillich (ed.) *Humanitarian Intervention and the United Nations*: 178 (1973).
126 Note, op. cit.: 495.
127 Reisman, 'Sanctions and Enforcement,' in C. Black and R. Falk (eds) *The Future of the International Legal Order* 3: 850 (1971).
128 Ibid.: 333.
129 Note, op. cit.: 498.
130 L. Goodrich, E. Hambro and A. Simons, *Charter of the United Nations*: 344 (3rd ed. 1969).
131 Note, op. cit.: 501.
132 Waldcock, op. cit.: 467.
133 Akehurst, 'The Use of Force to Protect Nationals Abroad,' *Int'l Rel.* 5: 3 (1977).
134 N. Ronzitti, op. cit.: 1.
135 J. Stone, *Aggression and World Order*: 43, 95–96 (1963); Bowett, op. cit.: Lillich, op. cit.: 336; Reisman and McDougal, op. cit.: 177.
136 J. Stone, op. cit.: 43.
137 Reisman and McDougal, op. cit.: 172–175; McDougal and Reisman, 'Response by Professors McDougal and Reisman,' *Int'l Law.* 3: 438, 444 (1969).
138 Note, op. cit.: 491.
139 Reisman and McDougal, op. cit.: 172.
140 Note, op. cit.: 493.
141 *UN Charter*, Article 55 and 56.
142 Reisman and McDougal, op. cit.: 174–175.
143 Note, op. cit.: 493. See Reisman and McDougal, op. cit.: 174–175.
144 McDougal and Reisman, op. cit.: 438, 444.
145 Ibid.: 444.
146 N. Ronzitti, op. cit.: xiii, 1; Akehurst, op. cit.: 3.
147 See notes 37, 102, and 114 above.
148 See notes 119–145 above.
149 See note 101 above.
150 See above.
151 North Sea Continental Shelf Cases (FRG v. Den.) (FRG v. Neth.), 1969 *ICJ* 4: paras 73, 74.
152 Ibid.

8 HUMANITARIAN INTERVENTION

1 Lane, 'Mass Killing by Governments: Lawful in the World Legal Order?' *NYU J. Int'l L. & Pol.* 2: 239 (1979).
2 Cited by N. Ronzitti, *Rescuing Nationals Abroad Through Military Coercion and Intervention on the Grounds of Humanity*: 98 (1985).
3 See Chapter 6 and 7 above.
4 According to Professor Verwey, 'It is not at all self-evident what is meant, legally speaking, by "humanitarian intervention."' Verwey, 'Humanitarian Intervention,' A. Cassese (ed.) in *The Current Legal Regulation of the Use of Force*: 58 (1986).
5 For other definitions and characterizations of 'humanitarian intervention,' see

Akehurst, 'The Use of Force to Protect Nationals Abroad,' *Int'l Rel.* 5: 9 (1977); Akehurst, 'Humanitarian Intervention,' in H. Bull (ed.) *Intervention in World Politics* 112 (1984); L. Brilmayer, *Justifying International Acts* 139–141 (1989); Baxter, in R. Lillich (ed.) *Humanitarian Intervention and the United Nations* 53 (1973); Chopra and Weiss, 'Sovereignty Is No Longer Sacrosanct: Codifying Humanitarian Intervention,' *Ethics & Int'l Affrs.* 6: 95 (1992); Flinterman, 'Humanitarian Intervention, or How Long Must the World Stand Idly By?' *NJCM Bull.* 3: 13 (1978); Lillich, 'Forcible Self-Help by States to Protect Human Rights,' *Iowa L. Rev.* 53: 325, 347–351 (1967); Moore, 'The Control of Foreign Intervention in Internal Conflict,' *Va. J. Int'l L.* 9: 205, 264 (1969); N. Ronzitti, op. cit.: xiv; David Scheffer, 'Challenges Confronting Collective Security: Humanitarian Intervention,' in D. Scheffer, R. Gardner and G. Helman, Post-Gulf War Challenges to the UN Collective Security System: Three Views on the Issue of Humanitarian Intervention: 1–13 (1992); F. Tesón, *Humanitarian Intervention:* 5 (1988); Verwey, op. cit.: 59; and Note, 'Resort to Force by States to Protect Nationals,' *Va. J. Int'l L.* 21: 485 (1981).

For a useful discussion of the definitional parameters of 'humanitarian intervention,' see Farer, 'Humanitarian Intervention: The View from Charlottesville,' in R. Lillich (ed.) *Humanitarian Intervention and the United Nations:* 150–151 (1973).

6 Akehurst, op. cit.: 15.
7 Ibid.
8 N. Ronzitti, op. cit.: xv; Akehurst, op. cit.: 105.
9 Moore, op. cit.: 205, 264. According to Professor Akehurst, humanitarian intervention 'is frequently described as applicable only when human rights have been violated on a massive scale.' Akehurst, 'The Use of Force to Protect Nationals Abroad,' *Int'l Rel.* 5: 13.
10 See, e.g. L. Brilmayer, op. cit.: 141; Levitin, 'The Law of Force and the Force of Law: Grenada, the Falklands, and Humanitarian Intervention', *Harv. J. Int'l L.* 27: 652 (1986); Scheffer, op. cit.: 12; Verwey, op. cit.: 66.
11 Verwey, op. cit.: 59; Scheffer, op. cit.: 5, 9. This would seem an extremely unlikely prospect, however.
12 Verwey, op. cit.: 59.
13 Akehurst, op. cit.: 13–16; Bowett, 'The Use of Force for the Protection of Nationals Abroad,' in A. Cassese (ed.) *The Current Legal Regulation of the Use of Force:* 49 (1986); N. Ronzitti, op. cit.: xiv–xv; Note, op. cit.: 485.

Tesón characterizes 'intervention to protect nationals' as a 'rescue mission,' and distinguishes such action from a true 'humanitarian intervention.' F. Tesón, op. cit.: 5.
14 Akehurst, 'Humanitarian Intervention,' in H. Bull (ed.) *Intervention in World Politics* 113 (1984); N. Ronzitti, op. cit.: xiv–xv. See also F. Tesón, op. cit.: 142–146.
15 Cf. N. Ronzitti, op. cit. xv.
16 Ibid.: xvii.
17 Akehurst, op. cit.: 113.
18 For more detailed reviews of state practice, though less comprehensive ones, see Akehurst, op. cit.: 95–99; N. Ronzitti, op. cit.: 93–106; F. Tesón, op. cit.: 155–200; and Verwey, op. cit.: 60–65.
19 N. Ronzitti, op. cit.: 92. Cf. Akehurst, op. cit.: 99; and Akehurst, 'The Use of Force to Protect Nationals Abroad,' *Int'l Rel.* 5: 10 (1977).
20 According to Bowett, 'we have no true example of a clear reliance on this right of intervention by any State since 1945.' Bowett, op. cit.: 50.
21 On the Arab intervention in Palestine, see Akehurst, op. cit.: 10–11; M. Donelan and M. Grieve, *International Disputes, Case Histories 1945–1970:* 48ff. (1973); A. Gerson, *Israel, the West Bank and International Law:* 17ff. (1978); N. Ronzitti, op. cit.: 93–95; and Verwey, op. cit.: 61.

22 The intervention was also justified in terms of protection of nationals. See Chapter 7 above.
23 *UN SCOR, 292nd mtg, May 15, 1948* 3: 3.
24 *UN SCOR, 301st mtg, May 22, 1948* 3: 3, 7.
25 N. Ronzitti, op. cit.: 95.
26 *UN SCOR, 292nd mtg, May 15, 1948* 3: 25.
27 N. Ronzitti, op. cit.: 94.
28 Akehurst, op. cit.: 11; and Akehurst, 'Humanitarian Intervention,' in H. Bull (ed.) *Intervention in World Politics: 96 (1984).*
29 Ibid.
30 Verwey, op. cit.: 61.
31 Akehurst, op. cit.: 99; Akehurst, 'The Use of Force to Protect Nationals Abroad,' *Int'l Rel.* 5: 7 (1977); Verwey, op. cit.: 61; N. Ronzitti, op. cit.: 30–32; and M. Zacher, *International Conflicts and Collective Security*: 238 (1979). See also Chapter 7 above.
32 Statement by the Belgian representative, M. Loridan in *UN SCOR, 873rd mtg, July 13–14, 1960* 15: 34.
33 The supporters of Belgium 'declared that, since Belgium had intervened for humanitarian reasons, it was not possible to consider it as an aggressor.' N. Ronzitti, op. cit.: 31–32.
34 Akehurst, 'Humanitarian Intervention,' in H. Bull (ed.) *Intervention in World Politics*: 99 (1984).
35 M. Whiteman, *Digest of International Law* 5: 522 (1965). Congolese Foreign Minister Bomboko had consented to the Belgian action, but had subsequently been overruled by Prime Minister Lumumba. Akehurst, 'The Use of Force to Protect Nationals Abroad,' *Int'l Rel.* 5: 7 (1977).
36 Verwey, op. cit.: 61.
37 F. Tesón, op. cit.: 155–200. In his discussion of state practice, Tesón aspires to 'spell out the conditions that define genuine, legitimate humanitarian interventions.' Ibid.: 157.
38 See generally Akehurst, op. cit.: 7–8; Akehurst, 'Humanitarian Intervention,' in H. Bull (ed.) *Intervention in World Politics* 100 (1986); Brownlie, 'Humanitarian Intervention,' in J. Moore (ed.) *Law and Civil War in the Modern World:* 22 (1974); Fairley, 'State Actors, Humanitarian Intervention, and International Law: Reopening Pandora's Box,' *Ga. J. Int'l & Comp. L.* 1038: 48–50 (1980); Lillich, op. cit.: 338–340; Reisman and McDougal, 'Humanitarian Intervention to Protect the Ibos,' in R. Lillich (ed.) *Humanitarian Intervention and the United Nations*: 185 (1973); N. Ronzitti, op. cit.: 78–79; Verwey, op. cit.: 61–62; G. von Glahn, *Law Among Nations* 168 (1970); and Weisberg, 'The Congo Crisis 1964: A Case Study in Humanitarian Intervention,' *Va. J. Int'l L.* 12: 261 (1972). See also Chapter 7 above.
39 Verwey, op. cit.: 61–62.
40 G. von Glahn, op. cit.: 168.
41 See Chapter 5 above.
42 N. Ronzitti, op. cit.: 78–79.
43 Akehurst, 'The Use of Force to Protect Nationals Abroad,' *Int'l Rel.* 5: 7 (1977); N. Ronzitti, op. cit.: 79.
44 *UN SCOR, 1174th mtg, Dec. 14, 1964* 19: 2.
45 *UN SCOR, 1176th mtg, Dec. 15, 1964* 19: 4–5; *UN SCOR, 1183rd mtg, Dec. 22, 1964* 19: 14; and *UN SCOR, 1177th mtg, Dec. 16, 1964* 19: 19, 26.
46 *British Practice in International Law*: 131–132 (1964); Akehurst, op. cit.: 7–8.
47 See Gerard, 'L'operation Stanleyville-Paulis devant le Parlement belge et les Nations Unies,' *Revue Belge de Droit International* 3: 265 (1967).
48 *UN SCOR, 1170th mtg, Dec. 9, 1964* 19: 28. Sudan opposed humanitarian

intervention in 1979, however. Akehurst, 'Humanitarian Intervention,' in H. Bull (ed.) *Intervention in World Politics*: 114 (1984).

49 Professor Verwey, for example, argues that 'the primary objective of US and Belgian policy from the beginning' was 'to destroy the rebel stronghold' in the Congo. It was clearly in the interests of the intervening states, he maintains, to bolster the precarious position of the Tsjombe government: 'it was not by coincidence that when [the intervening states'] troops departed, the rebels' "capital" was in the government's hands, their fighting capacity had been flattened, a mercenary strike force against them could be assembled, and Tsjombe's prospects in the civil war had been remarkably improved, not in the last place by providing him with air power and logistical support.' Verwey, op. cit.: 62.

50 US Representative Adlai Stevenson in *UN SCOR, 1196th mtg*: 14. For the US Legal Adviser's justification see Meeker, 'The Dominican Situation in the Perspective of International Law,' *Dep't S. Bull.* 53: 60 (1965).

  For scholarly analyses, see Akehurst, op. cit.: 100–101; Akehurst, 'The Use of Force to Protect Nationals Abroad,' *Int'l Rel.* 5: 11 (1977); Bogen, 'The Law of Humanitarian Intervention,' *Harv. J. Int'l L.* 7: 296 (1965); Brownlie, op. cit.: 221; Dore, 'The US Invasion of Grenada: Resurrection of the "Johnson Doctrine?"' *Stan. J. Int'l L.* 20: 173 (1984); Ehrlich, 'The Measuring Line of Occasion,' *Stan. J. Int'l Stud.* 3: 27, 35–37 (1968); Fenwick, 'The Dominican Republic: Intervention or Collective Self-defense,' *Am. J. Int'l L.* 60: 287 (1966); Franck and Rodley, 'After Bangladesh: The Law of Humanitarian Intervention by Military Force,' *Am. J. Int'l L.* 67: 287 (1973); McLaren, 'The Dominican Crisis: An Inter-American Dilemma,' *Can. Y.B. Int'l L.* 4: 178 (1966); Nanda, 'The United States Action in the 1965 Dominican Crisis: Impact on World Order – Part 1,' *Denver L.J.* 43: 439 (1966); N. Ronzitti, op. cit.: 32–35; Slater, *Intervention and Negotiation: The United States and the Dominican Revolution*: 203 (1970); Thomas and Thomas, *The Dominican Republic Crisis* (1972); and Verwey, op. cit.: 62–63.

51 N. Ronzitti, op. cit.: 33.

52 Akehurst, 'Humanitarian Intervention,' in H. Bull (ed.) *Intervention in World Politics*: 100 (1984); N. Ronzitti, op. cit.: 33.

53 Akehurst, 'The Use of Force to Protect Nationals Abroad,' *Int'l Rel.* 5: 11 (emphasis added) (1977).

54 A. Chayes, Ehrlich and A. Lowenfeld, *International Legal Process*: 1169 (1967).

55 Dore, op. cit.: 180.

56 Akehurst, op. cit.: 12–13; Akehurst, 'Humanitarian Intervention,' in H. Bull (ed.) *Intervention in World Politics* 96–97 (1984); Brownlie, 'Thoughts on Kind-hearted Gunmen,' in R. Lillich (ed.) *Humanitarian Intervention and the United Nations*: 139 (1973); Farer, op. cit.: 149, 157; T. Franck, *Nation Against Nation*: 166–167 (1985); Franck and Rodley, op. cit.: 275; Franck and Rodley, 'The Law, The United Nations, and Bangla-Desh,' *Israel Y.B. Human Rts.* 2: 142 (1972); Friedmann, 'Conference Proceedings,' in R. Lillich (ed.) *Humanitarian Intervention and the United Nations*: 114 (1973); *International Commission of Jurists Report, The Events in East Pakistan, 1971* 8: 59–62 (1972); Mani, 'The 1971 War on the Indian Subcontinent and International Law,' *Indian J. Int'l L.* 12: 83, 85 (1972); Nanda, 'A Critique of the United Nations Inaction in the Bangladesh Crisis,' *Denv. L. J.* 49: 53 (1972); Nanda, 'Self-Determination in International Law: The Tragic Tale of Two Cities,' *Am. J. Int'l L.* 66: 321 (1972); Nawaz, 'Bangla-Desh and International Law,' *Indian J. Int'l L.* 11: 459 (1971); T. Oliver, *The United Nations in Bangladesh* (1978); Reisman, 'Conference Proceedings,' in R. Lillich (ed.) *Humanitarian Intervention and the United Nations*: 17–18 (1973); N. Ronzitti, op. cit.: 95–97; Salzberg, 'UN Prevention

of Human Rights Violations: The Bangladesh Case,' *Int'l Org.* 27: 115 (1973); F. Tesón, op. cit.: 179–188; Verwey, op. cit.: 63–64.

57 N. Ronzitti, op. cit.: 95. See also Akehurst, op. cit.: 96.
58 *Int'l Comm. Jur. Report,* op. cit.: 7–14; Nawaz, op. cit.: 251.
59 F. Tesón, op. cit.: 180–181.
60 N. Ronzitti, op. cit.: 95.
61 *Int'l Comm. Jur. Report,* op. cit.: 20–21.
62 F. Tesón, op. cit.: 181.
63 Ibid. For specific accounts, see *Int'l Comm. Jur. Report,* op. cit.: 27–42; Salzberg, op. cit.: 115, 116; Schanberg, 'Pakistan Divided,' *For. Aff.* 50: 126–127 (1971).
64 *Int'l Comm. Jur. Report,* op. cit.: 26–27.
65 The Pakistan government claimed that no more than two million refugees had fled. Keesing's *Contemporary Archives* 24990 (1971). Prime Minister Gandhi suggested that East Pakistani refugees had totaled ten million. 'Ghandhi, India and the World,' *For. Aff.* 50: 70–71 (1972).
66 F. Tesón, op. cit.: 182; *Int'l Comm. Jur. Report,* op. cit.: 43–44.
67 Akehurst, op. cit.: 96; Akehurst, 'The Use of Force to Protect Nationals Abroad,' *Int'l Rel.* 5: 12 (1977).
68 See passages cited by Franck and Rodley, 'After Bangladesh: The Law of Humanitarian Intervention by Military Forces,' *Am. J. Int'l L.* 67: 275, 276.
69 See, e.g. *UN SCOR, 1606th mtg, Dec. 16, 1971* 26: 15.
70 Akehurst, op. cit.: 12; 'Humanitarian Intervention, in H. Bull (ed.) *Intervention in World Politics* 96 (1984). Cf. Bowett, op. cit.: 50.
71 F. Tesón, op. cit.: 186.
72 Verwey, op. cit.: 63.
73 Ibid.
74 Frey-Wouters, 'Conference Proceedings,' in R. Lillich (ed.) *Humanitarian Intervention and the United Nations* 107 (1973).
75 Akehurst, op. cit.: 96; N. Ronzitti, op. cit.: 96–97.
76 Meuffels, *De Verenigde Naties en de Handhaving van de Vrede– The United Nations and the Maintenance of Peace* 144 (1980); Vadney, op. cit.: 380–381; Verwey, op. cit.: 64; and Zacher, *International Conflicts and Collective Security* 276 (1979).
77 Verwey, op. cit.: 64. See also, *N.Y. Times,* Dec. 8, 1975: 9.
78 Verwey, op. cit.: 64.
79 See Meuffels, op. cit.: 144; Verwey, op. cit.: 64; and Zacher, op. cit.: 276.
80 Vadney, op. cit.: 380–381.
81 Meuffels, op. cit.: 144; Vadney, op. cit.: 484–485; Verwey, op. cit.: 64; and Zacher, op. cit.: 276.
82 Verwey, op. cit.: 64. South Africa also claimed to have a right of counter-intervention. Ibid.
83 See, e.g. Akehurst, op. cit.: 95–99; N. Ronzitti, op. cit.: 92–106; and F. Tesón, op. cit.: 155–200.
84 Ibid.
85 *UN SCOR, 1906th mtg, Mar. 31, 1976* 31: 20–22, 30.
86 Akehurst, op. cit.: 97–98; Lane, op. cit.: 239; N. Ronzitti, op. cit.: 98–101; Vadney, op. cit.: 507–511; Van der Kroef, 'Cambodia: From "Democratic Kampuchea" to "People's Republic,"' *Asian Survey* 29: 731 (1979); and Warbrick, 'Kampuchea: Representation and Recognition,' *Int'l & Comp. L. Q.* 30: 234 (1981).
    See also the letters of Alfred Rubin and Eugene V. Rostow published in *N.Y. Times,* Mar. 20, 1979: 18; and *N.Y. Times,* Apr. 10, 1979: 18.
87 N. Ronzitti, op. cit.: 98.
88 Lane, op. cit.: 239. According to Professor Vadney, between five hundred thousand

and one million persons died in Kampuchea as a result of disease, famine, and Khmer Rouge atrocities. Vadney, op. cit.: 511.

89 N. Ronzitti, op. cit.: 98–99.
90 Ibid.: 99.
91 Vadney, op. cit.: 509; N. Ronzitti, op. cit.: 99.
92 Ibid.: 98.
93 See especially *UN SCOR, 2108th mtg, Jan. 11, 1979* 34.
94 Akehurst, op. cit.: 97; N. Ronzitti, op. cit.: 99. See *UN SCOR, 2108th mtg, Jan. 11, 1979.*
95 Akehurst, op. cit.: 97; N. Ronzitti, op. cit.: 99.
96 For a more detailed account, see Akehurst, op. cit.: 97; and N. Ronzitti, op. cit.: 99–101.
97 Akehurst, op. cit.: 97.
98 N. Ronzitti, op. cit.: 101.
99 *UN SCOR, 2112th mtg, Jan. 15, 1979* 34.
100 During the course of General Assembly deliberations, a number of states observed that it was illegal to intervene in another state's territory, despite the commission of grave human rights violations by a local sovereign. N. Ronzitti, op. cit.: 101. *YB of the UN* 33: 290 (1979).
101 N. Ronzitti, op. cit.: 101.
102 Akehurst, op. cit.: 98.
103 Akehurst, op. cit.: 99.
104 Vadney, op. cit.: 509–511.
105 F. Tesón, op. cit.: 159–200. Professor Verwey also does not discuss the Vietnamese use of force. Verwey, op. cit.: 60–65.
106 For legal analyses of the intervention, see Akehurst, op. cit.: 98–99; Burrows, 'Tanzania's Intervention in Uganda: Some Legal Aspects,' *The World Today* 35: 306 (1979); Chaterjee, 'Some Legal Problems of Support Role In International Law: Tanzania and Uganda,' *Int'l & Comp. L. Q.* 30: 755 (1981); Hassan, 'Realpolitik in International Law: After Tanzanian Ugandan Conflict: Humanitarian Intervention Reexamined,' *Willamette L. J.* 17: 859 (1980–81); Reisman, 'Coercion and Self-Determination: Construing Article 2(4),' *Am. J. Int'l L.* 78: 642, 644 (1984); N. Ronzitti, op. cit.: 102–106; F. Tesón, op. cit.: 159–175; Umozurike, 'Tanzanian Intervention in Uganda,' *Archiv des Volkerrechts* 20: 301 (1982); and Wani, 'Humanitarian Intervention and the Tanzanian-Ugandan-War,' *Horn of Africa* 3: 18 (1980).
107 N. Ronzitti, op. cit.: 102.
108 H. Kyemba, *State of Blood:* 9 (1977); Amnesty International, *Human Rights in Uganda, Report, June 1978, Doc. AFR 59/05/78.*
109 F. Tesón, op. cit.: 163. See also Ullman, 'Human Rights and Economic Power: The United States v. Idi Amin,' *For. Aff.* 56: 529 (1978); M. Richardson, *After Amin, The Bloody Pearl* (1980); and *Int'l Com. Jur. Report, Uganda and Human Rights* (1977).
110 F. Tesón, op. cit.: 159.
111 *Keesing's Contemp. Arch.:* 29669 (1979); S. Kiwanuka, *Amin and the Tragedy of Uganda:* 123 (1979).
112 *Keesing's Contemp. Arch.:* 29669 (1979).
113 C. Legum (ed.) *Africa Contemporary Records* 11: B427 (1978–79).
114 N. Ronzitti, op. cit.: 102.
115 F. Tesón, op. cit.: 160.
116 *Keesing's Contemp. Arch.* 29761 (1979).
117 Ibid.
118 C. Legum (ed.) op. cit.: 11: B433. See also N. Ronzitti, op. cit.: 102.
119 Ibid.: 103.

120 Tanzanian control of the capital was complete by April 22, 1979. Hassan, op. cit.: 880–881.
121 Ibid.
122 *Africa Research Bull. – Political, Social and Cultural Series* 16: 5223 (1979).
123 *Le Monde*, Apr. 14, 1979, cited by N. Ronzitti, op. cit.: 103.
124 N. Ronzitti, op. cit.: 103.
125 *Africa Research Bull. – Political, Social and Cultural Series* 16: 5223 (1979). Emphasis added.
126 Wani, op. cit.: 24. According to Professor Tesón, 'The world sighed with relief at the fall of Idi Amin.' F. Tesón, op. cit.: 170.
127 Wani, op. cit.: 24.
128 N. Ronzitti, op. cit.: 104; F. Tesón, op. cit.: 165–166.
129 *Keesing's Contemp. Arch.* 25: 29670–29761 (1979); *Africa Research Bull. – Political, Social and Cultural Series* 16: 5154–5155, 5186 (1979).
130 N. Ronzitti, op. cit.: 104.
131 *Africa Research Bull. – Political, Social and Cultural Series* 16: 5224 (1979).
132 *Keesing's Contemp. Arch.* 25: 29840–29841 (1979).
133 F. Tesón, op. cit.: 167. Other supporters of the legality of the Uganda intervention are Professors Reisman and Umozurike. See Reisman, op. cit. and Umozurike, op. cit..
134 F. Tesón, op. cit.: 167–168.
135 N. Ronzitti, op. cit.: 102–106, 110. Akehurst rejects the 'humanitarian intervention' interpretation in part because Tanzania 'seems [not] to have invoked the "right" of humanitarian intervention to justify its actions.' Akehurst, op. cit.: 98. See also Hassan, op. cit.; and Wani, op. cit.
136 Tanzania's self-defense justification was of dubious legality. According to Tesón: 'A use of force in self-defense is not punitive in character and therefore cannot have been a "continuation." Had Tanzania acted in self-defense she would have had to stop after repelling the Ugandan initial attack.' F. Tesón, op. cit.: 173.
137 *Annuaire Français de Droit International* 25: 908 (1979); Akehurst, op. cit.: 98; Rousseau, 'Chroniques de Faits Internationaux,' *RGDIP* 83: 1058 (1979); F. Tesón, op. cit.: 175–179; and Wauthier, 'France in Africa; President Giscard d'Estaing Ambitious Diplomacy,' in C. Legum (ed.) op. cit.: 12: 120.
138 F. Tesón, op. cit.: 177–178.
139 N. Ronzitti, op. cit.: 92–106; Verwey, op. cit.: 60–66.
140 Akehurst, op. cit.: 98. Akehurst cites *Annuaire Français de Droit International* 25: 908–910 (1979).
141 F. Tesón, op. cit.: 176.
142 Statement of September 24, 1979, to the French television, cited by Rousseau, op. cit.: 365.
143 F. Tesón, op. cit.: 176. See, e.g. Rousseau, op. cit.: 365; Wauthier, op. cit.: 120.
144 F. Tesón, op. cit.: 177.
145 Ibid.: 178.
146 Ibid.: 175.
147 *Keesing's Contemp. Arch.*: 29933 (1979).
148 Ibid.
149 *N.Y. Times*, Sept. 24, 1979: 12.
150 Ibid.
151 Books on the Grenada invasion include: S. Davidson, *Grenada; A Study in Politics and the Limits of International Law* (1987); W. Gilmore, *The Grenada Intervention* (1984); and J. Moore, *Law and the Grenada Mission* (1984).
    Articles include: Boyle *et al.*, 'International Lawlessness in Grenada,' *Am. J. Int'l L.* 78: 172 (1984); Dieguez, 'The Grenada Invasion: "Illegal" in Form, Sound as Policy,'

NYUJ Int'l L. & Pol. 16: 1167 (1984); Dore, op. cit.; Doswald-Beck, 'The Legality of the US Intervention in Grenada,' *Neth. Int'l L. Rev.* 31: 362 (1984); Fraser, 'Grenada: The Sovereignty of the People,' *W. Indian L. J.* 7: 205 (1983); Gordon *et al.*, 'International Law and the United States Action in Grenada,' *Int'l L.* 18: 331 (1984); Joyner, 'Reflections on the Lawfulness of Invasion,' *Am. J. Int'l L.* 78: 131 (1984); Karas and Goodman, 'The United States Action in Grenada: An Exercise in Realpolitik,' *U. Miami Inter-Am. L. Rev.* 16: 53 (1984); Levitin, op. cit.; Moore, 'Grenada and the International Double Standard,' *Am. J. Int'l L.* 78: 145 (1984); Nanda, 'The United States Intervention in Grenada – Impact on World Order,' *Cal. Westrn Int'l L. J.* 14: 395 (1984); Quigley, 'The United States Invasion of Grenada: Stranger than Fiction,' *U. Miami Inter-Am. L. Rev.* 18: 271 (1986–87); Riggs, 'The Grenada Intervention: A Legal Analysis,' *Mil. L. Rev.* 1: 1 (1985); Smart, 'Revolutions, Constitutions and the Commonwealth: Grenada,' *Int'l & Comp. L. Qtly.* 35: 950 (1986); Vagts, 'International Law Under Time Pressure: Grading the Grenada Take-Home Examination,' *Am. J. Int'l L.* 79: 169 (1984); Waters, 'The Invasion of Grenada, 1983, and the Collapse of Legal Norms,' *J. Peace Research* 23: 229–246 (1986); and Wheeler, 'The Grenada Invasion: Expanding the Scope of Humanitarian Intervention,' *Bos. C. Int'l & Comp. L. Rev.* 8: 413 (1985).
    See also F. Tesón op. cit.: 188–200; and Verwey, op. cit.: 65.
152 Beck, 'The McNeil Mission,' *Nav. War Col. Rev.* 42: (1991); *Wash. Post*, Nov. 6, 1983: A1.
153 Moore, op. cit.: 153–156.
154 See, e.g. Ibid.: 145, 159–161.
155 See Chapter 5 above.
156 See, e.g. F. Tesón, op. cit.: 188–200.
157 R. Reagan, *An American Life*. 449–458 (1990).
158 A. Payne *et al.*, *Grenada; Revolution and Invasion*: 168 (1984).
159 See Moore, op. cit.: 153.
160 [This reference has been deleted from the text.]
161 For a discussion of the Reagan Administration's rationale, see F. Teson, op. cit.: 191–195.
162 See, e.g. 'President's Remarks, Oct. 25, 1983,' *Dept St. Bull.* 83: 67 (1983); 'Secretary Shultz's News Conference, Oct. 25, 1983,' *Dept St. Bull.* 83: 69–72 (1983).
163 *Dep't St. Bull.* 83: 73 (1983).
164 White House Statement, Nov. 3, 1983 in ibid.: 78.
165 F. Tesón, op. cit.: 192.
166 'Letter of Davis Robinson to Edward Gordon,' in Moore, *Law and the Grenada Mission*: 125–129 (1984).
167 Ibid.
168 N. Ronzitti, op. cit.: 92.
169 See Verwey, op. cit.: 66.
170 Professor Verwey's 1986 study of nine interventions came to a similar conclusion. See Verwey, op. cit.: 66.
171 Bowett, op. cit.: 60. According to Professor Akehurst, 'humanitarian intervention has been invoked by states on a surprisingly small number of occasions since 1945.' Akehurst, op. cit.: 99.
172 N. Ronzitti, op. cit.: 108–109.
173 White House Statement, op. cit.: 78.
174 Robinson to Gordon Letter, op. cit.: 128.
175 *Africa Research Bull. – Political, Social and Cultural Series* 16: 5223 (1979).
176 Ibid.: 5224.
177 Akehurst, op. cit.: 96; Akehurst, 'The Use of Force to Protect Nationals Abroad, *Int'l Rel.* 5: 12 (1977); Bowett, op. cit.: 50.

178 N. Ronzitti, op. cit.: 109.
179 See, e.g. ibid.
180 Ibid.
181 Ibid.
182 Whiteman, *Digest of Int'l Law* 5: 522 (1965).
183 *UN Doc. S/PV. 2112, Jan. 17, 1979*: 27.
184 N. Ronzitti, op. cit.: 109, 110; Akehurst, 'Humanitarian Intervention,' in H. Bull (ed.) *Intervention in World Politics* 99 (1984).
185 Ibid.: 99.
186 The general lack of state enthusiasm for the concept of 'humanitarian intervention' was also manifested during the drafting of UN Resolution on the Definition of Aggression. N. Ronzitti, op. cit.: 106–108, 110.
187 *UN SCOR, 1607th mtg, Dec. 5, 1971* 26.
188 N. Ronzitti, op. cit.: 110.
189 Ibid.: 109–110.
190 See authorities cited in notes 207–231 below.
191 Akehurst, op. cit.: 106; 'The Use of Force to Protect Nationals Abroad,' *Int'l Rel.* 5: 3 (1977); Levitin, op. cit.: 632; N. Ronzitti, op. cit.: 1.
       See generally M. Akehurst, *A Modern Introduction to International Law.* 313–314 (2nd ed. 1971); J. Brierly, *The Law of Nations.* 413–432 (6th ed. 1963); I. Brownlie, *International Law and the Use of Force by States.* 432–434 (1963); P. Delima, *Intervention in International Law.* 210–218 (1971); L. Henkin, *How Nations Behave.* 135–164 (2nd ed. 1979); P. Jessup, *A Modern Law of Nations.* 100–150 (1948); H. Kelsen and R. Tucker, *Principles of International Law.* 64–87 (2nd ed. 1966); Oppenheim, *International Law* 2: 154 (7th ed. by Lauterpacht, 1952); Verdross, *Hague Recueil* 83: 1 (1953) 14; Wehberg, *Hague Recueil* 78: 7, 70; Wright, 'The Legality of Intervention Under the UN Charter,' *Proc. Am. Soc'y Int'l L.* 51: 79, 86 (1957).
192 Akehurst, 'Humanitarian Intervention,' in H. Bull (ed.) *Intervention in World Politics.* 106 (1984). See generally R. Higgins, *The Development of International Law Through the Political Organs of the United Nations.* 167–230 (1963); Fonteyne, 'Forcible Self-Help by States to Protect Human Rights: Recent Views from the United Nations,' in R. Lillich (ed.) *Humanitarian Intervention and the United Nations.* 197 app. B, 209–216 (1973).
193 Note, op. cit.: 487; N. Ronzitti, op. cit.: 1.
194 Note, op. cit.: 487. Ian Brownlie's work is exemplary of the 'restrictionist' school. See I. Brownlie, op. cit.: 273; Brownlie, 'Humanitarian Intervention,' in J. Moore (ed.) *Law and Civil War in the Modern World.* 217, 219 (1974); and Brownlie, 'Thoughts on Kind-hearted Gunmen,' in R. Lillich (ed.) *Humanitarian Intervention and the United Nations.* 139, 146 (1973).
195 Note, op. cit.: 487.
196 See, e.g. Ibid.: 265–268.
197 Ibid.: 271–272; H. Kelsen and R. Tucker, op. cit.: 66–67.
198 Legal scholars debate whether a customary right to humanitarian intervention existed before 1945. See I. Brownlie, *International Law and the Use of Force by States.* 339–341; M. Ganji, *International Protection of Human Rights.* 22–24 (1962); N. Ronzitti, op. cit.: 89–91; F. Tesón, op. cit.: 157–159; and Verwey, op. cit.: 59–60.
       Restrictionists seem generally to believe that the existence of such a right is 'somewhat dubious.' N. Ronzitti, op. cit.: 92.
199 Friedmann, op. cit.: 115.
200 Note, op. cit.: 490.
201 See the 'Declaration on the Inadmissibility of Intervention in the Domestic Affairs of

States and the Protection of Their Independence and Sovereignty,' *GA Res. 2131*, *UN GAOR* 20, *Annexes* (Agenda Item 107) 3: 9, *UN Doc. A/6220* (1965); and the 'Declaration on principles of International Law Concerning Friendly relations and Co-operation Among States in Accordance with the Charter of the United Nations,' *GA Res. 265*, *UN GAOR Supp.* (No. 28) 25: 121, *UN Doc. A/8028* (1970).

202 See, e.g. H. Lauterpacht, *International Law and Human Rights* 397–408 (2nd ed. 1973); Fonteyne, op. cit.; H. Kelsen and R. Tucker, op. cit.: 67 n. 59.

203 See Chapter 5 above.

204 See Lillich, op. cit.: 337 n. 76. See also McDougal, 'Authority to Use Force on the High Seas,' *Nav. War Col. Rev.* 20: 28–29 (Dec. 1967); and Bowett, op. cit.

  According to Professor Lillich, 'unless one relies exclusively upon Article 51 to justify the protection of nationals, ... any rationale allowing interventions to protect nationals also authorizes humanitarian interventions generally.' Lillich, 'Humanitarian Intervention: A Reply to Ian Brownlie and a Plea for Constructive Alternatives,' in J. Moore (ed.) *Law and Civil War in the Modern World* 241 n. 76. (1974).

205 Note, op. cit.: 496. According to Professor Bowett, 'the preservation of the inherent right of self-defense is wholly irrelevant to the argument about humanitarian intervention.' Bowett, op. cit.: 49.

206 Restrictionists assert that human rights and other UN purposes 'are permanently subordinated to the dominant purpose of maintaining international peace and security.' As a result, 'no state can claim to be advancing these purposes when it breaches the peace to promote other interests, for they simply have no legitimate independent existence outside the context of international peace.' Farer, 'Law and War,' in C. Black and R. Falk (eds) *The Future of the International Legal Order* 3: 31 (1971).

207 Reisman and McDougal, op. cit.: 172–175; McDougal and Reisman, 'Response by Professors McDougal and Reisman,' *Int'l Law.* 3: 438, 444 (1969); and F. Tesón, op. cit.: 131.

208 F. Tesón, op. cit.: 131.

209 Note, op. cit.: 491.

210 Reisman and McDougal, op. cit.: 172.

211 Note, op. cit.: 493.

212 *UN Charter* articles 55, 56.

213 Reisman and McDougal, op. cit.: 174–175.

214 Note, op. cit.: 493. See Reisman and McDougal, op. cit.: 174–175.

215 McDougal and Reisman, op. cit.: 438, 444.

216 Ibid.: 444.

217 Fonteyne, op. cit.: 205–236; and Reisman and McDougal, op. cit.: 179–183. See also Brownlie, 'Thoughts on Kind-hearted Gunmen,' in R. Lillich (ed.) *Humanitarian Intervention and the United Nations*: 141–142 (1973).

218 Note, op. cit.: 492. See also Lillich, op. cit.: 332–334; Reisman and McDougal, op. cit.: 179.

219 Lillich, op. cit.: 328.

220 M. Reisman, *Nullity and Revision*: 848 (1971).

221 Lillich, op. cit.: 335; Reisman and McDougal, op. cit.: 138; F. Tesón, op. cit.: 138.

222 Note, op. cit.: 495.

223 Reisman, 'Sanctions and Enforcement,' in C. Black and R. Falk (eds) *The Future of the International Legal Order* 3: 850 (1971).

224 Ibid.: 333.

225 F. Tesón, op. cit.: 138.

226 Akehurst, 'The Use of Force to Protect Nationals Abroad,' *Int'l Rel.* 5: 3 (1977).

227 N. Ronzitti, op. cit.: 1.

228 Lillich, op. cit.: 336; Reisman and McDougal, op. cit.: 177; J. Stone, *Aggression and World Order*. 43, 95–96 (1963); and F. Tesón, op. cit.: 131.
229 F. Tesón, op. cit.: 131. In reflecting on the Tanzanian intervention in Uganda, Tesón notes:

> There must be something deeply wrong with an international legal system that protects tyrants like [Idi] Amin. As I have tried to show, the answer is not that international law is wrong. Rather, the answer is that absolute noninterventionism resulting from a broad construction of article 2(4) of the United Nations Charter simply does not, and should not, represent international law.
>
> Ibid. 167

230 Reisman and McDougal, op. cit.: 177.
231 J. Stone, op. cit.: 43.
232 Verwey, op. cit.: 66. Emphasis in original.
233 Akehurst, op. cit.: 12; Akehurst, 'Humanitarian Intervention,' in H. Bull (ed.) *Intervention in World Politics*. 96 (1984); Bowett, op. cit.: 50.
234 N. Ronzitti, op. cit.: 109.
235 See sources listed in note 191.
236 F. Tesón, op. cit.: 167.
237 See Chapter 7 above.

9 RESPONDING TO TERRORISM

1 N. Ronzitti, Rescuing Nationals Abroad: 140 (1985).
2 *N.Y. Times*, Feb. 3, 1981: A13.
3 This excludes the more modest steps taken by the US in response to the *Achille Lauro* episode. Here, American warplanes forced down the Egyptian airliner which was transporting the *Achille Lauro* terrorists. See *N.Y. Times*, Nov. 20, 1985: A3, col. 4; *N.Y. Times*, Nov. 25, 1985: A12, col. 4. The case will also be examined below.
4 In Benghazi, the principal targets were Benina Air Base and the Jamahiriya Barracks. The Tripoli attack focused on the Tarabulus (El-Assiziya) Barracks, Sidi Bilal training camp, and Tripoli Military Airfield. Gordon,' Pentagon Details 2-Pronged Attack,' *N.Y. Times*, Apr. 15, 1986: A1; *Dept. State Bull.* 86: 8 (1986).
5 Among the dead was Muammar Qadhafi's stepdaughter. Two of the Colonel's sons were injured. *N.Y. Times*, Apr. 19, 1986: 5.
6 Speech by Ronald Reagan, 'International Terrorism,' *US Dept of State Bureau of Public Affairs Spec. Rep. No. 24, 1986*: 1.
7 Intoccia, 'American Bombing of Libya,' *Case W. Res. J. Int'l L.* 19: 190; Seymour, 'The Legitimacy of Peacetime Reprisal as a Tool Against State-Sponsored Terrorism,' *Nav. L. Rev.* 39: 223 (1987).
8 *N.Y. Times*, Apr. 17, 1986: 23.
9 'The Libyan Equation,' *National Review*, May 23, 1986: 13.
10 *N.Y. Times*, Apr. 16, 1986: 16.
11 Intoccia, op. cit.: 189.
12 *N.Y. Times*, Apr. 16, 1986: 1.
13 *N.Y. Times*, Apr. 22, 1986: 1.
14 *N.Y. Times*, Apr. 22, 1986: 14.
15 *UN Doc. S/18018/Rev.1* (1986). The vote on the draft resolution was: 9 in favor (Congo, Ghana, Madagascar, Trinidad and Tobago, the United Arab Emirates, Bulgaria, China, the Soviet Union, and Thailand); 5 against (US, Britain, France, Australia, and Denmark); and 1 abstention (Venezuela). *UN Doc. S/PV.2682*. 43 (1986).

16 See Roberts, 'Self-Help in Combatting State-Sponsored Terrorism: Self-Defense and Peacetime Reprisals,' *Case W. Res. J. Int'l L.* 19: 243 (1987); Intoccia, op. cit.: 177; McCredie, 'The April 14, 1986 Bombing of Libya: Act of Self-Defense or Reprisal?' *Case W. Res. J. Int'l L* 19: 215 (1987); Baker, Terrorism and the Inherent Right of Self-Defense (A Call to Amend Article 51 of the United Nations Charter), *Houston J. Int'l L.* 10: 25 (1987); Paasche, 'The Use of Force in Combatting Terrorism,' *Columbia J. Transnt'l L.* 25: 377 (1987); Schachter, The Extra-Territorial Use of Force Against Terrorist Bases, *Houston J. Int'l L.* 11: 309 (1989); and Reisman, 'No Man's Land: International Legal Regulation of Coercive Responses to Protracted and Low Level Conflict,' *Houston J. Int'l L.* 11: 317 (1989).

17 Roberts, op. cit.: 243. According to von Glahn, the growth in terrorist activities is attributable to three factors: 1) 'the availability of an almost instant audience;' 2) the 'tacit or overt endorsement – and often support – of certain governments for certain terrorist groups,' and 3) the 'availability of new types of weapons.' G. von Glahn, *Law Among Nations* 348 (1992).

18 For example, Roberts' contention that sophisticated terrorist organizations 'pose one of the greatest threats to Western democracies' seems a bit overstated. Roberts, op. cit.: 247. What of the threats posed by such phenomena as nuclear proliferation, Third World debt, chemical warfare, petroleum supply disruption, and environmental collapse?

   According to Erickson, 'some writers have suggested that the United States might be far better served to ignore terrorism on the political level, both minimizing its inability to deter attacks and deflating the status of terrorists from international outlaws to common criminals.' R. Erickson, *Legitimate Use of Military Force Against State-Sponsored International Terrorism*: 38 (1989).

19 *US Dep't of State, Bureau of Public Affairs, International Terrorism* (1985). In 1985, a Rand Corporation study estimated that since the 1972 attack on Olympic athletes in Munich, terrorist incidents had risen at an annual rate of twelve to fifteen percent. *Wash. Post*, Dec. 3, 1985: A4, col. 4.

   In 1985, nine hundred and twenty-six lives were lost in more than eight hundred terrorist incidents around the globe. This represented a sixty percent increase over the incident rate of the previous two years. *Public Report of the Vice President's Task Force on Combatting Terrorism*: 1 (1986). See also 'Chronology of Major American-Related Terrorist Incidents, 1985,' *Dep't St. Bull.* 86: 13 (Aug. 1986) and Statement of the Secretary of Defense Caspar Weinberger before the opening session of the ABA's National Conference on Law in Relations to Terrorism, June 5, 1986, reported in *ABA Standing Committee Law and National Security Intelligence Report* 8: 8 (July 1986).

20 The phrase is the State Department's. G. Hastedt and K. Knickrehm, Dimensions of World Politics: 239 (1991).

21 These statistics include casualties suffered by terrorists themselves. *US State Department, Patterns of Global Terrorism, 1987* (1988). In 1987, nearly twenty-five percent of all attacks were directed against business facilities; government, military and diplomatic targets represented another twenty-four percent. Ibid.

22 Livingstone and Arnold, 'Democracy Under Attack,' in N. Livingstone and T. Arnold (eds) *Fighting Back: Winning the War Against Terrorism* (1986).

   In 1968, 'terrorists' reportedly inflicted fifteen US casualties; in 1988, two hundred and thirty-two US citizens were injured or killed during 'terrorist' attacks. Statistics compiled by the Office of the Coordinator on Anti-terrorism, US Dep't of State (1989), cited by Sofaer, 'Terrorism, the Law, and the National Defense,' *Mil L. Rev.*: 95 (1989).

23 Report on Combatting Terrorism: op. cit.: 4.

24 Martin and Walcott, *Best Laid Plans*: 126 (1988).

25 Report on Combatting Terrorism: op. cit.: 4.
26 As von Glahn notes, 'no two major calculations of the total number of terrorist acts committed in a given year agree because the calculators disagree as to what is a terrorist act.' G. von Glahn, op. cit.: 346. Similarly, Erickson observes: 'Absent an agreed-on definition, statistics must be compiled on the basis of assumptions about terrorism. Without a universal definition or standard of what terrorism is, all databases and statistical collections on terrorism are suspect.' Erickson, op. cit.: 25.
27 Jacobilis v. Ohio, *US* 378: 184, 197 (1963) (Stewart, J. concurring), cited by Roberts: op. cit.: 248.
28 As applied to actions by individuals, the term 'terrorism' appears to have been used first in an international penal instrument at the Third (Brussels) International Conference for the Unification of Penal Law held on June 26–30, 1930. Franck and Lockwood, 'Preliminary Thoughts Towards an International Convention on Terrorism,' *Am. J. Int'l L.* 68: 69, 73, fn. 23 (1974).
    In its 1954 Draft Code of Offenses Against the Peace and Security of Mankind, the International Law Commission introduced the concept of 'state sponsorship' of terrorism. *UN GAOR*, Supp. 9, 9: 11–12, *UN Doc. A/2693* (1972), cited by J. Murphy, *State Support of International Terrorism*: 5 (1989).
29 A. Schmid, *Political Terrorism: A Research Guide* (1983).
30 For descriptions of the numerous attempts to define terrorism, see Laqueur, 'Reflections on Terrorism,' *For. Aff.* 64: 86, 88 (1986); Levitt, 'Is "Terrorism" Worth Defining?' *Ohio Northern L. Rev.* 13: 97 (1986); J. Murphy, op. cit.: 3–43 (1989); and Sloan, 'Conceptualizing Political Terror: A Typology,' *J. Int'l Aff.* 32: 7 (1970).
31 Levitt, op. cit.: 97.
32 Schachter, op. cit.: 309. See also Dinstein, 'The Right of Self-Defence Against Armed Attacks,' in M. Sandbu and P. Nordbeck (eds) *International Terrorism: Report From a Seminar Arranged by the European Law Students' Association in Lund, Sweden, 1–3 October 1987*: 57 (1987).
33 W. Mallison and S. Mallison, 'The Concept of Public Purpose Terror in International Law: Doctrines and Sanctions to Reduce the Destruction of Human and Material Values,' *How. L.J.* 18: 12 (1974).
    According to Professor Joyner, terrorism's 'exact status under international law remains open to conjecture and polemical interpretation.' Joyner, 'Offshore Maritime Terrorism: International Implications and Legal Response,' *Nav. War Col. Rev.* 36: 20 (1983).
34 Baxter, 'A Skeptical Look at the Concept of Terrorism,' *Akron L. Rev.* 7: 380 (1974).
35 According to Professor Schacter, the lack of a commonly accepted definition 'does not mean that international terrorism is not identifiable. It has a core meaning that all definitions recognize.' Schachter, op. cit.: 309.
    Professor Dinstein argues that 'each scholar is entitled to submit his or her own working definition. As long as we remember that no definition is obligatory, and provided that we avoid a manifest incongruity or an internal contradiction, almost any definition will do.' Dinstein, op. cit.: 57.
36 'Political' objectives are construed broadly here to include 'terrorism for religious motives or ethnic domination.' Schachter, op. cit.: 309.
37 The State Department, for example, has defined terrorism as 'the threat or use of violence for political purposes by individuals or groups, whether acting for, or in opposition to, established governmental authority, when such actions are intended to shock, stun or intimidate a target group wider than the immediate victims.' *Office of Combatting Terrorism, US Dep't of State, Patterns of International Terrorism: 1982* (1983).
    Similarly, the Jonathan Institute's 1978 Jerusalem Conference on International

Terrorism adopted this definition: 'the deliberate and systematic murder, maiming and menacing of the innocent to inspire fear for political ends.' B. Netanayhu (ed) *Terrorism: How the West Can Win* : 9 (1986).

Professor Schachter has suggested this definition: 'the threat or use of violence in order to create extreme fear and anxiety in a target group so as to coerce them to meet the political objectives of the perpetrators.' Schachter, op. cit.: 309.

Yet another definition: 'the threat or use of violence with the intent of causing fear among the public, in order to achieve political objectives.' Intoccia: op. cit.: 177.

Professor von Glahn observes: 'the key element in all terrorist activity is a deliberate effort to create fear in order to persuade the ultimate target to accede to the terrorist's demands.' G. von Glahn, op. cit.: 347.

See also, Sandbu and Nordbeck, 'Introduction,' in M. Sandbu and P. Nordbeck (eds), *International Terrorism: Report from a Seminar Arranged by The European Law Students' Association in Lund, Sweden, 1–3 October 1987*: 13 (1987).

38 From the one hundred and forty definitions reviewed by Schmid, twenty-two common elements were identified. Of these elements, the most frequent were: violence or force; political purpose; terror or fear; threat; and anticipated psychological effects or reactions by third parties. Schmid, *Political Terrorism*: 76–77 (1983). See also *ELSA Seminar on International Terrorism*: 13 (1987).

39 Cassese, 'The International Community's "Legal" Response to Terrorism,' *Int'l & Comp. L. Qtly* 38: 598–599 (1989).

40 J. Murphy, op. cit.: 32–33.

41 According to a former Deputy Ambassador to the UN, 'with few exceptions, all terrorism is state-sponsored, state-implemented, or state condoned.' Johnson, 'Defusing the Radical Entente, The World and I,' *Washington Times Special edition*, Mar. 1986: 98. Cited by Roberts, op. cit.: 253.

See also N. Livingstone and T. Arnold, 'The Rise of State-Sponsored Terrorism,' in N. Livingstone and T. Arnold, op. cit.: 14; and Stuhl and Lopez (eds) *The State as Terrorist* (1984).

42 Murphy suggests that the twelve types of state involvement enumerated by DSI may be divided into two categories: 'state support' and 'state sponsorship.' J. Murphy, op. cit.: 33 (1989).

43 Ibid: 34.

44 Ibid.: 32–34.

45 Erickson, op. cit.: 33.

46 As noted above, scholars such as Murphy and Cassese contend that actions by official state organs may qualify as 'terrorist' acts. Such formulations, however, would expand the definition of 'terrorism' so that virtually any use of force by a state might conceivably be so labelled. For example, support of rebel groups, covert operations not involving proxies, and even overt aggression could all be considered acts of 'terrorism.'

According to Professor Murphy, 'the term "terrorism" is primarily applied to actions by private individuals or groups.' Murphy, op. cit.: 4.

47 For analyses of legal approaches to terrorism, see J. Murphy, *Punishing International Terrorists: The Legal Framework for Policy Initiatives* (1985); and J. Murphy and A. Evans, *Legal Aspects of International Terrorism* (1978).

For a compendium of the various treaties and conventions dealing with terrorism and terrorist acts, see R. Friedlander, *Terrorism: Documents of International and Legal Control*, Vols. I–III (1981); *Control of Terrorism: International Documents* (1979).

48 As we have contended throughout this book, the test of the existence of a rule of international law is the existence of authoritative and controlling state practice.

49 *Statute of the ICJ*, Art. 38, para. 1, secs. a, b, and c.
50 Ibid.
51 See, e.g. Friedmann, 'The Uses of "General Principles" in the Development of International Law,' *Am. J. Int'l L.* 57: 279–299 (1963); M. Hudson, *The Permanent Court of International Justice, 1920-1942*: 606–620 (1943).
52 G. von Glahn, op. cit.: 20.
53 Ibid.: 21.
54 Murphy, op. cit.: 11–14. Only a few states have adopted anti-terrorist statutes. 'Even when the term "terrorism" is expressly used in such national legislation, it is not always defined.' Murphy op. cit.: 12.
55 See, e.g. Paasche, op. cit.: 377; The argument of Professor Friedlander in International Law Association Paris Conference, Fourth Interim Report of the Committee on International Terrorism (1984), reprinted in *Terrorism: An Intl J.* 7: 129 (1985); and the argument of Abraham Sofaer, State Department Legal Adviser, made after US warplanes had intercepted an Egyptian airliner transporting the *Achille Lauro* terrorists. *N.Y. Times*, Nov. 20, 1985: A3, col. 4.
56 Sect. 404 of the Third Restatement (1986).
57 Paasche, op. cit.: 380.
58 Ibid.
59 After the Apr. 5, 1986 bombing of a Berlin nightclub, for example, Libyan Colonel Qadhafi termed 'heroic' the action which had wounded one hundred and fifty-four and killed two. Intoccia, op. cit.: 196.
60 *Geneva Convention on the High Seas, Apr. 29, 1958*, Art. 19, *UST.* 13: 2312, 2317, *IAS* No. 5200 5: 6, *UNTS* 450: 82, 92.
61 Schachter, op. cit.: 311. Cf. Cassese, op. cit.: 606.

We should be grateful that the idea that [terrorist] hijackers are pirates has never been accepted. Such an idea . . . would only serve to legitimize the use of force against anyone ideologically or politically opposed to the State purporting to exercise 'universal jurisdiction' and to escalate the spread of violence in the world. True, terrorists are in a way 'modern enemies of mankind,' and every state should endeavor to search for, try and punish them on its own territory. This, however, does not entail a license to use force in the territory of other States or against ships or aircraft of other States.

62 Cassese, op. cit.: 591; Dinstein, op. cit.: 59.
Two of the most comprehensive proposals that to date have failed to attain the force of law are: 1) the 1972 US Draft Convention on Terrorism, *UN Doc. A/C. 6/L*: 850 reprinted in *Int'l L. Materials* 11: 1382 (1972); and 2) the ABA Standing Committee on World Order Under Law, Div. of Public Service, *Model American Convention on the Prevention and Punishment of Serious Forms of Violence (July 1983)*.
63 (League of Nations) Convention for the Prevention and Punishment of Terrorism, Nov. 16, 1937, M. Hudson (ed.) *International Legislation* 7: 862 (1941), *League of Nations O.J.*: 19 (1938). Twenty-three states signed the instrument; only India ratified it. See *Doc. Inter-Allied Information Comm.* (1942), *Declaration of the Conference at St. James Palace*, Jan. 13, 1942, reported in *Am. J. Int'l L.* 37: 84–85 (1943).
64 Franck and Lockwood, op. cit.: 69, 73, n.23.
65 See Cassese, op. cit.: 591–592; Murphy, op. cit.: 9–11.
66 European Convention on the Suppression of Terrorism, Europ. T.S. No. 90; *Int'l L. Materials* 15: 1972 (1976). Done at Strasbourg on Nov. 10, 1976, entered into force on Aug. 4, 1978. Text also in *Am. J. Int'l L.* 15: 1272 (1976).

For a discussion of the European Convention, see Warbrock, 'European Convention on Human Rights and the Prevention of Terrorism,' *Intl & Comp. L. Q.* 32: (1983); and Cassese, op. cit.: 592–594.

67 Two other regional treaties of narrower focus have also entered into force: the 'OAS Convention,' which protects diplomatic, consular, and civil servants; and the 'Dublin Agreement,' which seeks to strengthen judicial cooperation among European states. Murphy, op. cit.: 9–11; McCredie, op. cit.: 221.

For texts of the agreements, see Convention to Protect and Punish the Acts of Terrorism Taking the Form of Crimes Against Persons and Related Extortion That Are of International Significance (OAS Convention), Feb. 2, 1971, *UST.* 27: 3949, *T.I.A.S.* No. 8413, *O.A.S.T.S.* No. 37: 6, *OAS Doc. OEA/Ser.A./17;* and Agreement on the Application of the European Convention for the Suppression of Terrorism (Dublin Agreement), Dec. 4, 1979, *Int'l L. Materials* 19: 325 (1980).

68 Dinstein, op. cit.: 59.

69 Convention For The Suppression of Unlawful Seizure of Aircraft (Hijacking), *UST.* 22: 1641, *T.I.A.S.* No. 7192, *Int'l L. Materials* 10: 133 (1971). Done at The Hague on Dec. 16, 1970; entered into force on Oct. 14, 1971.

70 Convention for the Suppression of Unlawful Acts against the Safety of Maritime Navigation, March 10, 1988, *I.M.O. Doc. SUA/CONF/15,* cited by Cassese, op. cit.: 592.

71 Convention for the Suppression of Unlawful Acts against the Safety of Civil Aviation (Sabotage), *UST.* 24: 564, *T.I.A.S.* No. 7570, *Int'l L. Materials* 10: 1151 (1971). Done at Montreal on Sept. 23, 1971; entered into force on Jan. 26, 1973.

72 Convention on the Prevention and Punishment of Crimes against Internationally Protected Persons, Including Diplomatic Agents, *T.I.A.S.* No. 8532, *Int'l L. Materials* 13: 41 (1977). Adopted by the UN General Assembly on Dec. 14, 1973; entered into force on Feb. 20, 1977.

73 International Convention Against the Taking of Hostages, *G.A. Res. 146* (XXXIV 1979), *Am. J. Int'l. L.* 74: (Jan. 1980), *Int'l L. Materials* 18: 1456 (1979). Adopted by the General Assembly on Dec. 17, 1979; entered into force on June 3, 1983.

74 IAEA Convention on the Physical Protection of Nuclear Material, 1979, reported in R. Friedlander, 'Terrorism: Documents of International and Legal Control,' Vol III: 583 (1981).

75 Art. 33, Constitution of the Universal Postal Convention, with Final Protocol, *UST.* 16: 1291, *T.I.A.S.* No. 5881.

76 Cassese, op. cit.: 592.

77 *UKTS* 9 (1910) Cmnd. 5030.

78 *UNTS.* 75: 31–83; (1950) *U.K.T.S.* 39 (1958), Cmnd. 550.

79 Protocol Additional to the Geneva Conventions of 12 August 1949, and Relating to the Protection of Victims of International Armed Conflicts (Protocol I), *Int'l L. Materials* 16: 1391 (1977). Adopted June 8, 1977; entered into force Dec. 7, 1978. Protocol Additional to the Geneva Conventions of 12 August 1949, and Relating to the Protection of Victims of Non-International Armed Conflicts (Protocol II), *Int'l L. Materials* 16: 1442 (1977). Adopted June 8, 1977; entered into force Dec. 7, 1978.

80 See, e.g. Geneva Convention Relative to the Protection of Civilian Persons in Time of War, *UST* 6: 3516, *T.I.A.S.* No. 3365, *UNTS* 75: 287, done at Geneva, Aug. 12, 1949, entered into force for the United States Feb. 2, 1956, Art. 3.

81 Ibid.

82 A major question raised by the four Geneva Conventions is under what specific circumstances an 'armed conflict not of an international character' in fact exists. Clearly, an ongoing civil war would constitute such an 'armed conflict.' It is uncertain, however, whether a non-international 'armed conflict' would exist if the only existing violence were that originating from the terrorist group itself.

83 N. Ronzitti, op. cit.: xiii; Mosler, 'The International Society as a Legal Community,' *Recueil des Cours* 140: (1974).
84 In favor: Austria, Belgium, Ecuador, France, Hungary, Japan, the Russian Federation, The United Kingdom, United States, and Venezuela. Opposed: None. Abstained: Cape Verde, China, India, Morocco, and Zimbabwe. *UN Doc. S/PV3063*, March 31, 1992; *S/RES/748* (1992).
85 See Lewis, 'Security Council Votes to Prohibit Arms Exports and Flights to Libya,' *N.Y. Times*, Apr. 1, 1992: A1, col. 4.
86 UNS.C. Res. 748, Mar. 31, 1992, reprinted in 'Resolution on Libya Embargo: Barring Takeoff and Landing 'to Any Aircraft,' *N.Y. Times*, Apr. 1, 1992: A12, col. 1.
87 Measures to Prevent International Terrorism, *G.A. Res. 40/61, UN GAOR Supp.* (No. 53) 40: 301, *UN Doc. A/40/53* (1985), reprinted in *Int'l L. Materials*. 25: 239 (1986).
   At the same time as the passage of the General Assembly resolution, the Security Council passed a resolution condemning all acts of hostage-taking and urging members to cooperate with one another against acts of terrorism. See *S.C. Res. 579 UN DOC S/INF/41* (1985).
88 Ibid. On the resolution Professor Schachter noted:

> It is true that the . . . resolution recognizes the inalienable right to struggle for self-determination and national independence in accordance with the UN Charter. Some Americans have suggested that this eviscerates the resolution. That is a regrettable and in my view, unfounded interpretation. The great majority of governments voted for that provision on the understanding that the 'struggle' for self-determination must conform to the Charter principles relating to the use of force and that international terrorism 'by whomever committed' is an international crime. The United States and the other western states acclaimed the resolution on that understanding. It is rather absurd for those opposed to terrorism to read into it an exception that is contrary to the main object of the resolution.
>
> Schachter, op. cit.: 310.

89 Dinstein, op. cit.: 61. Cf. Cassese, op. cit.: 605–606.
90 Possible responses to terrorism with state involvement include quiet diplomacy, public protest, international and transnational claims, economic sanctions, and military responses. J. Murphy, op. cit.: 2.
91 Scholars such as Professor Murphy have included 'interventions to protect nationals' or 'rescue missions' in their reviews of state practice. Ibid.: 85–108. Such forcible state actions will not be considered here, however, because their principal focus is typically upon rescuing nationals, not punishing terrorists *per se*. Hence, in Chapter 7 we have considered such terrorist-related 'interventions to protect nationals' as the 1976 Entebbe raid.
92 G. von Glahn, op. cit.: 352 (1992).
93 Sofaer, op. cit.: 109–110.
94 Not included in this chapter's review of state practice is the abduction by the United States of Fawaz Younis, an alleged Lebanese Shiite terrorist. In September of 1987, US Federal Bureau of Investigation agents arrested Younis in international waters in the Mediterranean after he 'voluntarily' boarded a vessel there. Although Lebanese Justice Minister Nabih Berri criticized the American action as 'an act close to piracy' and 'an attack on the honor of Lebanon,' it engendered little other international reaction. See *N.Y. Times*, Sept. 20, 1987, sec. IV: 20: col. 4; *Facts on File*, Oct. 2, 1987: 704–705; Sofaer, MLY, 103. The United States District Court for the District of Columbia dealt with the *Younis* case. See US v. Younis, 281 *F. Supp.* 896, 906–907 (D.D.C. 1988).

95 Cassese, op. cit.: 601.
96 *UN SCOR, 1738th Mtg.*, 35: *UN Doc. S/PV.1738* (1973).
97 *UN Doc. S/PV. 1738*, August 14, 1973: 28–30.
98 See J. Murphy, op. cit.: 99–102; Cassese, op. cit.: 601–603; A. Cassese, *Violence and Law in the Modern Age*. 62–75 (1988); Murphy, The Future of Multilateralism and Efforts to Combat International Terrorism, *Colum. J. Transnat'l L.* 25: 35, 80–83 (1986); Schachter, 'In Defense of International Rules on the Use of Force,' *U. Chi. L. Rev.* 53: 113, 140 (1986); McGinley, 'The *Achille Lauro* Affair – Implications for International Law,' *Tenn. L. R.* 52: 691 (1985); Constantinople, 'Towards a New Definition of Piracy: The *Achille Lauro* Incident,' *Va. J. Int'l L.* 26: 723 (1986); McCredie, 'Contemporary Uses of Force Against Terrorism: The United States Response to *Achille Lauro* – Question of Jurisdiction and Its Exercise,' *Ga. J. Int'l & Comp. L.* 16: 435 (1986); Paust, 'Extradition of the *Achille Lauro* Hostage-Takers: Navigating the Hazards,' *Vanderbilt J. Transnat'l L.* 20: 235 (1987).
99 Among those who argued that the US action was illegal were: Cassese, op. cit.: 73; and Schachter, op. cit.: 114, 140 (1986). By contrast, Murphy maintained that the action was lawful. J. Murphy, op. cit.: 64.
100 A. Cassese, op. cit.: 64.
101 *UN Doc. S/PV.2622*: 38–46 (Mr Kaddoumi).
102 *UN Doc. S/PV. 2622*: 53–55 (Mr Bein).
103 *UN Doc. S/PV.2622*: 32–38 (Said Sherifuddin Pirzada).
104 Cassese, op. cit.: 603–604.
105 *UN Doc. S/PV. 2651*, Feb. 4, 1986: 19–20.
106 Ibid.
107 *UN Doc. S/PV.2655/Corr. 1*, Feb. 18, 1986: 112–113.
108 'Israeli Commandos Seize Leader of a Pro-Iran Group in Lebanon,' *N.Y. Times*, July 29, 1989: 1, col. 1.
109 The previous Imam of Jibchit, Sheik Ragheb Harb, was killed in February of 1984 – allegedly by Israeli-backed militia. *Facts on File*, 1984: 529, A2.
110 'Israeli Commandos Seize Leader of a Pro-Iran Group in Lebanon,' *N.Y. Times*, July 29, 1989: 4, col. 1.
111 'Free Sheik, Group Warns, Or American Will Die,' *N.Y. Times*, July 31, 1989: A2, col. 1.
112 'Israel Dismisses Criticism,' *N.Y. Times*, July 30, 1989: 6, col. 5.
113 'Bush Criticizes Kidnapping,' *N.Y. Times*, July 29, 1989: 4, col. 6. British Prime Minister Margaret Thatcher was similarly critical.
114 'Israel Dismisses Criticism,' *N.Y. Times*, July 30, 1989: 6, col. 5. The Soviet Union called the Israeli action 'a major offense against Lebanese sovereignty.' *Keesing's Record of World Events, July 1989*: 36832.
115 *UN Doc. S/PV.2872*, July 31, 1989: 1–6.
116 *S/RES/638* (1989).
117 A Marine Lieutenant Colonel, Higgins had been head of the UN Interim Force in Lebanon (UNIFIL). He was captured in February of 1988 by the 'Organization for the Oppression of the Earth,' a Hezbollah front organization. On July 31, 1989, a grisly 30-second video was released showing a man who resembled Higgins hanging from a noose. It was then suspected that Higgins had been killed much earlier, however. *Keesing's Record of World Events, July 1989*: 36832.
118 An example of a recent covert assassination of an alleged 'terrorist' is the June 10, 1992 killing of Atef Bseiso, director of internal security in the Palestine Liberation Organization. One P.L.O. official subsequently charged: 'We are sure it is a Mossad operation and we are unfortunately also sure they received their information from their contacts within the French intelligence community.' By contrast, French officials speculated that Mr Bseiso had been killed by agents of the renegade

Palestinian group led by Abu Nidal. 'P.L.O. Says Slain Official Planned Covert Talks,' *N.Y. Times*, June 10, 1992: A6, col. 3.
119 O'Brien, 'Reprisals, Deterrence and Self-Defense in Counterterror Operation,' *Va. J. Int'l L.*: 462 (1990); Sofaer, op. cit.: 121.
120 Ibid. See 'P.L.O. Accuses Israel in Killing of Senior Arafat Deputy in Tunis,' *N.Y. Times*, Apr. 17, 1988: 1, col. 4; High 'Backing Seen for Assassination,' *Wash. Post*, Apr. 21, 1988: A1, col. 2; *UN SCOR, 2807th mtg.* 43: 6–15, *UN Doc. S/PV. 2807*(1988) (remarks by Ambassador Mestiri (Tunisia)).
121 'P.L.O. Accuses Israel in Killing of Senior Arafat Deputy in Tunis,' *N.Y. Times*, Apr. 17, 1988: 16, col. 3; 'Abu Jihad: A Strong Right Arm to Arafat Who Lived by the Sword,' *N.Y. Times*, Apr. 17, 1988: 16, col. 4.
122 *S.C. Res. 611, UN SCOR, Res. & Decs.* 43: 15, *UN Doc. S/INF/44* (1988).
123 *UN SCOR, 2810th mtg* 43: 26–31, *UN Doc. S/PV.2810* (1988) (remarks by Ambassador Okun United States).
124 O'Brien, op. cit.: 462.
125 Sofaer, op. cit.: 121.
126 'Israelis Kill Chief of Pro-Iran Shiites in South Lebanon,' *N.Y. Times*, Feb. 17, 1992: A1, col. 6; 'Israeli Raid Kills Hezbollah Leader,' *Wash. Post*, Feb. 17, 1992: A1, col. 4. The motorcade was travelling from a rally in Jibchit, the site, ironically, of Israel's abduction of Sheik Obeid in 1989. 'Eye for an Eye,' *The Economist*, Feb. 22, 1992: 31.
127 'Israelis Kill Chief of Pro-Iran Shiites in South Lebanon,' *N.Y. Times*, Feb. 17, 1992: A9, col. 1.
128 'Israeli Raid Kills Hezbollah Leader,' *Wash. Post*, Feb. 17, 1992: A1, col. 4.
129 'Israelis Kill Chief of Pro-Iran Shiites in South Lebanon,' *N.Y. Times*, Feb. 17, 1992: A9, col. 2.
130 'Israeli Raid Kills Leader of Hezbollah,' *Wash. Post*, Feb. 17, 1992: A33, col. 1.
131 'Sheik a Hero to Shiites, a Symbol of Terrorism to West,' *N.Y. Times*, Feb. 17, 1992 at A9, col 1.
132 'Murder by Mistake?' *Newsweek*, Mar. 20, 1992: 6.
133 Ibid.
134 Defense Minister Moshe Arens never explicitly acknowledged that Israel had sought to assassinate Sheik Musawi. Moreover, some Israeli officials conceded their regret that Musawi's family had perished in the operation. 'Israelis Kill Chief of Pro-Iran Shiites in South Lebanon,' *N.Y. Times*, Feb. 17, 1992: A9, col. 2; 'Israelis and Foes Trade Fire Near Border,' *N.Y. Times*, Feb. 18, 1992: A8, col. 2.
135 'Israelis Kill Chief of Pro-Iran Shiites in South Lebanon,' *N.Y. Times*, Feb. 17, 1992: A9, col. 3.
136 'US Urges Restraint,' *N.Y. Times*, Feb. 17, 1992: A9, col. 4.
137 'Israelis and Foes Trade Fire Near Border,' *N.Y. Times*, Feb 18, 1992: A8, col. 1. Iranian President Rafsanjani stated, 'This was a unique and unprecedented form of terrorism, shooting at a family and their companions from helicopters, but I believe that Lebanese groups are going to be logical and reasonable about a reaction.' 'Iran Urges Restraint,' *N.Y. Times*, Feb 18, 1992: A8, col. 3.
138 See Bowett, 'Reprisals Involving Recourse to Armed Force,' *Am. J. Int'l L.* 66: 1–36 (1972); O'Brien, op. cit.: 421–478.
139 These Israeli actions include:
     a. the Nov. 14, 1966 action against Jordan;
     b. the 'Samu incident' of Nov., 1966 (Syria);
     c. the Es-Salt Raid of August 4, 1968 (Jordan);
     d. the February 24, 1969 airstrike on bases in Damascas, Syria;
     e. the Es-Salt raid of March 26, 1969 (Jordan);

f. the south Lebanon raid of August 26, 1969;
g. the invasion of south Lebanon on May 12, 1970; and
h. the invasion of south Lebanon on September 2, 1970.

In each of these eight cases, the Israeli action was explicitly characterized by Professor Bowett as a response to 'Al Fatah' or 'terrorist' activities. For a selected list of reprisals (1953–70) which includes seven of the above cases, see Bowett, op. cit.: 33–36. On the February 1969 raid on bases in Damascas, see ibid.: 14.

140 These Israeli uses of force include:
a. the Lebanon incursion, February 1972;
b. the Lebanon incursion, June 1972;
c. strikes against Syria and Lebanon on September 7, 1972;
d. the Apr. 12, 1973 Beirut raid;
e. the Apr. 12–13, 1974 night raid on several Lebanese villages;
f. the May 16–21, 1974 attacks on PLO bases in Lebanon;
g. the May–June 1974 preventive/attrition air raids on PLO bases in Lebanon;
h. the December 2, 1975 air raids in northern and southern Lebanon;
i. the series of commando raids against PLO bases in Lebanon, spring 1980–spring 1981;
j. the 'July Mini-War of 1981' in Lebanon;
k. the air attack on PLO targets in Lebanon, Apr. 21, 1982;
l. the air attack on PLO targets in Lebanon, May 9, 1982;
m. the September, 1985 air raid on the Lebanese bases of PLO dissident Abu Musa; and
n. the Tunis raid, October 1, 1985.

See O'Brien, op. cit.: 426–443, 450–454, 460–462. To this list of fourteen Israeli 'forcible strikes against terrorist bases,' one might perhaps also add the Litani Operation (March 14–June 13, 1978) and the 1982 Lebanon War; however, in their size and military objectives, these actions would seem more to have resembled conventional uses of force. See ibid.: 445–450, 454–460.

141 'Israeli Planes Attack PLO in Tunis, Killing at least 30, Raid "Legitimate," US Says,' N.Y. Times, Oct. 2, 1985: A1, col. 6; 'Israel Calls Bombing a Warning to Terrorists,' N.Y. Times, Oct. 2, 1985: A8, col. 1. On the Tunis raid, see O'Brien, op. cit.: 460-462; Reisman, op. cit.: 329.
142 '3 Israelis Slain by Palestinians in Cyprus,' N.Y. Times, Sept. 26, 1985: A3, col. 4.
143 'Israel Calls Bombing a Warning to Terrorists,' N.Y. Times, Oct. 2, 1985 at A8, col. 1.
144 UN SCOR, 2615th mtg. 86–87 (remarks by Ambassador Netanyahu (Israel)), UN Doc. S/PV.2615 (1985).
145 O'Brien, op. cit.: 462.
146 S.C Res. 573, UN SCOR, Res. & Decs.: 40: 23, UN Doc. S/INF/41 (1985).
147 Reisman, op. cit.: 329.
148 UN SCOR, 2615th mtg 40: 111–112, UN Doc. S/PV.2615 (1985).
149 This figure is based on the reprisal studies of Bowett and O'Brien. For the twenty-three year period of 1966–88, these studies reported twenty-two cases which might arguably be said to have constituted 'state attacks against terrorist bases.' See Bowett, op. cit.: and O'Brien, op. cit.
150 These actions include:
a. the south Lebanon raid of August 26, 1969;
b. the invasion of south Lebanon on May 12, 1970;
c. the invasion of south Lebanon on September 2, 1970;
d. the Lebanon incursion, February 1972;
e. the Lebanon incursion, June 1972;
f. the strike against Lebanon on September 7, 1972;

g. the Apr. 12, 1973 Beirut raid;

h. the Apr. 12–13, 1974 night raid on several Lebanese villages;

i. the May 16–21, 1974 attacks on PLO bases in Lebanon;

j. May–June 1974 preventive/attrition air raids on PLO bases in Lebanon;

k. December 2, 1975 air raids in northern and southern Lebanon;

l. the series of commando raids against PLO bases in Lebanon, spring 1980–spring 1981;

m. the 'July Mini-War of 1981' in Lebanon;

n. the air attack on PLO targets in Lebanon, Apr. 21, 1982;

o. the air attack on PLO targets in Lebanon, May 9, 1982; and

p. the September, 1985 air raid on the Lebanese bases of PLO dissident Abu Musa.
See Bowett, op. cit.: and O'Brien, op. cit.

151 The term is Bowett's. Bowett, op. cit.: 1.

152 Ibid.: 2. On the legal status of reprisals, Bowett later observed tersely: 'there is a discrepancy between the formal principle and the actual practice.' Ibid.: *Am. J. Int'l L.*, 22. According to O'Brien, 'the Security Council in the years 1971 to 1989 continued the practice analyzed by Bowett in 1972.' O'Brien, op. cit.: 474.

153 Murphy, op. cit.: 102. On the action, see ibid.: 102–108; O'Brien, op. cit.: 463–467; Greenwood, 'International Law and the United States Air Operation Against Libya,' *W. Va. L. Rev.* 89: 933 (1987); Intoccia, op. cit.; McCredie, op. cit.; Boyle, 'Preserving the Rules of Law in the War Against International Terrorism,' *Whittier L. Rev.* 8: 735 (1986); Thornberry, 'International Law and Its Discontents: The US Raid on Libya,' *Liverpool L. Rev.* 8: 53 (1986); and Note, 'The US Raid on Libya: A Forceful Response to Terrorism,' *Brooklyn J. Int'l L.* 14: 187 (1988).

154 O'Brien, op. cit.: 464; Parks, 'Crossing the Line,' *US Naval Institute Proceedings* 112: 51–52 (1986); Intoccia, op. cit.: 179–180.

155 The US assault even prompted 'tens of thousands' of demonstrators in West Germany, Italy, Sweden and Great Britain to march in protest and to burn American flags. *N.Y. Times,* Apr. 20, 1986: A14, col. 1.

156 On the operation's political context, see Intoccia, op. cit.: 182–186.

157 O'Brien, op. cit.: 464.

158 See *UN SCOR, 2673–2680 mtgs, UN Doc. S/PV.2673–2680* (1986). For a summary of the Council's debates, see O'Brien, op. cit.: 463–467.

159 O'Brien, op. cit.: 464–465.

160 Ibid.: 465.

161 Parks, op. cit.: 45.

162 See *UN SCOR, 2674th mtg* 41: 13–19, *UNDoc. S/PV.2674* (1986) (remarks by Ambassador Walters [United States]).

163 See *UN SCOR, 2674th mtg* 41: 13–19, *UNDoc. S/PV.2674* (1986) (remarks by Ambassador Walters [United States]).

164 O'Brien, op. cit.: 466.

165 *UN SCOR, 2679th mtg* 41: 19–20, *UN Doc. S/PV.2679* (1986) (statement by Sir John Thomson [United Kingdom]).

166 Ibid.: 19–21.

167 'Thatcher: Reprisal Strikes Illegal,' *Wash. Post,* Jan. 11, 1986: A1, col. 1, cited by O'Brien, op. cit.: 466–467.

168 *UN SCOR, 2679th mtg 41: 22, 26–27, UN Doc. S/PV.2679* (1986) (statement by Sir John Thomson [United Kingdom]).

169 The resolution was sponsored by the Congo, Ghana, Madagascar, Trinidad and Tobago, and the United Arab Emirates. Also voting in favor of the resolution were Bulgaria, China, the Soviet Union, and Thailand. *UN SCOR, 2682d mtg* 41: 43, *UN Doc. S/PV.2682* (1986).

170 *G.A. Res. 41/38, UN GAOR Supp. (No. 53)* 41: 34, *UN Doc. A/41/53* (1986).

171 Excluded here from the category of 'forcible state responses to terrorism' are state interventions to protect nationals such as the 1976 Entebbe raid or the failed US attempt to rescue Americans held hostage in Iran.
172 See Bowett, op. cit.: O'Brien, op. cit.; and *supra.*
173 Bowett, op. cit.: 5–9. See also O'Brien, op. cit.: 471–472.
174 O'Brien, op. cit.: 471.
175 Ibid.
176 See, e.g. the bibliography in Erickson, op. cit.: 231–267 (1989).
177 See Chapter 5 above.
178 See notes 26–38 above.
179 Roberts, op. cit.: 249.
180 Cassese describes 'state terrorism;' others do not. See Cassese, op. cit.: 598; Murphy, op. cit.: 32.
181 Professor Coll suggests that any attacks 'directed specifically against military personnel and other agents of the state . . . are best described as implying acts of war,' providing the victim state 'with ample legal justification under the laws of war for responding.' He defines 'terrorism' narrowly as 'the explicit and deliberate (as opposed to collateral) destruction or threat of destruction of nonmilitary, non-governmental personnel in the course of political or other forms of warfare.' Coll, 'The Legal and Moral Adequacy of Military Responses to Terrorism,' *Proceedings Amer. Soc. Int'l L.*, 297–298 (1987).

Professor Schachter offers a contrary view: 'Terrorist acts are generally carried out against civilians, but extend to acts against governmental buildings, vessels, planes, and other instrumentalities.' Schachter, 'The Extraterritorial Use of Force Against Terrorist Bases,' *Houston J. Int'l L.* 11: 309 (1989). See also Green and Lador-Lederer, 'International Terrorism: Fourth Interim Report of the Committee of the I.L.A.' in *Terrorism: An International Journal* 7: 127 (1984); and Rubin, 'Terrorism and the Laws of War,' *Denv. J. Int'l Law & Pol.* 12: 219 (1984).
182 During the European Law Students' Association 1987 seminar on International Terrorism, for example, 'political motivation' did not come to be incorporated into the group's definition of 'terrorism.' Sandbu and Nordbeck, op. cit.: 13. Dinstein, op. cit.: 58–59.
183 Erickson, for example, criticizes a State Department definition of terrorism because it omits the modifier 'unlawful' to characterize terrorist violence. 'It is inconceivable,' he submits, that such violence 'could ever be other than illegal and criminal.' Erickson, op. cit.: 27. Professor Dinstein includes the modifier 'unlawful' in his definition of 'terrorism': 'any unlawful act of violence committed with a view to terrorizing.' Dinstein, op. cit.: 57.
184 The CIA and some scholars, for example, distinguish 'international terrorism' from 'transnational terrorism' based on whether the act is state sponsored. Erickson op. cit.: 31.
185 For a discussion of the problematic nature of the 'motive' concept, see Bowett, op. cit.: 3 and O'Brien, op. cit.: 423.
186 Professors Coll and O'Brien, for example, do not attempt to distinguish systematically terrorist acts within a state's borders from acts beyond its borders. See Coll, op. cit.: O'Brien, op. cit.
187 See, e.g O'Brien, op. cit.: 471; Roberts, op. cit.: 243.
188 Murphy, for example, considers only two 'major types' of armed responses: rescue missions and actions against supporting or sponsoring states. Murphy, op. cit.: 85–108. Cassese, by contrast, focuses on interceptions of aircraft transporting alleged 'terrorists.' Cassese, op. cit.: 601–604. Erickson writes of various state uses of force including: Israel's raid on the Beirut airport in 1968; the 1976 Entebbe rescue

mission; the Mogadishu rescue in 1977; the failed US rescue mission in Teheran of 1980; the Israeli attack on Iraq's Osirak reactor in 1981; the *Achille Lauro* incident of 1985; America's Libya raid in 1986; and Israel's raid on Tunis in 1987. Erickson, op. cit.: 6. Sofaer discusses hostage rescue, attacks on terrorists and terrorist camps, abductions, and assassination. Sofaer, op. cit.: 107–113, 116–121. Roberts lists four types of military responses: preemptive operations; search and recovery operations; rescue missions; and retaliatory operations. Roberts, 'Remarks,' *Proceedings Amer. Soc. Int'l. L.*, 318 (1987).

In this chapter's review of state practice, rescue missions have been excluded and assassinations with relatively clear state involvement have been included.

189 We include in our review the following scholars: Baker, Boyle, Cassese, Coll, Dinstein, Erickson, Frowein, Intoccia, McCredie, Murphy, O'Brien, Roberts, Rowles, Schachter, Seymour, and Sofaer.

190 Boyle, 'Remarks,' *Proceedings Amer. Soc. Int'l L.*, 294 (1987).

191 Sofaer, op. cit.: 96.

192 Rowles, 'Military Responses to Terrorirsm: Substantive and Procedural Constraints in International Law,' *Proceedings Amer. Soc. Int'l L.*, 314 (1987).

193 *Hague Academy of International Law, The Legal Aspects of Terrorism*, 1988. Frowein, *The Present State of Research Carried Out by the English-speaking Section of the Centre for Studies and Research*: 55–96 (1988).

194 Frowein, op. cit.: 64. Emphasis added.

195 Though he set out what we term a 'high threshold' argument, Professor Frowein appeared ultimately to dismiss it:

> The following principle would seem to describe the present state of law correctly: 'States shall not use force to protect their citizens who are under an imminent threat to their lives by terrorists on the territory of another State, unless that State fails to cooperate in order to remove the threat.
>
> Ibid.: 66.

196 Ibid.: 64–65; see also Sofaer, op. cit.: 93–94.

197 Boyle, op. cit.: 288–297, 319 (1987). In the same panel discussion, Professor Coll also briefly described the restrictionist argument. Coll, op. cit.: 300–301 (1987).

198 The Reagan Administration decision to intercept an Egyptian jet carrying the *Achille Lauro* hijackers was, argued Boyle, 'incredibly stupid and counterproductive.' The April 14, 1986 airstrike against Libya was a 'ruthless attempt to murder Qadhafi and his family.' Boyle, op. cit.: 290, 296.

199 Ibid.: 294. Emphasis added.

200 Ibid.: 293.

201 Coll, op. cit.: 302.

202 Ibid.: 307. Other scholars have likewise argued that the 'terrorism' phenomenon 'doesn't fit within normal concepts of self-defense' under Article 51. Murphy, 'Remarks,' *Proceedings Amer. Soc. Int'l L.*, 319 (1987).

According to Baker, 'invoking the right of self-defense in response to terrorism does not fit neatly into the requirement of article 51.' Baker, op. cit.: 47. And maintains Professor Murphy: Article 51 'deals with blatant armed attack, [but] does not extend easily to situations involving covert acts of terrorism.' Murphy, op. cit.: 319.

203 Coll, op. cit.: 307.

204 Ibid.: 298.

205 Ibid.

206 O'Brien, op. cit.

207 Ibid.: 470.

208 Ibid.
209 Coll, 'The Limits of Global Consciousness and Legal Absolutism: Protecting International Law from Some of Its Best Friends,' *Harv. Int'l L. J.* 27: 599, 606–613 (1986).
210 O'Brien, op. cit.: 470.
211 At no place in his article does O'Brien list systematically those acts engendering a state's right to respond in self-defense. In his account of law and state practice since 1971, however, he nevertheless discusses specific varieties of terrorist acts.
212 See, e.g. O'Brien, op. cit.: 426, 445–446.
213 See, e.g. ibid.: 431.
214 See, e.g. ibid.: 443–444 on the Entebbe incident.
215 See, e.g. ibid.: 460-461. Here, O'Brien discusses Israel's response to the murder of three Israelis in Larnaca, Cyprus by Palestinian terrorists.
216 Sofaer, op. cit.: 89.
217 Ibid.: Emphasis added.
218 Ibid.: Emphasis added.
219 Ibid.: Emphasis added.
220 Ibid.: Emphasis added. Sofaer noted, however, that attacks on a nation's citizens could not 'routinely be treated as attacks on the nation itself.' Ibid.
    Cf. Schachter, op. cit.: 311–312.

> Is an attack by terrorists on nationals of a particular state outside of that state an armed attack on the state? I submit that when such attacks are aimed at the government or intended to change a policy of that state, the attacks are reasonably considered as attacks on the state in question.
>
> Ibid.

221 Sofaer, op. cit.: 91.
222 Ibid.: 95–96.
223 Rowles, op. cit.: 307–317.
224 Ibid.: 314. Emphasis added. 'In general, I think there are very few situations in which military responses to terrorism are either legal or desirable.' Ibid.: 316.
225 Ibid.: 314.

> Arguably, military responses might be permitted in an extreme case calling for urgent action in anticipatory self-defense – if, for example, a terrorist group had a nuclear-armed missile aimed at Washington, was making launching preparations, and would probably launch if it learned of any approach for cooperation by the territorial state to bring its actions to a halt.

226 Ibid.: 314.
227 Ibid.: 313. Rowles said of the US raid on Libya: 'If 10,000 such attacks [as that upon the Berlin discotheque] were actually being launched, or a continuing campaign of such large-scale attacks was in progress, the United States might have had a colorable argument for bombing the terrorists' bases in Libya.'
228 Cassese, op. cit.: 589. Cassese challenged here Judge Sofaer's 1986 assertion that the 'law applicable to terrorism is not merely flawed, it is perverse.' Sofaer, 'Terrorism and the Law,' *For. Aff.* 64: 902–903 (1986). While conceding that 'the current legal regulation of responses to terrorism is far from satisfactory,' Cassese cited four causes for optimism: 1) 'there is a general consensus among the international community that terrorism is to be condemned'; 2) the international community appears to be moving closer toward a consensus definition of terrorism; 3) the international community has 'at least some conventional framework for rational, peaceful responses to terrorist activity'; and 4) the international community has 'rules limiting resort to military responses.' Cassese, op. cit.: 605–606.
229 Cassese, op. cit.: 596.

230 Ibid. Emphasis added.
231 Ibid. Cassese's emphasis.
232 Ibid. 596. Cassese would seem to exclude 'major' though isolated attacks from those terrorist acts constituting 'armed attacks.'
233 According to Professor Dinstein, 'three conditions must be met if self-defence is to be admissible under customary international law: necessity, proportionality, and immediacy.' Dinstein, op. cit.: 65. For the 'necessity' requirement to be satisfied under the UN Charter, an 'armed attack' must occur.
234 For a brief discussion of timeliness, see Erickson, op. cit.: 144.
235 Boyle doer not explicitly use the words 'immediate' or 'on-the-spot.' However, his meaning is clear from the context of his comments. Boyle, op. cit.: 294–295.
      On the 'immediacy' concept, Cf. Maizel, 'Intervention in Grenada', *Naval L. Rev.* 35: 73 (1986).
236 Boyle, op. cit.: 294.
237 Ibid. Emphasis added. Cf. Rowles, op. cit.: 313. 'Reprisals . . . are clearly and unequivocally prohibited by modern international law.' Ibid.
238 Boyle, op. cit.: 294–295.
239 Bowett, O'Brien, Intoccia, Rowles, and Seymour all acknowledge that contemporary scholarly opinion rejects that legitimacy of reprisals. Bowett, op. cit.: 1; O'Brien, op. cit.: 421; Intoccia, op. cit.: 199; Rowles, op. cit.: 309, 313; Seymour, op. cit.: 224.
240 Baker, op. cit.
241 Baker, op. cit.: 34. Emphasis added. Citing Schachter, 'The Lawful Resort to Unilateral Use of Force,' *Yale J. Int'l L.* 10: 292 (1985).
242 Baker, op. cit.: 34. Citing Gordon, 'Article 2(4) in Historical Context,' *Yale J. In'tl L.* 10: 278 (1985).
      Cf. Dinstein, op. cit.: 63–64. 'States – unlike human beings – cannot respond instantaneously. If John Doe assaults Richard Roe today, the latter may not wait until tomorrow before resorting to force in self-defence. A State, as an artificial (juristic) person acting through its organs, cannot be expected to act with similar celerity . . . Immediacy, therefore, should not be taken literally.'
243 Cassese, op. cit. Cassese never explicitly used the term 'immediacy' *per se.*
244 op. cit.: 597.
245 op. cit.: 596.
246 Cf. Intoccia, op. cit.: 202.

> The temporal nature underlying the Webster formulation is an element which requires a response to be made close in time to an attack or imminent threat. Without such an element, self-defense would sanction armed attacks for countless prior acts of aggression and conquest. The difficulty in defining a precise time limit – either before or after the executive of an aggressive act – does not impugn the fundamental principle. What emerges from the temporal aspect of the traditional formulation is the requirement that a forceful response be made in *reaction to an immediate threat, after practical peaceful options have been expended.* Emphasis added.

247 Coll, op. cit.: 297–307 (1987); O'Brien, op. cit.: 421–478; Sofaer, op. cit.: 89–123. See also Roberts, op. cit.: 318.
248 Coll, op. cit.: 302.
249 op. cit.: 302.
250 According to Coll, '[I]t is important to make the point that military responses to terrorism are essentially defensive in character; their spring is not aggressive, but on

the contrary, the prevention and long-term deterrence of that particular form of aggression that operates through terrorist strategy and tactics.' ibid.: 302.

251 Ibid.: 300.
252 Ibid.: 302.
253 Ibid.: 302–303.
254 O'Brien, op. cit.: 421–478.
255 Ibid.: 469.
256 Ibid.: 421, 475. Cf. Roberts, op. cit.: 318. 'There is little difference between the [self-defense and reprisal] concepts. The traditional positive view of self-defense and negative view of reprisal is impractical and counterproductive. Instead, both reprisal and self-defense should be analyzed under a single reasonableness criterion.'
257 O'Brien, op. cit.: 476. Seymour argues, by contrast:

> [F]orceful responses from victimized nations against terrorists or states sponsoring terrorism for the purpose of deterring further terrorism should more properly be termed 'reprisals,' rather than 'self-defense.' The concept of self-defense should not be stretched beyond recognition in order to serve as a legal basis for actions which can be described more accurately, and more honestly, as reprisal.
>
> Seymour, op. cit.: 240.

258 O'Brien, op. cit.: 476. 'Both forms of self-defense may be needed.'
259 Sofaer, op. cit.: 97.
260 Ibid.: 98.
261 Ibid.: 95. Emphasis added.
262 'The UN Security Council in several cases, most involving Israel, has judged proportionality by comparing the response on a quantitative basis to the *single attack* which preceded it.' Schachter, op. cit.: 315. Emphasis added.
263 Intoccia, op. cit.: 205–206.
264 Ibid. Emphasis added.
265 Ibid.: 206. Emphasis added. Intoccia would appear to permit deterrent action, however: 'the principle of proportionality requires only that such a level of force be exercized as is necessary to reasonably deter or abate offending aggressive action.'
266 Ibid. Citing Bowett, op. cit.: 4.
267 Another supporter of the 'cumulative' approach has been Yehuda Blum, Israeli Ambassador to the United Nations from 1978–1984, and subsequently professor of international law at Hebrew University in Jerusalem. Erickson, op. cit.: 143.
268 Roberts, 'Self-help in 'Combatting State-Sponsored Terrorism: Self-Defense and Peacetime Reprisals,' *Case W. Res. J. Int'l L.* See Erickson, op. cit.: 143–144.
269 Roberts, op. cit.: 282. Emphasis added.
270 Ibid. Emphasis added.
271 Ibid. Emphasis added.
272 Professor Dinstein seemed in his 1987 paper also to favor the 'deterrent' approach. He contends that 'The insistence on proportionality does not mean that a small-scale armed attack must necessarily be absorbed in silence. It does mean that any use of counterforce in self-defence must be attuned to the magnitude of the original attack.' However, 'defensive reprisals' as 'proportionate forcible measures short of war are admissible in response to low-intensity armed attack.' Dinstein, op. cit.: 66. To be legitimate, they must 'be designed not for retribution but for *future protection.*' Ibid. 67. Emphasis added.
  In his 1989 address, Judge Sofaer also advocated a deterrent notion of proportionality: States should not be 'expected . . . to accept a continuation of

unlawful aggression because of a tit-for-tat limit on military response.' Sofaer, op. cit.: 98. To buttress this view, Sofaer cited Schwebel's dissent in the *Nicaragua* case: 'He explained that an action is proportional when it is necessary to end and to repulse an attack, not just when it corresponds exactly to the acts of aggression.' Ibid.: 97. Citing *Nicaragua v. United States*, 1986 *ICJ*: 269–270, 367 (Diss. Op. Schwebel, J.).

273 O'Brien, op. cit.: 477.
274 O'Brien, op. cit.: 472. Emphasis added.
275 Coll, op. cit.: 299.
276 Ibid. Professor Edwin Smith asked Coll:

> Would your interpretation of article 51, requiring military response to be of the minimum force necessary to persuade the target to desist in its activities, use an objective or subjective measure in determining the appropriate amount of force; i.e., force sufficient to persuade a reasonable terrorist to reform as opposed to force sufficient to persuade an unreasonable fanatical terrorist to reform?

> Coll replied: 'The answer is not entirely clear, but in some cases the subjective standard might be appropriate.' Ibid.: 320.

277 Schachter, op. cit.: 315.
278 Ibid.
279 Ibid.
280 Ibid. Emphasis added. See also Schachter, 'The Right of States to Use Armed Force,' *Mich. L. Rev.* 82: 1620, 1637 (1984). Cf. McCredie, op. cit.: 230–231.
281 Baker, op. cit.: 47. Emphasis added. According to Professor Baker, to determine an action's proportionality, its referent or 'yardstick' must be determined:

> There is the specific incident which may have just occurred, but there may also be numerous prior attacks, and the unknown but certain future attacks. If each of the terrorist attacks is viewed in isolation, then responses such as the Libyan bombings [by the United States in 1986] can easily be seen as disproportionate. But, when responding to a continuing series of attacks such a myopic view is inapproporiate.'

282 The 'uninvolved' have been variously characterized as 'non-combatants,' 'civilians,' and 'the innocent population.' See Schachter, McCredie, and Coll.
283 Schachter, op. cit.: 315. Cf. Intoccia, op. cit.: 211. 'While each nation is under an obligation to conduct military operations in a manner which minimizes damage to civilians, no international rule exists which obligates a nation to forgo a legitimate miltary target simply because injury to civilian personnel might take place.'
284 Sofaer, op. cit.: 109. McCredie's notion of discrimination would appear to be a bit more stringent: any target for response, he contends, 'must be virtually free of a civilian presence.' McCredie, op. cit.: 241.
     Professor Baker notes that an 'inevitable outcome of [counter-terror] responses is that they also endanger the lives of people other than the terrorists themselves.' Baker, op. cit.: 47, citing Blum, 'The Beirut Raid and the International Double Standard: A Reply to Professor Richard A. Falk,' *Amer. J. Int'l L.* 64: 137 (1970).
285 O'Brien, op. cit.: 477. Professor Coll, too, noted that military measures '[o]bviously . . . should avoid collateral damage to innocent population.' Coll, op. cit.: 305.
286 Boyle, op. cit.: 296.
287 Intoccia, op. cit.: 211. Cf. Paasche, op. cit.: 400; and McCredie, op. cit.: 240.
288 Intoccia, op. cit.: 211.
289 For an excellent discussion of state responsibility, see Erickson, op. cit.: 95–126.

290 McCredie, op. cit.: 241. Emphasis added. He added that chosen targets must also be 'virtually free of a civilian presence, and the response must be proportionate to the alleged injury.'

291 Ibid.: 233.

292 Ibid.: 218.

293 Cassese, op. cit.: 597.

294 Ibid.: 598.

295 Ibid.: 599–600.

296 Baker, op. cit.: 36.

297 Ibid.: 36.

298 Ibid.: 38.

299 Sofaer, op. cit.: Cf. Coll, op. cit. According to Coll, sponsoring states 'that furnish financial or military support for terrorist activities are engaged in aggression. Their failure to respond to diplomatic requests to cease their aggressive behavior should justify military measures by the victim state.' Similarly, 'once it becomes reasonably evident that the *harboring state* is unable or unwilling to act, the injured state should be free to use the minimum of force required to stop the terrorist threat.' Coll, op. cit.: 305. See also Erickson, op. cit.: 97–103.

300 Sofaer, op. cit.: 103.

301 Ibid.: 108.

302 See also Erickson, op. cit.: 103–106.

303 Sofaer, op. cit.: 105.

304 Ibid.

305 Coll, op. cit.: 307.

306 Baker, op. cit.: 25.

307 See above. See also Bowett, op. cit. and O'Brien, op. cit.

308 North Sea Continental Shelf Cases (F.R.G. v. Den.) (F.R.G. v. Neth.), 1969 *ICJ* 4: paras 73, 74.

309 It could be argued that both states have had the most compelling *causes* and most extensive *capacities* to take forcible action.

310 Bowett, op. cit.: 2.

311 O'Brien, op. cit.: 474–475. O'Brien cites McDougal's definition of law as 'the conjunction of common expectations concerning authority with a high degree of corroboration in actual practice.' McDougal and Lasswell, 'The Identification and Appraisal of Diverse Systems of Public Order, reprinted in M. McDougal and Associates, *Studies in World Public Order*, 13–14 (1960).

312 Employing a somewhat different approach, O'Brien concluded in 1990: 'Prudence reflecting political and military reality will no doubt limit the cases of counterterror operations comparable to those of the Israelis, but when the necessity is sufficient, such actions may be mounted.' O'Brien, op. cit.: 475.

10 INTERNATIONAL LAW AND THE RECOURSE TO FORCE: A SHIFT IN PARADIGM

1 D. Moynihan, *On the Law of Nations*: 19 (1990).

2 The OECS action in Grenada and the Warsaw Pact action in Czechoslovakia come immediately to mind.

3 See Chapter 1 for our discussion of authority and control.

4 Arend, 'International Law and the Recourse to Force: A Shift in Paradigms,' *Stan. J. Int'l L.* 27: 1 (1990).

5 Although it is nearly impossible to categorize scholars as *absolutely* falling into a particular school, some individuals seem to be more clearly 'legalists.' Such scholars

would include: Michael Akehurst, Ian Brownlie, and Louis Henkin. See, M. Akehurst, *A Modern Introduction to International Law*: 256–261 (6th ed. 1987); I. Brownlie, *International Law and the Use of Force by States* (1963); L. Henkin, *How Nations Behave*: 135–164 (2nd ed. 1979).

6 Professor Alberto R. Coll refers to this approach as 'legal absolutism.' He explains that 'legal absolutism is best defined as a general tendency on the part of some international law theorists to interpret the United Nations' rules against aggression in such an expansive manner as to prohibit absolutely the use of force in international relations with a few narrowly drawn exceptions.' Coll, 'The Limits of Global Consciousness and Legal Absolutism: Protecting International Law from Some of its Best Friends,' *Harv. J. Int'l L.* 27: 606 (1986). Coll continues to explain that '[t]he norm around which interpreters of the legal absolutist tradition rally is the prohibition against force in international relations embodied in article 2(4) of the United Nations Charter.' Ibid.: 607 (footnote omitted). Thus, 'one dimension of legal absolutism is a highly *expansive* interpretation of article 2(4), [and] another is a highly *restrictive* view of the "self-defense" exception to article 2(4) contained in article 51 of the Charter.' Ibid.

7 Henkin, 'The Reports of the Death of Article 2(4) Are Greatly Exaggerated,' *Am. J. Int'l L.* 65: 544, 547 (1971).

8 L. Henkin, *How Nations Behave*: 146 (2nd ed. 1979).

9 Gordon, 'Article 2(4) in Historical Context,' *Yale J. Int'l L.* 10: 271, 275 (1985).

10 Ibid.

11 Ibid.

12 See notes 45–87 below and accompanying text.

13 As noted in Chapter 3, the international community has *seemed* to reaffirm the authority of the Charter norms on the use of force.

14 For example, Professor Schacter explains:

> It is not difficult to think of recent cases in which the rule against the use of force was probably violated. Consider some of the recent hostilities in: Afghanistan, Angola, Cambodia, Chad, Falkland Islands, Grenada, Iran–Iraq, Lebanon, Mozambique, Nicaragua, Vietnam. In each of these places, foreign states employed military force for one reason or another, generally claiming legal justification in the language of the UN Charter.

Schachter, 'In Defense of International Rules on the Use of Force,' *U. Chi. L. Rev.* 53: 113, 117–118 (footnote omitted). Schachter argues that '[t]he quality of these justifications varies' and concludes that

> most outsiders view many of these legal contentions skeptically, primarily because states, in substantiating their claims, frequently seem to cite carefully chosen, if not fabricated, sets of facts. Thus, the legal justifications offered by states are often perceived as rationalizations contrived after the decision to intervene had been made.

Ibid.: 118–119

Professor Richard Falk goes even further in commenting on the violations of the Charter norms on the use of force:

> The conclusion is that the legal effort to regulate recourse to force in international relations has virtually collapsed in state-to-state relations, including such institutional settings as those provided by the United Nations. Representative expressions of this legal collapse include: the Soviet invasion of Afghanistan in late 1979; the laissez-faire approach to the Iran–Iraq War throughout its five years; Israel's discretionary and frequent reliance on

retaliatory and preemptive uses of force against its Arab neighbors; and the United States government's blatant reliance on extensive 'covert operations' to overthrow the Sandinista government together with its brazen repudiation of the authority of the International Court of Justice (ICJ) in the Nicaraguan conflict.

Falk, 'The Decline of Normative Restraint in International Relations,' *Yale J. Int'l L.* 10: 263, 264 (1985).

15 See, e.g. L. Henkin, op. cit.: 146–164; Franck, 'Who Killed Article 2(4)? Or: Changing Norms Governing the Use of Force by States,' *Am. J. Int'l L.* 64: 809 (1970); Schachter, op. cit.: 116–119.

16 In support of the contention that these uses of force represent violations of a reasonable interpretation of Article 2(4), see the following: on Guatemala, Bowen and Hughes, 'Guatemala, 1954: Intervention and Jurisdiction,' *Int'l Rel.* 4: 78 (1972); on the Suez Crisis, Wright, 'Intervention, 1956,' *Am. J. Int'l L.* 51: 257, 267–274 (1957); on Hungary, T. Franck, *Nation Against Nation*: 62–70 (1985); on the Bay of Pigs, Falk, 'American Intervention in Cuba and the Rule of Law,' *Ohio St. L. J.* 22: 546 (1961); on Goa, Wright, 'The Goa Incident,' *Am. J. Int'l L.* 56: 617, 628 (1962); on the Dominican Republic, Nanda, 'The US Action in the 1965 Dominican Crisis; Impact on World Order' *Denver L. J.* 43: 439 (1966); *Denver L. J.* 44: 225 (1967); on Czechoslovakia, Goodman, 'The Invasion of Czechoslovakia, 1968,' *Int'l Law.* 4: 42 (1969); on the 1973 Middle East War, O'Brien, *The Conduct of Just and Limited War*: 286 (1981); on North Vietnam, Moore, 'The Lawfulness of Military Assistance to the Republic of Viet-Nam,' *Am. J. Int'l L.* 61: 1 (1967); on Kampuchea, Franck, op. cit.: 225–226; on Afghanistan, ibid.: 226–228; on Tanzania, ibid.: 228, 229; on the Falklands, Coll, 'Philosophical and Legal Dimensions of the Use of Force in International Law,' in A. Coll and A. Arend (eds) *The Falklands War: Lessons for Strategy, Diplomacy, and International Law*: 34–51 (1985): on Grenada, Joyner, 'Reflections on the Lawfulness of Invasion' *Am. J. Int'l L.* 78: 131 (1984); on Panama, Farer, 'Panama: Beyond The Charter Paradigm', *Am. J. Int'l L.* 84: 503 (1990); on Iraq's invasion of Kuwait, see notes below and accompanying text.

17 L. Henkin, op. cit.: 146.

18 Professor O'Connell has contended that '[a] treaty which is a dead letter may be said to be terminated.' D. O'Connell, *International Law*: 266 (1970). Similarly, Professor Franck asserts that 'the international system recognizes the principle of desuetude, which sweeps away the litter of discarded norms.' T. Franck, *The Power of Legitimacy Among Nations*: 173 (1990) (footnote omitted).

19 See Chapter 3 above.

20 This seems to be the approach taken by the majority of international legal scholars. Such scholars would include Derek Bowett, Myres McDougal, John Norton Moore, W. Michael Reisman. See, D. Bowett, *Self-Defence in International Law* (1958); M. McDougal and F. Feliciano, *Law and Minimum World Public Order* (1961); Moore, 'The Secret War in Central America and the Future of World Order,' *Am. J. Int'l L.* 80: 43, 80–92 (1986); Reisman, 'Coercion and Self-Determination: Construing Charter Article 2(4),' *Am. J. Int'l L.* 78: 642 (1984).

21 This would seem to be the position taken by scholars such as Moore and Bowett, op. cit.

22 Coll, 'The Limits of Global Consciousness and Legal Absolutism: Protecting International Law from Some of its Best Friends,' 27 *Harv. J. Int'l L.* 27: 509, 613 (1986).

23 Ibid.: 620.

24 Ibid.

25 Professor Schachter, who believes that the law is much greater than a narrow 'core,'

has nevertheless acknowledged the existence of such a 'core.' He explains that 'the rules have a core meaning that governments and legal experts generally accept. Thus it is perfectly clear that states may not invade others for gain or domination, a principle affirmed in the judgments of the Nuremberg and Tokyo trials.' Schachter, op. cit.: 102.

26 Professor Eugene Rostow, for example, contends that 'the Charter of the United Nations is going the way of the Covenant of the League,' but argues that '[f]or the Western nations to abandon the Charter as a guide to their own behavior under the pressure of the Soviet thrust for power would be a catastrophe, signalling the complete breakdown of the state system as a system of peace.' Rostow, 'The Legality of the International Use of Force by and from States,' *Yale J. Int'l L.* 10: 286, 290 (1985).

27 Ibid.: 290.

28 See M. Akehurst, *A Modern Introduction to International Law:* 259–260 (5th ed, 1984); Schachter, 'The Right of States to Use Armed Force,' *Mich. L. Rev.* 82: 1620, 1624 (1984).

29 The Kellogg-Briant Pact, Aug. 27, 1928, 46 Stat. 2343, T.S. No. 796, *L.N.T.S.* 94: 57.

30 Franck, 'Who Killed Article 2(4)? Or: Changing Norms Governing the Use of Force by States,' *Am. J. Int'l L.* 64.

31 Ibid.: 835.

32 Ibid.

33 Ibid.

34 Ibid.: 809.

35 T. Franck, *The Power of Legitimacy Among Nations:* 32 (1990) (footnotes omitted).

36 Ibid.: 78.

37 Ibid.

38 As early as 1958, Professor Julius Stone contended that

> any implied prohibition on Members to use force seems conditioned on the assumption that effective collective measures can be taken under the Charter to bring about adjustment or settlement 'in conformity with the principles of justice and international law.' It is certainly not self-evident what obligations (if any) are imported where *no* such effective collective measures are available for the remedy of just grievances.

J. Stone, *Aggression and World Order:* 96 (1958) (footnote omitted) (emphasis in original). More recently, Professor Rostow has argued that '[a]t this moment ... it is impossible to determine whether Article 2(4) of the Charter is an operative legal norm.' Rostow, op. cit.: 290 (1985). He recognizes that violations, especially those committed by the Soviet Union, have stripped it of much of its force, but concludes that 'it has not yet disappeared either as an influence on state behavior or as an aspiration for international law.' Ibid. Even Professor Reisman has come close to contending that Article 2(4) is no longer good law. Reisman, Criteria for the Lawful Use of Force in International Law, op. cit.

39 See notes 11–18 above and accompanying text.

40 See notes 27–28 above and accompanying text.

41 The late English jurist J. L. Brierly explained that

> [t]he doctrine of positivism ... teaches that international law is the sum of the rules by which states have *consented* to be bound, and that nothing can be law to which they have not consented. This consent may be given expressly, as in a treaty, or it may be implied by a state acquiescing in a customary rule.
> J. L. Brierly, *The Law of Nations:* 51 (6th Waldock ed. 1962).

42 This approach follows the famous dictum of the *Lotus* case, in which the Permanent Court of International Justice issued a classical statement of the positivist approach:

> International law governs relations between independent States. The rules of law binding upon States therefore emanate from their own free will as expressed in conventions or by usages generally accepted as expressing principles of law and established in order to regulate the relations between these co-existing independent communities or with a view to the achievement of common aims. Restrictions upon the independence of States cannot therefore be presumed.

'The Lotus Case' (Fr. v. Turk.), 1972 *P.C.I.J.*, ser. A, No. 10.

43 *UN Charter*, Art. 51.

44 Under pre-Charter customary international law, as noted in Chapter 5. The *Caroline* case was often regarded as having established the criteria for anticipatory self-defense. Under the *Caroline* principles, for an action to be permissible anticipatory self-defense, it must meet both the test of necessity and the test of proportionality.

45 Numerous international legal scholars have specifically affirmed the right of anticipatory self-defense. See, D. Bowett, op. cit. Brownlie, 'The Use of Force in Self-Defence in International Law,' *Brit. Y. B. Int'l L.* 37: 183 (1961); McDougal, 'The Soviet Cuban Quarantine and Self-Defense,' *Am. J. Int'l L.* 57: 597 (1963).

Some scholars who support the permissibility of anticipatory self-defense argue that the *Caroline* principles still apply. See e.g., Schachter, 'The Lawful Resort to Unilateral Use of Force,' *Yale J. Int'l L.* 10: 291, 293 (1985). Italian scholar Antonio Cassese seems to suggest a similar approach:

> One might perhaps draw the conclusion that consensus is now emerging that under Art. 51 anticipatory self-defence is allowed, but on the strict conditions that (i) solid and consistent evidence exists that another country is about to engage on a large-scale armed attack jeopardizing the very life of the target State and (ii) no peaceful means of preventing such attack are available either because they would certainly prove useless owing to the specific circumstances, or for lack of time to resort to them, or because they have been exhausted. However, the risks of abuse should lead us to interpret this construction of Art. 51 very strictly and consider it as giving only very exceptional licence.

Cassese, 'Return to Westphalia? Considerations on the Gradual Erosion of the Charter System,' in A. Cassese, op. cit.: 405, 515–516.

Others have felt that the criteria suggested by the *Caroline* case are too constraining in the contemporary international system. Professor William V. O'Brien, for example, has contended that '[t]he authority and relevance of this famous dictum [the *Caroline* case] have been exaggerated.' W. O'Brien, op. cit.: 132. According to him,

> the formula for the necessity of defense – instant, overwhelming, and leaving no choice of means and no moment of deliberation – is more rhetorical than substantive. Particularly unjustified is the implied requirement that there be no time for any other choice than the one taken.

Ibid.: 132–133

O'Brien notes that during 'the Cuban missile crisis, the United States had weeks to formulate its case of the necessity to take measures deemed imperative to meet the threat.' Ibid.: 133. In consequence, he argues that '[s]ome threats must be met instantly, but some may be met after protracted calculation.' Ibid. Because of this, O'Brien suggests a 'better formula for anticipatory self-defense' consisting of three criteria: first, '[t]here must be a clear indication of an intent on the part of the alleged aggressor to attack'; second, '[t]here must be adequate evidence that preparations for the attack have advanced to the point where it is imminent'; and third, '[t]he advantages of a preemptive attack must be proportionate to the risks of precipitating a war that might be avoided.' Ibid.

46 See Chapter 3.
47 Ibid.
48 Professor O'Brien details the opposition in the Security Council to reprisals, see O'Brien, 'Reprisals, Deterrence and Self-Defense in Counterterror Operations,' *Va. J. Int'l L.* 30: 435–443, 463–467 (1990).
49 Professor O'Brien explains that

> [t]he distinction between actions taken in self-defense and actions taken to punish antecedent armed attacks as a self-help sanction of the law is unrealistic, given the lack of Security Council enforcement of the UN *jus ad bellum* legal regime and the competing just war/just revolution doctrines and practices in the contemporary international system.
>
> Ibid.: 475–476.

He argues that

> [e]ven if the Security Council and international legal doctrine conceded that, in the absence of effective collective security, some form of reasonable reprisal should be recognized, it would be difficult, if not impossible, to obtain a consensus on which uses of force were delictual and which were sanctions of the UN *jus ad bellum* law regime. Ibid.: 476.

O'Brien concludes that '[a] more sensible approach would be to assimilate armed reprisals into the right of legitimate self-defense.' Ibid.

50 See Chapter 3.
51 Ibid.
52 Professor Reisman explains:

> The basic policy of contemporary international law has been to maintain the political independence of territorial communities so that they can continue to be able to express their ongoing desire for political organization in a form appropriate to them. Article 2(4), like so much in the Charter and in contemporary international politics, supports and must be interpreted in terms of this key postulate. Each application of Article 2(4) must enhance opportunities for ongoing self-determination. Though all interventions are lamentable, the fact is that some may serve, in terms of aggregate consequences, to increase the probability of the free choice of peoples about their government and political structure. Others have the manifest objective and consequence of doing exactly the opposite.
>
> There is, thus, neither need nor justification for treating in a mechanically equal fashion, Tanzania's intervention in Uganda to overthrow the Amin despotism, on the one hand, and Soviet intervention in Hungary or Czechoslovakia to overthrow popular governments and to impose an undesired regime on a coerced population, on the other. Nor should the different appraisal of these cases by the international legal system occasion any surprise.
>
> Reisman, op. cit.: 282–283.

Reisman's point seems to be that the international community accepts intervention that supports the right of the people to determine their own government in the traditional 'western' way. The problem with this approach is that too many states assert the right to promote other brands of self-determination. There simply is not a consensus that only *one* type of self-determination is permissible. See Chapter 3.

53 See Chapter 3.

54 One element of Argentina's justification for the invasion was that the British had illegally seized the Falklands in the 1830s. See Coll, 'Philosophical and Legal Dimensions of the Use of Force in the Falklands War,' in A. Coll and A. Arend (eds) *The Falklands War: Lessons for Strategy, Diplomacy, and International Law.* 39 (1985). See also Schachter, 'The Right of States to Use Armed Force,' *Mich. L. Rev.* 82: 1627–1628.

55 See Chapter 3; see also, Wright, 'Intervention, 1956,' *Am. J. Int'l L.* 56: 257, 261 (1957).

56 See Chapter 3.

57 See Chapter 3.

58 On the invasion of Kuwait, see generally, Murphy, 'Iraqi Force Invades Kuwait, Thrust Toward Capital,' *Wash. Post,* Aug. 2, 1990: A1, col. 4; 'Invading Iraqis Seize Kuwait and Its Oil; U.S. Condemn Attack, Urges United Action,' *N.Y. Times,* Aug. 3, 1990: A1, cols 3–6.

59 'Excerpts from Iraq's Statement on Kuwait,' *Wash. Post,* Aug. 9, 1990: A18, col. 1.

60 The Iraqi statement explained that '[o]ne of the most egregious criminal acts of colonialism was its partition of the homeland, which was a single homeland the day Baghdad was the capital of all Arabs'. Ibid.

61 Ibid.

62 *UNSC Res. 660,* reprinted in, *I.L.M.* 29: 1323, 1325. See Lewis, 'UN Condemns the Invasion with Threat to Punish Iraq,' *Wash. Post,* Aug. 3, 1990: A10.

63 *UNSC Res. 661,* reprinted in *I.L.M.* 29: 1323, 1325; see also, 'Text of the Resolution for Sanctions on Iraq,' *N.Y. Times,* Aug. 7, 1990: A9, col. 6; Tyler, 'UN Security Council Votes Embargo on Iraq; Saddam Says Seizure of Kuwait Is Permanent,' *Wash. Post,* Aug. 7, 1990: A1, col. 4.

64 *UNSC Res. 662,* reprinted in *I.L.M.* 26: 1323, 1327; see also 'Resolution Says Iraq Must Reverse Step,' *Wash. Post,* Aug. 10, 1990: A30, col. 1. See also Chapter 4.

65 Ibid.

66 As noted in Chapter 4, this Resolution

> AUTHORIZES member states cooperating with the Government of Kuwait, unless Iraq on or before January 15, 1991, fully implements, as set forth in paragraph 1 above, the foregoing resolutions, to use all necessary means to uphold the Security Council Resolution 660 and all subsequent relevant Resolutions and to restore international peace and security in the area.

S.C. Res. 678, reprinted in, 'Text of UN Resolution on Using Force in the Gulf,' *N.Y. Times,* Nov. 30, 1990: A10, col. 1. Even though the resolution does not specifically mention the use of force, it is clear from the negotiations surrounding its adoption, that its intent was to provide authorization for states to use force if necessary. See Lewis, 'UN Gives Iraq Until Jan. 15 to Retreat or Face Force: Hussein Says He Will Fight,' *N.Y. Times,* Nov. 30, 1990: A1, col. 6; Goshko, 'UN Authorizes Use of Force Against Iraq,' *Wash. Post,* Nov. 30, 1990: A1, col. 4.

Previously, the Council had adopted Resolution 665 authorizing the use of force to maintain a naval blockade. This Resolution

> CALLS UPON those member states cooperating with the Government of Kuwait which are deploying maritime forces to the area to use such measures commensurate to the specific circumstances as may be necessary under the authority of the Security Council to halt all inward and outward maritime

shipping in order to inspect and verify their cargoes and destinations and to insure strict implementation of the provisions related to such shipping laid down in Resolution 661 (1990).

S.C. Res. 665, reprinted in *I.L.M.* 29: 1323, 1329; see also, 'Text of Resolution by UN Security Council,' *N.Y. Times*, Aug. 26, 1990: A15, col. 3. Once again, even though force was not specifically mentioned, it was clear from the negotiating record that the intent was to permit its use. 'UN Votes Use of Force to Halt Iraqi Trade,' *N.Y. Times*, Aug. 26, 1990: A1, col. 6. See also, Sciolino, 'How US Got UN Backing For Use of Force in the Gulf,' *N.Y. Times*, Aug. 30, 1990: A1, col. 4.

Throughout the course of the conflict, the Security Council has adopted numerous resolutions. In addition to those already mentioned, these include *UNSCR Res. 666*, reprinted in *I.L.M.* 29: 1323, 1330 (allowing foodstuffs to be transported to Iraq under the coordination of the United Nations); *UNSC Res. 667*, reprinted in ibid.: 1332 (condemning Iraqi actions against diplomatic missions and diplomatic personnel); *UNSC Res. 680*, reprinted in ibid.: 1334 (imposing an air blockade on Iraq).

67 The United States Ambassador to the United Nations, Thomas Pickering, made these inevitable comparisons:

There is something repugnant, chilling and vaguely familiar about the statement issued yesterday [August 8, 1990] by the Iraqi Revolutionary Council. We have heard that rhetoric before. It was used about the Rhineland, the Sudetenland, about the Polish Corridor, about Mussolini's invasion of Ethiopia and about the Marco Polo Bridge incident in China. ... The world community did not react. The result was global conflagration. We here will not and cannot let this happen again.

Quoted in Goshko, 'UN Declares Annexation of Kuwait "Void,"' *Wash. Post*, Aug. 10, 1990: A5, A30, col. 3.

68 The international relations theorist Robert Lieber provides a partial lists of armed conflicts that have taken place since 1945. R. Lieber, *No Common Power.* 250 (2nd ed. 1990). None of these uses of force was justified solely on the basis of a desire for territorial aggrandizement.

69 But see, Cassese, op. cit.: 509.

70 As noted in Chapter 2, under the pre-League international legal regimes, states had a sovereign right to go to war. L. Oppenheim, *International Law* 2: 178 (7th ed. 1952) ('War was in law a natural function of the state and a prerogative of its uncontrolled sovereignty'). There were legal restrictions on uses of force short of war, but these were often not successful. See J. Brierly, *The Law of Nations*: 397 (H. Waldock ed. 1981).

71 See below for a discussion of the end of the Cold War.

72 See, e.g. 'Goshko, 'UN Summit Stresses Global Cooperation,' *Wash. Post*, Feb. 1, 1992: A1, col. 4; McFadden, 'Leaders Gather in New York to Charter World Order,' *N.Y. Times*, Jan. 31, 1991: A1, col. 6 (discussing special Security Council meeting convened at Head of State level to explore the future of international cooperation).

73 See below.

74 See below.

75 See Arend, 'The Role of the United Nations in the Iran–Iraq War,' in C. Joyner (ed.) *The Persian Gulf War: Lessons for Diplomacy, Law and Strategy* (1990).

76 *UNSC Res. 619* (Aug. 9, 1988); Lewis, 'UN Plans 250 Peacekeepers for Gulf,' *N.Y. Times*, Aug. 6, 1988: A3.

77 See 'Security Council Supports Direct Talks Between Iran and Iraq,' *UN Chronicle*: 21 (June 1990).

78 See Coll, 'Saddam Offers to Conclude Full Peace with Iran,' *Wash. Post*, Aug. 16, 1990: A1, col. 6.
79 See Arend, op. cit.: 203–204.
80 See 'Namibia: Independence At Last,' *UN Chronicle*: 4–12 (June 1990).
81 See 'Central America Peace Process Progresses,' *UN Chronicle*: 15–17 (June 1990).
82 Ibid.: 16.
83 Ibid.
84 See '"Big Five" Agree on UN Role in Cambodia,' *UN Chronicle*: 18 (June 1990); Prial, 'Five UN Powers Announce Accord on Cambodia War,' *N.Y. Times*, Aug. 29, 1990: A1, col. 2.
85 See 'New Round of Talks on Western Sahara,' *UN Chronicle*: 20 (June 1990).
86 See Chapter 4.
87 See M. Whiteman, *Digest of International Law* 12: 361–422 (1971) for a discussion of United Nations' actions against Rhodesia.
88 See ibid.: 422–439 for an examination of action taken against South Africa.
89 See above.
90 '"Big Five" Agree on UN Role in Cambodia,' *UN Chronicle*: 18–20 (June 1990).
91 See, e.g. Keller, 'Bush and Gorbachev Say Iraqis Must Obey UN and Quit Kuwait,' *N.Y. Times*, Sept. 10, 1990: A1, col. 6.
92 See I. Claude, *Swords Into Plowshares*: 245–285 (4th ed. 1971).
93 Lewis, 'World Court Plan Meets Difficulties,' *N.Y. Times*, Jun. 24, 1990: 9, col. 1.
94 Weiss and Kessler, 'Moscow's UN Policy,' *For. Pol'y*: 94, 99 (1990).
95 Ibid.: see also, M. Gorbachev, *Realities and Guarantees for a Secure World* (1987); D. Puchala and R. Choate, *The Challenge of Relevance*: The United Nations in a Changing World Environment: 14–23 (1989).
96 Statement by the President of the Security Council, UN Doc. S/23500, Jan. 31, 1992 (emphasis added).
97 An Agenda for Peace: Preventative Diplomacy, Peacemaking and Peace-Keeping, Report of the Secretary-General pursuant to the statement adopted by the Summit Meeting of the Security Council on 31 January 1992, UN Doc. A/47/277, S/24111, Jun. 17, 1992 [hereinafter cited as An Agenda for Peace].
98 Ibid. at para. 23.
99 Ibid. at para. 24.
100 Ibid. at para. 25.
101 Ibid. paras. 26–27.
102 Ibid. at paras. 28–32.
103 Ibid. at para. 33.
104 For a discussion of this decline, see e.g. Horelick, 'US–Soviet Relations: Threshold of a New Era,' *For. Aff.* 69: 51 (1990); Kirkpatrick, 'Beyond the Cold War,' *For. Aff.* 69: 1 (1990).
105 International Convention on Civil and Political Rights, entered into force Mar. 23, 1976, *U.N.T.S. 999*: 717.
106 Freedom House, the independent human rights monitoring organization, had classified all these states as 'Not Free.' See, 'The Map of Freedom,' Freedom at Issue 112: 31–33 (1990).
107 See Stent, 'Doctrinal Discord,' *The New Republic*: 16 (Jan. 8 and 15, 1990).
108 Professor Angela Stent explains:

> Communist Parties are disintegrating, their leaders jailed for corruption and reviled by outraged populations in mass street demonstrations. New coalition governments are struggling to survive. And behind this turmoil stands Mikhail Gorbachev. He engineered the downfall of the 40-year-old Soviet empire,

personally intervening to secure the resignations of hard-line leaders in East Germany, Bulgaria, and Czechoslovakia, after encouraging the earlier Polish and Hungarian renunciation of the Communist monopoly on power.

. . .

He [Gorbachev] actively intervened when countries going their way did not move fast enough from repression to democracy. He pushed recalcitrant Eastern European apparatchiki toward political pluralism, allowing the legalization of alternative parties and the abolition of the leading rule of the Communist Party.

Ibid.

109 Franck, 'Secret Warfare: Policy Options for a Modern Legal and Institutional Context,' Paper presented to the Conference on Policy Alternatives to Deal with Secret Warfare: International Law, US Institute of Peace, March 16–17, 1990: at 17.
110 Ibid.: 17–18.
111 Ibid.: 18
112 Ibid.
113 Ibid. Professor Franck has further developed these ideas. See, Franck, 'The Emerging Right to Democratic Governance,' *Am. J. Int'l L.* 86: 46 (1992).
114 'Survey Update,' insert in *Freedom at Issue* 112 (1990). Even though any attempt to categorize the freedom of states is inevitably subjective, Freedom House seems to use criteria similar to certain rights defined in the International Covenant. As Dr Joseph E. Ryan explains, '[t]he *Survey's* understanding of freedom is broad, and encompasses two sets of characteristics grouped under political rights and civil liberties.' Ryan, 'Survey Methodology,' in ibid.: 10. According to Ryan,

Political rights enable people to participate freely in the political process. By the political process, we mean the system by which the polity chooses the authoritative policy makers and attempts to make binding decisions affecting the national, regional or local community. In a free society this means the right of all adults to vote and compete for public office, and for elected representatives to have a decisive vote on public policies. A system is genuinely free or democratic to the extent that the people have a choice in determining the nature of the system and its leaders.

Ibid.

Freedom House has developed a check list to determine if a regime meets the criterion of political rights. Ibid. Ryan also explains the other criterion, civil liberties. According to him, '*Civil liberties* are the freedoms to develop views, institutions and personal autonomy apart from the states.' Ibid.: 11. Dr Ryan explains that

[t]he checklist for civil liberties begins with a requirement for free and independent media, literature and other cultural expressions. In cases where the media are state-controlled, but offer pluralistic points of view, the *Survey* gives the system credit. The checklist also includes the rights to have open public discussion and free private discussion, and freedom of assembly and demonstration.

Ibid.

115 Freedom House includes the following states in the 'Not Free' category: Afghanistan, Albania, Angola, Benin, Brunei, Bulgaria, Burkina Faso, Burma, Burundi, Cambodia, Cameroon, Cape Verde, Central African Republic, Chad, China (PRC), Comoros, Congo, Cuba, Djibouti, Equatorial Guinea, Ethiopia, Gabon, Ghana, Guinea, Guinea-Bissau, Haiti, Iran, Iraq, Kenya, North Korea, Laos, Lebanon, Lesotho, Liberia, Libya, Malawi, Maldives, Mali, Mauritania, Mongolia,

Mozambique, Niger, Oman, Qatar, Romania, Rwanda, Sao Tome and Principe, Saudi Arabia, Seychelles, Somalia, Sudan, Syria, Tanzania, Togo, the Soviet Union, the United Arab Emirates, Vietnam, Yemen [South Yemen at the time of the Report], Zaire, 'The Map of Freedom – 1990,' in ibid.: 31. See also, *Amnesty 1990 Report* (1990) (Annual Report on the state of human rights by Amnesty International).

116 See above. Professor Anthony D'Amato seems to support the contention that this regime was an illegitimate 'tyranny.' He argues that

> if any of the forms of government become in the Aristotelian sense corrupted, resulting in tyranny against their populations – and I regard 'tyranny' as occurring when those who have monopolistic control of the weapons and instruments of suppression in a country turn those weapons against their own people – I believe that intervention from outside is not only legally justified but morally required.

D'Amato, 'The Invasion of Panama Was a Lawful Response to Tyranny,' *Am. J. Int'l L.* 84: 516, 519 (1990) (footnotes omitted).

117 With the exception of a few close allies of the United States, most states in the international system were quite critical of the invasion. For example, the Yugoslav Ambassador to the United Nations told the Security Council that the action was a '"gross violation of sovereignty".' Schwartz, 'World Criticism of US Intervention Mounts,' *Wash. Post*, Dec. 22, 1989: A29, col. 1, A33, col. 3. The Ethiopian Ambassador termed the invasion '"unnecessary flexing of big-power muscle".' Ibid.: col. 4. The Swedish Foreign Ministry claimed the US action was a '"violation of fundamental principles of international law".' Ibid.: col. 5. Even the Secretary-General of the United Nations, Javier Perez de Cuellar, stated that he '"could not but oppose the recourse to force".' Ibid.: A29, col. 4. In addition to these and many other individual statements condemning the action, the Organization of American States went on record criticizing the invasion. See Goshko and Isikoff, 'OAS Votes to Censure US for Intervention,' *Wash. Post*, Dec. 23, 1989: A7, col. 5. Moreover, but for the vetoes of the United States, Great Britain, and France, the United Nations Security Council would have adopted a resolution condemning the action. Schwartz, 'US, Allies Veto UN Council Censure,' *Wash. Post*, Dec. 24, 1989: A16, col. 1.

118 See above.

119 I am grateful to Jeffrey Hovenier of Georgetown University for emphasizing this point.

120 Professor Henkin has explained that '[h]istorically, how a state treated persons within its territory was its own affair.' Henkin, 'The Internationalization of Human Right,' *Proc. Gen. Educ. Sem.* 6: 7 (1977), reprinted in, L. Henkin, R. Pugh, O. Schachter, and H. Smit, *International Law: Cases and Materials* 981 (2nd ed. 1987).

121 See ibid.: 996–1001.

122 Professor John Norton Moore has consistently emphasized the point that for the right of self-defense to be meaningful, it must be a 'real' right. States must be able to provide for 'effective' self-defense. See Moore, 'The Use of Force in International Relations: Norms Concerning the Initiation of Coercion,' in J. Moore, F. Tipson and R. Turner, *National Security Law* 85, 87–89 (1991).

Index

abductions 147–50
Achille Lauro incident 148–9
Action with Respect to Threats of the
   peace, Breaches of the Peace, and
   Acts of Aggression 31–2, 47–51
aggression: and force 34; indirect 90,
   196; prohibitions 21; and
   self-defense 23; state 168
aircraft interceptions 148, 149, 156
Akehurst, Michael 33, 119, 122, 130
America: *see* US
Amin, Idi 123, 124
Anglo-Iranian Oil Company 95
Angola 120–1
Antelope case 16
anticipatory self-defense: Article (51)
   72–3, 219 (n7); case studies 74–9;
   contemporary state practice 73–9;
   Grenada 64; Grotius 15; legal status
   71, 79, 259–60 (n45); publicists' view
   157; *see also Caroline* case
Aquinas, Thomas 14
Arab states, and Israel 44, 95
Argentina 45
Aristotle 12–13
armed attack 90, 196
assassination 150–2, 156
Augustine 13–14
authority, international law 3–4, 9–10,
   206 (n47), 206–7 (n48)
Awami League 118

Baker, James 93
Baker, Mark 163, 166, 168
Bangladesh 118
'Barracuda' Operation 125
Baxter, Richard 140
Begin, Menachem 71

Belgium 96–7, 115–17, 231 (n49)
belligerency 81–2
blockade 62, 75
Bodin, Jean 16
Bokassa, Jean-Bedel 125–6
bombing, La Belle discotheque 154,
   161–2
Boutros-Ghali, Boutros 56, 58, 66,
   191
Bowett, Derek: anticipatory
   self-defense 74; counter-terrorism
   152, 157; humanitarian intervention
   129; reprisals 42; self-defense 107
Boyle, Francis 159–60, 163
Britain: *see* UK
Brownlie, Ian 21, 42, 74, 106
Bush, George 1, 93, 102, 150
Bush Administration 42

'Call to Amend Article 51' (Baker) 163
Cambodia 98, 112, 121–3
Caroline case 18, 72, 75–6, 79, 164, 259
   (n44)
Carter Administration 100–1
Cassese, Antonio: anticipatory
   self-defense 259–60 (n45); response
   to terrorism 162, 163; terrorism 145,
   168; terrorist actors 141, 142
Cassin, René 77
Central Africa 125–6
Central America 87, 189
Certain Expenses of The United Nations
   case 67
Chayes, Abram 62, 75
Cicero 13
civil conflict 37, 80, 81–6
Coll, Alberto: Article (2(4)) 182–3;
   deterrence 166; reprisals 164;

self-defense 160; terrorism 249
(n181), 252–3 (n250)
collective security 51, 58
collective self-defense 31, 36, 89
collective use of force 51–2, 57
competence de guerre 17, 188
conflict: civil 37, 80, 81–6; international
37–9; mixed 37, 80, 87–92
Congo 96–7, 115–17, 231 (n49)
Constantinople Convention 44
contemporary state practice 73–9,
103–5, 110–11, 128–31, 147–59
contra rebels 41–2, 80, 81, 92
control 9–10, 206 (n47)
Corfu Channel case 80
counter-intervention 88–91
counter-restrictionists: anticipatory
self-defense 73, 74, 78–9;
humanitarian intervention 132–5;
protection of nationals 106–9
counter-terrorism 152, 157, 160, 167,
171
covert action 38, 197
Cuba, and Angola 120
Cuban Missile Crisis 62, 74–6
cujus regio ejus religio 16
cumulative proportionality 165
customary international law 6–7; norms
9; reprisals 17; self-defense 72,
218–19 (n4); terrorism 144; and
United Nations Charter 30
Cyprus 100

De Jure Belli ac Pacis (Grotius) 15
De Res Publica (Cicero) 13
debt collection, and force 18–19
decolonization 86
'Definition of Aggression' Resolution
40–1, 48, 221 (n16)
democratic governance, right to 192
Democratic Kampuchea 112, 121–3; *see
also* Cambodia
deterrent action 253 (n272)
deterrent proportionality 165, 166
Dinstein, Yorum: deterrence 253
(n272); self-defense 218–19 (n4);
terrorism 145, 146–7; war 23
Dominican Republic 97–8, 117
Dore, Professor 117

East Pakistan 118–19
East Timor 119–20

Eban, Aba 76
economic sanctions 190
ECOWAS (Economic Community of
West African States) 65
Egypt 44–5, 76, 95–6, 114–15
'El Dorado Canyon' Operation 138, 154
El Salvador 89
El Wazir, Khalil 150–1
enforcement action 49, 61–2
enforcement mechanisms 133–4
Entebbe 99

Falk, Richard 90, 256–7 (n14)
Falklands War 45
First World War 19
force 35–6; and Charter provisions
32–4; and contract debts 18–19;
lawful uses 185–6, 196–201; national
policy 23–4; normative orientation
11; permissible 108, 134–5;
restrictions 11, 195–6; against
terrorism 147–57; unlawful uses
187–8, 201
force short of war 17–18
Foreign Relations Law, US 144
France 44, 125–6
Franck, Thomas 184–5, 192
Freedom House 193, 264 (n114)
Frowein, Professor 159

General Assembly: *see* UN General
Assembly
general principles of law 7, 143
Geneva Conventions, Common Article
(3) 145
geopolitics 117, 127–8, 129
Ghana, and Cuban Missile Crisis 75–6
Gordon, Edward 180–1
Grenada: invaded 41, 64–5, 101, 126–8;
US 101, 126–8, 212 (n44), 221–2 (n18)
Grotius, Hugo 15
Gulf War 53–5

Hague Convention (1907) 19
Hall, William Edward 17
Henkin, Louis 180, 181–2, 219 (n7)
hijacking 148–9
Hobbes, Thomas 16
Holsti, K J 3
holy war 11–12
hostages 100–1, 116, 138
human law 14

human rights 109, 195; abuse 128; protection 112, 113, 132–3; and UN Charter 86; *see also* humanitarian intervention

humanitarian intervention 112–14; circumstances 128–9; collective use of force 113; customary right 133–4; and geopolitics 117, 127–8; illustrations 114–28; international law 94; *jus ad bellum* 136; legality 131–7; Realpolitik motives 120; responses 130–1; restrictionists 131–2, 136; self-defense 167; self-determination 113–14; and state consent 113–14, 116–17; state justification 129–30; state practice 128–31; UN Charter 109; UN Security Council 55, 56

imminent attack 196
imperialism 13
India 118, 130, 135
Indonesia 119–20
injustices, correction 43–5, 179, 186–7
insurgency 81–2
international conventions 6
International Court of Justice: Article (38) 5–6, 7; as international institution 39; *Nicaragua* case 35, 87–8, 89; USSR 190
International Covenant on Civil and Political Rights 193
international institutions 8–9, 39, 177, 189
international law 206 (n47); contemporary 260–1 (n52); norms 2; test 9–10; traditional sources 5–9
intervention 94; circumstances 103–4; and civil conflict 81–6; lawfulness 37–8; and mixed conflict 87–92; norms 80–1; scope 104; state justification 105; state practice 103; *see also* humanitarian intervention
Intoccia, Gregory 165, 167–8
Iran, US hostages 100–1, 138
Iraq: international inspections 55; invading Kuwait 1, 53, 190; and Israel 71, 77–9
Israel: aircraft interception 148, 149, 156; and Arab states 44, 95; assassinations 150–2, 156; and Egypt 44–5, 76, 114–15; force against

terrorism 156–9; kidnapping 150; military strikes 152–3; Osarik reactor 71, 77–9; and Palestinian conflict 114–15, 135; self-defense 149; and Uganda 99; and United Arab Republic 76–7

Johnson, Lyndon 117
Joyner, Christopher C 91
jus ad bellum 2, 4; future 194–202; humanitarian intervention 136; international terrorism 172–3; League of Nations 22; recommended 195–6, 201–2; UN Charter 131
'Just Cause' Operation 93, 102
just war period 11–15
justice, over peace 34, 40–5, 85, 179, 191–3, 210 (n14)

Kampuchea 112, 121–3; *see also* Cambodia
Kashmir 74
Kellogg-Briand pact period 22–4
Kennedy, John F 74–5
Khmer Rouge 112
kidnapping 150
Korean War 52–3
Kuwait 1, 53, 190

La Belle discotheque 154, 161–2
Larnaca airport 100
League of Nations 4, 19–22
Lebanon 98–9, 150, 155
legal obligation, new 193–4
legitimacy of regimes 192, 193
Levitt, Professor 140
liberation: *see* national liberation
Liberia 58, 65, 102–3, 217–18 (n107)
Libya 43, 55, 138–9, 154
Lieber, Robert J 3
Lillich, Professor 133
Locke, John 15

Mallison, W and S 140
Mauritania 99–100
Mayaguez 98
McCredie, Jeffrey 168
McDougal, Myres 34, 109, 132–3, 171
McGovern, George 112
Meeker, Leonard 62, 75
Middle East, protection of nationals 95–6

Middle East War (1967) 76–7
military coalition 54
military contingents 66
military sanctions 50–1
Military Staff Committee 50–1, 57–8
military strikes 152–3, 154–5
mixed conflict 37, 80, 87–92
Moore, John Norton 11, 63–4, 84, 85,
    265 (n122)
Murphy, John 141–2
Musawi, Abbas 151–2

Namibia 189
Nasser, Gamal Abdel 44, 76
national liberation 41, 86, 123, 184
national policy, and force 23–4
nationals, protection of 201, 202;
    customary rule, pre-Charter 107–8;
    humanitarian intervention 113–14;
    illustrations 94–103; legality 105–10,
    111; Middle East 95–6; Panama 93;
    state practice 103–5
natural law approach 14
Naulilaa case 17
naval blockade 62, 75
necessity 18, 164
Nicaragua 41–2, 80, 81, 90–1
Nicaragua case 35, 73, 80, 88, 89, 196,
    197
non-intervention 131–2; neutral 84–5,
    86, 92
Noriega, Manuel 93, 102
norms/rules 29, 203–4 (n19)
North Sea Continental Shelf principle
    171
nuclear weapons 38–9
Nyerere, Julius 123, 124

OAS (Organization of American States)
    117
OAU (Organization of African Unity)
    124
Obeid, Abdul Karim 150
O'Brien, William V: assassinations 150;
    Caroline case 259–60 (n45);
    counter-terrorism 157, 160, 167, 171;
    deterrent proportionality 165, 166;
    justice 210 (n14); reprisals 42, 152;
    self-defense 160, 164
observer groups 66
observer states 130–1
OECS (Organization of Eastern

Caribbean States) 64, 127
Operation 'Barracuda' 125
Operation 'El Dorado Canyon' 138, 154
Operation 'Just Cause' 93, 102
Operation 'Sharp Edge' 103
Operation 'Urgent Fury' 101, 126–8
opinio juris 9
Organization of African Unity (OAU)
    124
Organization of American States (OAS)
    117
Organization of Eastern Caribbean
    States (OECS) 64, 127
Origen 13
Osarik reactor 71, 77–9

Paasche, Franz 144
pacificism 13
pacta sunt servanda 7
Pakistan 74, 118–19
Palestine conflict 114–15, 135
Palestinians 100, 148–9, 152
Panama 42, 93, 101–2, 193
paradigms 204–5 (n23)
paradigmatic shift 4–5, 194
Paris, Pact of 22–4
Paris Peace Conference 19
Parsons, Anthony, Sir 79
peace, over justice 34, 40–5, 92, 177–8
Peace of Westphalia 16
peacekeeping 59, 65–7, 179
Perez de Cuellar, Javier 150
permissible force 108, 134–5
Persia 95; see also Iran
Persian Gulf Conflict 1–2
piracy, and terrorism 144
Politics (Aristotle) 12
positivism 10, 14, 16
positivist period 15–19
post-Charter obligation 185–8
post-Charter self-help paradigm 5,
    178–88, 194; see also self-help
post-Cold War era 188–94
post-Second World War battles 3
Power of Legitimacy Among Nations,
    The (Franck) 184
preemptive action 43, 78
preventative diplomacy 191
pro-democratic paradigm 194–5
proportionality 14, 18, 72, 165–6
proportionate counter-intervention rule
    88–90, 92

protection of nationals 201, 202;
    customary rule, Pre-Charter 107–8;
    and humanitarian intervention
    113–14; illustrations 94–103; legality
    105–10; Middle East 95–6; Panama
    93; state practice 103–5
publicists 8, 157–70

Qadhafi, Colonel 43, 138, 154, 167
quarantine 62, 75

racism 86
ratification of treaties 6
Reagan, Ronald 43, 138
Reagan Administration 41–2, 92, 101,
    126
rebels, support 197–8
refugees 55
regimes, legitimacy 192, 193
regional intervention 60–5
Reisman, W Michael: Article (2(4))
    107–8; enforcement mechanisms
    133–4; human rights 86, 109, 132–3;
    international law 260–1 (n52);
    self-determination 186; Tunis Raid
    153
reprisals 17–18; forcible 42–3, 152;
    permissible 158, 164, 185–6;
    self-defense 253 (n256)
'Reprisals, Deterrence and Self-Defense
    in Counter-Terror Operations'
    (O'Brien) 160
response to terrorism: attributability
    200; legal assessment 170–1;
    proportionate 165–6; targets 166–9,
    200; timely 162–5
restrictionists: anticipatory self-defense
    73, 74, 78; humanitarian intervention
    131–2, 136; protection of nationals
    93, 105–6, 109–10, 111; state practice
    110, 111
Roberts, Guy 139, 158, 165
Ronzitti, N 117, 121, 123–4, 125, 128
Rowles, James 159, 161–2
Russell, Frederick 13

Sahara, Western 99–100
sanctions 48–9, 50–1, 190
Schachter, Oscar: force 256 (n14);
    proportionality 166; self-defense 167,
    210 (n10); self-determination 244
    (n88); terrorism, international 140,

144, 249 (n181)
Schmid, Alex 140
secession 82
Security Council: see UN Security
    Council
self-defense 18; aggression 23; Article
    (51) 31, 36, 108; collective 31, 36, 89;
    customary international law 72,
    218–19 (n4); humanitarian
    intervention 167; Israel's against
    terrorism 149; just war period 12;
    lawful 185–6, 196–201; regional 61;
    as right 107, 265 (n122); and
    terrorism 159–62, 198–201;
    thresholds for 159–62; UN Security
    Council 33; US response 138, 154–5;
    see also anticipatory self defense;
    reprisals
self-determination 40–2, 85–6, 91–2,
    186; foreign intervention 84, 194;
    and humanitarian intervention
    113–14; regional intervention 63–5;
    UN Charter 244 (n88)
self-help 5, 17, 19, 44, 188
'Self-Help in Combating
    State-Sponsored Terrorism' (Roberts)
    165
Serbia 55
'Sharp Edge' Operation 103
Sierra Leone 58
Socialist bloc 41; see also USSR
Sofaer, Abraham 159, 160–1, 164–5,
    168–9, 253–4 (n272)
Somalian Civil War 55–6
South Africa 120–1
sovereignty 4, 7, 15–17, 39–40
Soviet: see USSR
state aggression 168
state involvement, terrorism 141–2,
    152–3, 158, 168–9
state practice, contemporary 73–9,
    103–5, 110–11, 128–31, 147–59
Stone, Julius 134–5, 258 (n38)
Suarez, Francisco 14
Suez Canal 44, 96
Summa Theologiae (Aquinas) 14
Syria 44, 76

Tanzania 123–5, 129–30, 238 (n229)
target states, intervention 130–1
targets, for response to terrorism
    166–9, 200

Taylor, Charles 65
territorial annexation 187–8, 201
territorial integrity 130
terrorism: defined 38, 139–42, 240–1
    (n37), 249 (n181); forcible response
    147–57; international law 143–7; *jus
    ad bellum* 172–3; lack of analytical
    framework 157–9; and the law
    143–7, 162–9, 251 (n228); responses
    138–9, 162, 163, 252–3 (n250);
    scholarly opinion summarized
    169–70; and self-defense 159–62,
    198–201; state involvement 141–2,
    152–3, 158, 168–9; and state practice
    147–57, 155–9; statistics 239 (n19);
    UN Charter 145–6, 170–1
'Terrorism, The Law, and the National
    Defense' (Sofaer) 164
terrorist actors 141, 142
terrorist acts 141, 143–7
Tertullian 13
Tesón, Professor: Central Africa 125–6;
    enforcement mechanisms 133–4;
    Grenada 127; human rights 132;
    humanitarian intervention 116, 119;
    jus ad bellum 136; Kampuchea 123;
    Tanzania 238 (n229); Uganda 123,
    125
text writers 8, 157–70
Timor, East 119–20
tit-for-tat proportionality 165
treaties 6; Kellogg-Briand 22–4;
    obligations 180–1, 182; ratification 6;
    and terrorism 144–5; UN Charter 30
Tunis raid (1985) 152–3

Uganda 99, 123–5
UK 44, 95–6, 97
UN (United Nations) 4; collective uses
    of force 52–6; peacekeeping 66;
    permanent members 51–2;
    strengthening 190–1; successes
    189–90
UN Atomic Energy Commission 73–4
UN Charter 29–30; approach 182–4;
    enforcements 47; failures 178–9;
    force 30–45, 56–8; humanitarian
    argument 109; *jus ad bellum* 131;
    legal obligation 177; legal paradigm
    4–5; regional arrangements 60–5;
    self-determination 244 (n88);
    terrorism 145–6, 170–1; value

hierarchy 177–8
UN Charter Articles: (1) 132–3; (2(4)) 1,
    30–6, 75, 86, 131–2, 134–5, 145–6,
    177, 179–85, 195; (39) 48, 50; (40) 50;
    (41) 48, 49; (42) 32, 48, 49; (43) 32,
    57; (47) 51; (51) 31, 36, 38, 54, 61,
    72–3, 74, 78, 108, 131–2, 159, 160,
    219 (n7); (52) 60; (53) 32–3, 60–1,
    62–3; (54) 61; (55) 132, 133; (56) 132,
    133; (106) 32; (107) 32–3
UN Charter Preamble 132–3
UN Commission on Human Rights 112
UN General Assembly 59–60; Interim
    Committee 59; Libya 155;
    peacekeeping 66–7; resolutions 8–9,
    34–5, 146–7; as Security Council
    substitute 178–9
UN Iran–Iraq Military Observer Group
    189
UN Observer Group in Central America
    189
UN Security Council: force authorized
    31–2, 33, 201; and human rights 113;
    humanitarian intervention 55, 56
UN Security Council Resolutions 8; (82)
    52; (83) 52; (84) 52–3; (387) 120–1;
    (479) 34; (573) 153; (638) 156; (660)
    1, 2, 53, 54, 187; (661) 1, 53, 54;
    (662) 1, 53, 187, 215 (n36); (664) 1;
    (665) 1, 54; (666) 2; (667) 2; (668) 2;
    (678) 54, 187; (687) 55, 215 (n45);
    (688) 55; (748) 146; (794) 56
unification 82
United Arab Republic 76–7
United Nations: *see* UN
'Uniting for Peace' Resolution 59–60,
    66–7
unrest, low intensity 81
'Urgent Fury' Operation 101, 126–8
US: *Achille Lauro* hijackers 148–9;
    Cambodia 98; citizens as targets 140;
    Congo 231 (n49); Dominican
    Republic 97–8; force against
    terrorism 156–9; Grenada 101, 126–8,
    212 (n44), 221–2 (n18); humanitarian
    justification 129; Iran 100–1; Iraq 1;
    Liberia 102; Libya 138–9, 154;
    Panama 93, 101–2, 193; Unified
    Military Command 52–3
USSR 120–1, 190–1

value hierarchy 34, 177–8, 179, 191–3

Vattel, Emerich de 15
Verwey, Professor 116, 120, 135, 231
    (n49)
veto 52, 57, 178
Vietnam 87, 90, 121
Vitoria, Francisco 14
von Glahn, Professor 143

Walters, Vernon 149, 153, 154
war: as instrument of international
    policy 23; morality/legality 13, 14–15;
    and sovereign state system 16–17
wars of secession 82
wars of unification 82
Warsaw Pact 41
Western Sahara 99–100
Westphalia, Peace of 16
Williams, Abiodun 65
World War I 19

Zanzibar 97
Zionists 114–15